L.L. Bean

Ultimate Book of Fly Fishing

L.L. Bean
Ultimate Book of Fly Fishing

Fly Fishing

Dave Whitlock

Fly Casting

Macauley Lord

Photographs by Jim Rowinski

Fly Tying

Dick Talleur

THE LYONS PRESS

Guilford, Connecticut
An imprint of The Globe Pequot Press

First Lyons Press paperback edition, 2005

The Lyons Press is an imprint of The Globe Pequot Press.

Originally published by The Lyons Press as *L.L. Bean Fly-Fishing Handbook*, *L.L. Bean Fly-Casting Handbook*, and *L.L. Bean Fly-Tying Handbook*

10 9 8 7 6 5

Printed in China

ISBN 978-159228-891-5

The Library of Congress has previously cataloged an earlier (hardcover) edition as follows:
The L.L. Bean ultimate book of fly fishing / Macauley Lord, Dick Talleur, Dave Whitlock.
p. cm.
Contents: L.L. Bean fly-fishing handbook/ Dave Whitlock—L.L. Bean fly-casting hand-book / Macauley Lord—L.L. Bean fly-tying handbook / Dick Talleur.
ISBN: 1-58574-632-0 (hc)
Fly fishing—Handbooks, manuals, etc. I. Talleur, Richard W. II. Whitlock, Dave.
III. Title
SH456.L67 2002
799.1'24—dc21 2002073191

Contents

Acknowledgments

Welcome to the special world of fly fishing. In recent years, fly fishing has become increasingly popular as more people discover its magical qualities. After over 50 years of fly-fishing experience, most spent teaching either family, friends, business associates, or the general public, I've come to the conclusion that it is a sport that nearly anyone who loves nature and the outdoors can enjoy. And the 10-plus years that I worked with the L.L. Bean Fly-Fishing Schools were certainly among the most significant that I've experienced learning and teaching the sport.

This handbook is a direct result of those experiences. A lot of people helped me develop these teaching methods as well as this handbook and I'd like to take this opportunity to recognize and thank them.

Leon Gorman and Scott Sanford for giving me the opportunity to represent L.L. Bean and to develop the L.L. Bean Fly-Fishing Schools.

Tom Ackerman, Brock Apfel, and Mike Verville for helping me with school coordination and instruction.

John Bryan, Don Davis, Rob Crawford, Pat Jackson, Dwight Lander, John Meadow, Joe Murray, Joe Robinson, and Joan Whitlock for the very special work they each did as instructors and contributors to the schools and the handbook.

Nick Lyons and his outstanding editorial staff for all the editions of this handbook. Their patience and attention to detail have made my instructions and illustrations much easier to study and use.

My wife, Emily Whitlock, for her encouragement, wonderful advice, superb photography, and editing, which helped make this edition so much more effective for the readers and students of fly fishing.

And my heartfelt thanks to the L.L. Bean Fly-Fishing School students for teaching me how to instruct fly fishing with maximum effectiveness . . . and for enriching my life with their time, warmth, enthusiasm, and fishing stories!

—*Dave Whitlock*

A teacher learns mostly from others, some from his own experience, and passes the knowledge on. Those from whom I've learned include some of the great names in casting: Jim Green, the dean of West Coast casting instructors, whose 1975 film, *Secrets of Fly Casting*, taught me how to accelerate the rod and whose confidence in me as a casting instructor changed my life; Mel

Krieger, fly casting's poet, whose vision to raise the standards for casting instruction came to fruition in the Federation of Fly Fishers' Casting Instructor Certification Program. Mel's book, *The Essence of Fly Casting*, set the standard for all casting books to come. I have also been fortunate to learn from Joan Wulff, an extraordinarily innovative and graceful mentor to casters for more than half a century, who continues to share her visionary teaching methods with us; Lefty Kreh, whose wonderful style with a fly rod and sincere affection for all fly fishers has made him the Pied Piper of our sport; and Gary Borger, who helped me control my backcast in West Yellowstone in 1981 and whose books, articles, and videos have raised the bar for fly fishers and their teachers everywhere. All of my teachers and mentors may find things in this book with which they disagree, perhaps passionately. May they understand . . .

No teacher could have a better education than my 12 years of casting colloquy with the gifted instructors of the L.L. Bean Fly-Fishing School. They have included Dave Whitlock, Joe Robinson, John Kluesing, Dave Hagengruber, John Sharkey, Ellen Peters, Brian Golden, and Joe Codd. To hear us discuss casting, you'd have thought we were trying to agree on a rewrite of the Ten Commandments. During those times, it was often Pat Jackson who cheerfully reminded us that we were only talking about fly casting.

Joe Codd provided early comments on the tone of this book. It is better for his suggestions. Dana Dodge provided a punch line, perhaps the only one. Steve Meyers, author, guide, and friend of rivers, was invaluable during our photo shoot in Colorado. If only he could have kept it from snowing every day.

Known to the pros as the best unheralded casting instructor on the continent, Bruce Richards of Scientific Anglers provided fly lines that photograph and cast beautifully. Rich Best of G. Loomis provided the great white rod. Bill Gammel, his father's greatest student, told me the story of Jay Gammel's last cast. Captain Brock Apfel guided me over many new waters. When an injury kept me from casting, Kyle Whyet prayed for me, and my wife, Carol, wouldn't let me fall.

Jim Rowinski proposed this book and asked me to write it. He's also the one who brought me to the L.L. Bean Fly-Fishing Schools many years ago. If it weren't for Jim, I might have a real job.

—*Macauley Lord*

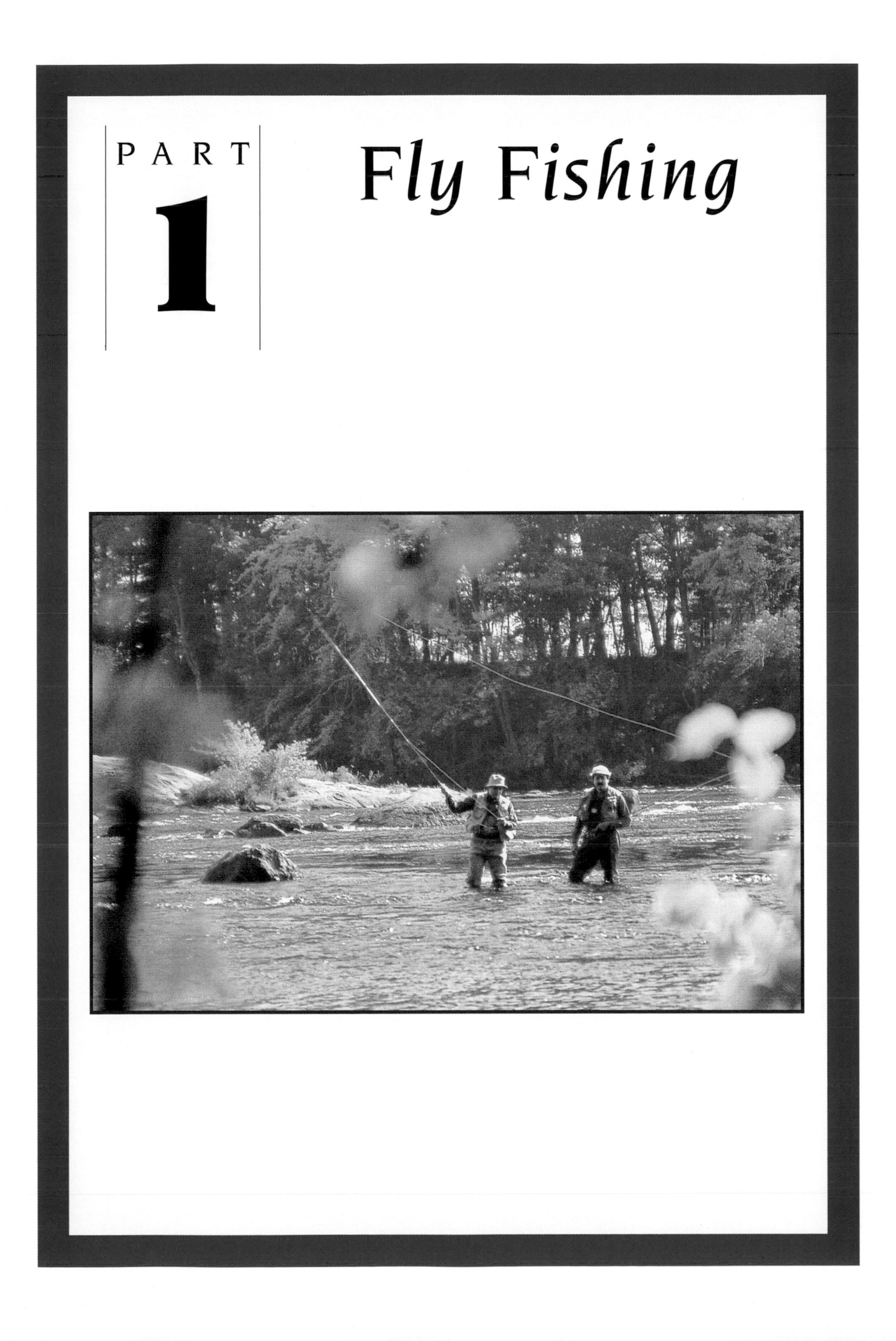

PART 1

Fly Fishing

Introduction: The Joy of Fly Fishing

One summer afternoon some years ago, Dave Whitlock and I fly fished up a little feeder creek in Yellowstone Park. It was a warm afternoon and we were in no particular hurry—which is the best way to fish—so we fished together and then alone, and we talked a lot, and we caught a few trout. Dave did most of the catching.

The particular brand of fly fishing we did was unusual and I had not done it before. Big fish had come up into this feeder stream from a larger, famous river whose temperature got quite high in August. The fish, Dave told me, were in the stream for relief from the heat, not food. You had to tempt them with a fly they could not refuse. He suggested a grasshopper, which is a mouthful, and he gave me a new version of his famous Dave's Hopper. Dave is one of America's most innovative fly tyers and—had I been a trout, and as they proved—this fly looked good enough to eat.

Dave showed me how to approach a bend pool, how to stand 15 feet back from the bank, how to cast so that merely the leader fell on the water. These were special techniques, local refinements. He gently corrected a hitch or two in my casting and helped me perfect a knot—for he is a deft instructor.

About five o'clock, beneath a stand of lodgepole pine, we picked some small wild strawberries, sat on the mossy ground, looked up at a singularly blue sky, talked about the fish we'd seen and caught, compared notes. We were both smiling broadly at the exquisite pleasure of the past few hours. He said he wished everyone had a chance to spend at least one afternoon like this—back in wild country, with a good friend, learning a new technique or two, fly fishing to difficult trout, catching a few. Fly fishing was at the heart of it. Twenty years earlier, I said, before I fly fished, the day would have been impossible. The particular peace and pleasure I felt were intricately connected to the brand of fishing I practiced—the rhythmic cast, with rod and line becoming extensions of my arm; the subtle drop of the fly, which imitated a natural insect; the intimate knowledge of the stream and our quarry that we needed to fish this way. And I was still learning. That was part of fly fishing, too: It became more and more fascinating and (no matter how good you got) there was always something new to learn. The afternoon had been a blend of satisfactions: skills already mastered and new skills that I had learned—none of them difficult to learn, though once I'd thought so.

We used equipment that was balanced and understood. Line, reel, and rod were matched, and could do our bidding. The simple and lovely act of casting a fly—in this case one tied by Dave—was in itself rewarding. We had to stalk the fish, in gorgeous surroundings, and we had to know why they were here and

Brook trout leaping down on Dave's Hopper.

on what they might feed. You could not merely chuck out a bait or lure and chance a fish coming by. We had to "read" the water, know our fish, actively hunt them. We were more closely connected to the subtle web of nature than we could possibly have been through any other pastime I could imagine. We were more involved—physically and mentally—than had we practiced any other fishing method. The wild strawberries we ate—which were soft, bright crimson, astonishingly sweet—were only the most palpable symbol of our connection with the natural world.

Dave and I were ourselves an example of the magic fly fishing weaves. He lives in Arkansas and I in a large eastern city; for him, fly fishing is a way of life, a consummate art to be practiced with cunning and increasing skill; for me it is that, too, but also a respite from the work and tension of cities. As the modern world has become more and more mechanized, crowded, even harsh in its metropolitan pressures, I have grown to love fly fishing the more and to appreciate its gifts, for itself and as a sorely needed tonic. It demands such happy skill of hand and eye, knowledge of the fish's world, imagination; it always challenges and refreshes me. Dave and I were from sharply different worlds—rural and urban—and may even have fly fished for different reasons; but we shared an absolute joy in this special art of angling. Fly fishing had brought us together, taught us a common language, made us friends.

Too many people avoid fly fishing because they think it is too difficult to learn. Some take it up without proper instruction and then drop it. This little handbook is an antidote. It has one simple purpose: to be a clear and eminently practical introduction to the sport. It seeks to take the mystery out of fly fishing and to make it accessible to a vast number of people who might otherwise avoid the sport.

To my mind, this handbook does the job with unique skill. That's not surprising. For the 25 years Dave's been teaching fly fishing, 10 have been spent working with the L.L. Bean Fly-Fishing Schools System. It has been a happy and successful venture. With the company's encouragement and support, Dave has developed a variety of new teaching techniques; he has refined his own considerable skills as an instructor; and he has found the simplest and most effective ways to get people started fly fishing. Since his methods worked so well with hundreds of students,

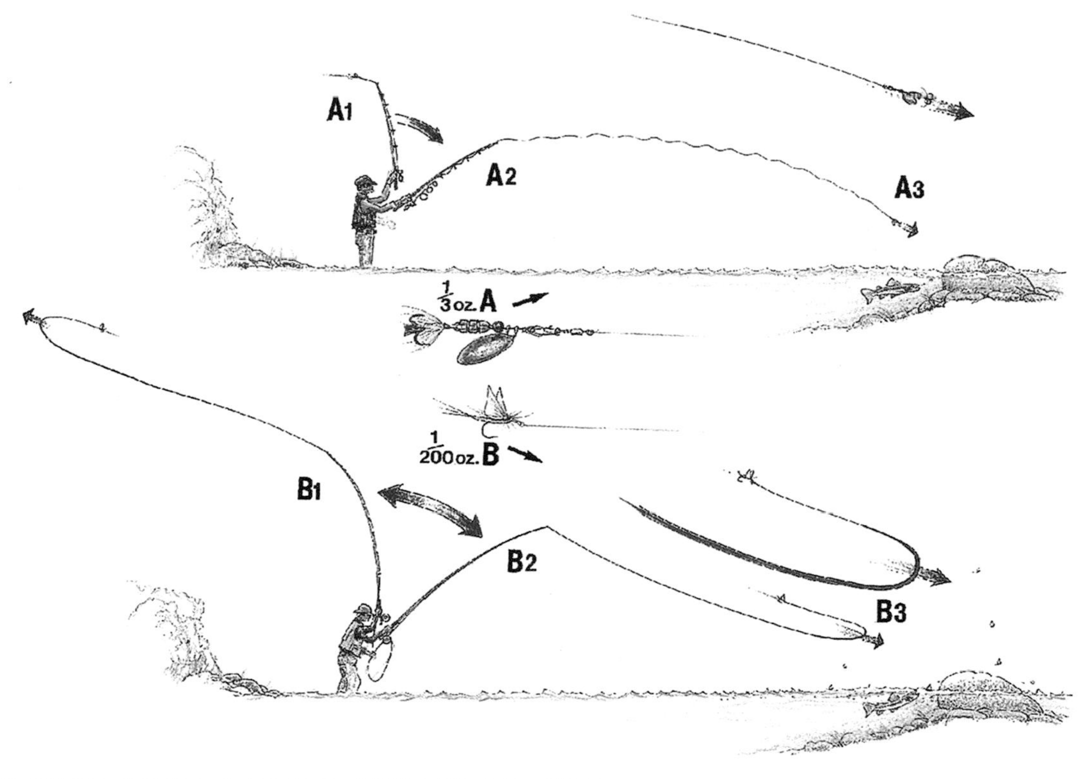

CONVENTIONAL CASTING AND FLY CASTING
In CONVENTIONAL CASTING (called bait casting or plug casting), the rod movement (A1) sends a weighted lure (A3) into motion, and the lure then pulls the almost weightless line (A2) after it. In FLY CASTING the rod movement (B1) sends a weighted fly line (B2) into motion, and the fly line then pulls the almost weightless fly (B3) after it.

L.L. Bean thought they ought to be in print; the result, I think, is like spending a weekend fishing with Dave.

Dave will introduce you to fly tackle, fly casting, fishing tactics, fly tying, and other tools and skills that will make this sport of limitless interest to you, regardless of your age, sex, income, or athletic ability. You will learn that it is not beyond your ability to cast well and with accuracy, and that with a little patience and practice you can tie your own flies—and then catch fish on them—and that this will double your fly-fishing pleasure. Dave will surprise you by showing how many different species can be caught on a fly—not only trout but also bluegill, bass, bluefish, on up to sailfish and even marlin; fly fishing can be practiced not only in rivers but also in ponds, lakes, estuaries, and the ocean. Since Dave is a skilled artist, he has supported his text with a multitude of helpful line drawings and charts. In all, this book can provide the down-to-earth basic instruction you need to get you catching fish on a fly. And this time it's in full color.

Once you've learned the fundamentals, you will want to go on and learn more—for fly fishing can become a finely tuned art. And in a short time you'll know why millions of anglers consider fly fishing the most versatile and challenging—as well as the most enjoyable—way to sportfish. As my afternoon with Dave on that haunting western stream reminded me, it is also a singularly compelling way to enjoy the outdoors.

—Nick Lyons

Understanding Fly Tackle

Fly fishing is a purely *personal* and manual method of sportfishing that involves the casting, presentation, and manipulation of an artificial fly to hook, play, and land fish. Fly fishing is unique because the tackle components—rod, reel, line, leader, and fly—are used differently from the ways tackle is used in such other popular angling methods as spin casting, spinning, and bait casting. In fly fishing, you use the fly rod to cast a length of handheld, weighted line that propels an almost weightless lure (the fly) to the fishing area. Other methods employ a *propelled* weighted lure to pull an almost weightless line off the reel.

THE FLY ROD

The **fly rod** is designed to control (with mechanical advantage) the uniquely linear-shaped and weighted **fly line.** Fly rods are generally longer and more supple than other fishing rods to allow optimum performance in casting and in leader and fly presentations, as well as in their correct manipulation on water.

The **fly reel's** function is to hold the excess fly line and backing line during casting and fishing. Once a fish is hooked, the reel, acting as a winch, allows line to be extended or retrieved as you play the fish.

The **leader,** a light, nearly invisible extension of the heavy, highly visible fly line, aids in presenting and manipulating the fly.

Flies, which can imitate any type of natural fish food (such as insects, smaller fish, shrimp, leeches, frogs, or even plant parts), are cast and manipulated near the fish with the fly rod and line. The feel, visual pleasure, and control you receive from holding the sensitive rod in one hand and the bare fly line in the other hand while casting, presenting the fly to the target, puppeteering the fly, and then striking and fighting the fish are personal, sensitive experiences that surpass all other methods of fishing.

This seemingly simple manual method actually has nearly limitless possibilities—far more than other methods that use live bait or artificial lures. The most noticeable reason for this is that the fly has no significant weight. This allows the fly fisher to imitate the whole range of fish food sizes, from 1/16 inch to 10 inches or more.

A fly-fishing outfit has five main tackle components: the fly, the leader, the line, the rod, and the reel. These components work together most efficiently when they are balanced, or matched to one another. Thanks to agreements by fly-tackle manufacturers, most components are uniformly coded with the information you need to assemble well-matched fly tackle.

THE FLY LINE

The fly line, with its linear casting weight, is the key component of the fly-tackle system. The fly line appears, to the user of other casting methods, to be unusually thick. This is because weight and taper are built into a fly line to aid in casting and making the line float or sink. Line diameter does not necessarily correspond to line weight or strength, as is the case with the lines used in other angling methods.

Fly-line sizes are standardized, or calibrated, according to a code adopted by the American Fishing Tackle Manufacturers Association (AFTMA). An AFTMA fly-line size is calculated by weighing the first 30 feet of the line (excluding the tapered tip of the line); lines are measured in grain-weight units from 60 to 850 grains.

Fly lines are available in weights ranging from 1 to 15, with weights 1 through 12 covering most of the fly fisher's needs. The four most popular line weights are 5, 6, 7, and 8. The 6-weight floating line is today's best-selling fly line.

All modern fly lines are clearly marked and coded on their containers with the

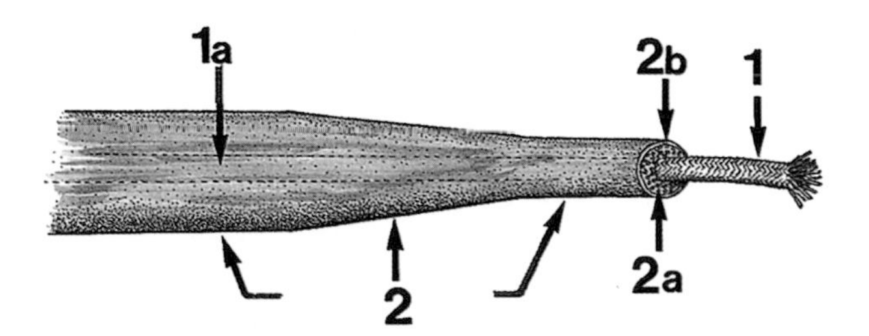

Composition of Modern Fly Line

1. Braided level core.
1a. The core gives the fly line most of its strength.
2. The coating provides most of the fly-line weight, shape, and size.
2a. The composition of the coating determines fly-line density.
2b. The coating finish reduces friction in rod guides, air, and water.

AFTMA line weight and other design and use codes. The *design*, *weight*, and *density* of the fly line determine how the fly is cast and the depth at which the fly is fished.

Most modern fly lines are constructed with a central core of level braided nylon or similar synthetic material. The **core** provides strength, a portion of the line's weight, and the foundation for layers of coating. The **coating** generally consists of one or more layers of a molded PVC plastic or vinyl material and provides the line with a durable shape (or taper), the majority of its weight and flexibility, its density, and its color. The coating also has a very smooth, *low-friction* surface for line movement through the rod's guides, your hands, the air, and water. Some premium fly lines are even impregnated with lubricating

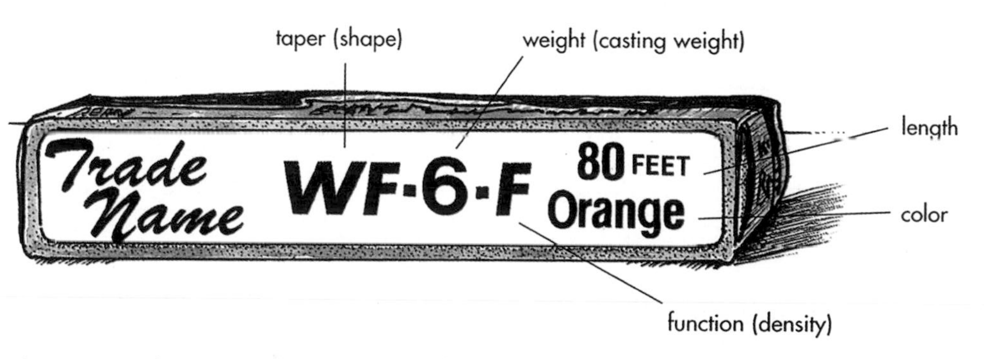

The AFTMA Fly Line Code as it is typically printed on the fly-line box.

agents that gradually seep from the line to make it more friction-free.

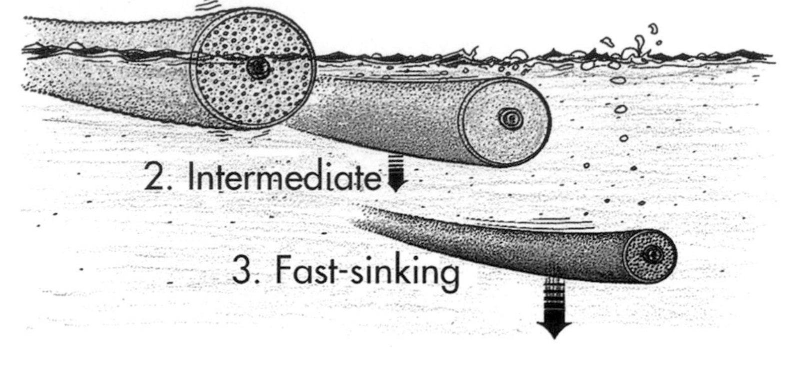

This cross-sectional diagram shows the water positions of three fly-line densities of the same weight.

Fly-Line Densities

There are three main fly-line densities: floating, intermediate, and sinking.

The **floating line** (F), buoyant to ride on top of the water, is usually the first line a beginning fly fisher purchases. It is used primarily when fishing dry flies (floating flies), but it is also often used with wet flies, streamers, or nymphs (sinking flies) in shallow water, generally less than 10 feet.

The **intermediate line** (I) is just slightly heavier than water so that it sinks slowly. This fly line is most useful for fly fishing with wet flies and nymphs at shallow depths for trout, panfish, bass, bonefish, and tarpon. An intermediate line can be dressed with line flotant to make it float. The old silk fly lines were all intermediates and required frequent coating with paraffin to make them float.

Sinking lines can be subdivided into sinking-tip and full-sinking lines.

The **sinking-tip line** (F/S) is just that: The first 5, 10, or 15 feet (the tip) of the line sinks and the remainder of the line (the belly) floats. The sinking-tip line is becoming very popular as a second line. It allows you to fish floating/diving flies, wet flies, nymphs, streamers, and bottom-crawling flies with ease, yet it has many of the more desirable casting characteristics of a floating line. It is much easier for beginners to use than a full-sinking line. Sinking-tip lines are excellent for fishing flies at depths of 2 to 10 feet.

Sinking-tip fly lines are available in several tip-density choices, with sinking speeds of slow (I), medium (II), fast (III), or extra fast (IV and V). Faster-sinking (or higher-density) tips keep the fly deeper during a retrieve or while it is drifting in current.

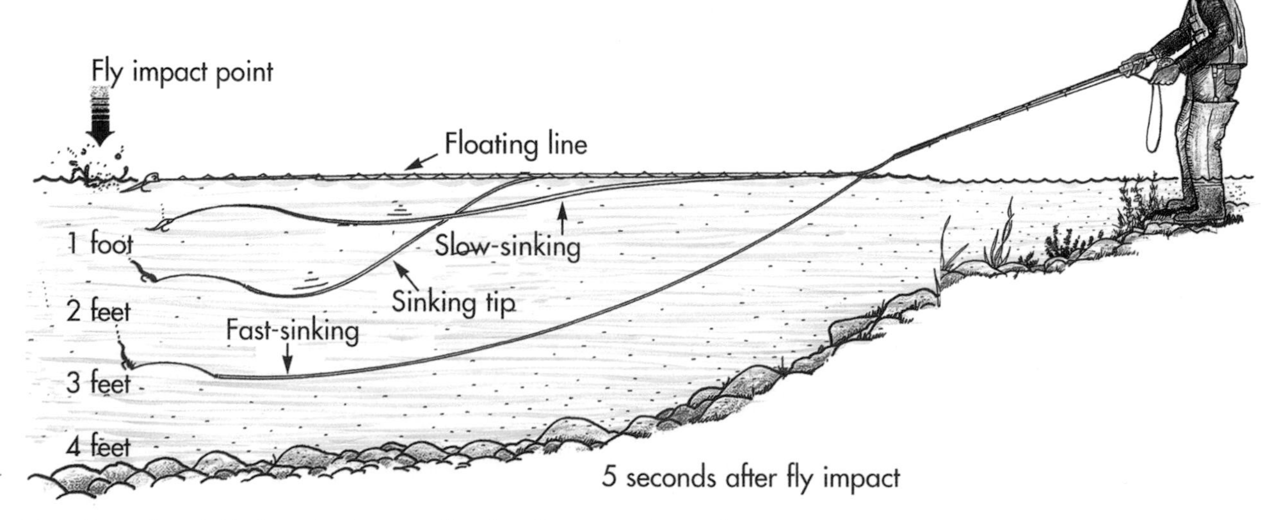

The effect of each fly-line density on a fly after five seconds on the water.

The **full-sinking line** (S) is used to pull a fly down to a depth of as much as 30 feet. Sinking lines are useful for standard casting and retrieving techniques as well as for trolling. As with sinking tips, different densities are available to provide a choice of sinking rates from slow to very fast. Most of the density variation is created by impregnating the fly line's coating with lead, tungsten, or other heavy-metal particles.

These three main fly-line styles—floating, intermediate, and sinking—of identical AFTMA line weights will have different diameters. The floating line will have the largest diameter and the sinking line the smallest. This is a function of water displacement versus density. Because 30 feet of floating line weighs the same as 30 feet of sinking line, the floating line must be larger in diameter in order to float. The thicker floating line will *feel* lighter than a sinking line of the same weight, but it is not. It also will not cast quite as far as the sinking line with an equal amount of effort. This happens simply because the floating line's greater surface area creates more drag on the rod's guides and in the air.

Fly-Line Shapes

Most fly lines are made in one of three shapes: level, double taper, or weight forward. Each design has characteristics that you should understand in order to choose the right line for your needs. Although a fly line is more complex in makeup and higher in price than monofilament spinning line or braided bait-casting or trolling line, with proper care it will last considerably longer (usually three or four years) than other fishing lines.

The **level line** (L) has a level braided core and a level molded coating throughout its length. It works well for casting and roll-casting short distances (20 to 40 feet). Because the *tip* of a level line is so heavy and large in diameter compared to the other line shapes, it limits your ability to make delicate or complex presentations. Generally, we do not recommend using a level fly line to learn proper fly-casting and presentation methods.

The **double-taper line** (DT) is tapered for several feet on each end and has a uniform diameter in the midsection. The tapered tip permits more delicate and controlled presentation of the leader and fly than does the uniform tip of the level line. The double taper is well suited for most short- and medium-distance fly casting and roll-casting. Its larger midsection, however, hinders the shooting of line for distance casting (over 60 feet). The double taper has the advantage of a longer life than the other tapered designs, for it can be reversed on the reel when the front tapered end begins to wear out.

The **weight-forward line** (WF) has a tip taper generally identical to the tip of a double-taper line. It has a short, heavy midsection tapering to a long, lighter, level shooting section behind. The weight-forward line casts well at short and intermediate distances, and because of its more advanced design, it will cast farther and more easily than the level or double-taper design. Roll-casting distance, however, is limited to approximately 40 to 50

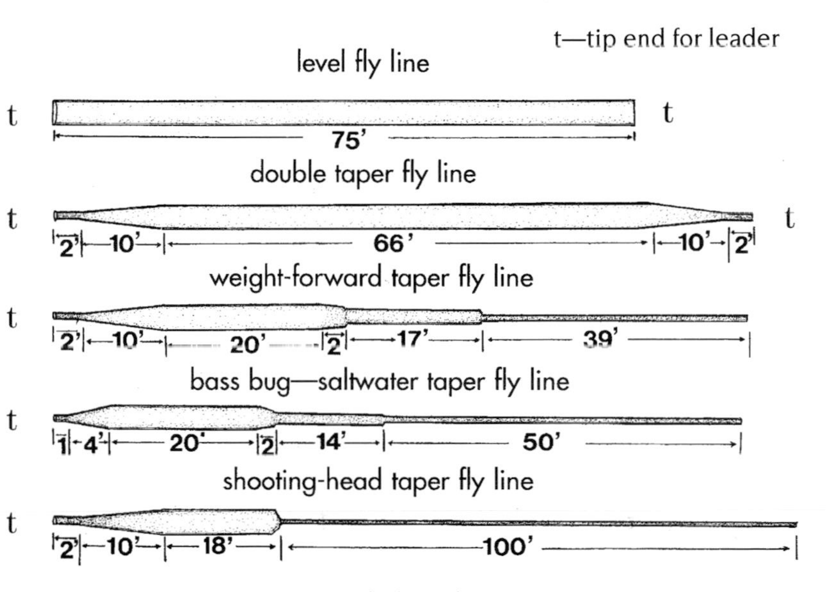

These are the five most common fly-line shapes.

feet. Beyond that distance, the smaller shooting-line section reduces roll-casting efficiency. Although it cannot be reversed for longer life as the double taper can, the weight-forward line is the most versatile line design.

There are six important modifications of the weight-forward taper: the long belly, rocket taper, bass-bug taper, saltwater taper, nymph taper, and Wulff triangle taper.

The **long belly** is just that—a longer belly or midsection that enables more line to be carried more easily in the air. Long-belly lines were designed to help make longer casts using modern graphite fly rods.

The **rocket taper**, designed by Leon Chandler of the Cortland Line Company, is a weight-forward line with a longer front taper for more delicate presentations, and good roll-casting and shooting performance.

Bass-bug and **saltwater tapers** (floating only) are more or less identical. They have a short, blunt, tip taper with a heavy, short midsection and a long, thinner shooting section. These lines are designed to cast larger, heavier, more wind-resistant flies quickly on stiff leaders at short to medium distances (20 to 70 feet) while minimizing false casts. They are excellent performers in the windy conditions that are so common around bass lakes and salt water.

Nymph tapers (floating only) are weight-forward lines with a blunt, very buoyant tapered tip specially designed to maximize the casting and mending of sinking nymphs, split shot, and strike indicators. A nymph taper also shoots line easily to minimize false-casting while nymphing.

The **Wulff triangle taper** (floating only) is a weight-forward line designed by Lee Wulff. It has a continuous tapering belly or midsection designed to load the rod well and carry the energy to the loop very efficiently. Because this concept is so different from that of standard level-belly weight forwards, triangle-taper lines have a very distinctive feel. These lines also have an ease of roll-casting.

The **shooting-head line** (SH) is a special-purpose modification of the tapered or level line. To create a shooting-head line, the first 30 feet (the *head*) of a level or tapered line is spliced to 100 feet of 20- to 30-pound-test monofilament or to a special, very small-diameter level fly line (the *shooting* line). The shooting head, with its nearly frictionless shooting line, is designed for casting long distances (70 to 120 feet). The shooting head is relatively difficult to use, however, and is not a good choice for beginners.

Fly-Line Colors

The visibility of the fly line to the angler affects overall fly-fishing performance and success. White, pastel, or fluorescent lines are easier for the fly fisher to see than dark or

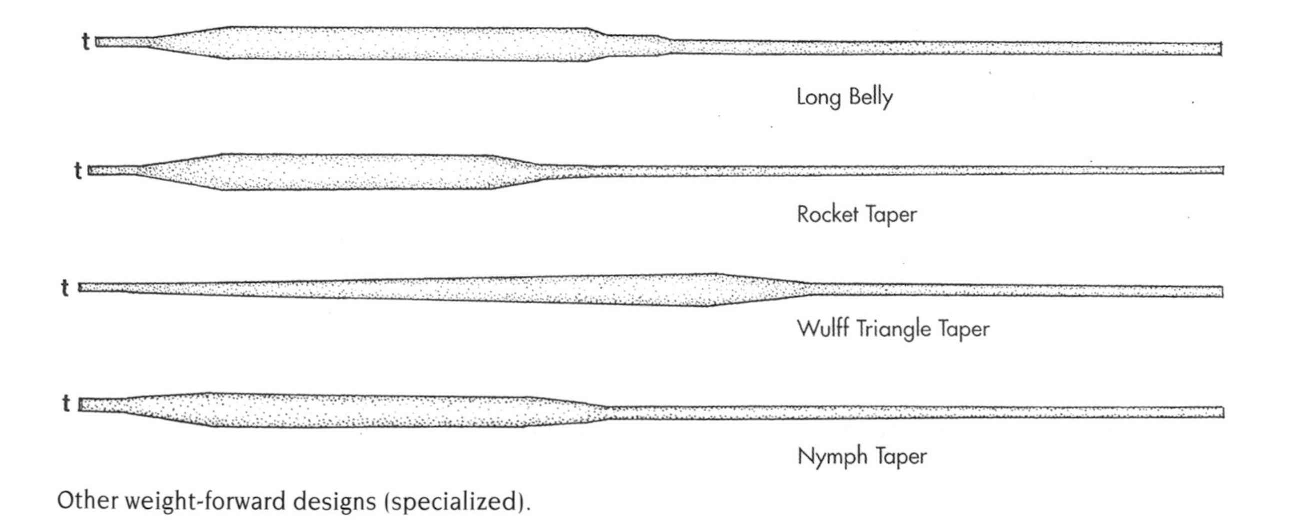

Other weight-forward designs (specialized).

Fly-Line Colors

1. Hi Viz for maximum visibility, accuracy, and linc control.
2. Pastels offer good visibility, accuracy, and line control, yet are less offensive to fish than Hi Viz.
3. Dark colors for low visibility and maximum casting and fishing stealth.

neutral colors, such as brown, green, or gray. This allows greater control over casting and fishing the fly. But lighter colors are more visible to the fish, which increases the chance of scaring them. In bright light, a fly line in the air actually looks larger than it is, and when a fly line is on or beneath the water, the fish may see it as an unnatural object and become frightened. Dark or neutral colors are less visible above and on the water, so there are some real choices to make.

We recommend that the beginning fly fisher choose a highly visible line to enhance the learning of basics in casting, presentation, and fishing techniques.

Fly-Line Weights

The size, or weight, of the fly line you choose should be based on the flies you are going to use (hook size, weight, and wind resistance). Generally speaking, the smaller line sizes (weights 1, 2, 3, 4, and 5) are best suited to flies tied on size 8 to 28 hooks. The medium line sizes (6, 7, and 8) are best for size 1/0 to 12 flies. The large line sizes (8, 10, 11, and 12) are best for size 5/0 to 4 flies. Keep in mind that very wind-resistant or heavily weighted flies will require a larger line size than these general parameters. Windy conditions may also make it necessary to use a line one or two weights heavier to cast the same fly correctly. The line size choice is determined by the line's ability to control the fly. If the fly controls the line, you will have casting problems.

For the best line to begin your fly fishing—say, for the first one to three years—we recommend a *floating, weight-forward, 6- or 7-weight,* if you plan to seek good instruction from a professional or a fly-fishing school. If this type of assistance is not available to you, we recommend a *floating double taper,* which is initially easier to use. Six- or 7- weight fly lines and matched fly tackle are the most practical for all-around fly fishing in fresh water.

THE LEADER

The leader provides a low-visibility link between the heavy fly-line tip and the fly. Of almost equal importance, the leader should also assist the fly line's front taper in casting and presenting the fly and letting the fly float, swim, or sink in the most natural manner. To do this, the leader must continue the line tip's taper down its length to its tip. The tapered leader has three parts—the butt, midsection, and tip.

The **butt** section is the largest in diameter, and it resembles the fly-line tip in flexibility and density—continuing the taper of the fly line.

The **midsection** continues the leader's length for deception; it also provides the most drastic taper area.

The **tip** joins the tapering midsection with a smaller-diameter length of level monofila-

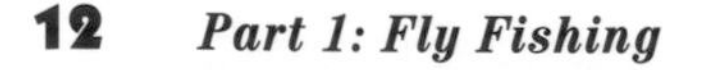

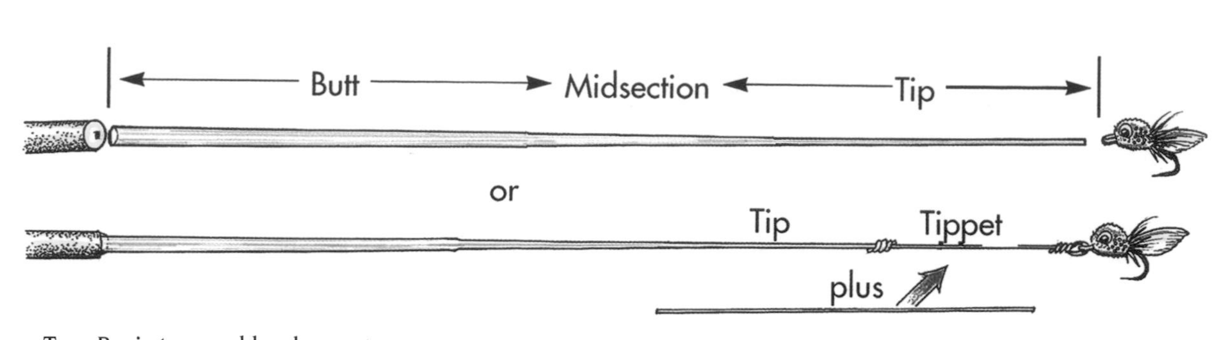

Top: Basic tapered leader parts.
Bottom: Optional tippet section attached.

ment. The tip is usually 12 to 24 inches long; this provides the maximum fish-deceiving length while helping to give a natural movement to the fly in the water. To extend or prolong the tapered leader's life or uses, additional monofilament may be tied to the leader's tip. This addition is called the **tippet.** Though its purpose is simple, it often confuses the new fly fisher.

A **shock,** or **bite,** tippet is a short section (3 to 12 inches long) of very heavy monofilament (30- to 100-pound test) or metal wire that is added at the fly to prevent fish with sharp teeth or body parts from cutting off the fly. A bite tippet is used for such species as bluefish, tarpon, shark, barracuda, muskellunge, and pike.

Understanding the Tippet

The tippet can be used simply to lengthen the leader, or it can be used to add a smaller-diameter section of monofilament to improve fish deception or to allow the use of a smaller fly. A tippet may also be added to repair or replace part of the tip.

Wind knots often occur in the tip or tippet during the course of a day's fishing, as does abrasion damage or breakage. These conditions are corrected by cutting out the problem section and replacing it with a new one. The tippet is usually 18 to 24 inches long. Tippet material is sold in convenient, pocket-sized spools, individually or in sets, with about 10 to 25 yards of material on each spool. The spools are usually well marked to indicate monofilament diameter and breaking strength. It's a good idea to use tippet material of the same make as the leader. Different tippet brands may be softer or harder than your leader; a mismatch will weaken knots.

Types of Leaders

The **knotted compound-tapered** leader is made by tying together sections of nylon monofilament that differ in diameter to create a desired taper and length. The ability to tie your own tapered leaders can save you money and allow you to experiment with tapers. A

Tippet spool detail. Label indicates tippet size, diameter, pound-test strength, and amount of tippet on spool.

LEADER TIPPET AND FLY SIZE
(For optimum casting, presentation, and fishing performance)

Leader Tip or Tippet (Diameter in thousandths of an inch)	*X Code*	*Pound Test*	*Fly-Hook Sizes*
.003	8X	1.2	24, 26, 28, 32
.004	7X	2	20, 22, 24, 26
.005	6X	3	16, 18, 20, 22
.006	5X	4	14, 16, 18
.007	4X	6	12, 14, 16
.008	3X	8	10, 12, 14
.009	2X	10	6, 8, 10
.010	1X	12	2, 4, 6
.011	0X	14	1/0, 2, 4
.012	X1	15	2/0, 1/0, 2
.013	X2	16	3/0, 2/0, 1/0, 2
.014	X3	18	5/0, 4/0, 3/0, 2/0
.015	X4	20	6/0, 5/0, 4/0, 3/0

Based on monofilament nylon, Aeon, and L.L. Bean product

Note: This chart is a simple guideline. Fly-hook wire sizes, hook-shank lengths, extra weighting, and material designs, as well as variations in leader-material stiffness, all affect performance. In situations where water is very clear and calm and fish are very selective, longer, smaller-diameter leaders and tippets are more effective because they are less visible and allow the fly to look and act more natural.

drawback, however, is that knots can catch on rod guides or plant life, which can cause fish loss, casting tangles, and leader breakage.

The **braided leader** has a butt and midsection of braided strands of monofilament and a knotted or glued tip section of level nylon monofilament. The **twisted leader** is similar except the strands are twisted rather than braided.

Although braided and twisted leaders are designed to be more flexible and cast better, we have not found this to be the case in most situations.

The **knotless tapered** leader, a continuous length of extruded tapering monofilament, is the most popular and least troublesome design in our experience at the L.L. Bean Fly-Fishing Schools and for actual fly fishing. Knotless tapered leaders provide greater freedom from casting tangles, snags, and knot or glue failures.

Level leaders function reasonably well if precise presentation is not necessary, especially short ones (2 to 6 feet) used on sinking-tip or full-sinking fly lines.

Tapered leaders are made in 4-, 6-, 7½-, 9-, 10-, 12-, and 16-foot lengths. The longer leaders, 7½ through 16 feet, are generally used with floating lines. The 7½-foot leader is good for very narrow streams, waters with a rough surface, or murky waters. The 9-foot length is best for general conditions. The 12- and 16-foot lengths are best for very clear waters with calm surfaces.

Leader with bite tippet and fly attached.

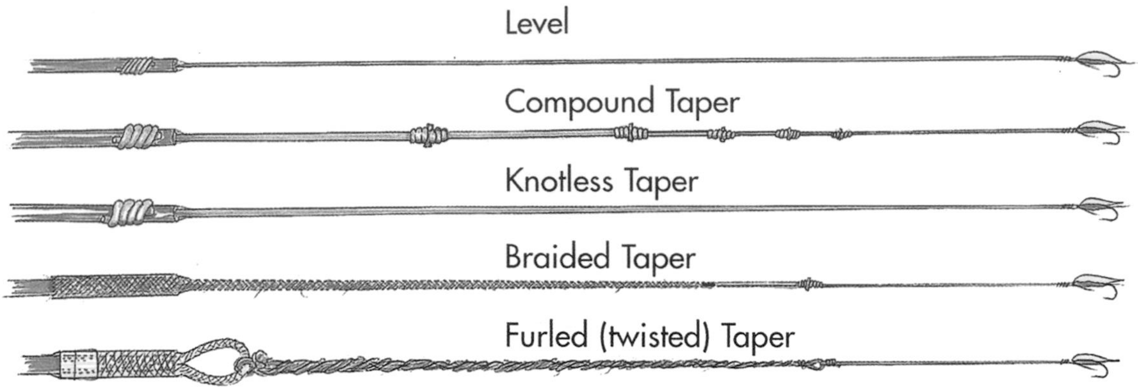

Level

Compound Taper

Knotless Taper

Braided Taper

Furled (twisted) Taper

Five common leader designs.

For sinking-tip and full-sinking fly lines, 2-, 4-, and 6-foot lengths are most useful. Because nylon monofilament is only slightly denser than water and thus resists sinking, the shorter the leader, the more effective the sinking portion of the line will be in bringing the fly to the desired depth.

Most knotless tapered leaders are sold today as all-purpose leaders or specific-purpose leaders, such as nymph, bass, saltwater, or sinking line. The all-purpose leader is generally recommended for beginning fly fishers; as your skills and interest increase, the specific-purpose leaders become preferable.

Fluorocarbon Leaders and Tippets

An alternative to nylon monofilament offers some truly significant improvements for leaders and tippets: polyvinylidene fluoride or, more simply, fluorocarbon. Compared to the best nylon it is less visible, denser (sinks faster), more abrasion resistant, unaffected by ultraviolet radiation, and has better knot strength when wet.

Still, compared to nylon, it's also more expensive, harder to tie knots with, not as strong, and only available in level filaments. Tapered leaders must be hand-tied. Fluorocarbon is probably most practical as an alternative material when its specific properties are needed over those of nylon.

BACKING

Backing is a length of braided line that is attached and wound onto the reel spool and then attached to the end of the fly line.

The purpose of backing is to provide extra line in case a fish is strong enough to pull off

FLY LINE AND LEADER CHART

Type of Fly Line	*Leader Length (Feet)*	*Where to Use*
Floating (L, DT, WF)	6 to 7½	Narrow, weedy, brushy creeks (15 to 20 feet wide) and small ponds
Floating (L, DT, WF)	7½ to 9	Most creeks, streams, ponds, and lakes
Floating (L, DT, WF)	9, 12, 16	Very clear, calm, shallow, slow-moving spring creeks, ponds, and lakes
Floating bass and saltwater (WF)	7½ to 9	Most bass, pike, and panfish streams, ponds, lakes, and saltwater areas
Sinking tip (WF)	4 to 6	Most waters listed above from 3 to 10 feet deep
Full sinking (WF, SH)	2 to 6	Most waters listed above 4 to 30 feet deep

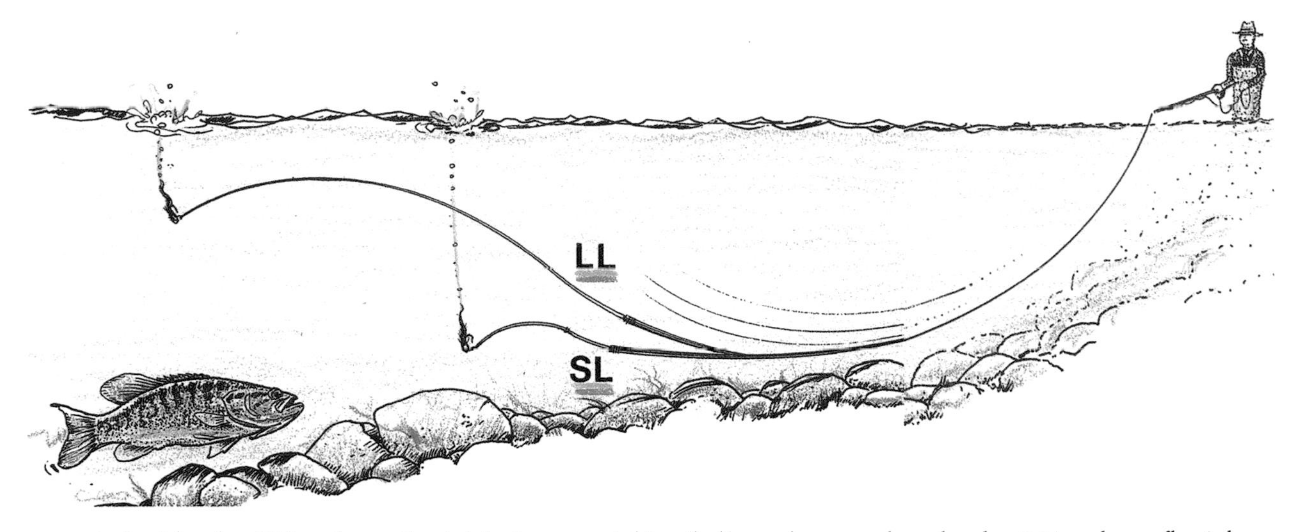

A short leader (SL) makes a fly sink faster on a sinking fly line, whereas a long leader (LL) makes a fly sink slower.

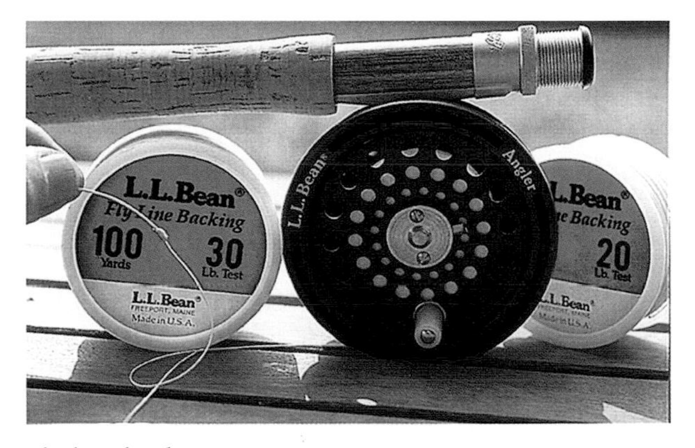

Fly-line backing.

more than the fly line (a fly line is usually 80 to 120 feet long). Backing also serves to fill the reel spool's excess capacity. This setup allows the reel to retrieve the fly line more efficiently and also allows the fly line to be stored on the reel in relatively large coils. These large coils make straightening the fly line easier, and a straight, coil-less fly line casts and fishes better.

The amount of backing used is dictated by the reel-spool capacity, the fly-line size, and how far a fish might run when hooked. We recommend that any fly reel have at least 50 yards of backing on it. Twenty-pound test is best for smaller line weights (1 to 6), and 30-pound test for line sizes 7 to 12.

The ideal line for backing is braided, low-strength Dacron or Kevlar (12-, 20-, or 30-pound test) attached to the reel spool and then to the end of the fly line. Braided nylon fishing line will also work. *Never* use nylon monofilament for backing: It is prone to tangles and can damage the reel spool.

THE FLY ROD

The traditional symbol of the sport, the long, slender, and graceful fly rod is second only to the fly line in importance. The responsive fly rod gives you the control and feel that make casting, fishing, and catching fish on flies so much fun.

The fly rod transfers energy and control from the fly fisher to the line, leader, and fly.

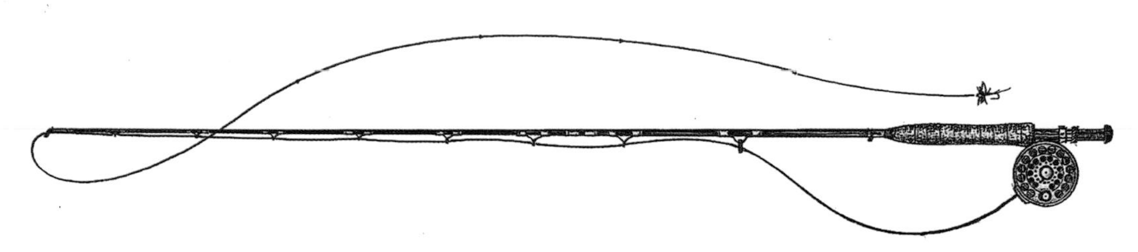

Rod length, taper, and action are specifically designed for this purpose. Bait-casting or spinning rods will not perform well for fly fishing.

The fly rod must be matched with the correct fly-line weight for optimum performance in fly casting and presentation. Most fly rods manufactured in the past 25 years have the correct line-matching information printed on them just forward of the handle and hookkeeper. Usually, the line-weight range is given along with the rod's length and approximate weight.

Specifications listed on a fly rod include rod length and recommended line weight.

The above illustration shows the typical rod specification markings: Model Code Number 907, 9 feet, 3⅛ ounces, 7-weight line. (Note that the Model Code Number 907 indicates a 9-foot rod and a 7-weight line.) Some manufacturers recommend two line weights. The lighter size is usually for more delicate presentations or for sinking or sinking-tip lines. The heavier is better for floating lines, windy conditions, and casting larger flies.

There are seven parts to a fly rod:

The **butt section** is the part of the rod from the handle to one-third of the way up the rod's length. The stiffest part of the rod, the butt mainly adds length and strength to the rod and creates leverage.

The **midsection** is the middle third of the rod's length. This section generally contains the flexing or casting power of the rod.

The **tip** is the top third of the rod's length and is the most flexible part. The tip is principally for shock absorption when striking and landing fish.

The **handle** includes the butt cap, the reel-seat lock for attaching the fly reel in place, the cork grip (also called the handle or rod-hand grip), and the handle check cap. Some heavier rods also have a **fighting** or **extension butt** immediately behind the reel seat.

There are three basic designs of reel seats: *down-locking*, *up-locking*, and *slide band*. The up-locking reel seat is generally the most dependable choice.

The **hookkeeper** is a wire ring or other simple device that holds the fly's hook safely in place when the outfit is rigged but the angler is not fishing.

The **guides** hold and control the line on the rod during casting. The guides include the *stripper* (or stripping) guide, which is the first guide up the rod from the rod handle and which should be made of a low-friction, hard material. The stripper guide's large inside diameter reduces friction, tangles, and surface wear between line and guide. The *snake* guides hold the fly line close to the rod during casting. Snake guides are light and nearly friction-free to allow easy casting and retrieving of line. The *tip-top* guide holds the fly line at the end of the rod, and, like the other guides, it is designed to be practically friction-free

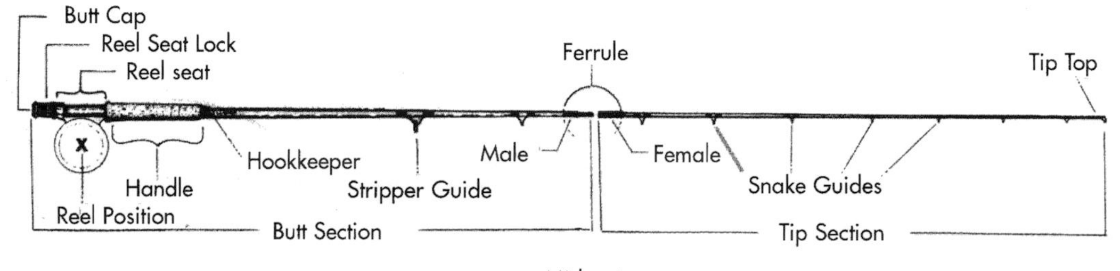

Fly-rod reel seat types: (left to right) slide band, down-locking, up-locking, up-locking with small extension or fighting butt.

and also to prevent tangling of the line on the end of the rod.

The **ferrule** is a connection between rod sections. This allows the long fly rod to be easily disassembled for storage. Most fly rods are two- or three-piece, but some break down into as many as six sections for storage or packing convenience. Most ferrules on modern graphite fly rods are made of graphite composites that are lighter and flex more than the older metal ferrule designs.

Most modern fly rods are made of from one of three materials. Each material has different performance characteristics and different production costs. The right fly rod for you depends on the type of fishing you will be doing, your level of skill in fly fishing, and what you can afford. The three rod materials are bamboo, fiberglass, and graphite. Combinations of graphite, glass, boron, and/or Kevlar are sometimes used to manufacture composite rods.

Hookkeeper.

Today's **bamboo** or **split-cane rods** are combinations of traditional craftsmanship

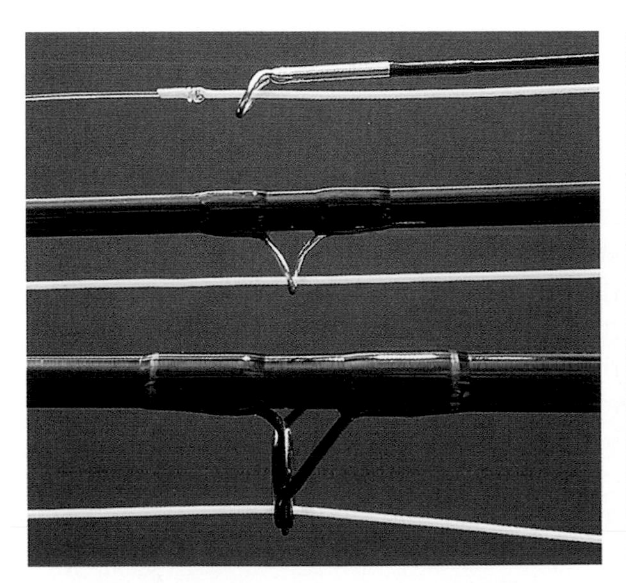

Fly-rod guides: (top to bottom) tip-top, snake guide, stripper guide.

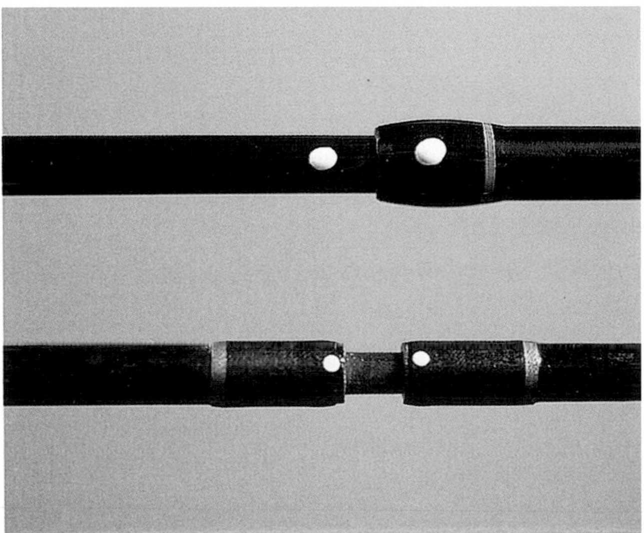

Fly-rod ferrules: sleeve ferrule (top), spigot ferrule (bottom).

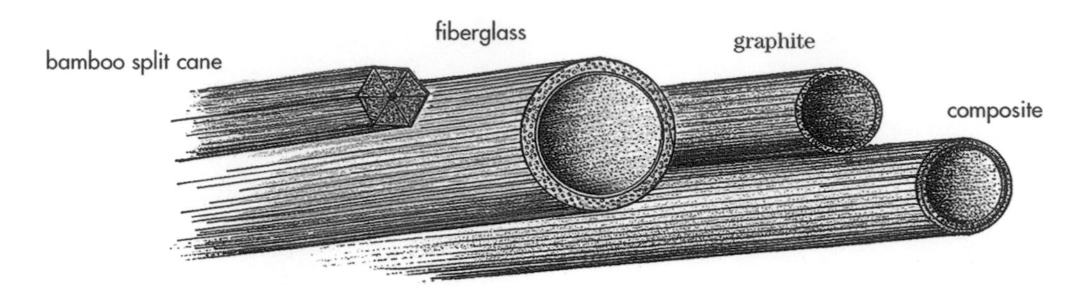

Fly-Rod Blank Materials
All four blank diameters are in the perspective of one fly-line weight. Colors are usually natural; some rods are painted to give a more interesting or attractive fishy finish.

and modern technology. Those built from high-quality Tonkin cane are lovely to look at and can be very enjoyable to fish with. They are expensive, however, and require considerable care. Those impregnated with special resins tend to require less care, seldom warp, and are more durable. Practically speaking, however, the bamboo fly rod is only for those who are willing to trade light weight and performance of graphite rods for beauty, feel, craftsmanship, and aesthetics. Lighter-line-weight bamboo fly rods (2- to 5-weights) are the most practical for fly fishing today.

Fiberglass rods replaced bamboo in popularity, durability, and affordability after World War II. Today they are becoming more rare than bamboo rods due to the greater popularity of graphite fly rods.

Graphite (carbon fiber) rods completely dominate the fly-rod market. They are lighter, more sensitive, more powerful, and more forgiving than either bamboo or glass rods. Each year better and more reasonably priced carbon fibers are being manufactured, and graphite fly rods are constantly being improved. Well-made, inexpensive models make it possible for anyone to own an excellent-casting fly rod. We highly recommend graphite for your first fly rod.

Rod Action

The "feel" of a fly rod when it is flexed, cast, mended with, or used to hook and battle a fish is generally described as the rod's *action* or *performance.* This feel is of considerable interest to fly fishers at all levels. The main categories of action are fast, medium, and slow.

Fast-action rods feel stiff when flexed. When the fly line is cast, the rod unflexes or straightens rapidly.

Medium-action rods are more limber when flexed than fast-action, unflex a little slower, and seem smoother. A medium-action rod bends more than a fast-action under the same line weight.

Slow-action rods are very limber and feel rather willowy as they flex and unflex. A slow-action rod bends much more than a fast- or medium-action, especially in the mid- and butt sections.

Regardless of their action, all fly rods should flex progressively from tip to butt under varying loads. This flex produces excellent performance at casting distances of 20 to 80 feet and casts a wide range of fly sizes and weights. When you are fishing the fly, the tip is used to move and animate the fly. When you are setting the hook on a fish, the tip is the principal energy absorber. The midsection and the butt are the energy transmitters. Once the fish is hooked, the rod becomes a lifting and pulling tool. It also transmits the fish's movements to your hand and absorbs the shock of the fish's more violent movements.

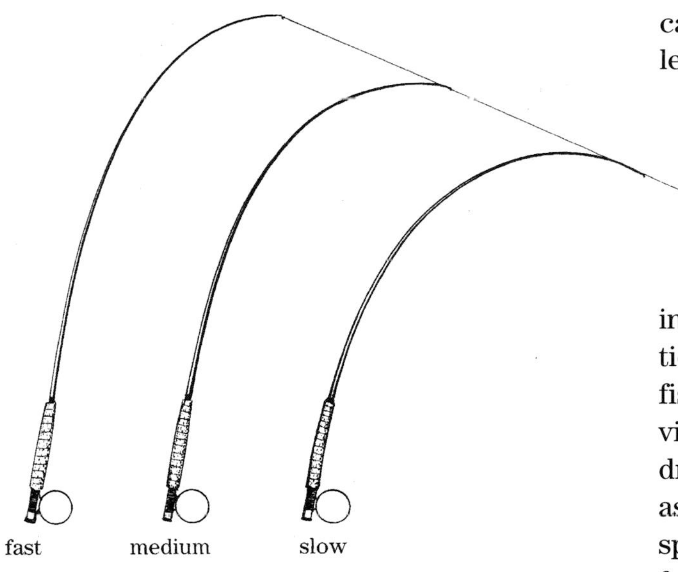

This is how fly rods of different actions flex under identical loads.

The Most Versatile Fly Rod for Beginners

A medium-action, progressively loading fly rod is the best rod with which to learn the sport. Medium action is the most adaptable to a person's individual timing and reflexes. The beginner's rod should be 8 to 8½ feet long, designed to cast a 6- or 7-weight line. This combination is light, sensitive, and provides ample power to cast from 20 to 60 feet. With it you can fish most flies designed for trout, panfish, and small- to medium-sized bass.

After you begin to master the basic fly-casting strokes, qualified instructors will be able to advise you on which action best suits your own reflexes and coordination level. Generally, the quicker your own reaction time, the faster the rod action that will suit you. A person who tends to be relaxed and to have a smooth, slow reaction is better suited to a medium- or slow-action rod; someone with very quick reflexes will probably be more successful with a fast-action rod. Once you are properly matched with a rod, your skill as a caster should progress rapidly. As your casting skill improves, you will be able to cast well with a wider range of fly-rod actions, lengths, line weights, and fly sizes.

THE FLY REEL

The primary function of a fly reel is to contain the backing, the fly line, and the leader. Other functions are to retrieve line and aid in fighting fish. While you are fighting a fish, the reel provides a variable degree of resistance (called drag) that helps tire a strong-swimming fish as it pulls line off the reel. A fly reel, unlike spinning or casting reels, performs no casting function.

The reel is positioned and locked onto the fly rod directly behind and under the rod-hand grip. In this position it counterbalances the rod's weight during casting and fishing and so helps prevent hand and arm fatigue. It also eliminates most fly-line tangles. There are three basic types of fly reels: the single action, the multiplier, and the automatic.

Types of Reels

The **single-action** reel is a simple direct-drive winch with a one-to-one ratio. One complete revolution of the reel's handle causes the reel spool to make one complete revolution.

A well-designed single-action fly reel should be lightweight and corrosion resistant. It should have an adjustable drag to prevent line from free-spooling when it is pulled out by the angler or a fish. Another useful component is an exposed, flanged spool for palming or finger-dragging to increase pressure on a running fish. An audible-click drag is useful to let you hear how fast a fish is taking out line.

A single-action reel should also have interchangeable spools. A properly sized spool will hold the fly line that matches the rod you intend to use, plus 50 to 100 yards of backing. A spool with perforated sides is lighter than one

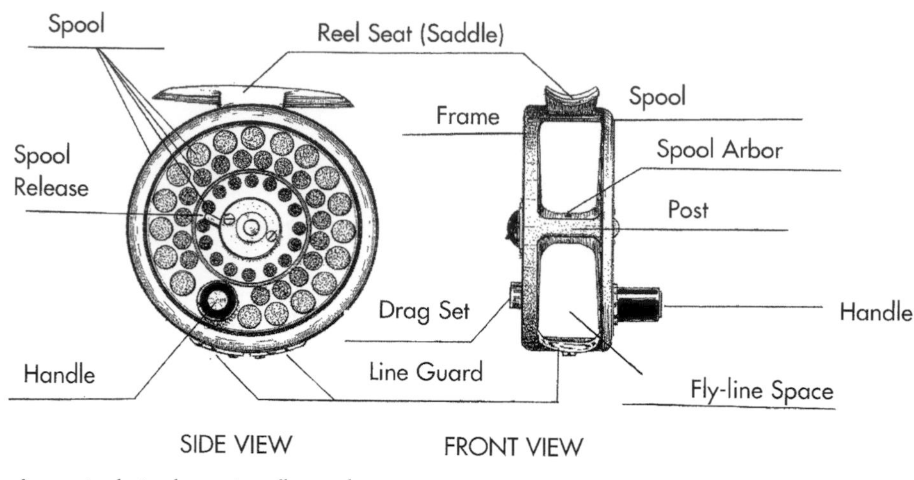

The parts of a typical single-action fly reel.

with solid sides, and allows wet line to dry when stored on the spool.

The **multiplier** reel is similar in design to a single-action reel, except that it has a complex, geared winch with a one-to-greater-than-one handle-to-spool ratio. One turn of the handle causes the spool to revolve 1½ to 3 times. Such a fly reel is most useful when fast or long line retrieves are routinely necessary.

The **automatic** reel is designed to rewind line automatically. If you have ever used a roller type of pull-down window shade, you know the principle. As you pull fly line off the reel, the action puts tension on a built-in coil spring. Then you can quickly and mechanically wind the line back onto the spool by lifting a spool-spring tension lever.

The automatic fly reel has very limited capacity for line and backing and offers no quick-change, extra-spool options. Because of its spring-loading design, it has a very coarse and nonadjustable drag system. Only a limited amount of fly line can be pulled directly off the reel without releasing the spring tension. This limitation is troublesome if you need to pull additional line or backing off the reel. The automatic is quite heavy and mechanically unreliable in many fly-fishing situations. It is best suited for fly fishing where short casting is used, fast retrieves are needed, and the fish

Fly reels: (left to right) single action, multiplier, and automatic.

> **Beginner's Outfit**
>
> The outfit we recommend for most people over 14 years old is a 6- or 7-weight, 8½-foot graphite two-piece fly rod with a medium-fast action; a single-action fly reel with 50 to 100 yards of 20-pound-test Dacron backing; and a floating weight-forward 6- or 7-weight fly line with a 7½- or 9-foot knotless tapered leader. This is the best all-around outfit for all things—flies, fish, your strength, and conditions. For a younger or smaller person, an 8-foot, 5- or 6-weight rod and line is best.

does not take line off the reel. People who have the use of only one hand or a disabled hand, however, can fly fish successfully with the automatic fly reel.

The single-action reel is the most popular and practical choice for most fly fishing. We recommend this type of reel in a size that will hold a 6- or 7-weight fly line and the appropriate amount of backing.

FLIES

The **fly** is an artificial lure designed either to imitate natural fish foods or to otherwise stimulate a fish into striking. The term *fly* stems from fly fishing's origins in Europe where live insects impaled on hooks were used to catch trout, grayling, and other species. Later, artificial imitations of live insects were conceived. Today the term *fly* doesn't necessarily mean an imitation of an insect, but rather covers a wide variety of artificial fishing lures.

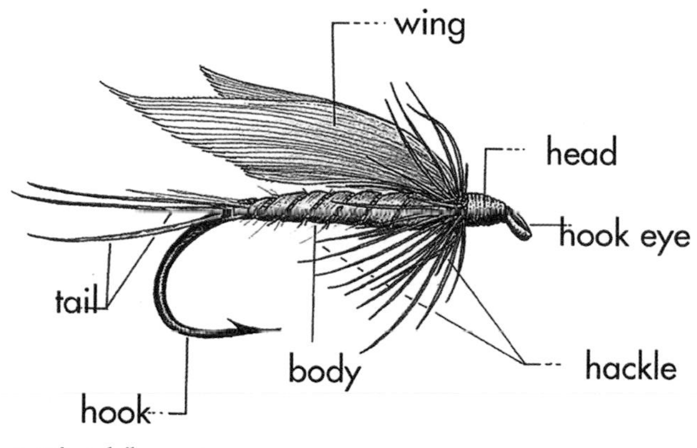

Artificial fly parts.

The fly seldom weighs more than 1/32 ounce and usually weighs less than 1/64 ounce. Fly lengths are from 1/16 inch to 10 inches. Flies are handmade, usually on a single, light hook using lightweight, natural and/or synthetic materials such as feathers, furs, threads, flosses, latex, plastics, wood, foam rubber, and waterproof cements.

There are five important aspects in a good artificial fly: size, action, shape, color, and odor. Each of these is sensed and investigated by the fish before it is lured into trying to eat the fraud.

Size is extremely important, especially so when the food a fly imitates is less than an inch long. **Action** is important, too, because a fly must seem alive or otherwise in a natural state. **Shape** adds an impressionistic or realistic imitation of the food form. **Color** enhances the imitation by increasing visual recognition and attracting the fish. Though flies are not usually "scented" with fish food odors, it is important that the fly have a neutral or natural **odor** not disliked by fish.

Types of Flies

The two general types of fly designs are floating (dry) flies and sinking (wet) flies.

The **floating,** or **dry,** fly rides on or in the water's surface. Floating flies come in a wide range of sizes, color patterns, and shapes, and may imitate aquatic or terrestrial insects, small animals, reptiles, amphibians, or even plant seeds.

The floating fly's effectiveness is determined by its shape, the material from which it is made, and how it is manipulated by the angler on the water's surface. The flies listed below can be fished many ways, from sitting motionless on the surface to fluttering, wiggling, popping, diving, or skipping across the

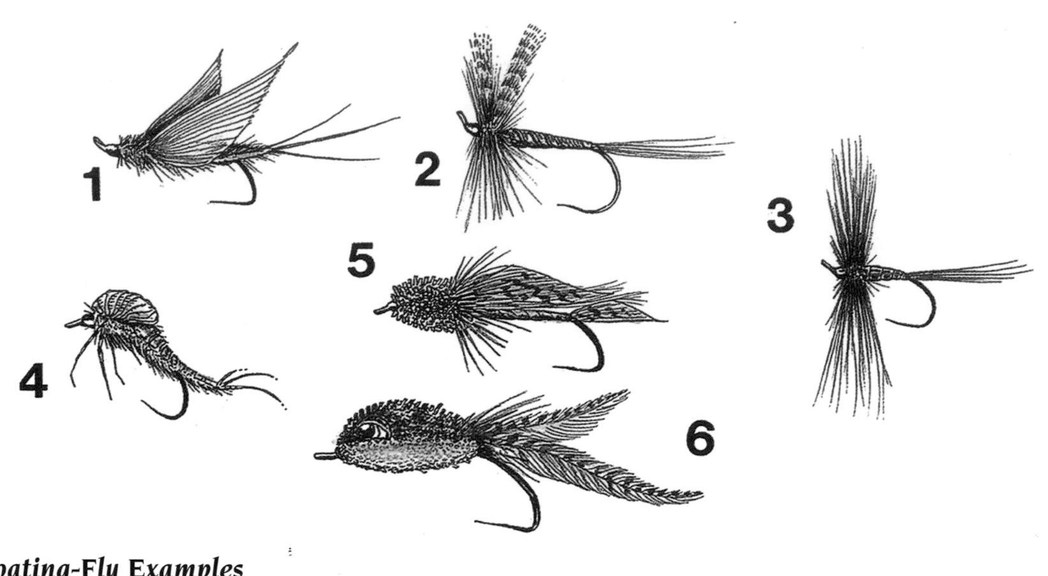

Floating-Fly Examples
1. No-hackle dry fly.
2. Hackled dry fly.
3. Skater dry fly.
4. Floating-emergent nymph.
5. Muddler minnow.
6. Deer-hair frog.

surface. These lifelike actions imitate natural floating foods and so attract the fish.

Floating flies are usually effective during warmer weather when both terrestrial (land-based) and aquatic (water-based) foods are more active and abundant. Adult aquatic insects (such as mayflies, caddisflies, and midges) and terrestrial insects (such as ants, grasshoppers, and beetles) are far more active during warmer weather. At times, minnows and nymphs (immature aquatic insects) also gather at the water's surface to feed, to flee underwater predators, or to hatch (nymphs). During times of such surface activity, floating flies that imitate what are normally subsurface foods can be effective. Floating-fly designs include:

1. Hackled dry flies
2. No-hackle dry flies
3. Wakers
4. Bass poppers
5. Hair bugs
6. Muddlers
7. Spiders
8. Skaters
9. Divers
10. Sponge bugs
11. Floating nymphs
12. Terrestrial insects

Sinking, or **wet,** flies are designed to imitate a wide range of submerged terrestrial or aquatic organisms. Sinking flies may also be designed to stimulate a reflex response that makes fish strike.

Sinking-fly materials are either water absorbent or heavier than water, so the fly sinks. The fly's shape and density and the fishing method used determine how deep it is fished. Sinking-fly designs include:

1. Traditional wet flies
2. Soft-hackle flies
3. Nymphs
4. Streamers

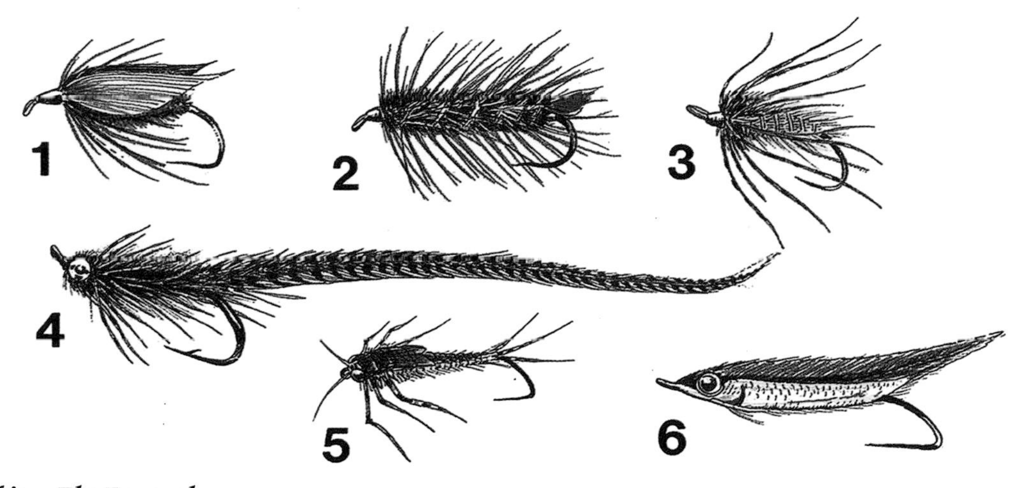

Sinking-Fly Examples

1. Wet fly.
2. Woolly worm fly.
3. Soft-hackle fly.
4. Eelworm.
5. Nymph.
6. Matuka mylar streamer.

5. Egg flies
6. Attractors
7. Worms
8. Bucktails
9. Woolly Worms
10. Eelworm streamers
11. Leeches
12. Emergers
13. Woolly Buggers
14. Crayfish

Sinking flies are more effective than floating flies overall because most of the time fish feed under the water's surface. That's because underwater food is generally more abundant and easier for the fish to detect. Besides, a fish feeding under the surface exposes itself to fewer predators than one feeding on the surface.

2 Assembling Fly Tackle

It is easy to assemble fly tackle properly, but at first the several components of the tackle system—the rod, reel, backing, fly line, leader, tippet, and fly—might seem confusing. With practice, it will all become second nature.

The accompanying diagrams should give you a clear picture of how to set up the complete tackle system used in most fly fishing. You might find it valuable also to seek out the help of someone who already fly fishes.

The instructions are divided into two parts: first the initial reel and line-components assembly, using the fly-rod butt section, and then the complete assembly for actual fishing.

FLY-LINE SYSTEM COMPONENT ASSEMBLY

The first thing to do is learn the knots and connections of the fly-line system. Strong, small, smooth, easy-to-make junctions are absolutely necessary for high performance. The connections that we recommend and use are neat, strong, and easy to do yourself. We think they are among the best yet developed.

Study the diagram. Notice that there are six parts to the fly-line system: the fly reel, braided backing, fly line, leader, tippet, and fly. To join these parts efficiently, there are five connections. For four of these, the same knot is used—the Duncan loop (also called the uni-knot). For the other connection, the tippet to leader, use the double surgeon's knot.

The connections we will be making are:

1. Backing to reel.
2. Backing to fly line.
3. Leader to fly line.
4. Tippet to leader tip.
5. Tippet end to fly.

To set up your system, select a well-lighted tabletop surface and a comfortable chair. Have on hand a small pair of needle-nose pliers with smooth jaws, scissors, fingernail clippers, several size 8 to 10 darning needles, a needle vise or an L.L. Bean Knot Tool Kit, and an emery stone. Have ready your fly rod's handle section, fly reel, a spool of backing, fly line, leader, tippet material, and a large fly or hook.

Remove the fly-rod butt section from its protective tube and cloth case. Check your reel to make sure that its drag system is set to operate correctly when used with the hand with which you intend to hold its handle. Most new fly reels are convertible to right- or left-hand wind. Most come from the manufacturer

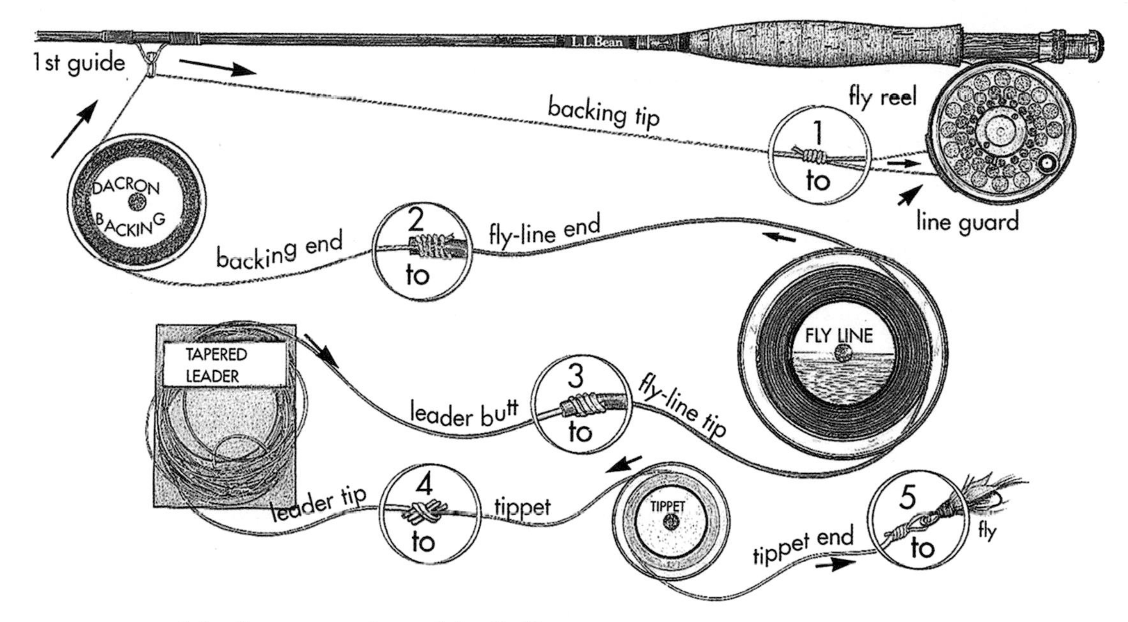

The components and the five connections of the fly-line system.

set up to operate with right-hand wind. If you wish to use the other hand, refer to the reel's instructions or ask a knowledgeable friend or salesperson to help you convert the rod. We *strongly* recommend that you use the hand you do *not* cast the rod with to control the fly reel—that is, if you cast right-handed, retrieve with your left hand. With this arrangement, you need not switch hands after casting to begin fighting a fish or retrieving line.

Backing to Reel

Place the fly reel on the fly-rod handle with the reel handle on the side that you intend to use for retrieve and the reel's *line guard* facing forward. Tighten the reel seat so that the reel does not rock from side to side or move forward or backward. Use finger pressure only—avoid using a wrench or pliers to tighten the reel-seat lock rings. When the reel is mounted on the rod, you can easily reel on backing, line, and leader because the rod butt provides a convenient handle.

The next step is to put the backing on the reel. Remove 5 or 6 feet of backing from the spool and place its tag end down through the stripper guide toward the handle, then through the reel's line guard, and finally twice around the spool spindle. (This is simpler and faster to do if you remove the reel spool from the reel's frame. Be sure to pass the line through the line guard before attaching it to the spool.)

Make sure that the backing end passes in and out at the same place and not between one or two of the reel's frame posts; otherwise, you'll find it impossible to tie the line to the spool. Pull at least 12 inches of backing through the reel; this will be enough to tie the Duncan loop. (See the diagram *Backing to Fly Reel.*) *Be sure you snug the knot tightly down on the spool's spindle; it must not slip on it.*

Knot #1: Backing to Fly Reel with Duncan Loop

1. Pass the backing line through the line guard of the reel and then twice around the reel spool and back out to the line guard—leaving 8 to 12 inches of tag end for the knot.
2. Form a large loop with the tag end toward and then away from the reel.
3. The tag excess should now be about 6 to 8 inches long.
4. With the tag end, make four wraps away from the reel, through the loop and standing line, as shown here.

5. Pull on the **tag** to tighten the knot over the line.
6. Pull hard on the line to slide and tighten the line against the spool spindle. Clip off the excess tag end. Make sure that the knot loop is absolutely tight against the spindle.

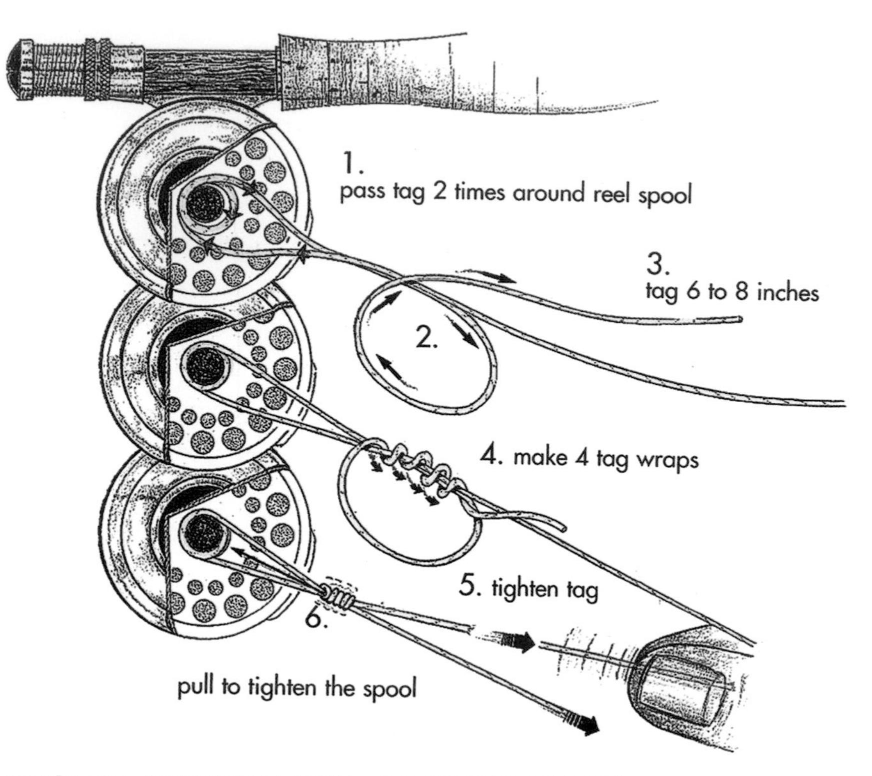

KNOT #1: DUNCAN LOOP—BACKING TO FLY REEL

You are now ready to wind the backing onto the reel spool. Place a pencil, pen, or wooden dowel through the center hole of the backing spool. If help is available, have someone hold the backing spool by the pencil; if you're alone, place the pencil between your knees for control and tension. *Always wind the reel's handle forward*—clockwise with your right hand, counterclockwise with your left. Use just enough tension between backing spool and reel spool to ensure that the backing is firmly wrapped on the fly-reel spool.

As you wind on backing, try to position the consecutive winds on the spool evenly, going from one side to the other and back. Use your rod hand's index finger to control tension and position the backing on the spool.

You should fill the spool with backing to a level that leaves enough space to hold the fly line plus a fingertip's clearance between the reel post and fly line. This may be hard to judge. If you're in doubt, ask an experienced fly fisher or your tackle dealer how much backing your particular reel needs with the fly line you have. Remember, a floating line takes up more space than the same weight and length of sinking line.

Backing to Fly Line

After placing the proper amount of backing on the reel, you are ready to attach the fly line to the backing. If the fly line is wound on a plastic storage spool, find the end and pull off about 24 inches of fly line. If the fly line is only coiled loosely around the plastic spool, carefully remove any twist-ties, then find the end and pull out the fly-line length. Most manufacturers include in the container directions for unspooling their fly line. With a weight-forward line, you must tie the backing to the back or shooting portion of the fly line; most manufacturers mark this with a small printed tab. For level or double-taper fly lines, it does not matter which end you use first. Try to locate the top or upper end, however, for easiest unwinding.

To attach the backing to the fly-line end, follow the *Backing to Fly Line* diagram, which is simply a modification of the *Backing to Fly Reel* knot.

Knot #2: Backing to Fly Line with Duncan Loop

1. Lay 10 inches of backing alongside the end of the fly line.

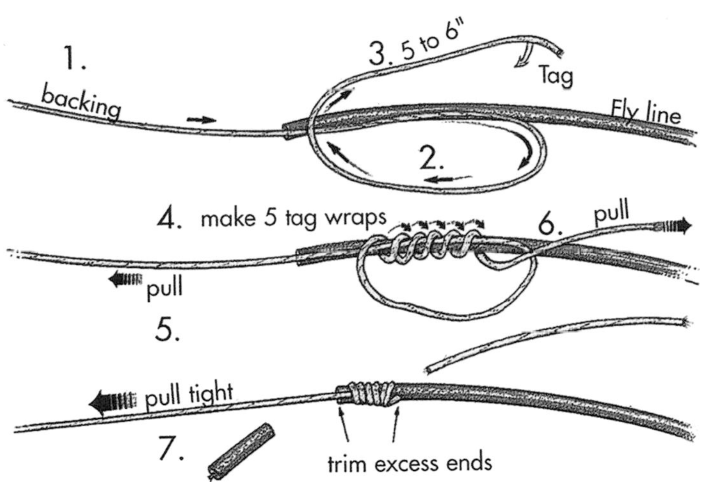

KNOT #2: DUNCAN LOOP—BACKING TO FLY LINE

2. Loop the tag end back toward the fly-line end to form a 2-inch loop.
3. The tag end of the backing should be 5 or 6 inches long.
4. With the tag end of the backing, make five wraps over the fly line and through the loop back from the fly-line end.
5. Grasp the fly line and wraps, then carefully pull on both sides of the backing to close the slack in the loop. Take care not to allow the knot to slip off the end of the fly line.
6. Pull on the tag end to tighten the knot wraps and loop firmly against the end of the fly line. Try to keep the knot wraps close together but not overlapping.
7. Pull the backing tight and trim the excess fly line and backing so that you have a neat, trouble-free knot. Coat the knot and fly-line end with a flexible waterproof cement to make the connection smoother and stronger.

With the backing attached to the fly line, carefully wind it onto the reel spool, firmly but not tightly. Leave about 4 feet of the fly line loose off the reel for the leader-to-fly-line connection. Should your reel spool be too full of backing to accept the entire fly line with room for your little finger between the fly line and the reel's frame posts, you must do one of two things: Remove the fly line, cut the backing-to-fly-line knot, and remove some part of the backing so that the fly line fits the spool; or, if you are putting on a level or weight-forward line, you can cut off as much as 10 to 12 feet from the level running line without affecting casting or fishing performance. The advantage of the latter is that it allows for more backing.

Leader to Fly Line

If the leader is coiled and stored in a package, remove it carefully. Place three or four fingers inside the leader coils and spread your fingers. With your other hand, carefully unravel the leader, butt section first, while maintaining finger tension on the remaining coils until the leader is completely uncoiled. This simple procedure will prevent some time-consuming tangles. Now, using your hands, stretch and stroke the leader's butt section to remove some of the nylon's coil memory. This makes tying it to the fly line much faster and easier. Put a simple, single overhand knot 2 or 3 inches from the butt end of the leader. This will ensure against a couple of errors that you might make as you attach the leader to the fly line.

Fly-Line Tip to Leader Butt Match: (left to right) Leader is too flexible = poor performance; leader and fly line are same stiffness = excellent performance; leader is stiffer than fly-line tip = poor performance.

For optimum casting performance, the fly-line tip and leader-butt junction should be of the same general flexibility. Good-quality leaders are usually designed with butts that match the fly-line tips. If your leader butt is too stiff, here's what to do to make it match: Stroke it with a smooth-jawed pair of needle-nose pliers to flatten the leader slightly. This will make the butt more flexible to match the fly-line tip.

Attach the leader butt to the fly-line tip by following the steps in the *Leader to Fly Line* illustration.

Knot #3: Leader to Fly Line with Duncan Loop

This method works with knotless tapered leaders (with no tippet added yet) and braided hollow-core fly lines.

1. Begin with a size 8, 9, or 10 crewel or darning needle.
2. Insert the needle's eye end into the core of the fly line's tip ¼ to ⅜ inch; then push it out the side of the coating, as shown.
3. Pass 1 inch of the leader tip through the eye of the needle. If the tip is too large, shave 1 or 2 inches of it with a razor blade until it is small enough to pass through the eye.
4. Pull the needle and end of the leader out of the tip of the fly line.
5. Pull the leader through the line tip to about 6 or 8 inches from the end of the butt.
6. With the end of the butt, form a loop next to the fly line, away from the tip end of the line.
7. Holding the leader butt loop and fly line firmly, make four snug, close-spaced wraps beginning at the exit hole, around the fly line and through the loop as shown. Make sure that you wrap the leader butt *away* from the fly-line tip end.
8. Take great care to keep the leader-butt wraps tightly in place while pulling the

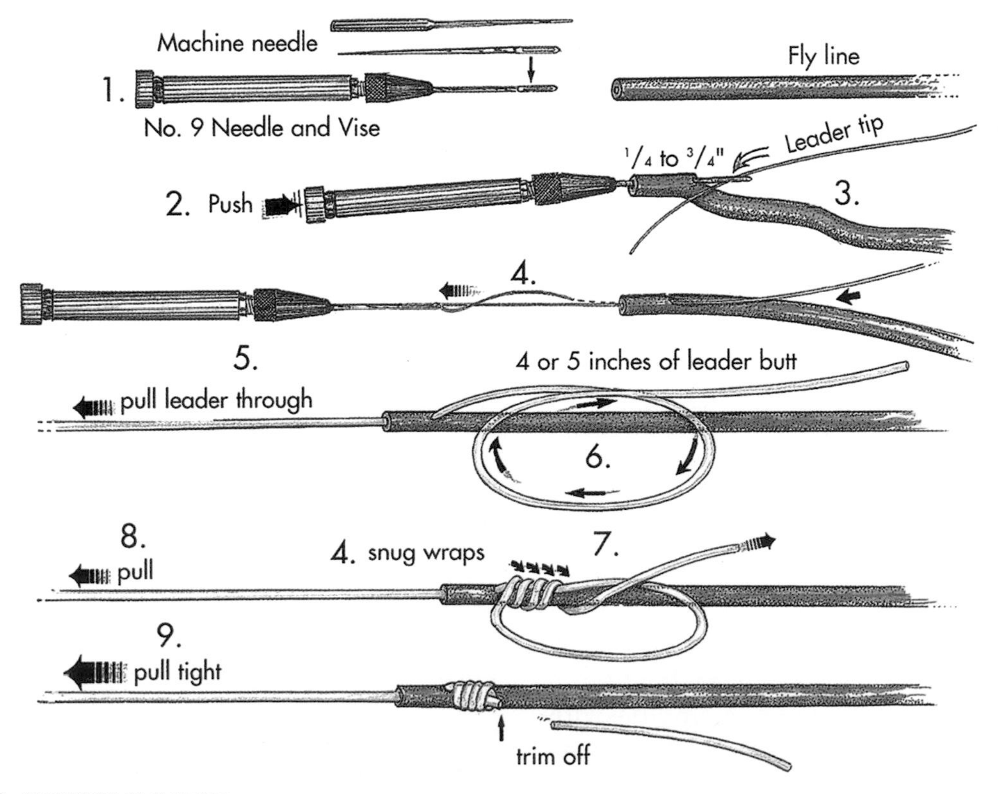

KNOT #3: DUNCAN LOOP—LEADER TO FLY LINE

leader in order to snug up the knot's wraps and loop.

9. Make one more extra-hard pull on the leader to snug it completely; then trim the excess leader-butt tag close to the knot. To make the knot smoother, coat it and the tip of the line with a fast-drying, flexible, waterproof cement, such as Zap-A-Gap or Dave's Flexament.

Note: If you have a knotted tapered leader, follow these steps (and see *Knotted Leader to Fly Line* diagram).

1A. Hold the leader-butt end so that it curves up.

1B. Using a *new*, very sharp razor blade, stick the side of the butt end at a 90-degree angle, 2 inches from the end. Then change the angle to 10 degrees and slowly shave a portion away.

1C. Continue to rotate the butt and shave the end two or three times or until ½ inch of the end will pass through a size 8 or 9 darning-needle eye.

1D. Dull the needle point with a stone so it will pass easily inside the braided core of the fly line. Using a pin vise to hold the needle for steps 1D and 2A will help.

2A. Push the needle point ¼ inch into the fly-line tip core and then out through the side of the line up to the needle eye. Place the leader butt through the eye ½ inch and crimp.

2B. Pull the needle completely through the side of the line. Clear the leader from the eye, then *carefully* pull 6 to 8 inches of the leader through the line tip. Then go to step 5 of the *Leader to Fly Line* instructions.

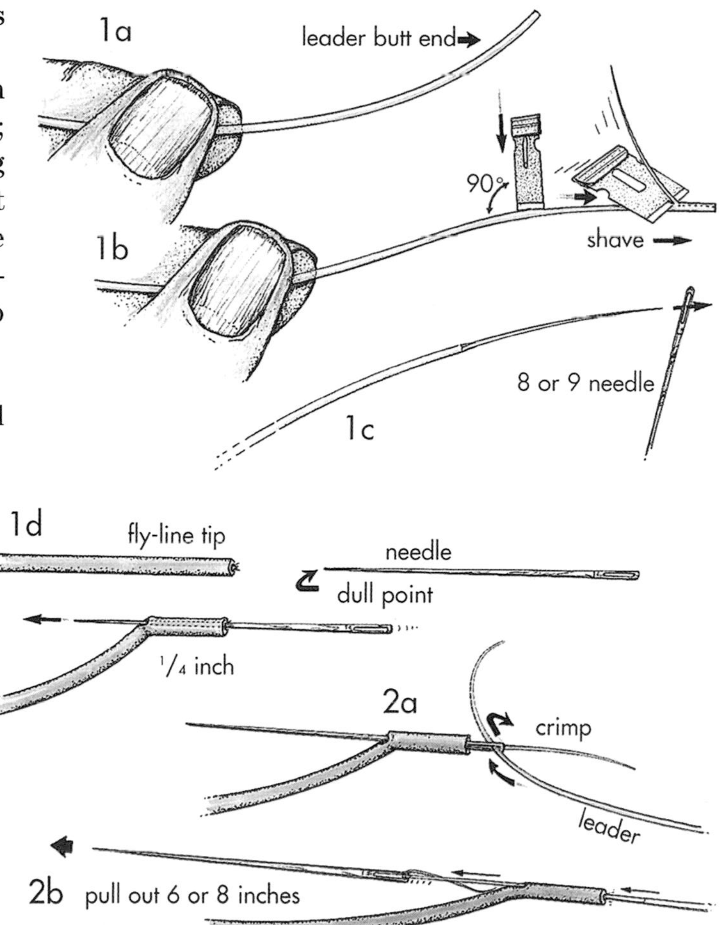

KNOT #3A: KNOTTED LEADER TO FLY LINE

Other leader-to-fly-line options: If your line has a solid core, such as lead core, monofilament, Kevlar filament, or twisted filament, tie the leader to this with the Duncan Loop Knot #2 (*Backing to Fly Line*) method.

Note that two options besides the Duncan loop are included. One is a special Zap-A-Gap cemented leader-to-line connection that, when properly done, gives you a simple, smooth, and strong alternative. The other is a braided loop, which is popular for fast, loop-to-loop leader changing or because some folks do not wish to tie knots. There are also several gadgets for attaching the leader to the fly line that we don't recommend. The metal eyelets with a barbed point and the plastic connectors are apt to fail. Besides, making the connections shown here takes about the same amount of time as installing the gadgets—and they are smaller, smoother, and much more dependable and efficient.

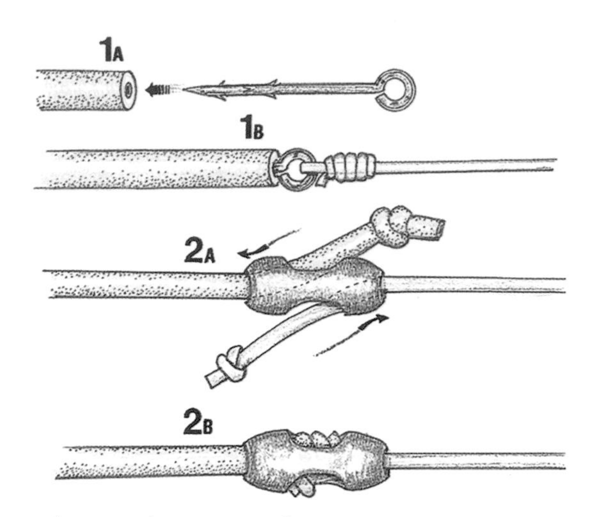

Leader To Fly-Line Gadget Connectors

1A. Insert the metal barbed eyelet into the fly-line tip end.

1B. The leader butt is tied to the eyelet with a clinch knot.

2A. Pass the line and butt ends through the connectors and form a simple single overhand knot in the end of each. Trim excess ends.

2B. Now pull both line and leader knots inside the connector.

5. Remove the needle and pull the knotless leader, tip section first, through the fly-line tip until only 3 or 4 inches of butt remain outside the needle hole.
6. Using 50- to 100-grit sandpaper, thoroughly roughen a ½-inch section of the leader butt next to the fly-line tip. *Note:* If the leader-butt end has been straightened, the line-to-leader connection will also be straight.
7. Place a small drop of Zap-A-Gap on the roughened section and spread the glue evenly over it with the nozzle of the glue bottle. *Move immediately to the next step.*
8. Now quickly grip the exposed leader butt by the overhand knot with pliers or forceps and, holding the fly-line tip with a firm grip, give a quick, short pull on the leader-butt end to pull the roughed section just inside the fly line.

Zap-A-Gap Fly Line to Leader Connection, Option #1

Splicing the leader and fly line together with Zap-A-Gap is a no-knot option to using Knot #3. This glue has been thoroughly tested for superior waterproof bonding between nylon monofilament leaders and fly lines. Properly bonded, the fly line or leader butt will break before the connection fails.

1. Insert the eye of a size 8, 9, or 10 crewel or darning needle into the fly-line tip core. Use a pin vise to hold the needle.
2. Push the needle ½ inch up inside the fly-line core, then out the side of the coating.
3. Insert an inch of knotless leader tip (whose butt end has been straightened) through the needle eye.
4. Now pull the needle and leader tip out of the fly-line tip.

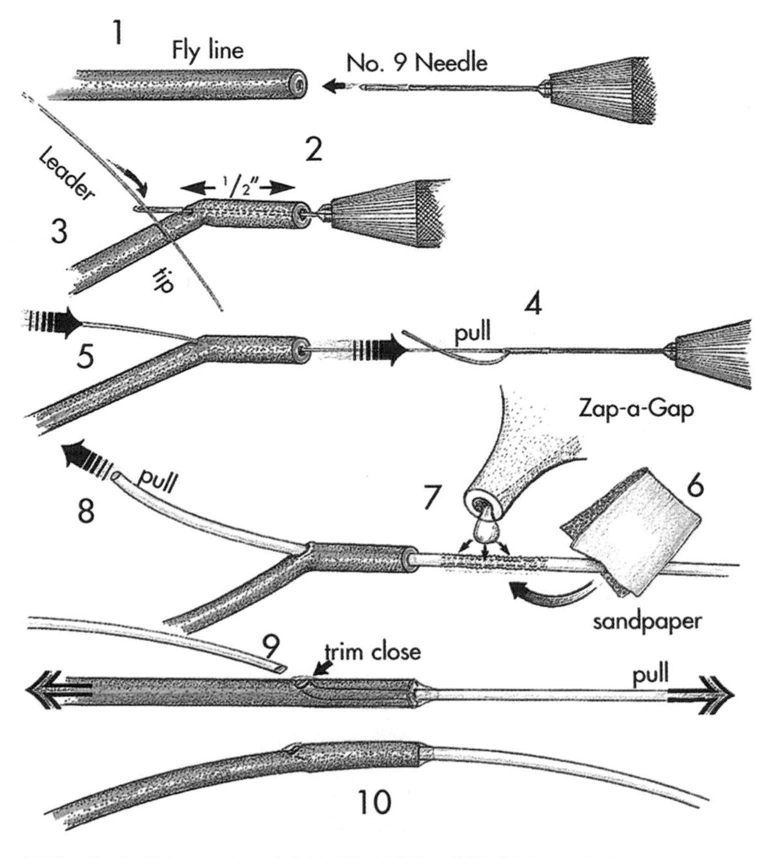

ZAP-A-GAP—LEADER TO LINE CONNECTION (*Option #1*) (Designed by Joe Robinson of Austin, Texas.)

9. Allow 15 to 20 seconds for the Zap-A-Gap glue to cure and form a permanent bond. Trim off the exposed excess butt end flush with the fly-line coating. After trimming, place a tiny amount of Zap-A-Gap over the hole. Give a few sharp tugs on the leader butt and fly line to pull the end of the trimmed butt inside the fly-line core for a smooth surface finish.

Note: A small excess of glue may remain at the fly-line tip. If you allow this to dry for about 30 seconds, it will provide a smoother link at the junction of fly line and leader butt. The glue drying may be accelerated to one second if you apply a catalyst called Zip Kicker. Zap-A-Gap is available through L.L. Bean as well as at fly-fishing, hardware, and hobby shops. It is distributed through Wapsi Fly Company, Route 5, Box 57 E, Mountain Home, AR 72653 and Umpqua Feather Merchants, P.O. Box 700, Glide, OR 97443.

The Speedy Nail Knot Connection, Option #2

The speedy nail knot is a fast option to attach a knotless leader or a leader-butt section to the fly line. It will not work on compound knotted leaders or braided-butt tapered leaders.

1A. With your left index finger and thumb, hold the fly-line tip and lay the point end of a small needle or toothpick next to the line tip.

1B. Place the leader tip next to the fly-line tip so that it extends 1 or 2 inches beyond the fly-line tip.

1C. Place the butt end of the leader next to the fly-line tip, with the butt end extending to the left past the needle eye 2 or 3 inches.

2. With your left index finger and thumb, grasp the fly line, needle, leader tip, and leader butt firmly about 1 inch behind the fly-line tip end. With your right hand, wrap the leader-butt section that is extending to the *right* of the left finger firmly over and around the fly line, needle, and leader-butt and tip sections, six to eight wraps, progressively to the left. *Note:* The purpose of the needle is to give stiffness to make the wraps possible.

3A. Without letting the wraps loosen, slip your left finger and thumb carefully over the wraps and hold them in place with a firm squeeze.

3B. With your right finger and thumb, pull the leader-tip end to the right, until the entire leader (except the leader-butt tag) slides under the wraps.

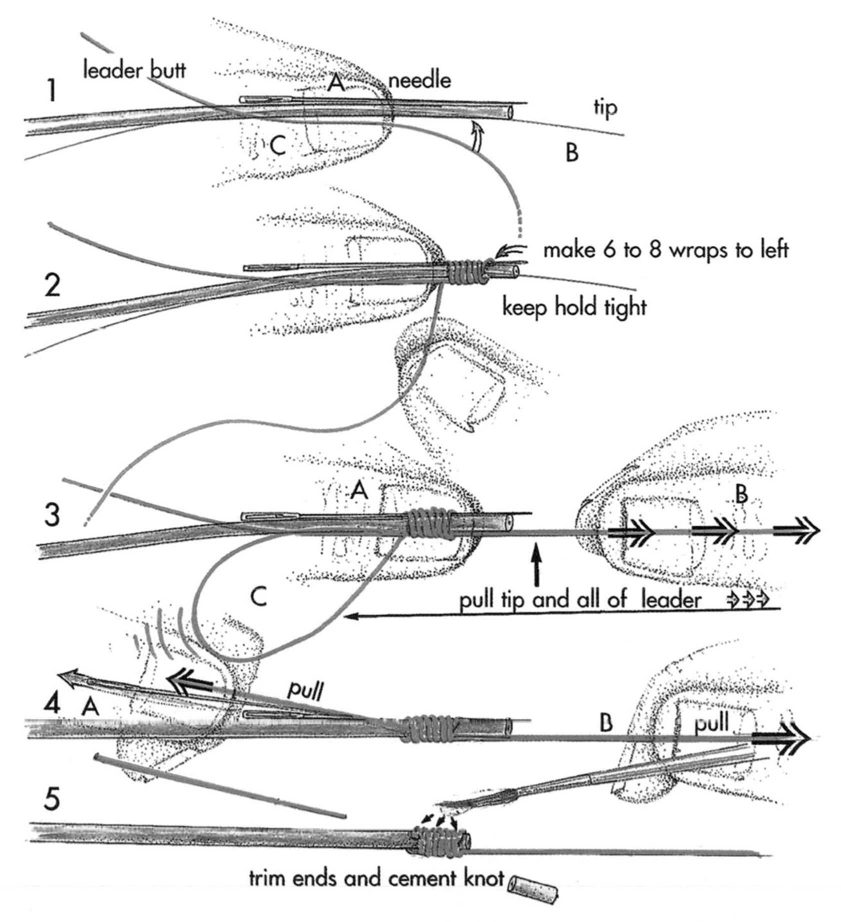

SPEEDY NAIL KNOT—LEADER TO LINE CONNECTION (*Option #2*)

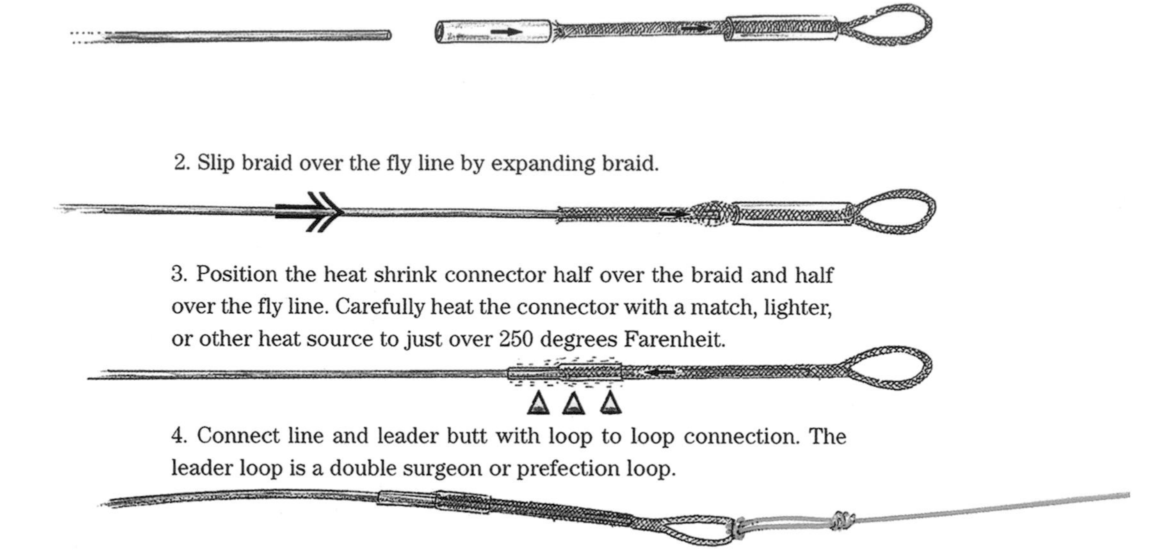

SLIP-ON BRAIDED LOOP—LEADER TO LINE CONNECTION (*Option* #3)

3C. As you pull the leader through the wraps, be careful to keep the leader loop from twisting and tangling on itself or on your left hand.

4A. Continue holding the knot wraps firmly with your left hand. Using your right hand, pull on the tag end of the leader butt to tighten the wraps a bit more. Continue holding the knot wraps with your left hand and use your right hand to pull the needle to the left to remove it.

4B. With your right hand, pull on the leader tip to further tighten the wraps onto the fly line. When you are sure the wraps are tight, release the left-hand grip, and pull both the leader-butt tag and the leader-tip end to completely tighten the knot on to the fly-line tip.

5. Trim off the ends of the fly-line tip and the leader-butt tag. I'd advise also coating the fly line with a flexible, waterproof cement to make the knot and tip smoother so that the connection will pass through the rod guides more easily.

Tippet to Leader Tip

For connecting two sections of nylon monofilament line, whether for making a knotted tapered leader or tying tippet to tip, the *surgeon's knot* is superior to the popular blood or barrel knot. It is stronger, smaller, faster, and much easier to tie, as well as less sensitive to size or hardness mismatches. Practice this knot on level, 10- to 12-pound-test tippet material or scrap fly line before using it on your tapered leader tip.

It's good practice to add a tippet section to your new knotless tapered leader before you use it; about 18 inches is ideal. This addition requires only one small, dependable surgeon's knot, and it will significantly prolong your leader's life for two reasons. First, tying on flies uses up the inexpensive tippet rather than the expensive tapered leader; most knots use up 3 to 6 inches each time you change flies. Second, most leader damage, especially that due to abrasion or "wind knots," occurs on the 12 inches or so of your leader next to the fly. Your leader will last many times longer when you initially add a tippet.

Knot #4: Tippet to Leader Tip with Double Surgeon's Knot

1. Place the leader tip and tippet section ends side by side in opposite directions, overlapping about 5 to 7 inches each.

2. With the lines together, twist and form a 2-inch-diameter common loop. Pass the leader-tip tag and the tippet's long end through the loop.
3. Pass both through the loop once more. Wet the loop wraps with your lips.
4. Tighten the knot by first pulling on the long sides of leader and tippet, then on the tag ends. Trim the excess tag ends. *Note:* If you are tying together two different types of nylon, it is best to make a third pass with both through the loop to prevent the harder type from cutting the softer type. For additional strength and efficiency, coat this knot with Zap-A-Gap.

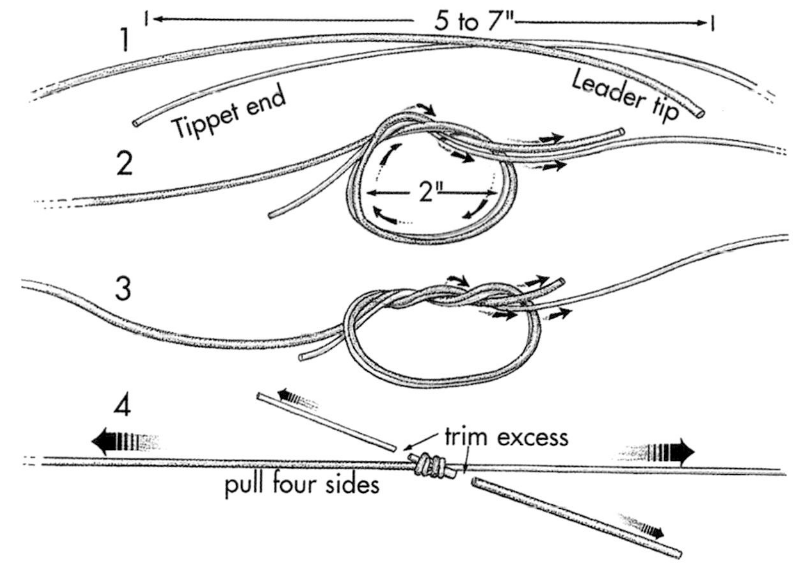

KNOT #4: DOUBLE SURGEON'S KNOT—TIPPET TO LEADER

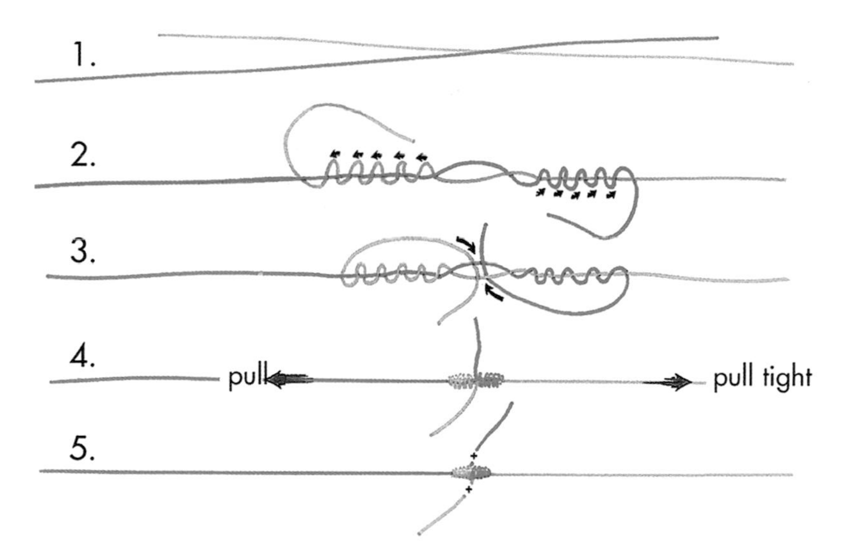

KNOT #4A: BLOOD KNOT (BARREL KNOT)—OPTIONAL TIPPET-TO-LEADER-TIP KNOT

1. Cross and parallel 6 to 8 inches of leader tip and tippet.
2. Take each tag end and wrap or twist it four or five times around.
3. Now pass the tag ends through the loop that is between the two tippet wraps.
4. Wet the wraps and pull both leader and tippet long ends apart smoothly to draw the knot wraps tight.
5. Test the knot wraps with several sharp tugs. This also draws the knot down smaller and tighter. Clip the tags close to the knot. For superior performance and strength, lightly coat this knot with Zap-A-Gap.

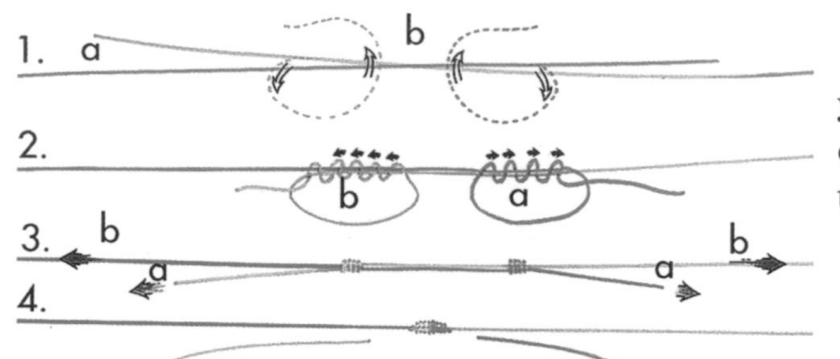

KNOT #4B: DOUBLE DUNCAN LOOP—
OPTIONAL TIPPET-TO-LEADER KNOT

1a. Place the leader-tip tag and tippet tag so that they cross each other with a 4- to 6-inch overlap.
1b. Form a loop with the tag end of the leader.
2a. With the leader tag end, form a three- or four-turn Duncan loop knot onto the tippet section.
2b. Repeat step 2a, using the tippet tag end.
3a. Wet and tighten each Duncan loop.
3b. Pull the leader and tippet in opposite directions to slide the two Duncan loop knots firmly together.
4. Pull the tags tight, then cut away the tag ends close to the knots.

Tippet End to Fly

Knot #5: Tippet End or Leader Tip to Fly with Duncan Loop Knot

1. Pass 6 to 8 inches of the tippet's tag end through the eye of the hook.
2. First toward, then away from the fly, form a 1½-inch-diameter loop with a tag.
3. Pass the tag through and around the loop and tippet five times; make sure the wraps are away from the fly.
4. Wet the wraps with your lips and snug the five wraps by holding on to the tag and pulling the fly as illustrated.
5. Tighten the knot by pulling very tightly on the tag end. The degree of tightening determines how easily the knot will slide on the tippet to form an open or closed loop. With a heavy tippet—over .011 inch—tighten the knot with pliers or hemostats.
6. Adjust the loop between fly and knot to the desired size for specific fly performance. Trim the excess tag.

This is a superb knot for tying all flies to your leader. It's fast and simple to tie and has excellent wet-knot strength. It can be tied in three configurations:

- A small open-loop knot for maximum fly action and good balance.

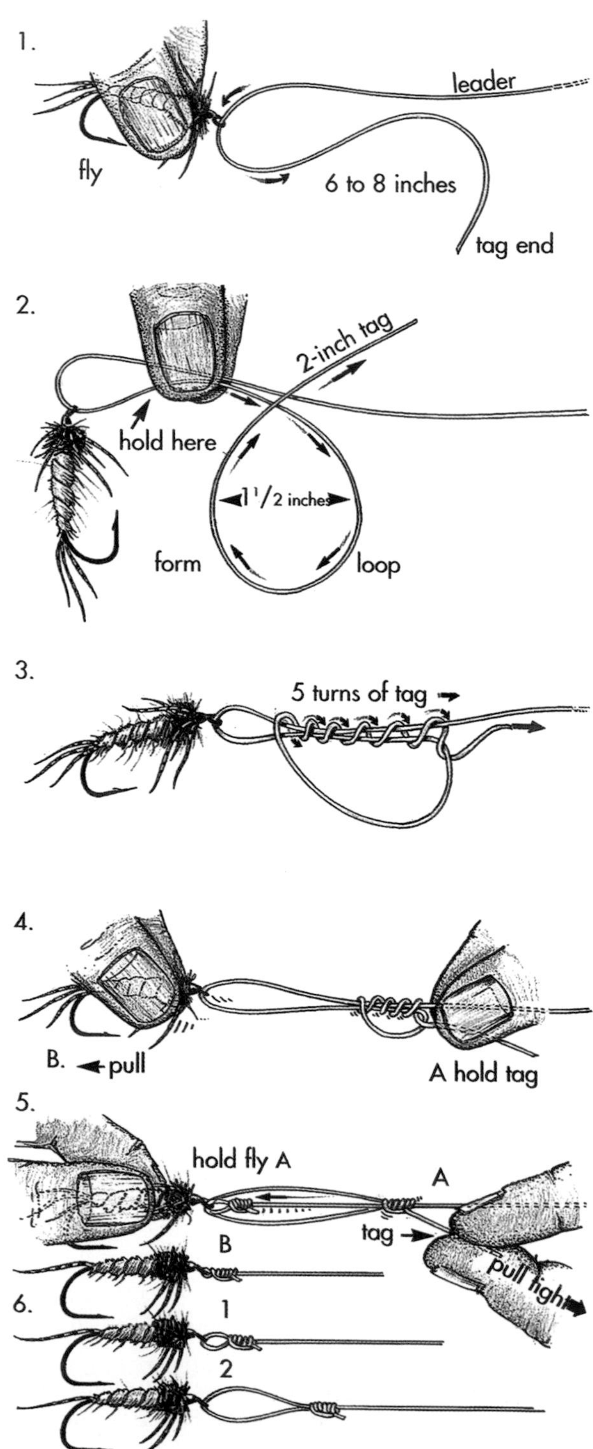

KNOT #5: DUNCAN LOOP—LEADER TIP OR TIPPET TO FLY

- A larger loop knot for slip-shock absorption with heavy fish or rod strikes.
- Tight against the hook eye to hold the leader hard against the fly.

Duncan Loop Options

When properly tightened, a Duncan loop may be positioned to perform several options:

1. Clinched down tight next to the fly—for leader control of the fly's attitude.
2. Small open loop—to allow the fly to move more independently of the leader for more lifelike action, balance, and floating or sinking ability.
3. Large open loop—for shock absorption when the leader is violently or excessively strained by fish, obstruction, or angler.

Before attaching your fly, practice tying the Duncan loop with some excess 10- or 12-pound-test monofilament until you become proficient with it; also practice forming various loop sizes. The tighter the knot, the less the loop will slip shut or closed on the fly's eye. If properly tightened, it will not slip closed during normal casting or retrieving but will be easily opened with your fingernails if it slips closed on the strike or fight.

Duncan Loop Options: (top to bottom) Knot is pulled tight against hook eye; small loop to allow fly to move more naturally; large loop to increase strike shock absorption.

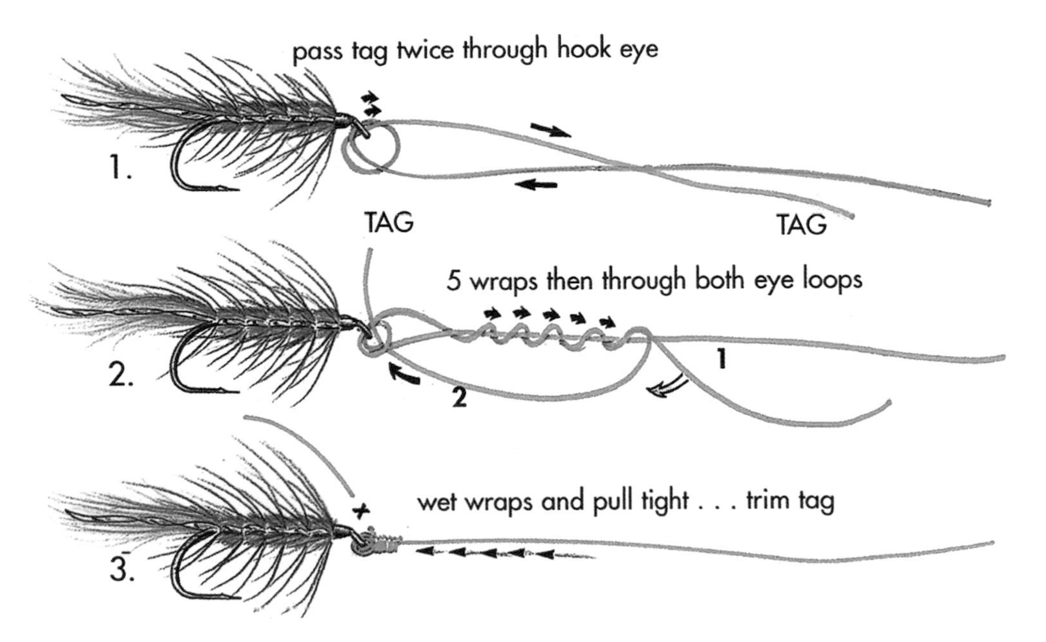

KNOT #5A TRILENE KNOT—OPTIONAL FOR LEADER TO FLY

This is a good, strong knot and especially practical to tie on fly sizes 10 and larger.

1. Pass the tag end of your tippet twice through the hook eye.
2. Make five wraps around the tippet with the tag, away from the hook. Bend the tag back toward the fly and pass it through both eye loops.
3. Wet the loops and wraps with your lips, then draw the knot down tightly by pulling on both the tag and the tippet. Cut away the excess tag end.

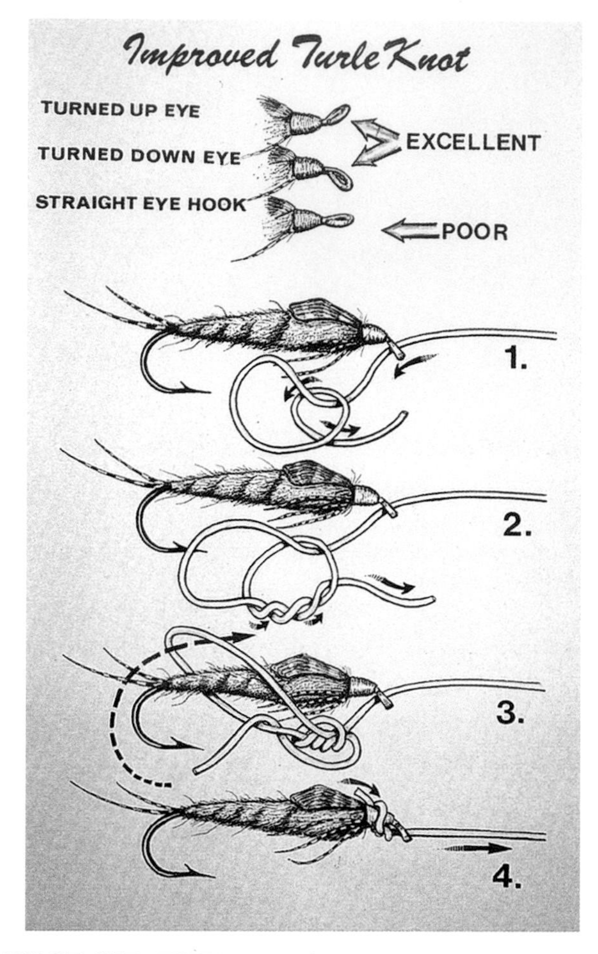

KNOT #5B: TURLE KNOT—OPTIONAL LEADER TO FLY

This knot works nicely on hooks with turned-up or -down eyes but poorly on straight-eyed hooks. Use it when you want your fly to swim exactly in line with your leader tip.

1. Pass 3 to 5 inches of the leader through the hook eye and form a loop with the tag end.
2. Tie a double overhand knot at the loop.
3. Pass the loop over the tail, hook, and fly body.
4. Snug the loop tightly around the fly head by pulling the leader tight.

Practice all these recommended connections as many times as it takes for you to feel comfortable doing them quickly, neatly, and correctly. This investment will reward you with more fishing time and more success. Fly-line scraps or old fly lines make excellent, easy-to-see-and-handle practice materials. For this, you can cut 8 or 10 feet of fly line from the back of a weight-forward or level fly line without in any way hurting its practical length.

The Life of Fly-Line Components

Your backing should last for many years. The fly line will usually not need changing for at least two or three years of normal use and care. The leader, though, requires changing two or three times a season, more often if you fish a lot. The tippet may need replacing several times a day, and certainly each time you go fishing.

The fly needs to be replaced or retied regularly during a fishing day. The backing-to-fly-reel knot needs to be tied only once, backing-to-fly-line knot every two or three years, leader-to-fly-line knot three or four times a season, tippet knot two or three times a day, and fly knot about one to ten times each fishing day. That's why practicing the surgeon's knot and the Duncan loop many times is important. All knots tend to weaken when they become wet, or with use or age. Test all knots regularly and retie the tippet and fly knots regularly.

Wind Knots

Wind or overhand leader knots are tied unintentionally as you cast, due to either fishing accidents or casting faults. The most common cause is rushing or overpowering the casting stroke, trying to compensate for the wind's

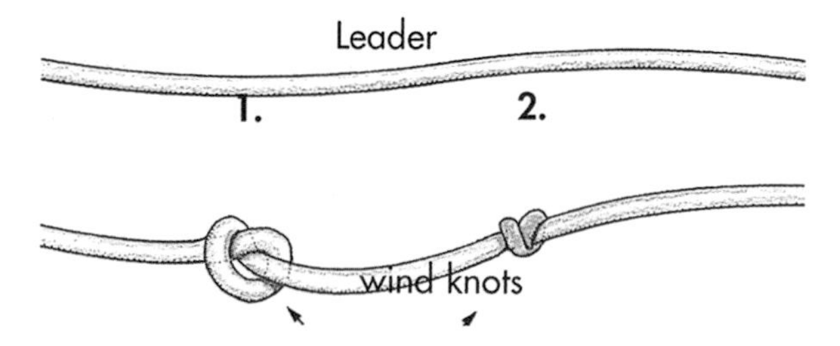

A knotless leader will be smooth if it's free of wind knots.

1. A wind knot that has not yet tightened can be removed by untying it.
2. A wind knot that has tightened has already damaged and weakened the leader and should not be untied. Instead, the leader must be repaired or replaced.

force against the cast—hence the name. Wind knots occur most frequently on the tip or tippet section of the leader. Though nearly invisible, they weaken the leader's strength by as much as 50 percent! This is because the overhand knot continues to tighten and cuts or squeezes itself when stressed. Wind knots must be removed. Those not yet tight can simply be untied. If a knot *is* tight, you must cut off the leader tip or tippet to the wind knot and either retie the fly at that point or replace the section removed with a new piece of tippet material using the double surgeon's knot, and then retie the fly to the new tippet. Wind knots occur less frequently on the heavier mid- or butt sections, but if they do, they may be untied or left there without severely weakening the leader. Check your leader frequently, especially on windy days or if you notice the leader or fly-line tip striking or tangling with each other. In chapter 3 we will discuss how to prevent wind knots from occurring.

Droppers

At times you may wish to use two or more flies—called *droppers*—at once. Droppers are most easily attached simply by leaving a 4- to 6-inch-long tag on the leader-to-tippet surgeon's knot. Tie the dropper fly to the long tag with a Duncan loop or a trilene clinch knot.

Bite or Shock Tippet

Some freshwater and many saltwater predator fish have sharp, cutting teeth, fins, or gill plates that can cut your leader at the fly. To fish for these species without losing a lot of flies, you'll need to tie on a short tippet section of wire or extra-thick monofilament that will resist being severed.

For most of these bite-tippet sections, 20- to 60-pound-test hard monofilament is ideal and preferred over the heavier and more kink-prone wire tippets. Nylon bite tippets should be made from straightened, hard types of nylon monofilament such as Mason or Maxima.

The Albright knot is effective for these nylon-to-extra-heavy-nylon or nylon-to-wire connections. Here are instructions for tying an improved, slip-proof version of this popular knot.

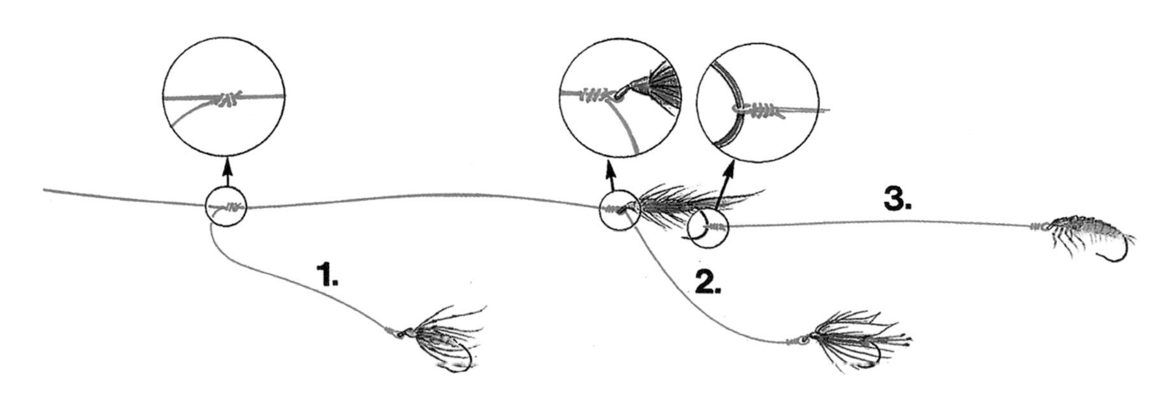

THREE TYPES OF DROPPER FLIES

1. Use a double surgeon's knot to tie the tippet to the leader tip, then tie the dropper fly onto the tippet tag end.
2. With a Duncan loop or trilene knot, tie the first fly onto the tippet. Using the tag end of the tippet, tie on the dropper fly.
3. Use a Duncan loop or trilene knot to tie the dropper fly to the hook bend. *Note:* The dropper length may be from 6 to 18 inches. The shorter lengths tangle less on the leader and other flies.

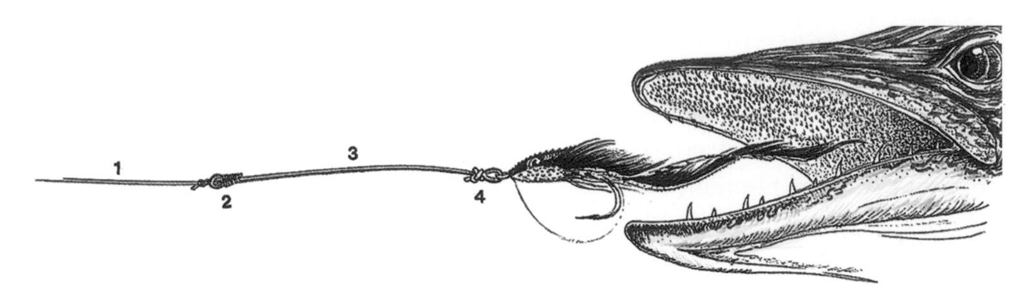

BITE TIPPET

Some fish have sharp teeth and require a tippet that they cannot cut through.

1. Leader tip.
2. Improved Albright knot—leader to bite tippet.
3. Heavy Mason mono bite tippet (30 to 60 pounds).
4. Bite tippet to fly—Homer Rhode loop knot.

Improved Albright Knot for Bite Tippet

1. Form a short loop with bite-tippet material and pass 8 to 10 inches of leader tip through the side loop.
2. Grasp and close the loop with your fingers and wrap the leader tip firmly and evenly around the loop end 12 times. Pass the leader tip through the loop as shown.
3. Pull the 12 wraps tight with the leader's end.
4. Wrap the leader's tip end around the leader three times and pass the tag end between the first wrap, then pull the wraps back tight against the bite-tippet loop.
5. Tug on both sides of the knot to further tighten and test, then clip the excess ends. Coating this knot with Zap-A-Gap is highly recommended.

Note: If you are using a .012-inch or larger leader tip, you may need pliers to tighten the wraps.

To attach the fly to the nylon bite tippet, use a Homer Rhode loop knot. This knot provides a fixed open loop that allows the fly to move freely, even though it is tied to thick, stiff material. Note, however, that this knot is *not* used with normal-diameter

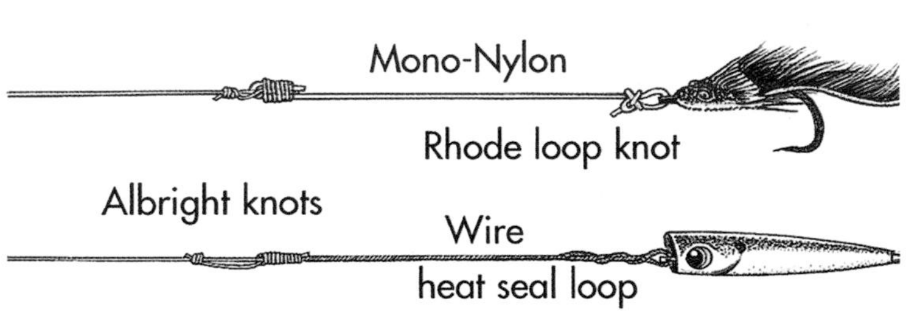

Two types of bite tippets: nylon and wire.

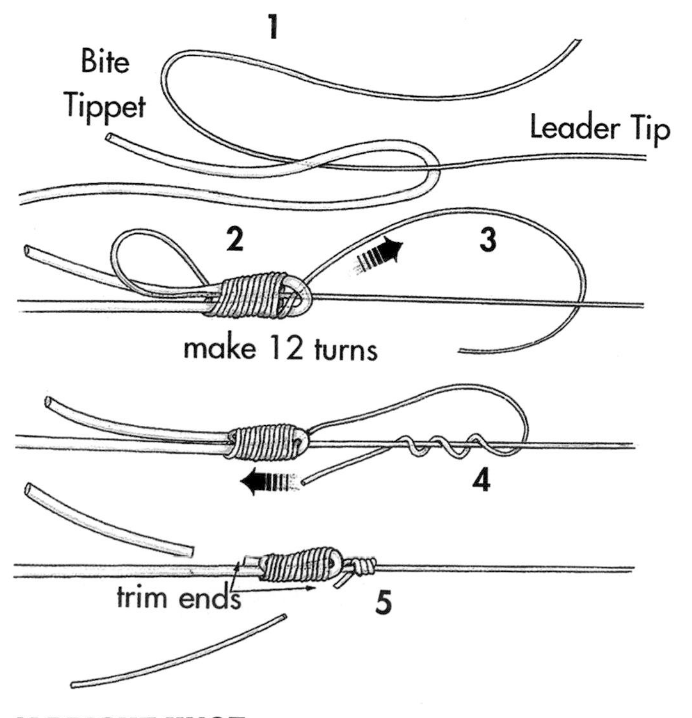

ALBRIGHT KNOT

tippet because it has only 50 percent knot strength.

Nylon Bite Tippet Fly Knot—Homer Rhode Loop Knot

1. Place a simple open overhand knot on the leader bite tippet about 3 to 6 inches from its tag end.
2. Pass the tag end through the eye of the hook.
3. Pass the tag end through the open overhand knot.
4. Snug down the overhand knot just in front of the hook eye as illustrated.
5. Take the tag end and pass it around the leader to . . .
6. . . . form a second snug overhand knot.
7. Work the second knot back to the first overhand knot. With pliers, pull the knot *very tightly* and trim off the excess tag.

Note: You can also use this loop knot for soft-braided wire tippet material if you tighten it correctly with pliers. Some fish can cut heavy hard nylon; for these you'll need braided wire coated with nylon. Attach the wire to the leader with the same improved Albright knot illustrated here.

To attach the fly to a nylon-coated braided wire, simply pass the wire through the fly's eye; twist it four to six times around itself and carefully heat the twists with a match flame or cigarette lighter until the nylon melts. Allow the wrap to cool and clip off the excess wire tag.

For other useful fly-fishing knots, I recommend Mark Sosin and Lefty Kreh's knot book, *Practical Fishing Knots*.

BITE-TIPPET MATERIAL AND SIZE GUIDE (FRESH AND BRACKISH WATER)

Smaller sizes of material are for smaller fish; the small size should be changed after you've caught one or two larger fish.

CHAIN PICKEREL 20- to 30-pound monofilament

NORTHERN PIKE 30- to 50-pound monofilament

MUSKIE 40- to 60-pound monofilament or 15- to 20-pound braided wire

GAR 15- to 25-pound braided wire

BOWFISH (grindle or dogfish) 30- to 40-pound monofilament or 15- to 20-pound braided wire

SNOOK 30- to 60-pound monofilament

TARPON 30- to 80-pound monofilament or 15- to 30-pound braided wire

SHARK 15- to 30-pound solid wire

BLUEFISH 30- to 60-pound monofilament or 15- to 30-pound solid wire

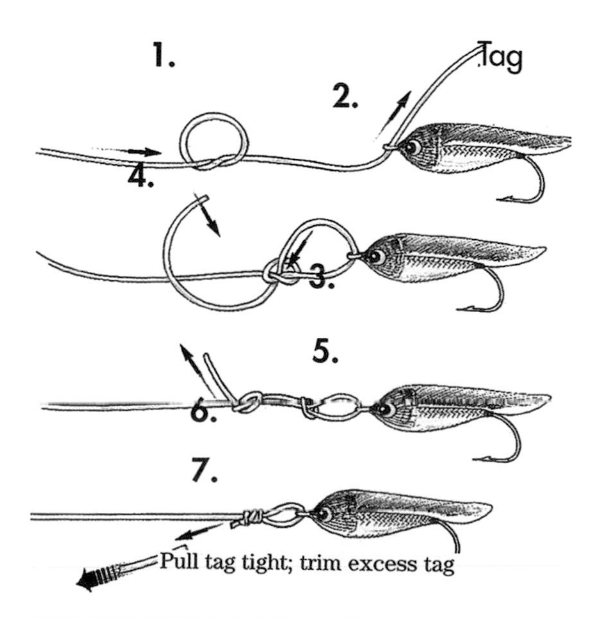

HOMER RHODE LOOP KNOT—NYLON BITE TIPPET TO FLY

Nylon-coated wire fly attachment. To seal wraps tight, carefully heat the wraps with a low flame.

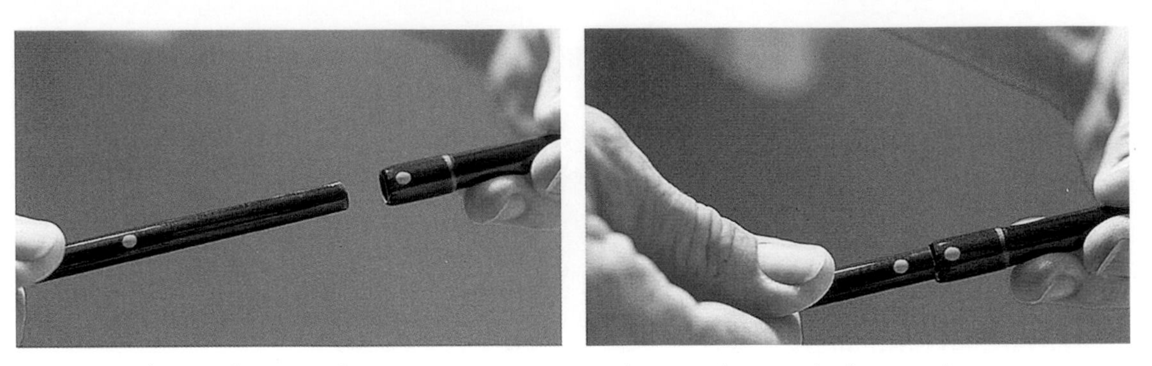

Fitting Rod Ferrules Together. Insert and twist to tighten. Make sure the line-up dots are even, or the rod guides are lined up straight.

ASSEMBLING FLY TACKLE FOR USE

Correct assembly of fly tackle can be simple and fast and will assure you of the best performance from your tackle.

Rod Assembly

Remove the fly rod from its protective tube and its cloth cover. Insert the rod's male ferrule into the female ferrule until you feel resistance. Align the guides on the different sections so they are in a straight line; you can adjust the alignment with a gentle twisting motion. Once the guides are aligned, apply a bit more push pressure to the ferrule to tighten the two pieces. Don't worry if the male ferrule seems a bit long; it is made this way to compensate for wear.

If the ferrules fit together loosely, take the rod apart and apply a thin film of beeswax or candle wax on the male ferrule; this will usually tighten up the fit without damage. If the ferrules feel gritty when you're putting them together, take them apart and clean them with soap and water. A cotton swab is excellent for cleaning inside the female ferrule.

Fly-Reel Attachment

Once the rod sections are together, attach the reel to the reel seat, making sure the spool handle is on your reeling hand's side. Finger-tighten the screw-locking ring. Rock the reel back and forth, then tighten the locking ring one more time. Next, find the leader tip on the reel and pass it through the lower-forward position of the reel. Holding the rod handle, pull out the entire length of leader plus 1½ times the rod length of fly line. Now place the reel-handle end of the rod on a clean, flat, nonabrasive surface (or have a companion hold it). If a clean surface is not available, place the rod handle and reel in your hat. Hold the rod near the ferrule and grasp the fly line 2 or 3 feet from the leader. Thread the doubled-over line through the guides toward the tip, taking care not to wrap the line around the rod between

Locate the leader tip and pass it out of the reel spool's lower front area as shown.

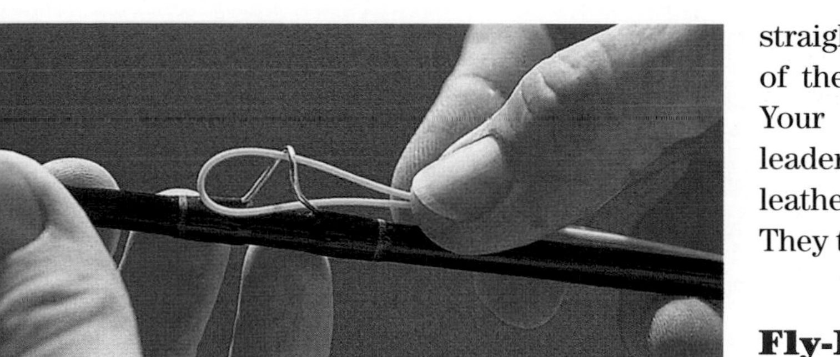

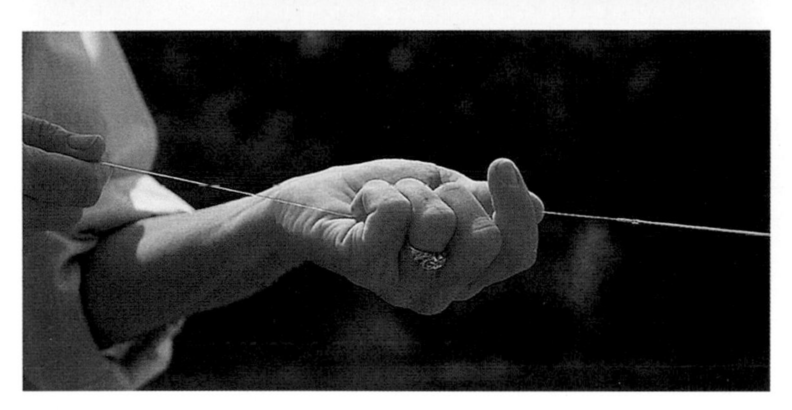

Top: Double the fly-line end and pass the loop through each rod guide.
Bottom: Correct method for holding, warming, and straightening leader. Note that the leader and line are held very taut while the other hand strokes the tight area.

the guides. If possible, hold the fly rod guides-up when threading the lines. Pull the loose line and leader through the guides as you advance toward the tip. When you have 2 feet of fly line through the tip-top, release it and give the rod a couple of quick casting motions. The loose line between the reel and tip will quickly clear the rod tip.

Leader Straightening

The leader and fly line will have developed a coil set from being stored on the reel spool. This set must be straightened for best performance. To do this, have someone hold the fly line near its tip or attach it to a door handle or other firm, smooth object. Stroke the leader with your hand until you feel it warm up. Hold the leader straight and tight for a few seconds as it cools to reset it in a straight condition. Repeat until most of the coils or kinks are removed. Your bare hand is a much better leader straightener than commercial leather or rubber straighteners. They tend to "burn" the leader.

Fly-Line Straightening

A straight fly line, without reel-spool memory coils, will cast farther and more accurately than one with such coils. It will also float better and, without coil slack, will improve strike detection and hook-setting.

Over a clean surface, pull 30 to 50 feet of fly line off the reel. Have someone hold one end or attach it to a firm structure. Then pull the fly line tight until you feel it stretch just a bit. Hold it stretched for several seconds, *slowly* release tension, and see if the line has straightened. If it hasn't, repeat this procedure or stretch and gently stroke the line surface. A fly line is particularly difficult to straighten when the air is below 45 degrees F. When air or water temperatures are near or below freezing, the fly-line finish becomes hard. Under such conditions, the line can easily crack during stretching or fishing. To prevent cold-temperature cracking damage, avoid excessive stretching.

This waterline picture demonstrates how a straight fly line floats while an unstraightened one sinks.

Wrap the fly line around a convenient, smooth object and then stretch and hold it for 10 to 20 seconds. Slowly release the tension.

Fly to Leader

Now you are ready to tie on the fly, using one of the knots previously recommended. If you are just going to practice casting, you can tie on a practice fly—one with neither point nor barb.

When you assemble your tackle, be sure to place the empty cloth sack back in the fly-rod tube and put the lid back on the tube. This will ensure that the cloth sack does not get wet or dirty and that neither it nor the lid gets lost.

DISASSEMBLING FLY TACKLE

Proper disassembly of fly tackle is also important. It helps you prevent damage and ensures that the tackle will be ready the next time you need it.

When you stop fishing, reel in your line and make a few short, rapid false casts to dry off the fly before removing it. Cut the fly from the tippet and place it in a hatband, on your fishing vest's fly patch, or in a well-ventilated fly box so it will dry completely.

To clean and dry your fly line immediately or shortly after use, lay it over the water or over a grit-free surface. With a clean cloth or paper towel in your rod hand, reel the fly line onto the reel spool while squeezing it with the towel. This removes most of the water and the dirty film that a line acquires during fishing. Always make sure when you reel the fly line onto the reel that it spools on firmly and evenly. Guide it with your rod hand, using moderate tension. Too-loose or uneven spooling may cause a bad tangle. If the fly line is wound on too tightly, however, it may kink or set in small loops or curls.

Leader Storage

As you wind the leader onto the fly reel, leave out about 4 to 6 inches of the tippet. This makes the fine tippet end much easier to find next time, and it also prevents the end from accidentally passing under the leader or line coils on the reel. If the leader does slip under the coil of line, it may form a half-hitch, causing a tangle and possible loss of a large fish.

Pass the end of the leader out of one of the reel-spool ventilation holes and back in another to keep it in place and prevent its getting lost in the spool.

With a clean rag, wipe your rod and reel clean and dry before storing them in their protective cases.

Fly-Reel Storage

Remove the reel from the reel seat, wipe it clean, and dry it with a towel. If you have been fishing in brackish or salt water, be sure to wash the salt deposits off the reel and fly line with fresh water. Wipe dry, then allow to air-dry for a few hours before storing. Place the reel in a well-ventilated bag or case to allow the damp fly line, backing, and internal parts of the reel to dry.

Disassembling the Fly Rod

Now disassemble the rod. If the ferrules seem stuck, have a companion help you separate them—both of you should hold on to a different section of the rod and then pull slowly. Wipe the rod clean and dry with a towel. Replace it in the cloth rod bag and protective case. Be sure not to get the inside of the rod case or the rod bag wet. When storing, leave the lid off the tube until you are sure that the rod bag, the inside of the rod tube, and the fly rod are completely dry. It is essential that the rod and cloth bag be dry.

Store your tackle in a dark, cool, dry area. Proper storage prevents damage and premature aging.

Always disassemble the sections of your fly rod when storing it in a boat, car, or cabin, or when carrying it through dense foliage. Car doors, house doors, feet, and tree limbs are famous for their ability to break fly rods. Many more fly rods are broken as a result of carelessness than by fish or fishing.

How to Fly Cast

Casting well is the key to the successes and pleasures of fly fishing. You must devote more time to practice than you might for other casting methods, but your rewards will be many times greater. There is a poetic, hypnotic, almost sensuous feeling to casting a fly well. A good fly caster seems graceful and artistically endowed, and with practice you can feel this way, too!

Learning to cast depends first on a clear understanding of the dynamics of propelling a *weightless* fly with the *linear* weight of the fly line using the *mechanical* control of the fly rod, your hand, your locked wrist, and your arm. To the casual observer—or even experienced spin and bait casters—a fly caster appears to be simply waving the rod and line back and forth through a series of graceful arcs. *This is completely incorrect.* Fly casting is a precisely timed and controlled cycle of stroking motions that energize and direct the line and fly along an accurate path to the water.

First, you must focus on directing the *line*, not the fly! The leader and fly are pulled along with the line. Next, always keep in mind that the line is *linear* weight (weight that is spread over a long distance) under the control of your arm and hand through the fly rod. Unlike the case of other casting methods, the reel is not used during fly casting.

To move linear weight efficiently, it must be *straight.* Consider a garden hose. If it's lying in loose coils on the ground, you can't move its whole length by holding one end and sweeping your arm. But if it's *straight* on the ground, you can move the entire length with a short sweep of your hand. This is the same principle that governs directing and moving a fly line.

The basic fly cast is performed with a length of fly line extended straight on the water in front of you. This is done in a four-part, continuous, timed sequence.

1. **Pickup.** Lifting the extended fly line up and off the water's surface with the fly rod.
2. **Upstroke** (backcast). Stroking the fly rod up and back by gradually accelerating and quickly stopping it to propel the lifted fly line, leader, and fly up and behind you—*straightening* the fly line for the next part of the cast.
3. **Downstroke** (forward cast). Stroking the fly rod forward and down by gradually accelerating and quickly stopping it to straighten, direct, and deliver the fly line, leader, and fly toward the target.
4. **Presentation.** Directing the fly, leader, and fly line down to the water target area using the fly rod and gravity.

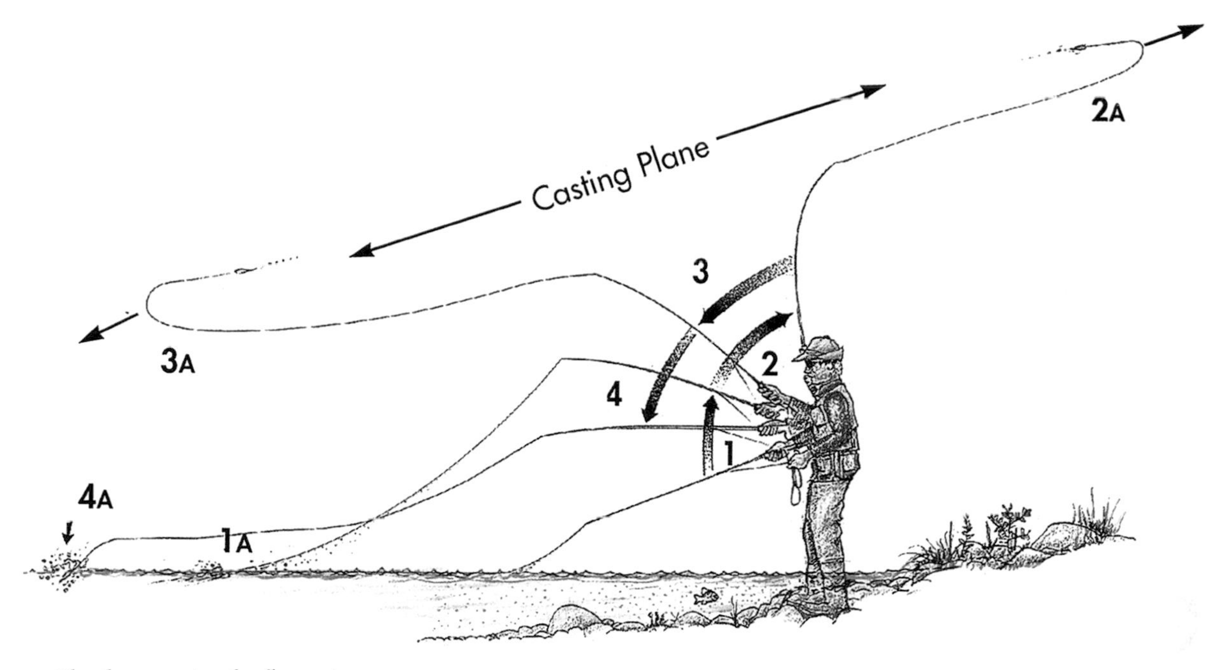

The four parts of a fly cast.

Study this casting procedure carefully to develop a strong visual concept of these crucial four parts.

The fly is not retrieved to the rod tip as is done in spinning and bait casting with weighted lures. A fly cast must be started with at least 20 to 25 feet of fly line extended—there has to be enough linear weight from the line to make the cast.

The path that the fly line follows backward and forward is more or less straight and at a constant angle. This is called the **casting plane.** If the line does not travel in this *straight plane,* the cast becomes inefficient.

The direction the fly line travels is controlled by the stroking rod, hand, and arm. During the upstroke and downstroke, the fly rod is gradually accelerated and abruptly stopped at the end of each stroke. After the stop, the fly line continues to move in the direction of the stroke, and as it does, it forms a moving U-shaped *loop* that rolls over itself until the fly line, leader, and fly are fully extended.

Because the heavy, relatively stiff fly line always moves *with and in the same direction as the tip of the fly rod,* the loop shape and the line's direction of travel are under the fly caster's direct control. Precise control of the fly rod's movement means precise control of the fly cast, as if the rod tip were a pencil marking on paper.

The Four Parts of a Fly Cast

1. Pickup (lift).
1A. Start step 2 when the leader begins to come off the surface.
2. The up-and-back casting stroke.
2A. Pause to allow the fly line, leader, and fly to unroll and straighten.
3. The down-and-forward casting stroke.
3A. Pause to allow the fly line, leader, and fly to unroll and straighten.
4. Presentation.
4A. Allow the fly, leader, and line to land on the water.

Loop control (both shape and direction) is the key to good fly casting. And the *path of the loop* (the casting plane) as it goes back and forth is the key to fly-casting efficiency and accuracy.

The four general loop shapes common to fly casting are *narrow, wide, open,* and *closed*

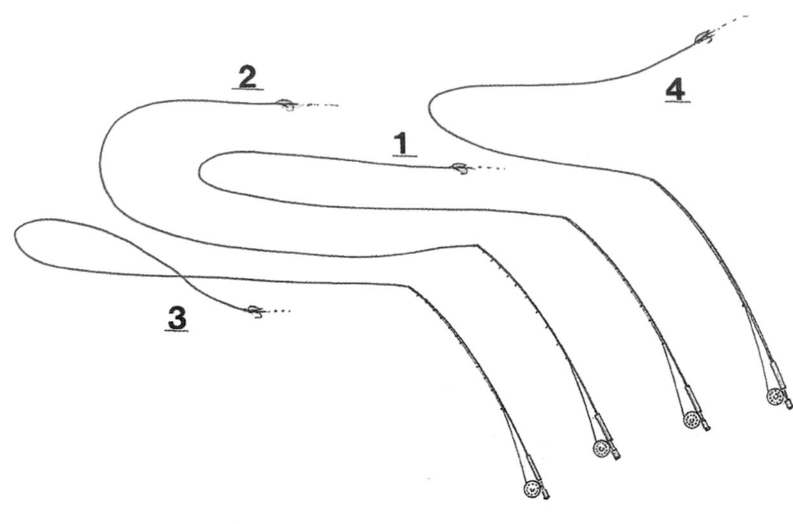

Four Loop Shapes

1. Narrow loop.
2. Wide loop.
3. Closed or tailing loop.
4. Open loop.

or *tailing*. These four loops and their many variations are direct results of timing and the arc that the rod tip follows during the power stroke. Or in other words, the moving rod tip forms the fly-line loop shape.

Which loop shape is correct? A narrow, or *tight*, loop is the most efficient for distance and best leader/fly delivery. The wide loop is less efficient because it moves more slowly and has more wind resistance, but it may be useful for some fly presentations. The tailing and open loops are deformities caused by poor casting dynamics and are seldom if ever desirable.

The simplest way to understand and relate loop shape and control to the fly rod and casting stroke is to use what is known as the clock system. Visualize yourself standing with a large clock face at your side. The nine o'clock position is forward (the direction you are facing), twelve o'clock directly above your head, three o'clock behind you, and six o'clock at your feet. The fly rod is the clock hand.

To form a **narrow loop,** begin your cast with a pickup (lifting) motion from the water—eight o'clock lifting to ten o'clock.

For the up-and-back power stroke, gradually accelerate the rod from ten to twelve o'clock and quickly *stop there*. The tight loop then forms, moving in the direction of the stroke up and behind you with the rod tip stationary at twelve o'clock.

Just as the line, leader, and fly straighten out above and behind you (turn your head back and watch this), initiate your forward-and-down power stroke by *gradually accelerating* the fly rod from twelve o'clock to ten o'clock. *Abruptly stop the rod at ten o'clock!* This allows the narrow loop to form and move forward and down toward the target area. It's that simple.

If you had stroked from ten o'clock to three o'clock (waved your rod through a larger arc) and then from three o'clock back to ten o'clock, you would have had two very wide, inefficient loops. This would not have taken your fly as far or as precisely as the narrow loop. Unfortunately, many beginning fly casters have the rod-waving concept or have had experience with other casting methods using weighted lures and often fall into bad loop-shape habits—with frustrating results. It's human nature, if a loop is formed causing the fly to fall short, to *increase* the rod arc and try to force the fly line to go farther. *Less* arc and *less* power are the solution!

The closed, or tailing, loop is the most undesirable loop shape. It's caused when the caster either starts the forward stroke too soon (before the line straightens out in back) or accelerates the cast too fast at first. In either case, the flexible rod tip dips sharply down, or *shocks*, with the sudden overload of line weight and power, causing a portion of the line moving with the stroke to do so as well. This deformed, closed loop often catches on itself near the end of the cast, causing leader and fly tangles, overhand or wind knots, and poor presentations.

Remember that the movement of the rod tip forms the loop's shape. If the rod tip dips

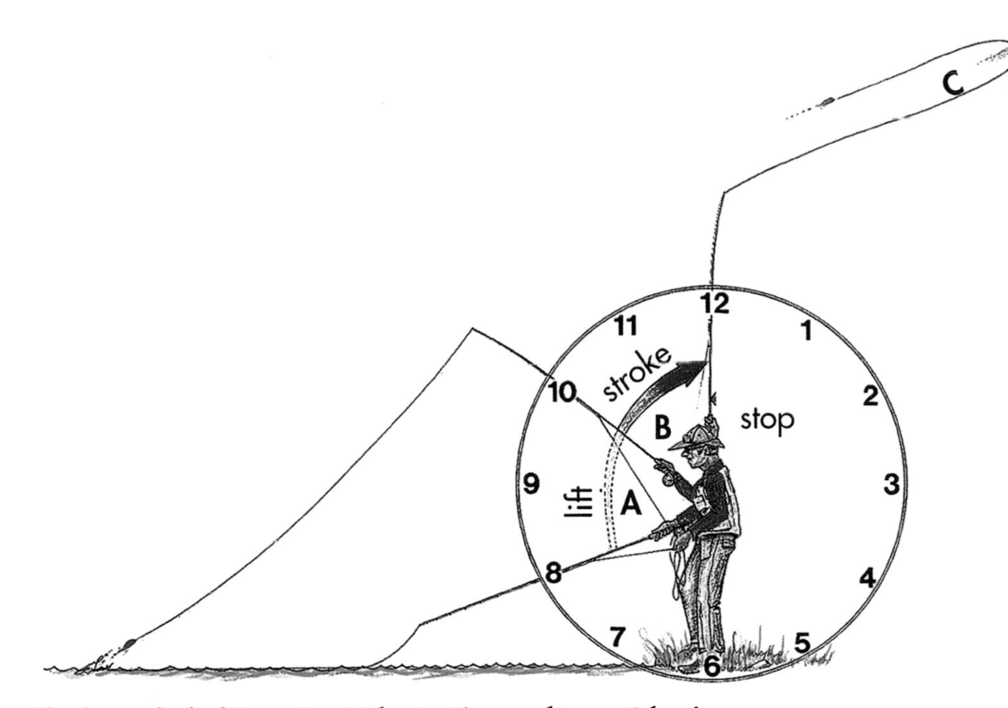

The Clock Method of Four-Part Fly Casting and Loop Shaping

A. Pickup: from eight to ten o'clock.

B. Up-and-back stroke: from ten to twelve o'clock and stop abruptly.

C. The result is a narrow loop in the correct casting plane.

steeply and then straightens, that's what the fly line must do. Here's the solution: If you gradually and smoothly accelerate the stroke, the tip shock is far less likely to deform the loop shape.

The beginning fly fisher's most common error is to wave the rod, creating very wide or open loops. Using the wrist to move the rod up and back or down and forward is often the culprit. To prevent problems, keep your wrist more or less locked. As fly fishers become better casters, they sometimes begin to *force* the rod for extra distance and so develop tailing loops.

The degree of tip flex during the power stroke has a definite effect on loop shapes. Slow-action rods consistently form wider loops and more tailing loops than those with medium action. Medium-action rods often form loops a bit wider than those of fast-action rods. Medium-fast or fast-action fly rods are best for beginners for casting tighter, high-speed loops and are less prone to tip shock and tailing loops.

BASIC FLY-CASTING PROCEDURE

To learn the correct basics of fly casting as quickly as possible, we strongly advise you to *refrain from trying to catch fish* while you *practice* fly casting. Otherwise you will blur your focus on correct techniques and may form bad casting habits. At our schools, we limit actual fishing until the students have practiced casting for *several* one- to two-hour sessions.

Before you begin, be sure that you understand the section on fly-casting dynamics. It's best to begin your fly-casting practice under the direction of a qualified instructor—preferably *not* a spouse or fly-fishing friend (who might cause unnecessary emotional pressure). If friends want to help, make sure that first they read and understand this section on fly-casting theory and method so they will speak the same language and not confuse you. It's better for you to understand this text and go it alone than to accept the help of an unqualified instructor. Learning any skill as complex as fly

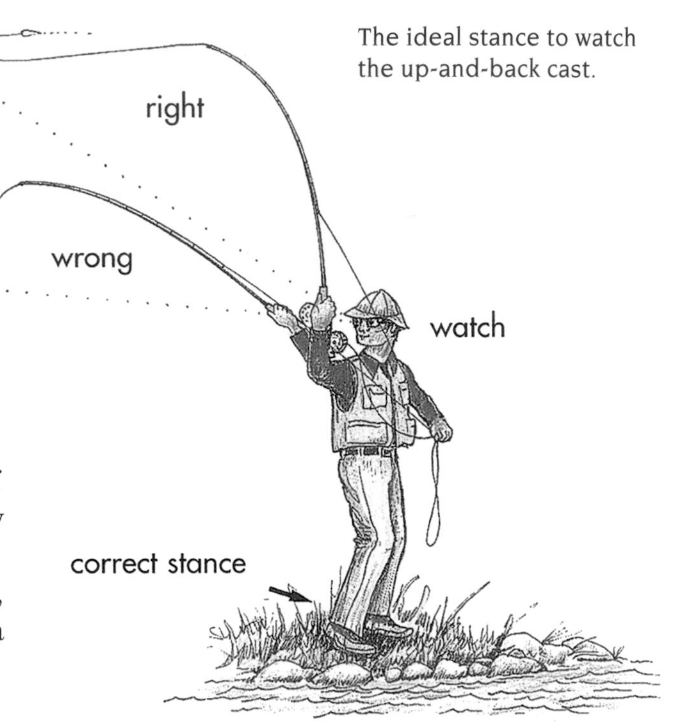

The ideal stance to watch the up-and-back cast.

casting may be accomplished in several ways. The best way *for you* may differ from another's. Be aware of this and don't get upset when you discover varying teaching methods.

There are some fine videotapes on fly casting available, such as *L.L. Bean's Introduction to Fly Fishing.* If possible, watch it and others as you learn how to cast. See the appendix for additional instructional materials, and see part 2 of this volume for an extended treatment of fly casting.

Choose for your practice an uncongested, calm, *nonflowing* water surface such as a pond, lake, or swimming pool. The area should also have an unrestricted space of at least 40 feet behind you and 20 feet to either side. If such an area is unavailable, you might practice on a lawn or gymnasium floor. If you are casting over muddy, rough, or oily surfaces, spread out a plastic ground sheet or canvas to protect your fly line from damage and dirt. In any instance, try to practice when there is little or no wind. If you cannot escape the wind, try to position yourself so that it blows from your left side if you cast with your right arm, and vice versa.

Five examples of highly visible, hookless practice flies. Try to match the fly type and size to your tackle and fish flies on or near the surface for best practice.

It's important when practicing fly casting to use a small, hookless practice fly. Without a fly, the tackle does not cast correctly, and this will misdirect your learning responses. To avoid accidents, use a fly that has had its hook point, barb, and bend removed; cut the hook off at the bend with a pair of pliers. Another option is to tie an inch or two of bright yarn or doubled pipe cleaner to the leader tip. Now straighten your leader and about 40 feet of fly line as described in chapter 2.

Hold the rod in your casting hand (your writing hand) and strip about 30 feet of line off the reel with your other hand. Let this line

Correct grip on the fly-rod handle to fly cast: thumb on top and four fingers wrapped around lower side of handle.

Alternative grip: Some fly-fishing instructors recommend placing the index finger on top of the rod, thumb to the side, and three fingers beneath the handle.

Incorrect grip for fly casting: This grip gives you minimal rod control and is very tiring.

Reel hand holds the fly line firmly as the line is cast with the rod hand.

fall to the ground at your feet. Grasp the fly and leader and pull about 25 feet of fly line out through the tip-top. Lay this line on the ground in a straight line behind you to its full length, including the leader.

Facing the direction in which you intend to cast, place your feet about 1½ feet apart and move your casting-arm foot a bit behind the other. If you are casting over water, stand at about water level and only a foot or two from the edge; be sure the area is clean so that the excess line does not tangle or become dirty. By positioning your feet as recommended, you will be standing slightly sideways of the direction in which you intend to cast. This stance is necessary to allow you to watch both your up cast and down cast unroll. *You cannot learn to fly cast well if you do not observe* both *your backward and forward casts.*

Hold the rod, reel, and line as shown in the accompanying illustration. Make sure that your thumb is on top of the rod handle and that you have positioned your grip on the handle comfortably. Avoid placing your index finger on the top of the handle, for this position will not give you the stability you need. Likewise, avoid placing your thumb on the side of the handle—this splits your control, and you do not want the rod to twist or rotate in your grip. Hold the fly line between the reel and the first stripper guide with your other hand to maintain line control.

The hand that holds the fly line while you cast and fish may be thought of as your reel hand. It performs many fly and fly-line control functions; at first, however, simply teach it to hold the line tightly between the reel and the first rod guide. (Study the photo.) If you release your grip on the fly line during the cast, the slack line will cause casting problems.

Before starting to cast, take a few slow, deep breaths and relax. With the fly rod in about the one o'clock position, cast forward, putting the fly in front of you in the water or grass. The fly line should be extended more or less straight on the area in front of you! Now begin to make the four parts of a fly cast—pickup, up-and-back cast, down-and-forward cast, and presentation.

Pickup (Lift)

With the rod tip straight forward and almost touching the water or ground (about eight o'clock), begin to lift your fly rod in a smooth, steady motion, raising your arm and fly rod, lifting the fly line off the water. This pickup motion should be slightly off the side of your casting shoulder and upward. Keep your *wrist locked* to avoid any rod-tip rotation as you lift with the rod and arm; resist the tendency to "rip" the fly line off the water with a nervous jerk. When all but the leader and fly are off the water, the rod angle should be somewhere around ten o'clock. Your line hand and arm should be held *slightly* forward and low, and kept relaxed through all four parts.

Up-and-Back Cast

Without pausing after the pickup, begin the up-and-back motion using mostly your forearm and locked wrist. You want to gradually accelerate the rod from ten o'clock to eleven o'clock to make sure the line is all straightened in front of you; this is often called *loading the rod.* Then between eleven o'clock and twelve o'clock, apply the faster, power portion of the stroke using the energy needed, say, to toss a golf ball that high and far behind you. To create

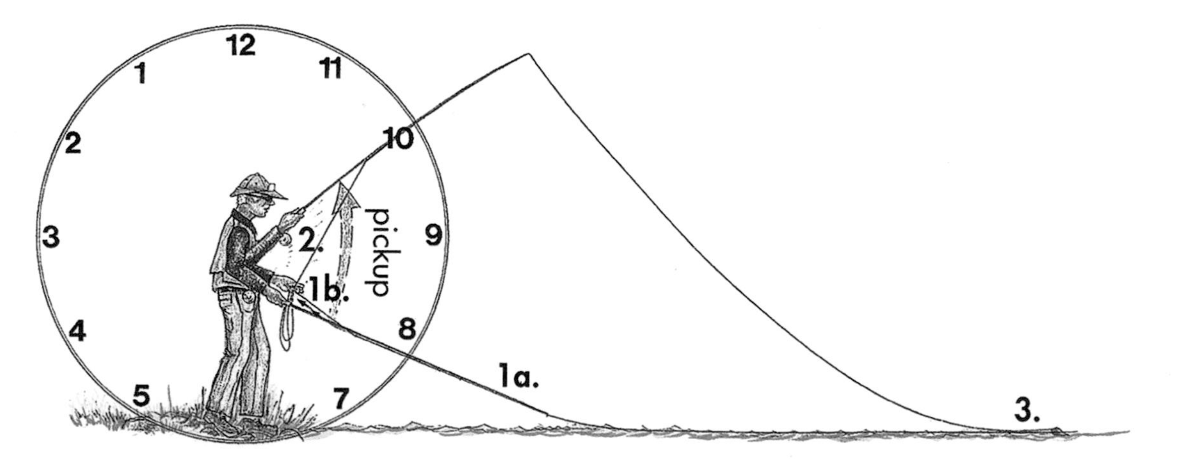

PICK-UP METHOD to Begin Cast

1a. Begin the pickup with the rod tip almost touching the water's surface and pointing toward the fly.

1b. With the fly-line hand, pull any slack out of the fly line between your hand and the fly.

2. Immediately after step 1b, begin to pick up the fly line from the water with a smooth, steady rod-lifting motion. Try to use your height and arm length to raise the line up into the casting plane rather than rotating the fly rod to a high angle. Study this diagram carefully.

3. Watch your fly-line tip/leader/fly area and try to pick up the line to at least this point; then, without pausing, allow the fly to leave the water smoothly to start your up-and-back cast so that the line and rod angle are in the best casting-plane position.

Note: The clock is reversed to show the casting arm movements of a right-handed caster.

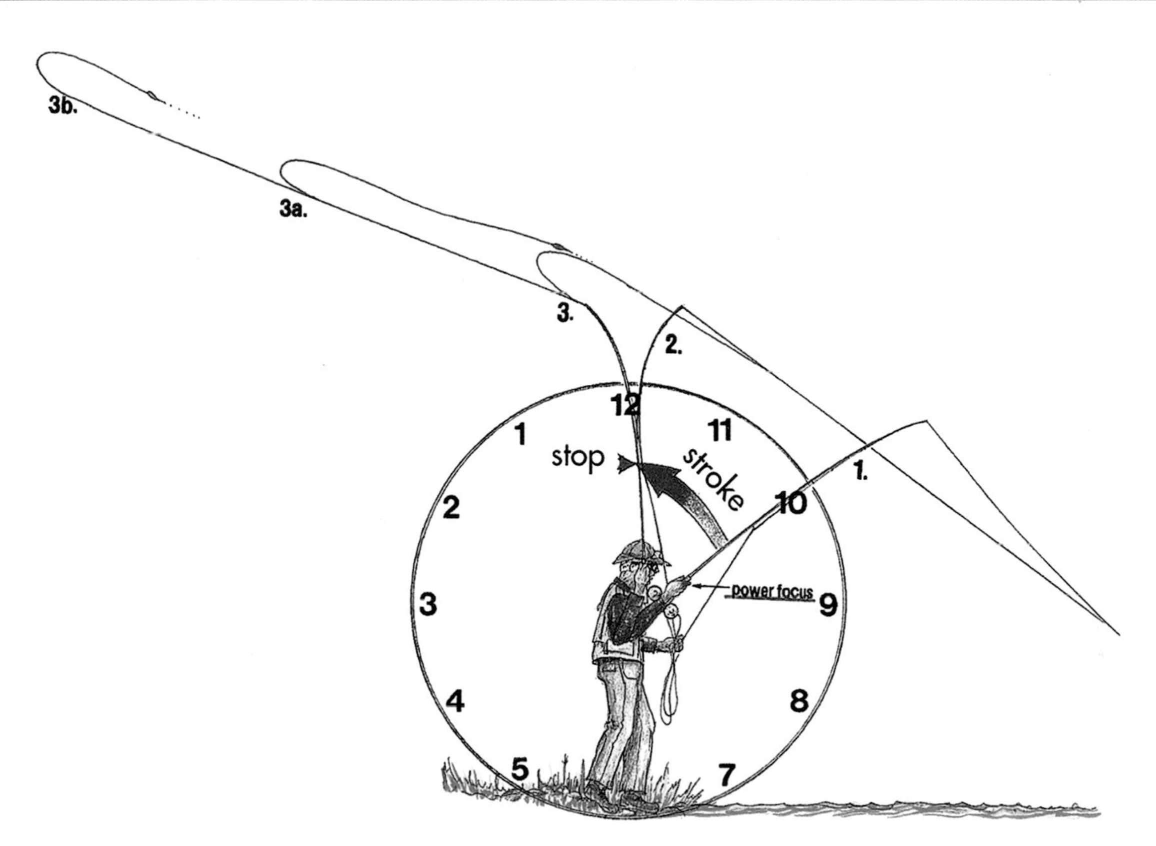

UP-AND-BACK CAST

1. Begin the stroke with a slow, smooth acceleration from approximately ten to eleven o'clock.
2. Stroke from eleven to twelve o'clock with maximum power and acceleration.
3. Stop the stroke abruptly at twelve o'clock. This causes a loop to immediately begin to form and move up and back past the rod tip.
3a. A narrow loop unrolls up and back.
3b. The up-and-back cast is complete and the forward-and-down cast should begin.

a good, tight loop, you must stop the rod abruptly at twelve o'clock. Focus your stroke energy on your index finger's pressure on the underside of the rod's handle. You're trying to cast the fly line up and over yourself from off the water so that it will *straighten* out above and behind you. During initial practices, *you must watch the fly line* to do so! This way you can see whether you have stopped at the right clock position and whether you have given the stroke enough power; you will then know precisely when to start the third phase, which is just *before* the leader and fly come straight back and begin to fall. Eventually, watching your up-and-back cast will not be necessary.

If you stand correctly, you can comfortably watch your up-and-back cast. This is an absolute must if you want to develop a correct and well-timed up-and-back cast and a precisely timed down-and-forward cast stroke. The trick to watching the up-and-back cast is to turn your head just before or as you start the pickup and quickly focus on the area where you want your up-and-back cast to end up. Don't try to focus and follow the cast as it leaves the water and moves past and behind you; your vision will usually blur, causing disorientation and discomfort. It helps to have the backcast area in shadow and free from glare.

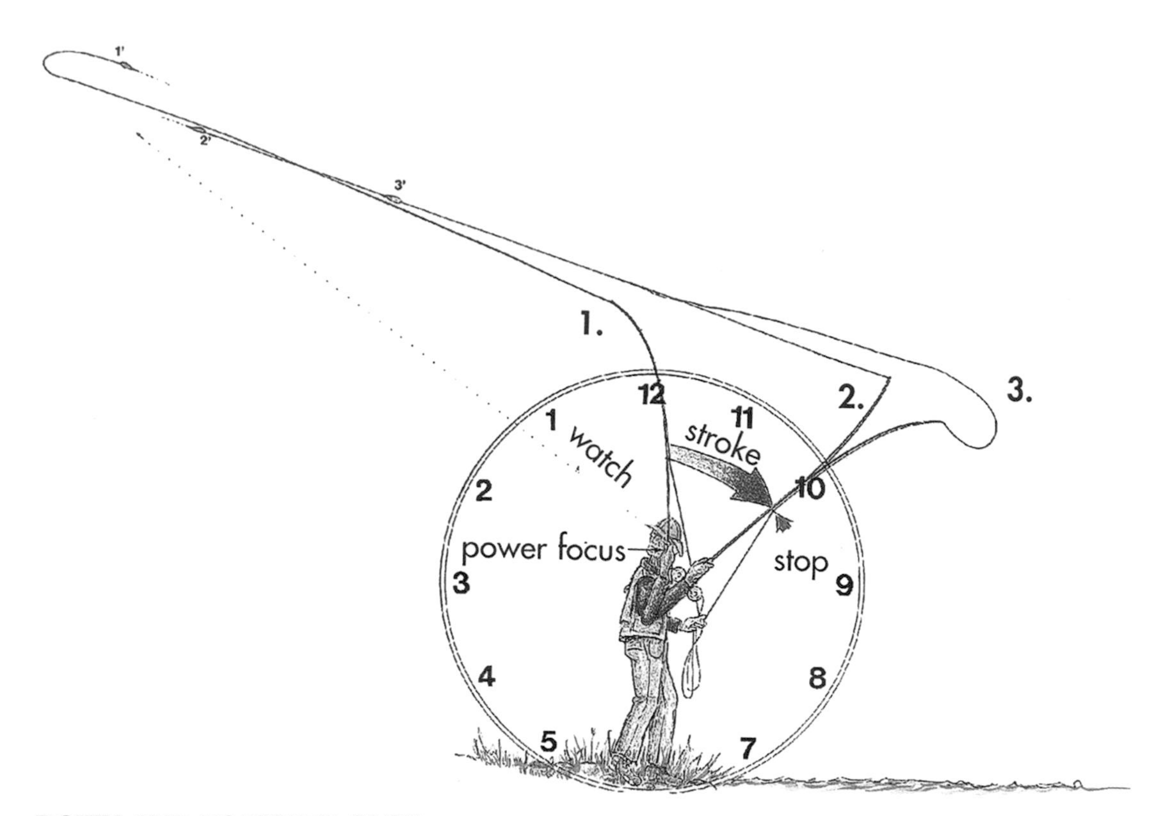

DOWN-AND-FORWARD CAST

1. You should be watching your fly, leader, and line tip. Just before they straighten, slowly begin a smooth stroke forward from twelve to eleven o'clock.
2. Stroke from eleven to ten o'clock with maximum power and acceleration, then stop abruptly at ten o'clock.
3. The forward-and-down stroke and stop forms the loop shape and determines the direction it will travel.

Down-and-Forward Cast

With your fly-rod tip at about twelve o'clock and as the fly line straightens out above and behind you, begin a slowly accelerating down-and-forward stroke, using mostly your forearm and locked wrist. You'll drift forward and down, slowly accelerating from twelve o'clock to eleven o'clock to ensure that the line is completely straightened out behind you (loading the rod) and to prevent shocking the tip. Next, apply the faster, power portion of the stroke between eleven o'clock and ten o'clock. Just as you focused your energy on your index finger for the up-and-back cast, focus the down-and-forward stroke energy on your thumb's pressure on the top of the rod's handle! Stop the rod motion abruptly at ten o'clock, *keeping the tip high at ten o'clock*, and watch the fly-line loop form and move forward past the rod and toward the water or ground.

Presentation

As the fly line, leader, and fly reach the extent of their length forward, begin to follow the falling line with your fly-rod tip down to around eight o'clock, until the fly line and fly rest on the water.

Repeat this four-part procedure for three to five minutes to get the feel of your tackle and casting. Stay relaxed and loose; don't hold your breath or rush the casting cycles. If your back or forward casts are weak or falling short, increase your stroke power. Remember, overcoming the water's hold on the fly

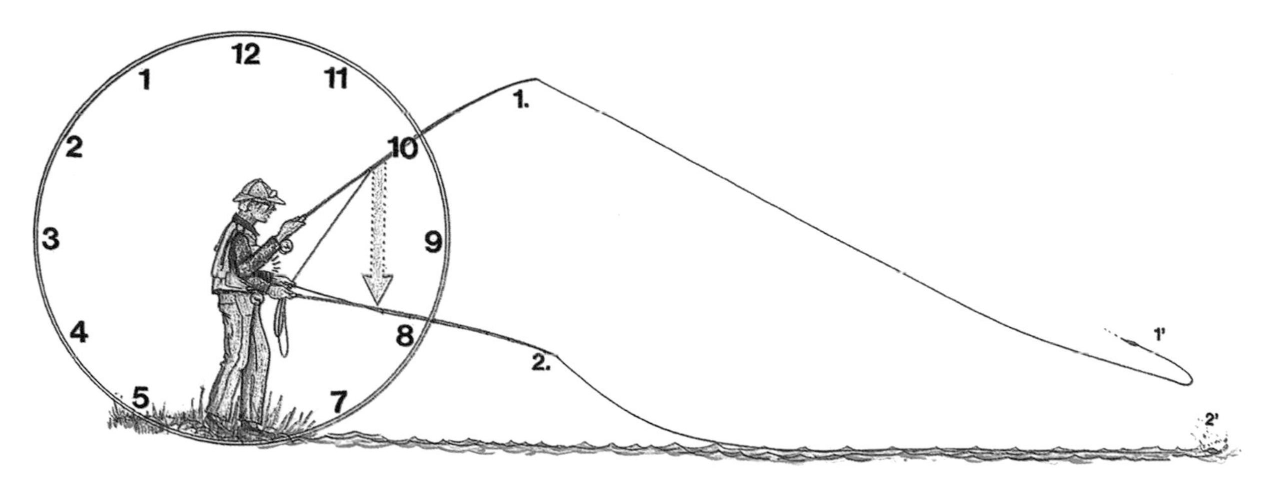

PRESENTATION

1. Keep the rod at ten o'clock until the loop completely unrolls and the fly is about 1 foot from the water.
2. When the fly settles on the water (2 feet), lower the rod to whatever position is required to either make the next pickup or fish the fly.

and overcoming gravity during the up-and-back cast takes *more power* than casting that same load downhill with gravity during the down-and-forward cast. Most beginning fly casters tend to reverse these power needs. Especially concentrate during your practice on keeping the ten o'clock to twelve o'clock arc in your back-and-forward casts to assure a good loop shape and *correct casting plane.*

The overhead or over-shoulder casting position is the best to begin with since it relates easily to the clock method. But as soon as you have a clear understanding of the clock and of loop shapes and casting planes, it's easier to

This front view of a fly caster shows the three main casting angles.

1. Overhead or shoulder cast.
2. Off-shoulder cast.
3. Sidearm cast.

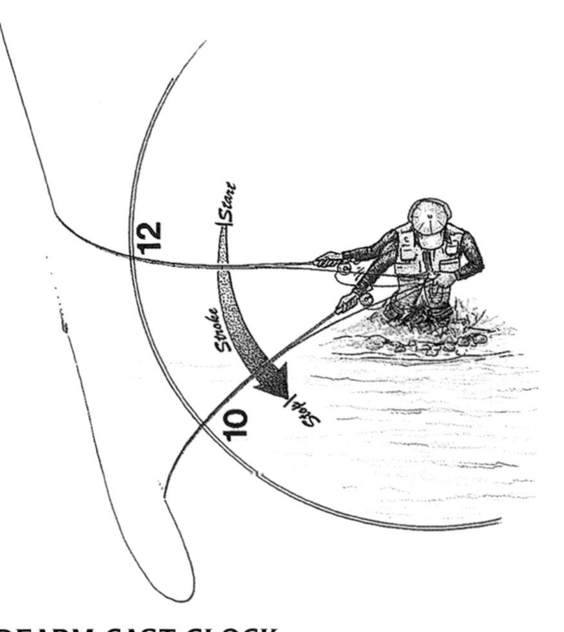

SIDEARM CAST CLOCK

For correct sidearm casting, visualize a horizontal clock. Angle the casting arm to the side and follow the same procedure as with overhead casting.

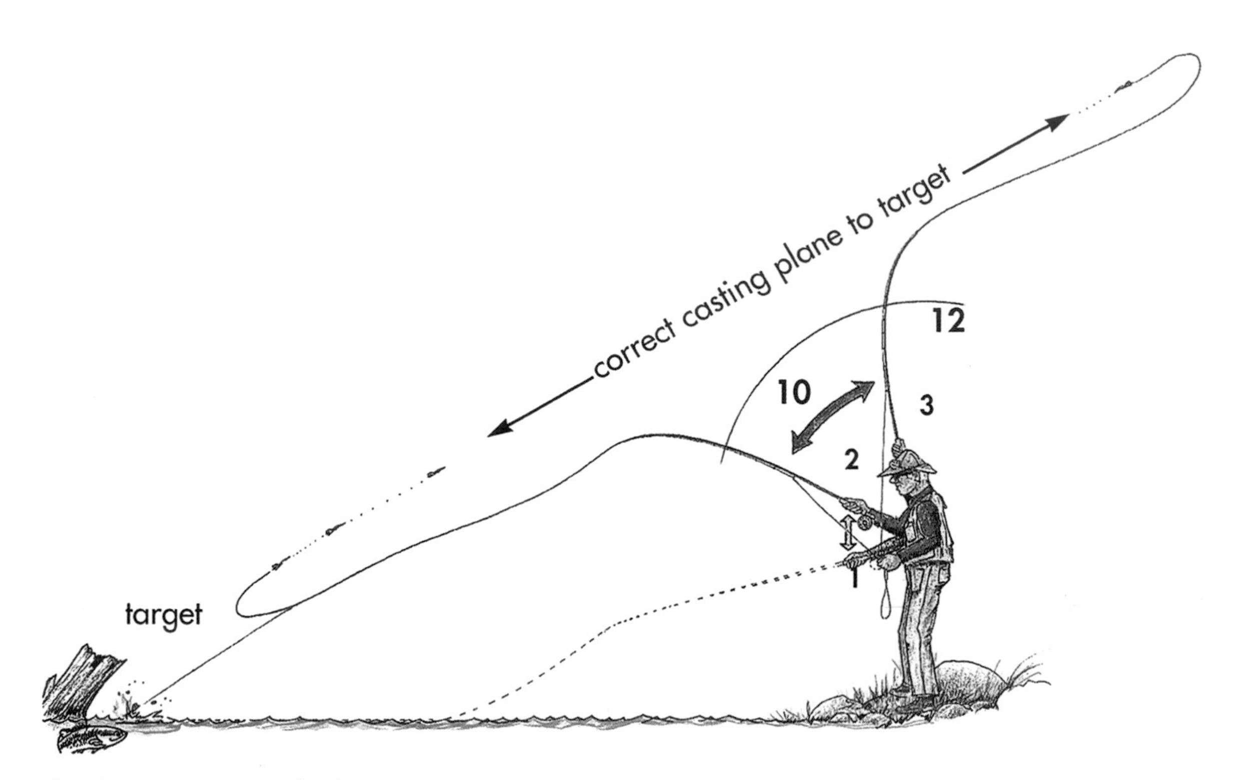

Practice to a target to obtain accuracy.

practice casting with an off-shoulder position. This is because your arm and shoulder muscles and reflexes are more comfortable and familiar with making off-shoulder or sideways strokes—with baseball bats, tennis rackets, and the like. Also, sidearmed, your fly line will travel a bit lower and more to the side, making it easier to watch your backcast and rod-tip position than when casting overhead. This cast angle also helps prevent the fly and fly line from striking the rod or you accidentally. Study the off-shoulder and sidearm casting diagram carefully.

When you actually fly cast for fish, you will use some form of sidearm position for most of your casts. This lower-angle cast is less hazardous, less affected by wind, and less visible to fish. But don't forget the clock angle; just imagine it tilted over at the same plane as the fly rod moving at your side.

As you get some feel for casting, let's add further suggestions. Place a hula hoop or dishpan on the surface to serve as a target. Look at this target as you begin each forward-and-down stroke, and make that stroke toward the target. It's not necessary to *hit* the target, but trying to will motivate you and develop your aim. Adjust your casting plane so that the loop travels straight toward the target and so that the fly strikes the target area just as the leader turns it over. Most fly presentations require the fly to either strike the target area directly or fall from 1 to 2 feet above it for a softer, more delicate landing.

To hit the target area with your fly, adjust the casting plane so that the fly travels in a more or less straight path to the target. Note that just as the fly and the leader straighten forward, the fly strikes the target area.

1. Pickup begins at eight o'clock to about ten o'clock; this is the beginning point of the casting-plane angle needed to hit the target.
2. Up-and-back stroke from ten o'clock to twelve o'clock so that the fly and line travel in the correct plane.
3. The down-and-forward stroke from twelve o'clock to ten o'clock puts the fly on target. Now lower your rod back to the first position in order to fish the fly.

Casting problem: Line, leader, and fly splash in a pile on the water. The rod is being stroked to the nine or eight o'clock position. Stop and hold the rod at ten o'clock until the line rolls out and the fly touches the water.

Casting problem: The line straightens forward too high and falls down and back into a pile. The forward-and-down stroke is angled too high (going forward-and-up).

If the fly and the line strike the water in a splashy pile short of the target, you're most likely bringing the rod tip too far down, perhaps to nine o'clock or eight o'clock, thus creating a "wide" loop and not allowing the fly line to extend to the target. Remember: *The fly line always follows the direction of the rod tip.*

If your line and fly go out high over the target and fall back toward you in a messy heap of fly, leader, and line tip, this is because your down-and-forward rod stroke is actually more forward-and-*up* and is ending too high ("high stroking"). This causes the fly line, leader, and fly to straighten out at a high angle; the leader and fly are then pulled back toward the rod tip by the falling line's weight. Most likely this high stroking is caused by your allowing the rod, during the up-and-back cast, to go too far back and down, to the two, three, or four o'clock position. This causes a change in the casting plane from ten/ twelve/ ten o'clock to ten/two/ twelve o'clock. This is the most common fly-casting error.

The Perfect Fly Cast

To make a perfect fly cast, each of these four steps must be accomplished correctly. It's natural for you to emphasize the down-and-forward cast most. But the single most important part of the cast is the pickup. If this is not correct, it is impossible to proceed with a perfect cast. This may surprise you, but there are relative values for each part of the cast:

1. Pickup—50 percent.
2. Up-and-back cast—25 percent.
3. Down-and-forward cast—15 percent.
4. Presentation—10 percent.

In our years at the L.L. Bean Fly-Fishing Schools, we have found that practically every incorrect casting habit or problem can be directly traced to an incorrect pickup.

FALSE-CASTING

After you've learned the four parts of the cast, it's time to try some false-casting.

False-casting is merely eliminating the presentation and pickup sequences for one or more casts while repeating the up-and-back and down-and-forward paths continuously. False-casting is used to extend fly-line length, to hold the fly in the air above the water until you pick a target, to change fly-line direction, or to remove water from a soggy floating fly. False-casting is also useful when practicing your loop control and fly-casting technique. When you are fishing, however, too much false-casting can cause fatigue and poor timing, as well as frighten fish. If you false-cast sparingly, it will serve you well.

To false-cast, eliminate the presentation part of the four-part cast, and as the line straightens forward above the water start another up-and-back cast. Don't let the fly hit the water, and in a back-and-forth casting cycle hold the fly up in the air. At first, using a short length of fly line (20 to 30 feet), practice doing just one false cast; then do two or three. False-casting can be tiring, so don't overpractice until you've built up your endurance.

As you practice, at this point resist the temptation to extend the fly-line length! Stay within about 20 or 30 feet or a length you feel comfortable using. Choosing a fixed target at a fixed distance will help you avoid the temptation. Using too much line will cause problems with timing, loop control, casting plane, presentation, and fatigue, and this will discourage you. Most of my fly fishing is done at 30 to 40 feet; longer distances are seldom required and are usually not as productive. In time, however, and with correct technique, you will be able to achieve much longer casting distances with ease.

Good fly casting is based not on strength but on proper timing and correct technique. Expert fly casters appear to make long casts effortlessly. This is because they do not throw the fly line with their arm speed but correctly energize (or load) and stroke the fly rod and then allow *it* to unflex and cast the fly line. Because many of us have used our arm's speed (as a short lever) to throw balls or rocks, we tend to try to throw the fly line and rod with arm speed as well. This is a mistake. Just use your shoulder, arm, wrist, and hand torque to energize the rod through the smooth, accelerating casting stroke. The fly rod is a fine casting tool that gives you so much leverage you need only a small amount of strength to fly cast. That's why you can fly fish effectively from age 9 to 90 (and longer).

ROLL-CASTING

Roll-casting is a forward cast without a backcast. Some fly-fishing instructors prefer to teach the roll cast first; I believe either order

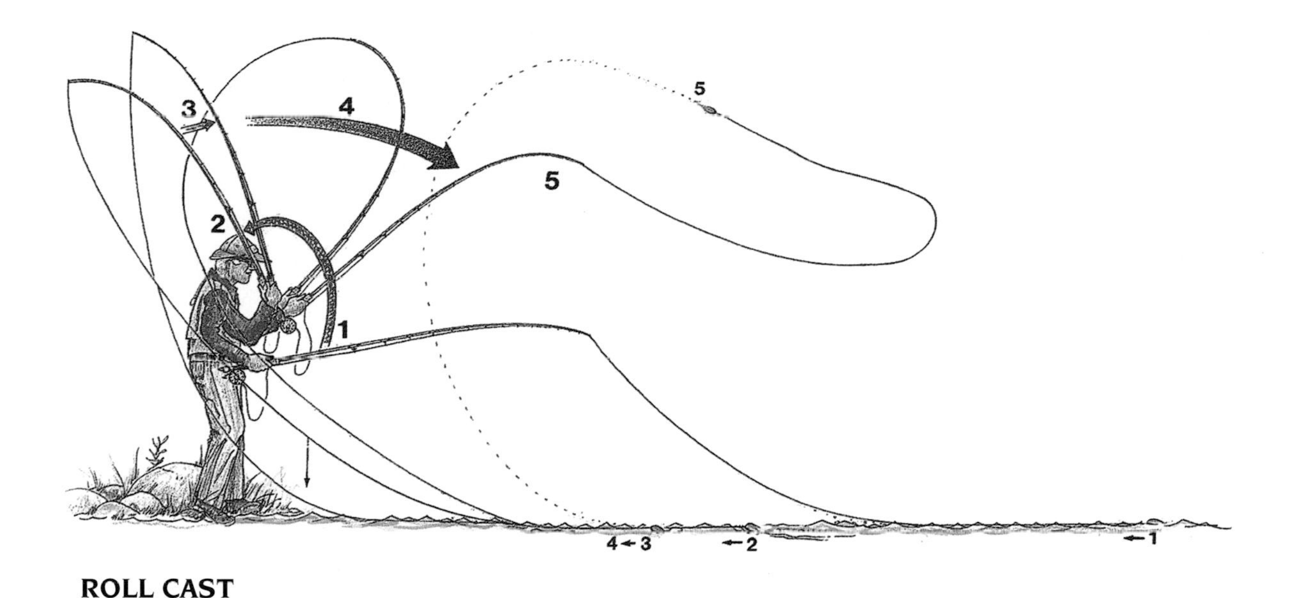

ROLL CAST

works nicely. It uses the same fly-casting dynamics and, like the false cast, merely modifies the basic four-part cast.

The roll cast must be practiced over water, never on dry surfaces. See the illustration above.

Pickup

This is the most important part. With the fly line extended forward on the water and your rod tip pointed low and toward the fly line, begin a slow arm- and rod-lifting motion that ends with your arm extended up and to the side, with the rod tip pointing at two o'clock. Do not rush; pause for a second or two. This pickup motion should slide the fly line, leader, and fly on the water toward and slightly to your side (the off-shoulder rod position). Do this pickup motion in slow motion. With the pause to the two o'clock position, the fly line you have lifted off the water will sag down beside and behind your shoulder.

Down-and-Forward Cast

After the pause, move your fly rod to the twelve o'clock position. From there begin the basic down-and-forward power stroke toward the target. Stop the tip abruptly at ten o'clock. There is a temptation at this point to lower or stroke the tip down too far, even striking the water with it. Don't let this happen or the fly line, leader, and fly will simply pile up on the water somewhere between the rod tip and target. You need to make a basic forward cast so that the fly-line loop will form and move forward with leader and fly. If the forward-rolling loop and fly fall short of straightening out, increase the power of your stroke and check that you are stopping your rod tip abruptly at ten o'clock.

Presentation

As the loop unrolls forward, the leader and fly follow it as the line falls to the water; after the fly and leader hit the water, follow the line down with the rod tip to the eight o'clock position. That is a completed roll cast.

Repeat this procedure a number of times. Because it's so important, once again we'll remind you: Don't rush the pickup. Don't accelerate the down-and-forward cast too abruptly, making the rod-tip arc go only from twelve o'clock to ten o'clock. Practice the roll cast until you feel confident with it, then try it in the sidearm and backhand casting positions.

The roll cast works without a backcast because it places the fly-line weight behind you with the two o'clock rod-angle pickup and pause. This pulls the remaining line and fly up and forward off the water, as the forward-moving loop passes over them. It is not a long cast, however—usually 20 to 40 feet, seldom over 50 feet.

The roll cast has almost unlimited uses in fly fishing. Here are some of its most important:

- When an obstacle is above or behind you, you can still make a forward cast without snagging your fly.
- It's the perfect method for picking up or straightening slack fly line.
- A modified roll cast allows you to swim a fly in any direction on the water.
- It makes lifting and pickup of a sinking-tip or full-sinking fly line easier.
- It aids in unhooking your fly when snagged on an obstacle.
- To make a slow, delicate fly presentation.
- To assist in hook-setting when excess fly-line slack is unavoidable.
- For repositioning your fly line if it should blow or drift too far to your side for safe or correct pickup.
- For making an easier down-and-forward cast when there is a strong wind at your back.
- For reaching your fly—to inspect or change it—without reeling or stripping in your fly line.

THE FLY-LINE HAND

As you hold the fly rod to cast, fish, hook, and fight fish, your other hand is in constant use. Let's add this hand into our casting practice. The fly fisher uses the fly-line hand on each cast to tighten the fly line on pickup, to extend more fly line when casting for extra distance, and to retrieve and animate the fly. If a fish strikes, the fly-line hand helps set the hook, control the line and fly reel throughout the battle, then, with net or bare hand, land the fish. Clearly the fly-line hand has a key role in fly fishing.

Before you begin your pickup, with the fly-rod tip at its lowest angle, use your line hand to remove any slack from the line. This simple tightening of the fly line will ensure a much more efficient pickup, and in turn a much better cast.

As you lift the line off the water with your rod and casting arm, hold the fly line tightly in your line-hand thumb and first finger, keeping your line hand and arm stationary. Better yet, use your line hand to make a short downward pull, or *haul*, just as you begin the up-and-back stroke. This simple technique will increase line speed, which helps move it off the water and upward, improving pickup efficiency.

Using the Line Hand for Extra Distance

To cast farther, add extra power to the down-and-forward stroke. As the overaccelerated line and fly move well forward of the rod tip, you should feel a slight line *tug* on your line hand. As this occurs, loosen your finger hold on the fly line, and the extended line weight will pull out more line from your hand proportional to its excess energy. This is called **shooting line.** For maximum effect, the line hand must be trained to sense this pull and release the line at precisely the right time. When you first try this, you will probably release the fly line *during the power stroke*, which will add slack and spoil the cast, actually reducing your distance. Delay the line release; watch the line move forward until you *feel* the tug.

When adding extra power to the down-and-forward stroke, you must still accelerate slowly and smoothly and maintain the rod-tip stop position at ten o'clock. If the rod goes lower on the stroke, you'll force the fly line to dive steeply at the water rather than unroll over it;

***Shooting* Out Extra Line**
Step 1: Hold extra line in your reel hand.

Step 2: When the forward-and-down casting stroke is completed and the line moves forward, relax your grip on the line coils and let them be pulled out by the extended forward moving line.

this shortens rather than lengthens the cast. Remember to watch the fly line move well forward. As it does, if you've given the cast enough extra power, you'll feel the fly line tug and release properly for the shoot. The more line you have extended, the better. Shooting line works because more weight pulls out more line.

Note: Never turn the fly line completely loose from your line hand's control as you cast and shoot fly line. Release the finger hold into a circle formed with your thumb and index finger. (See the photograph, bottom right.)

Establishing Absolute Line-Hand Control

As your fly nears the water, you should have control over it. This is done by establishing a **two-point** (two-hand) hold on the fly line. This allows you to control precisely the tension on the fly line for animating the fly, retrieving it, detecting strikes, hooking fish, and manually pulling the fish to you. *Mastering this two-point method is an absolute must for successful fly fishing.* Here's how to do it:

1. As the fly line, leader, and fly start to fall to the surface, begin to move your line hand toward your extended rod hand. Keep your eyes on the fly.
2. Extend the first or index finger of your rod hand down from its grip on the rod handle.
3. With your line hand's fingers, make direct contact with your rod hand's extended finger, placing the fly line across the extended finger. Now grasp the line with the rod hand's index finger and press it

Maintain your hold on the line as it shoots forward so you do not lose control of it as you attempt to fish or cast again.

One-point line control position for casting, hauling, and shooting fly line.

Two-point control position for retrieving fly line, setting the hook, and fighting a fish.

against the rod handle. Do not release your line hand's grip on the fly line. Now you are controlling the line in a two-handed hold.

4. With this two-point method, you have the best possible control on the line and fly for controlling initial slack and tension, animating the retrieving the fly, feeling the strike, setting the hook on a strike, and controlling slack and tension on the line as a hooked fish fights.

   If you have spin fished, an excellent way to understand this two-point control system is to consider the rod-hand index finger grip on the fly line as the bail of a spinning reel, and the line-hand grip as the spinning-reel handle. If you fail to close the bail or engage the handle, you have no line or lure control. That is what happens when you do not use fly fishing's two-point system.

5. Just as you begin the pickup for the next cast, release the rod hand's finger hold on the fly line.

A caution: As you initially practice two-point control, you will probably try to steer the fly line onto the rod finger by reaching with the rod hand (and fly rod) for the fly line. You'll quickly see that this doesn't work well. The *line hand* must move *to* the rod finger while keeping the fly rod in the correct fishing position.

Each time you cast and present the fly, establish your two-point control. Retrieve the fly by making a few short line strips with your line hand. Relax your rod-finger grip tension each time you pull on the line with your line hand. Then, as you reach for additional lengths of line *just behind your rod finger,* tighten your rod-finger grip so as not to allow the fly line to become slack. Always reach for more fly line *behind the hand.* Practice this with every cast until it is automatic. This is because you will need two-point control every time you fish a fly.

You can use two-point control to fight and pull in a small fish, but it's usually best to eliminate the excess line that accumulates between your hand and the reel. To prevent tangling, after you set the hook and have the fish under initial control, place the slack line in your rod hand's small finger and begin winding the line onto the reel, using the small fin-

To put fish "on the reel," use the two-point control hold while using your little finger to keep slack line tight as you reel it onto the reel spool.

Correct hand position to fight fish directly off the reel.

ger to provide tension and level-winding control for the spooling fly line. Make sure you have the fish *well hooked* and under *tight line control* before you attempt to reel up the slack fly line, then reel it up smoothly so that the fly rod's tip doesn't jiggle and possibly dislodge the hook from the fish's mouth.

Once all this slack is on the fly reel, release the rod finger's grip on the line. Now you can fight the fish from the reel, using cranking speed and your rod to control slack and line tension until the fish tires and is landed.

This may seem obvious to some, but others seem to miss this point: Most of the fly's movements on the water are the result of line-hand pulls and rod-tip movements. As you pull, you are shortening the amount of fly line you have extended. Try at this point to keep at least 20 feet of line extended to provide enough casting weight for the next cast. Then, as you make the next cast and want to extend the line and fly out farther, do so by overpowering and shooting out extra line, as explained earlier. One or more false casts may be necessary to extend the fly line longer distances. As you practice, try to work on each of these procedures.

OTHER CASTING TECHNIQUES

Besides basic casting and roll-casting, there are other techniques that you will want to master to fully enjoy fly fishing.

Shooting line is similar in purpose to working out line. As mentioned earlier, it is accomplished in either the backward or forward cast by using considerably more power than is needed to cast the line already extended. In either the backward or forward cast, slack line is fed out just as the moving loop reaches its end, thus pulling or shooting the extra slack out with it. The weight-forward taper is best for shooting out extra line. Generally, shooting out line reduces the number of false casts needed and adds casting distance.

Hauling is a technique for increasing line speed or overall fly-casting efficiency by using the power of both the rod arm and the line-hand arm. To accomplish a haul, the caster, just as the power stroke is applied with the fly rod, simultaneously pulls down, with the line hand, on the taut fly line below the first

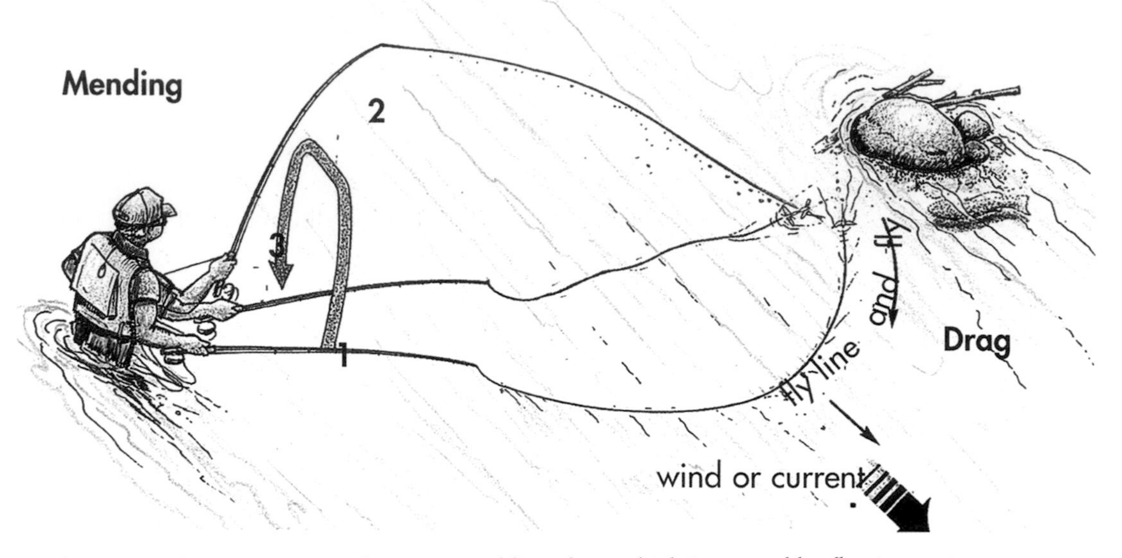

Mending is used to compensate for unwanted line drag, which is caused by flowing water or surface wind.

1. When unwanted drag begins to develop, lift the section of fly line causing drag off the water.
2. Using the rod, place the fly line in the opposite direction of the drag.
3. The rod is back into fishing position.

stripper guide. This pull—or haul—increases the line's forward or backward speed. **Double hauling** involves hauling on both the forward and backward strokes. Hauling should not be attempted until you have mastered loop control. Only then does it become a useful method for better line pickup and for making long, powerful casts. If you try hauling before you have mastered loop control, it will have an adverse effect on your overall casting ability.

Mending line is an extremely important technique for repositioning the line and leader on moving water to better control the fly. Mending is accomplished by using various rod-lifting and roll-casting rod movements. When you are fishing streams, mending line is about as important as casting.

The **sidearm cast** is a variation on the basic four-part or roll cast done by holding the rod to your side so that the line travels lower and the loop lies on its side. This allows you to keep the line low and out of the fish's sight, to keep it under the wind, or to cast under obstacles.

The **backhand cast** is simply an opposite sidearm cast. The rod and casting arm are placed across your body so that the line and fly are cast to that side. This gives you the advantage of the sidearm cast with another cast angle.

The **underhand cast** is basically a sidearm cast done with an underhand casting stroke so that the line and fly travel very low or skip over the water. This is an excellent way to present a fly very delicately.

The **skip cast** is simply a sidearm cast delivered with extra-fast speed and a low angle so that the fly hits the water and skips to the target. This is a great technique for casting a fly far back under low overhanging obstructions.

A **curve cast** bends to the right or left of you and is a variation on the standard forward cast. A portion of the line tip, leader, and fly curves to the right or left from the general direction of the power-casting stroke. Curve casts are useful when presenting the fly around surface objects or to prevent the leader and fly line from being seen by a fish as the fly passes overhead.

The **slack-line** or **serpent cast** is another variation on the standard forward cast, this one causing the line to fall on the water in a series of curves or S's. Such a cast allows the fly to float without dragging and is especially useful when casting across current or directly downstream.

The **reach cast** presents the fly to the target area and places a portion of the leader and fly line above or below the fly's position. It is especially useful when presenting a fly across a stream that has several current speeds. Reach-casting prevents the fly from dragging downstream faster than the water on which it lands. The reach cast is also considered a mend *during* the casting stroke—an in-air mend.

COMMON FLY-CASTING PROBLEMS AND SOLUTIONS

Proper fly-casting technique takes patience and practice to acquire. You will probably encounter difficulties along the way to achieving proficiency. Here are some of the most common problems that beginner and intermediate casters encounter. Each is followed by its solution.

Problem: Fly line, leader, and fly will not go out the desired distance (20 to 60 feet).
Solution: This is often the beginner's first problem, and it usually is caused by inefficient casting technique or improperly balanced tackle or both.

Make sure the rod and fly-line sizes are properly matched. Too light a line for a rod will cause casting problems of this nature. Check your four basic cast moves. Work on tighter loop control and better timing of power application on both the up-and-back and down-and-forward casting strokes. Also make sure you are using the correct casting plane for the distance that you are casting and for your height above the water.

Problem: Fly hits the water behind the caster.
Solution: This problem usually results from inefficiency in the up-and-back. Check to see that you are starting your pickup at eight o'clock and lifting the fly line off the water as your rod tip reaches the ten o'clock position. You want a smooth, slack-free line pickup at the beginning of the up-and-back stroke, and a

Wide up-and-back cast loop, and wide forward-and-down cast loop. Both these loops cause problems with distance and accuracy.

quick stop of the power stroke at the twelve o'clock position. *Check how far behind you the rod tip is going.* You may be waiting too long on the up-and-back cast to allow the line to straighten. Look back to see if your backcast falls or if it has enough power to unroll before it begins to fall behind you. Remember: It takes more power to cast up-and-back than down-and-forward.

Problem: Leader and line splash down too hard or before they completely unroll and straighten out.
Solution: This usually indicates that you are bringing the rod tip too low during your forward stroke, thus forcing line and leader to the water before the loop unrolls. Stop the power stroke higher and delay the rod's follow-through to the eight o'clock position until the fly lands on the water.

Problem: Fly, leader, and line strike the rod.
Solution: If the line or leader strikes the rod on the backward or forward cast, first angle the fly rod to the side to avoid most line-and-rod collisions. You may need more power or a smoother power stroke. When lifting line from the water, be sure to begin the pickup at the eight o'clock position, then lift the line by raising the rod butt and your arm before you begin the up-and-back stroke. Now simply apply more power to the power stroke when making the up-and-back or down-and-forward casts.

Problem: Tailing loop, in which the fly, leader, and line tangle together at the end of the casting stroke.
Solution: This problem usually results when an inexperienced fly caster begins a power stroke before the backcast loop unrolls. With more advanced casters, the problem is most commonly a result of applying power to the rod too quickly rather than allowing the power to increase smoothly through the stroke. This is especially common when you try to cast extra distance or into a strong wind. Watch your loop unroll, start the power stroke slowly, and gradually accelerate just as the line tip and leader are unrolling. Beginning a stroke too fast will shock the rod's tip and cause it to recoil, which drops that point of the fly line and forms a tailing loop.

Problem: Too wide a loop.
Solution: This problem results from a power-stroke arc that is too wide. The loop size is proportional to the size of the rod-tip arc. Using the clock method, practice the power-stroke arc between the ten o'clock and twelve o'clock positions.

Problem: Leader does not straighten and piles up on the water.
Solution: This is usually caused by either too wide a loop or your down-and-forward power-stroke direction being angled too high above the water. Try to apply power more down and toward the target, and tighten your loop.

Problem: Open loop.
Solution: This problem is caused by too wide a rod-tip arc when casting, or by starting the casting stroke too late, then exaggerating by

Tailing loop. This casting fault causes most wind knots and line/leader/fly tangles.

Fly-line loop unrolling forward too high above water caused by high stroking when the up-and-back cast has been angled too low. The line, leader, and fly usually fall short of the target and land in a pile.

lowering your tip too quickly after the power stroke. It may be solved in the same manner as the problem of casting too wide a loop. Also, make sure to leave the rod tip high (ten o'clock) until the fly and leader land on the water, so as not to pull the loop open.

Problem: Fly snaps off on your down-and-forward cast, and/or you hear a cracking noise on your backcast.

Solution: This happens when you start the down-and-forward cast too soon, before the line has unrolled and straightened behind you. This problem is very similar to the tailing-loop problem and can be corrected in the same manner. Get into the habit of watching your backcast, especially if you are encountering persistent casting problems. You will notice that the fly-snapping problem and line-cracking problem do not occur on the

Open loop. The loop has a wide, almost double-sized loop shape because the fly-rod tip is far too low. As a result, the presentation is sloppy.

Wide-looped up-and-back cast. This is caused by a rod angle of almost three o'clock. Watching the cast will help correct this fault.

forward loop, because you watch it unroll before beginning the next stroke.

Problem: Fly and leader twist and tangle.
Solution: This happens when you use a fly that spins as it is cast. Use a fly that is designed better, or use a larger-diameter, stiffer tippet. If you can't do either, make slower casts and reduce or eliminate false-casting. Large-hackle (size 12 or larger) dry flies and flies with long upright wings or split wings are usually the worst for twisting.

Wind Casting

Excessive wind from any direction may cause casting difficulties. In most instances, however, if you understand how wind affects casting, you can use the wind to your advantage.

Problem: When the wind is in your face, it blows the fly and line back at you when you cast forward.
Solution: To avoid this, increase the height and angle of the up-and-back cast. This tactic lofts the line into the wind, adding its force to the backcast, which enhances the forward-cast power. Make the down-and-forward cast more directly toward the water. Always form a tight loop when casting into the wind.

Problem: When the wind is at your back, it tends to slow and blow the fly line down, causing it to strike your back or the rod on a forward stroke.

Solution: Make a powerful sidearm, low-angle, tight-loop up-and-back stroke to reduce wind drag on the line and to keep the line out of the wind's full force—just the opposite of casting into the wind. On the forward-and-down stroke, make a higher-angle power stroke to let the wind's force lift and turn over the line, leader, and fly. If the wind is too strong for a good cast, simply make a forward roll cast to let the fly line roll and blow forward with the wind.

Problem: When the wind is from your casting-arm side, it blows the line across your body and head, often tangling up or hooking you.
Solution: To correct this, keep your rod arm high and angled over you to the other side or use a backhand casting technique. You can also use the opposite arm for casting. These adaptations place the line on the downwind side of you and prevent it from striking you.

Problem: When the wind blows from your free-arm side, the line is blown low and to the rod's side, causing a presentation problem or the possibility of hooking someone on that side.
Solution: To solve this problem, use a low sidearm cast to reduce the fly-line height, which avoids the wind's full force. The fly line is blown out farther to that side, so you only need to compensate for extra wind lead.

The wind's force against any cast is best countered using a very tight-looped and powerful (high-line-speed) cast. The modern graphite fly rod is a powerful, small-diameter, high-energy casting tool and thus is the best choice during windy conditions. If you regularly fly fish in very windy areas, you should also consider using heavier line weights and faster-action rods to gain more casting power against the wind. It is very hard to make long and accurate casts against strong wind (20 miles per hour or more). But if you follow these suggestions, there is no reason that you cannot enjoy fly casting in normal winds of 5 to 10 miles per hour.

Fly-Fishing Tactics

Fishing the fly is as important as casting the fly. Unless you intend to fly cast only in your backyard or to be a tournament fly caster, you will need to become a student of the ways of water and of fish and fish foods.

There are two types of fly-fishing water: still water and moving water. Lakes, streams, and oceans have both types. Still water is less common than moving water, even in a lake, because of wind and currents. Oceans have currents, tides, and inflows.

Presenting a fly in calm water involves casting to a certain spot and then allowing the fly to rest, or swimming it back toward you. In still water your fly, leader, and line remain motionless until you move them. The successful fly fisher works the fly at the right depth and with an action that imitates what the fish are feeding on. Drag is seldom a problem on still water unless the wind is blowing or you are moving, as in a drifting boat. Then you must adjust your retrieving technique as if you were fishing on flowing water.

Achieving good results in moving water requires many casting and presentation techniques. In such water, at or below the surface, the fly is fished by letting it simply move with the current's direction and speed, or is retrieved across, down, or directly against the current.

The natural movements of fish foods range from stationary to swimming up, down, or across currents. Imitating such actions with fly tackle is simple. At certain times and places, fish will respond aggressively to a fly fished with an unnatural action, but these instances are both less predictable and less common than are reactions to true imitations of natural fish food.

The fly fisher who prefers to fish moving water should be familiar with three basic fly presentations.

The **upstream presentation** is one in which the fly is cast upstream to or above the area in which you suspect a fish is waiting. Generally, the upstream presentation allows the fly to float or drift downstream at the speed, and under the control, of the water's flow.

The **downstream presentation** is one in which the fly is cast downstream just above or to the area that you suspect holds a fish. With this presentation, the fly can be retrieved upstream, retrieved to the right or left across the stream, or, by paying out fly line, allowed to drift downstream.

The **across-stream presentation** is one in which the fly is cast at an angle across the current to land just above where you suspect a fish is waiting. Variations on the across-stream presentation allow the fly to drift downstream, be retrieved upstream, or be retrieved across stream.

Practicing with water targets greatly speeds up learning the accurate presentations required to catch fish consistently.

APPROACHING YOUR QUARRY

Fly fishers must approach their quarry more closely and quietly than other anglers do to successfully present the fly. Most fly fishing is done either by walking along shorelines or by wading, and generally these approaches are the least complicated and most satisfying. However, some waters are too deep or distant to approach on foot. For these places the fly fisher must use a flotation device. Here are a few of the best alternative approach methods.

Float tubes are round or U-shaped one-person, portable, and inflatable flotation units in which the angler sits. They are propelled with swim fins or ankle paddles. Float tubes are excellent for approaching fish closely and quietly on sheltered, still water, but are not recommended or safe for flowing water. They are lightweight and economical and are also a good choice for ponds and lakes where it is difficult or impossible to launch other types of boats.

Float tubes are the most popular and economical means of safe and convenient personal flotation.

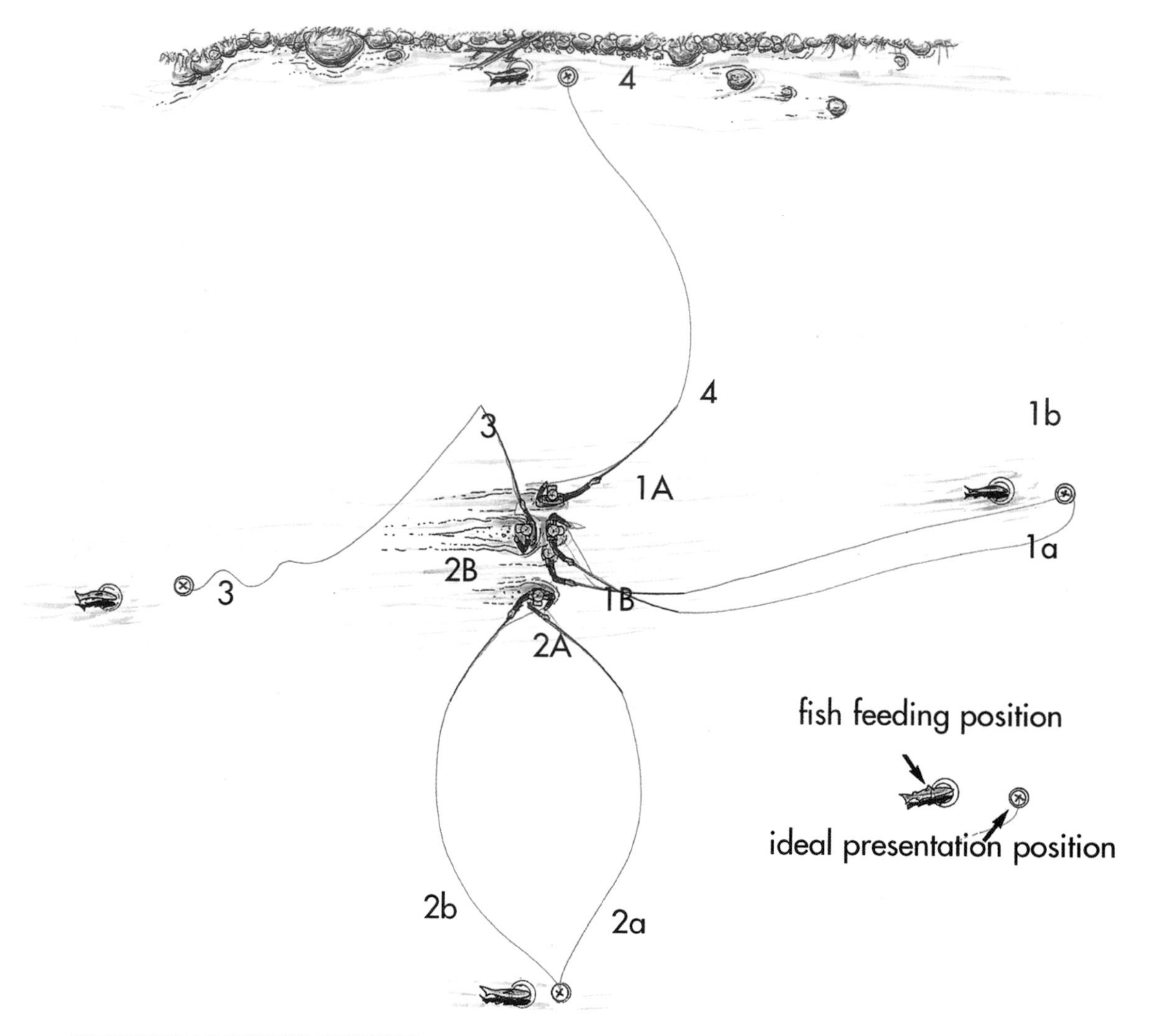

STREAM PRESENTATIONS

1. **Upstream to fish:** 1A. (the cast) 1a. (the presentation) Standing directly below the fish's position, make a curve cast. 1B. (the cast) 1b. (the presentation) Standing several feet to the right or left of the fish's position, make a straight cast.
2. **Across stream, right:** 2A. (the cast) 2a. (the presentation) Use an upstream reach cast when the fish is in a slower current than the fly line. 2B. (the cast) 2b. (the presentation) Use a downstream reach cast when the fish is in faster water than the fly line. Mending is recommended in both cases.
3. **Downstream:** Use a slack-line cast, short of the fish, then lower your rod as the fly floats toward the fish. (Do not stand directly above the fish if possible.)
4. **Across stream, left:** Casting toward the shoreline, use an upstream reach cast if the fish is in slower water than the fly line. Mending is also recommended to continue a long, drag-free drift.

Kick boats are portable and inflatable one-person craft that the angler sits *on* and propels with either swim fins or oars or both. Kick boats are larger and more buoyant than float tubes, so the angler sits higher above the water, with only the legs below the knees in the water; this usually makes it easier to cast and warmer when the water is cold. Kick boats can also move faster across the water. Most are for still water, but some can be used in rivers if you are a skilled boater and cautious about attempting swift and treacherous rapids. Another convenience is that there is room to carry extra equipment, often even a cooler.

A kick boat.

A distinct advantage to using a float tube or kick boat is that everyone gets to fish because no one has to "row the boat." Of course it's not possible, convenient, or desirable to use float tubes and kick boats in some fishing situations. The following devices require a rower.

Inflatable rafts are larger than kick boats and are designed to float or drift streams; they usually carry more than one person. They are powered by oars and/or small outboard engines. Rafts are a convenient method for fly fishing while drifting down a river or for getting to hard-to-reach wade-fishing areas.

Prams are small one- or two-person cartop boats that are propelled by oars or a small outboard motor. They are useful in sheltered still water and slow-flowing streams, or to reach wadeable water.

Canoes are one- and two-person lightweight, cartop craft that are traditional classics for fly fishing ponds, lakes, streams, and rivers. Canoes are easily paddled and can be adapted for small outboard motors to cover longer expanses of water. They are quiet, graceful, and beautiful boats to enjoy fly fishing from or to use to reach distant wading waters.

Johnboats are flat-bottomed wooden or aluminum boats with squared bow and stern and can usually accommodate two to four persons. They are powered by pole, paddle, electric motor, or gas engine. The flat bottom of a johnboat makes it ideally stable for reaching shallow waters and fly fishing, but it is not comfortable to use on high waves.

McKenzie River drift boats are rowboats that are specifically designed for floating or drifting streams and rivers. They are ideal for one or two fly fishers and an oarsman. They are flat bottomed and shallow drafted, and they offer precise maneuverability with oars. Many are fitted with specific devices for fly-fishing comfort—such as swivel seats and slots for standing anglers.

Bass boats are large, shallow-drafted, stable fiberglass or aluminum boats with casting decks on the bow and stern. They are powered by large gas engines and electric fishing motors. They are good craft for larger lakes,

Canoes are the ideal shallow-draft boats for one or two anglers to access good fly-fishing areas of lakes and streams with speed and quietness.

A johnboat.

McKenzie drift boats are very stable craft to drift streams with. You can cast from them or beach them and wade.

A bass boat.

especially when fly fishers must travel some distance to reach the waters they wish to fish.

Flats skiffs are similar to bass boats except with even shallower drafts and cleaner interiors—and they are a bit more seaworthy for fishing saltwater bays, flats, and brackish backwaters. For fly fishing, skiffs are usually poled, but some are also powered by electric fishing motors.

TECHNIQUES FOR FISHING FLIES

Artificial flies can deceive fish into mistaking them for the real thing. There are five basic kinds of flies: dry flies, wet flies, nymphs, streamers, and bugs.

Dry flies float on or in the surface to imitate terrestrial or aquatic insects. Generally, such insects float and move with the water's surface movements or with the wind's speed and direction. Dry flies are usually presented with a floating fly line and allowed to drift or float as naturally as possible. If the real insect is active on the surface, you should attempt to impart a similar action to the artificial. On the other hand, if the natural is inactive, the imitation should also be inactive. Wind, variable horizontal current speeds, or both of these forces will often cause drag on the fly line, leader, and fly. Drag causes the imitation to move unnaturally. It can usually be avoided by proper presentation and mending of the fly line.

Most dry flies are designed and tied with materials that allow them to float partly above or in the water's surface film. However, if not treated with a waterproofing agent such as silicone or paraffin, they usually will soon become wet and sink. This is especially true when a fly has undergone repeated dunkings or has caught many fish. Use a dry-fly spray or paste to waterproof the fly before you use it. Put on just enough to coat the entire fly very lightly. Sprays and liquids are a little easier to apply, but they are more expensive and do not last as long as the paste dry-fly flotants. Pastes will usually liquefy with the warmth of your fingers and solidify when fished.

If the dry fly begins to float too low or sink and does not improve after several water-removing false casts, retrieve it and blot with an absorbent paper or cloth towel, tissue, or chamois leather. Absorbing the excess water will lighten the fly and serve also to clean it. Apply another coat of dry-fly dressing, and the fly should float like new. An absorbent towel or chamois is also very useful for cleaning and drying the fly after you remove it—wet, slimy, and matted—from a fish's mouth.

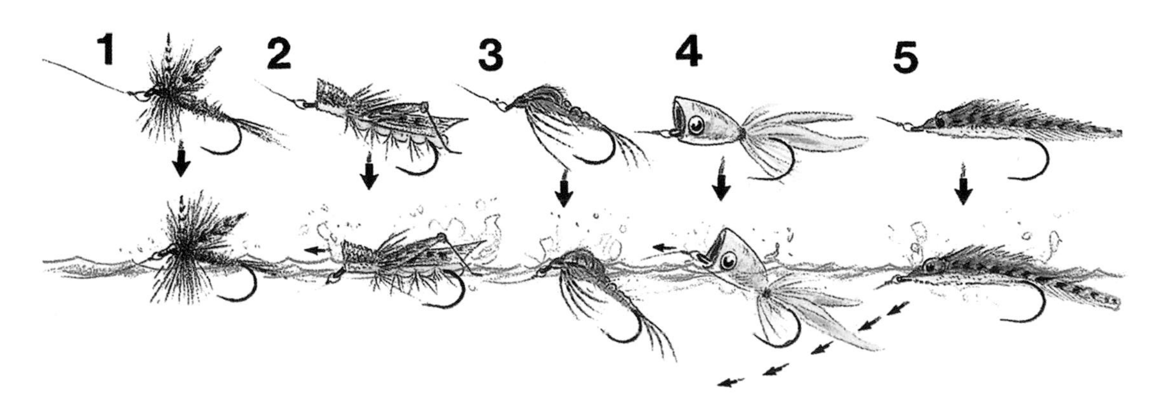

Examples of how **floating-fly designs** rest on or in the water's surface:

1. Hackled dry fly: Sits on the surface.
2. Grasshopper: Swims in the surface.
3. Emergent nymph: Hangs in the surface film.
4. Bass popper: Pops and swims across the surface.
5. Frog diver: Floats on and dives below the surface.

Wet flies sink just below the surface or deeper and generally imitate aquatic insects swimming, emerging, egg laying, or drifting helplessly in the water. Some wet flies also imitate small fish or submerged terrestrial insects. Wet flies can be fished with floating, sinking-tip, or full-sinking fly lines, depending upon the depth and angle of the desired fly movement. On calm water, wet flies are usually presented *on the far side* of where you suspect a fish is swimming. The fly is then allowed to sink to the right depth. Then, with whatever action and speed will imitate the natural insect or small minnow, the fly is retrieved to and past the fish. Many wet flies are made in highly colorful attractor or exciter patterns, especially those used for brook trout, bass, shad, panfish, salmon, and steelhead. These attractor flies are generally fished faster and in a less imitative manner in an attempt to attract and excite the fish.

Wet flies in moving water are generally presented *in front of and just above* the fish's position. They are drifted downstream or retrieved across or upstream, depending upon what they are designed to imitate and how they are meant to attract or excite the fish. Some wet-fly methods use more than one fly on the leader. (Check the regulations for the waters you fish.) Sometimes as many as six wet flies are used, although two flies are much more common. Multiple wet flies are usually fished on and just below the surface.

Nymphs are designed to be fished below the surface, including on the bottom, of either calm or moving water. Nymphs mainly suggest (give a general impression) or imitate (give a detailed impression) immature aquatic insects. But nymphs also may be used to suggest snails, scuds, leeches, crayfish, worms, and similar foods. Floating, intermediate, sinking-tip, and full-sinking fly lines are useful in various waters to fish nymphs. For shallow, still, and moving water from 1 to 6 feet deep, floating or intermediate lines are generally best. These lines allow the best overall fly action and control for nymphing. For medium depth (4 to 8 feet), especially in moving water, a sinking-tip fly line generally works best. For deeper water (8 to 20 feet), either still or moving, a full-sinking line generally performs best with nymphs.

In still water the nymph is cast *past* the fish's swimming path or holding area. It is allowed to sink to the desired depth, then it is animated with the method that best suggests the live natural food.

In moving water nymphs are fished in two basic ways. In the first method they are fished with a floating line. The nymph is cast *upstream* and allowed to sink and drift naturally downstream. The second way is with a sinking-tip or full-sinking line. The nymph is cast up and across stream to achieve the tight line-to-leader-to-fly contact needed to animate a nymph with a swimming action while retrieving it across or upstream.

Streamers are usually designed to be fished below the surface to suggest or imitate the small fish, minnows, eels, leeches, and so on, that are swimming or drifting in the water. However, streamers are sometimes fished at the surface to imitate the feeding or crippled action of a small fish. Streamers, like nymphs, can be fished with all four fly-line types depending upon the action and the depth desired. The sinking tip is generally the best all-around streamer fly line.

In still water the streamer is presented *near or beyond* the fish's position and is retrieved *past and away from* the fish with an action that suggests the natural creature's panic or vulnerability.

In moving water the streamer may be presented at all angles to suggest the natural food's movement. Most small fish are strong swimmers and can live in areas from top to bottom in a stream. Perhaps the most popular streamer presentation is casting across the current and retrieving with erratic swimming and pausing action as the fly swims and swings down and across the flow. This sideways mo-

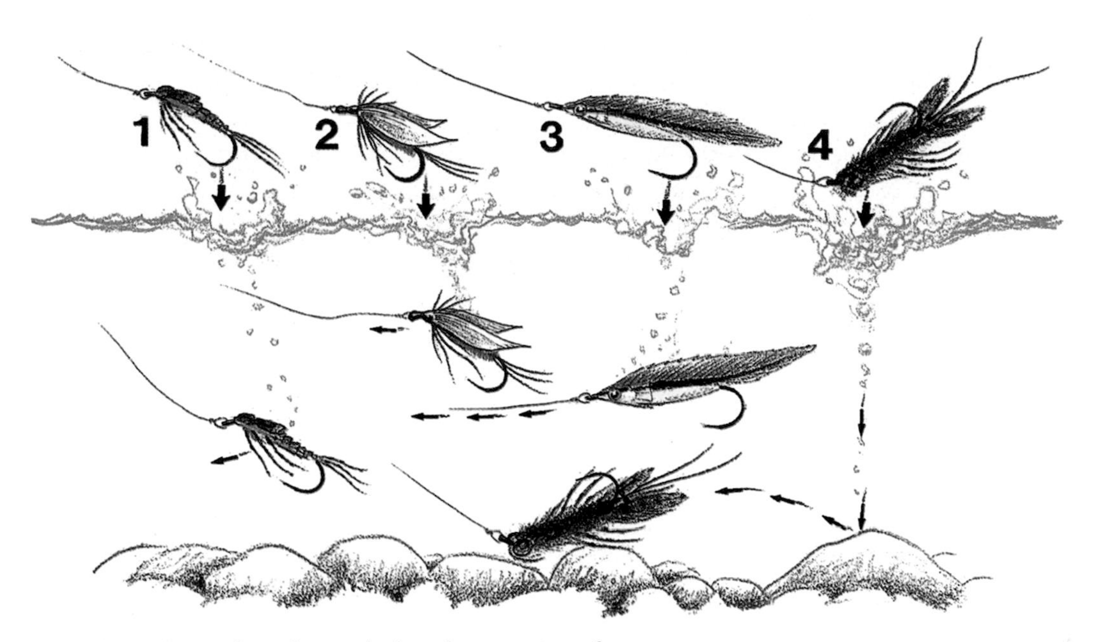

How **sinking flies** sink and swim below the water's surface:

1. Weighted nymph: Sinks and swims or drifts.
2. Wet fly: Sinks slowly and swims or drifts.
3. Streamer: Sinks and swims like a small fish.
4. Fast-sinking crayfish: Sinks to the bottom and crawls or swims near bottom.

tion suggests distress and vulnerability to a minnow-hungry fish. Once the streamer reaches the end of the drift, it is retrieved erratically upstream. Sometimes streamers are effective when cast upstream and allowed to drift downstream with the current, as if they were dying or helpless.

Wet flies, nymphs, and streamers perform best when they are tied using soft, water-absorbent materials. After they get wet, they take on the natural odors of the waters you fish. Before you begin fishing these three types, rub them on a wet alga-covered stone, on some aquatic vegetation, or on some silt taken from the bottom of the water you plan to fish. This simple wetting and deodorizing preparation will enhance your fly's ability to fool fish.

Bugs float on the surface and suggest larger insects, frogs, mice, crippled minnows, and so on. Bugs are fished with a floating or sinking-tip fly line. Use a floating line if you're fishing bugs just at the surface. A sinking-tip fly line, with a 4- to 6-foot leader, allows the fly to be fished at the surface, diving, swimming, or surfacing.

For stillwater fishing, bugs are generally presented *near or past* the fish's location. Often they are most effective when presented near structures such as the bank, lily pads, logs, or overhanging trees. When cast over an object, a bug can be hopped or made to fall into the water to suggest a natural terrestrial food falling into the water. Once on the surface, the bug is worked like a miniature puppet, being made to struggle or swim in an attempt to entice a strike. Usually, the more slowly these types of flies are moved, the more effective they are.

In moving water, bugs are generally cast at all current and eddy angles and fished with an action similar to what is used in still water. Line drag is avoided by casting-angle adjustments and line mending, as with dry flies. In moving water, bugs are usually fished near or off shoreline and surface structures.

Dropper flies (two or more flies) may be used on one leader to increase your chances of catching one or more fish on a cast. (Check regulations first.) Such combinations as two to four wet flies, wet fly and streamer, nymph and streamer, or dry fly and nymph are often more effective than a single fly. The larger, heavier fly should always be tied to the end of the leader and the smaller, lighter flies tied farther up the leader's tippet (except in the case of a dropper tied to the hook or eye of another fly). A dropper fly is attached to a leader by first tying a blood knot or surgeon's knot with a 4- to 6-inch tag of tippet material. The fly is often tied onto the long tag with a Duncan loop or improved clinch knot (see chapter 2).

By using two or three flies at one time on your leader's tip and tippet, you can learn what the fish's preference is from repeated catches on one of the flies. Many times two, three, or four flies will also have an "emotional" or exciting effect on fish that might ignore a single fly. Casting two or more flies is, however, a bit more difficult than casting one fly, and tangles are more frequent.

ANIMATING FLIES, DETECTING STRIKES, AND HOOKING AND FIGHTING FISH

Once you have learned to cast a fly correctly and accurately and can quickly establish the two-point control, your focus shifts to making the fly look desirable to the fish, detecting the strike, hooking the fish, tiring it, then landing it.

Fly animation is normally accomplished in either a passive or an active manner. The **passive** method involves simply letting the fly sit or drift with current or wind, allowing the fly to float or sink and move in the water more or less as would a helpless insect or injured live food.

The **active** method involves puppeteering the fly, either by pulling on the fly line with your line hand or by careful rod-tip movements. Perfecting these fly-animation techniques is fascinating and challenging, second only to casting for pure enjoyment. Seeing a fish leap to meet your fly as it falls to the water, intercept its drift, or chase and catch it is always thrilling.

Detecting these "bites" is the key to hooking fish. The first sense to use is your sight. Watch your fly if you can see it; if not, watch your leader, strike indicator, or fly line for any unnatural movement that might indicate a fish has taken the fly. Next, feel and listen for strikes. The line and rod provide you with a sensitive connection to the fly. Strikes may be no more than a slight tightening or loosening of the tension—a twitch or a series of tugs. You must recognize these and react *immediately* with a strike. If you delay for even a second, the fish will usually recognize a fake and spit it out.

The major mistake fly-fishing students make is in not concentrating on and reacting to these takes. At my schools I have students practice recognizing strikes by sight, feel, and sound, reacting quickly and reflexively.

Setting the Hook

When a fish takes a fly, you seldom have more than two or three seconds to hook it before it ejects the fake food. You must react quickly to make the point of the hook penetrate the fish's mouth. We call this **setting the hook.** Smaller and barbless hooks require less energy to hook most fish. Larger hooks require more energy or power even for the smaller fish.

Small flies (sizes 18 to 8) usually require finer leader tips to be most effective. Smaller hooks also require *less* energy to penetrate a fish's mouth skin. The light-leader, small-hook strike is a *quick* movement up and back with the fly-rod tip—not a slow pull. This up-and-back movement hooks the fish and puts the rod in a position to absorb any excess pulls from you or the fish that might break the leader or tear the fly out of the fish's mouth.

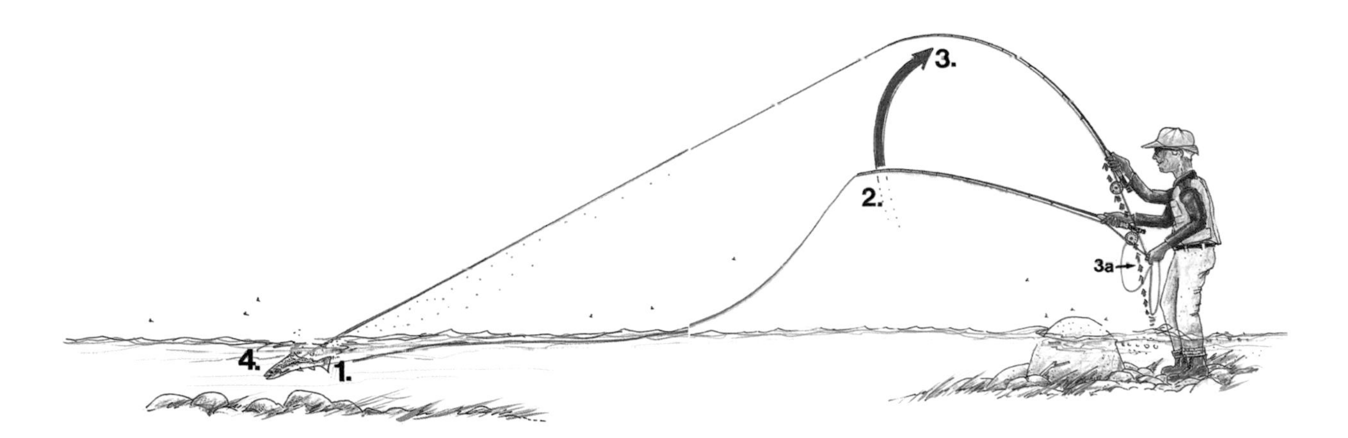

Small-Hook Strike and Set Procedure

1. Angler detects a fish strike by feeling it on the line or by seeing it.
2. The rod-tip position as strike occurs may be between eight and ten o'clock, depending on the type of water and fish.
3. Strike with the rod by quickly and crisply lifting and rotating the rod tip upward to eleven o'clock. The high tip position absorbs some of the excess energy to prevent breakoffs.

3a. As the rod is lifted up and the tip rotated, allow a few inches of slack fly line to slip from your line hand. This helps prevent the tippet from snapping and keeps the hook from bending or being pulled out of the fish.

4. The fish is hooked and begins to tire quickly against the spring of the high rod.

Large flies (sizes 6 to 5/0) usually require much more strike energy to penetrate the fish's mouth tissue, and also a different strike method than small hooks. The large fly hook is set with a quick line-hand pull on the fly line followed immediately by a stern back motion of the rod's mid- and butt sections while keeping the tip low and forward. This strike motion and low tip angle put much more force on the hook's point, causing the hook to move forward and penetrate a fish's mouth.

In both cases the hook penetrates faster if the strike begins with a quick move. Think of the difference between driving a nail into wood by striking it sharply with a hammer or just pushing on it.

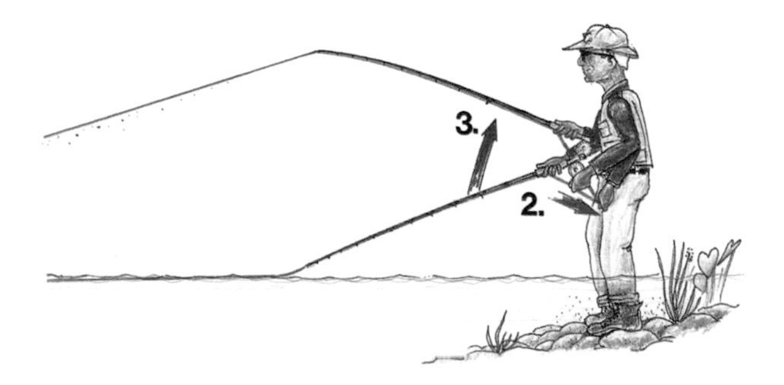

Large-Hook Strike and Set Procedure

1. Angler detects a strike by feeling or seeing it.
2. As you detect the strike, immediately pull the line taut with your line hand. Note that the rod tip is low and that the line is tight to the fish.
3. With stern force on the rod's mid- and butt sections, pull it back and up (to your side and back) to position 3 of the diagram (around ten or ten-thirty).
4. The fish is hooked and the rod is in an ideal position to assert more hooking force or leverage against the fish in order to tire it quickly.

When you see, feel, or even sense the fish take your fly, you must be prepared to set the hook *quickly!* Lack of concentration often prevents strike detection and quick reaction. It is important to practice striking and setting the hook until it becomes a *reflex action.* A pond full of small panfish such as bluegill or sunfish is ideal for this practice.

Remember, striking and setting the hook on most fish requires a quick tightening of the fly line with the rod and line hand. Larger or tough-mouthed fish require a stronger, harder rod strike performed while also pulling down on the fly line with your free hand. Very sharp barbless hooks are vastly more efficient in hooking fish than are dull or barbed hooks. For the same reason—less friction in penetrating the fish's mouth tissue—smaller hooks require less force to set than do larger hooks regardless of the fish's size. Overreacting when striking a large fish with a small line and a light leader will usually result in breaking the leader and losing the fish.

Landing Fish

Once the fish is securely hooked, it will struggle to escape. Landing small fish is rarely a problem. But larger fish have the size and strength to take out line, dive under cover, or break your leader. Your skill counters these maneuvers. This is one of the most pleasurable and exciting parts of angling.

Always maintain a taut line on the fish in order to keep the hook embedded and the fish under your control. Know the power of your rod and strength of your leader tip. Do not exceed these limits when fighting a large fish. Try to keep the rod at about a 45-degree angle above the water so that the rod tip can absorb the tension of the fighting fish on the hook and leader. If the fish pulls harder than your tackle can stand, let it pull out line until it tires, slows, or stops. Then immediately resume pulling it in.

Never force in a fish, but rather allow it to jump, swim, and struggle until tired. Don't try to boss a freshly hooked fish, or it is likely to panic and break away. Likewise, never underplay the fish. Use enough rod and line pressure to make the fish struggle and tire quickly. When fighting a fish in a stream or river, try to position yourself to its side or below it. Fighting a fish upstream will take longer and could give the fish the advantage it needs to get off the hook. It can also cause the fish to become overtired and drown.

It is a good practice, after you get a fish under control, to fight it directly from the fly reel, rather than to strip in slack line that might tangle around your feet or legs. This is especially true for larger fish. Do not just reel the fish straight in. Instead, pump the fish in with the rod, first lifting it up then reeling in line as you let the rod down.

When the hooked fish tires, it will begin swimming slightly on its side. *Do not reel the fish all the way to the rod tip.* Leave the leader outside the rod's tip-top, and leave at least a rod length of line and leader between you and the fish. That way the line and leader should have enough stretch to keep from breaking, and the knots will not hang in the guides if the fish makes an unexpected dash. This length also allows you to reach the fish as you land it.

When the fish is ready to be landed, it will reluctantly but calmly surface and lack the strength to dive away. Depending on its species, size, and location, several methods can be used.

Catch and Release

For various personal, sporting, or legal reasons, you may wish to release a fish. It is important for you to know how. To release a small fish, if the hook is visible in the fish's mouth, pull the fish close to you in the water. Then simply reach out, grasp the fly, and turn and twist the hook upward. The hook will disengage (this is especially easy if the hook is barbless) and the fish will turn head-down and swim away. If the hook is

The catch-and-release net is an ideal tool to land, unhook, and release a trout.

deeper, secure the fish by gently sliding your wet hand under its stomach and lifting without squeezing its body. Avoid putting your fingers inside the fish's mouth or through its gills to free the hook, and try not to lift the fish out of the water. Most fish, even small trout, have sharp teeth or gill rakers that can cause painful or even crippling cuts. Besides, fish are very likely to thrash when they feel your hands. This action can result in your hooking yourself or dropping the fish and injuring it. Use a hook-removal tool instead. With a hook disgorger or a hemostat, firmly grasp the fly and back the hook out. Quickly place the fish back in the water and give it time to regain its equilibrium and swim out of your hand.

When releasing a fish, never *throw* it back into the water. The fish is tired from the fight, and the shock of hitting the water lessens its chances of survival. A small landing net is very useful for landing and releasing small fish. To release a large fish (16 inches or more), use a specially designed catch-and-release landing net, with a soft, shallow bag, or carefully beach the fish if you don't have a net.

Netting: Lead the tired fish with steady, smooth rod pressure over the bag of a still, submerged net. As the fish's head comes over the net's bag, release the rod tension so that the fish's head will begin to sink into the net. At the same time, lift up the net to trap the entire body. Never come down on or from behind a fish with the net; this kind of approach can strike and frighten the fish and cause it to swim or leap away from the net. Keep most of the net's bag in the water until the fish calms down. Reach inside and unhook the fish, trying to keep its body and gills in the water.

Let the fish revive and swim out of the net bag under its own power; dumping or tossing a fish out of a net can injure it.

Beaching: When the fish surfaces and turns on its side, calmly and gently lead it with steady rod pressure to a gradually sloping, unobstructed shoreline. As the fish beaches itself in the shallows, relax the line pull. Unhook the fish and turn it around, gently coaxing it into deeper water. If the fish is too exhausted to right itself and swim, hold it upright (with your hand near the tail) until it does. Then let it escape your gentle hold under its own power.

Never pull a fish you intend to release completely out of the water onto the shore. If you must handle it, do so as tenderly as you would a human infant. Never hold a fish by sticking your fingers inside the gills. Try not to keep an exhausted fish out of the water any longer than you absolutely must. If you wish to show your catch to a companion or photograph it, keep the fish in the water until you actually show it or photograph it. I recommend that you prefocus and set the aperture before you photograph the fish; this can save precious time out of the water.

If the fish is hooked in the gills or throat, to ensure that it has the best chance to survive you should cut the leader at the hook eye, then release the fish. In time the fish's immune system and enzymes will reject the hook and the wound will heal. If hooking or hook removal causes continuous bleeding, the fish most likely will die.

Catch and Keep

If you plan to keep a fish, you should tire it thoroughly before attempting to land it. It is best to use a landing net on freshwater fish such as trout, bass, walleye, pike, and panfish. Most smaller saltwater fish can also be landed with a net.

Once the fish is in the net and calms down, you can remove the fly hook using the procedure already described for releasing a fish. If the fish is not put in a live well or on a stringer, it is best to kill it immediately. Do this by striking it several times on the top of its head, just behind the eyes, with a small club, or priest.

To beach a fish that you wish to keep, *thoroughly tire it out.* Follow the procedure described earlier for catch-and-release beaching, except use more force and beach the fish farther up on the shore. Extra tiring will prevent the fish from flopping back in. A sharp rap on the head will stun or kill a beached fish.

Many larger freshwater and saltwater fish that you wish to land and keep require the use of either a tailer or a gaff. A **tailer** is a device that is commonly used by Atlantic salmon anglers to disable and hold the salmon with its tail in a loop snare. A **gaff** is a large metal hook with a sturdy handle for hooking (gaffing) and landing a large fish. The gaff is a more brutal way to land a fish, especially if used to hook the fish's body, but it is sometimes necessary on strong, large, and dangerous fish such as shark, billfish, and tuna. Gaffs can be used to lip-hook larger fish without seriously wounding them if they are to be photographed and/or released. It is more difficult to use a gaff or tailer than to use a net or the beaching method. We do not advise using gaff or tailer without personal instruction from an experienced fly fisher or fishing guide.

The **priest**—actually a fancy club—is used to kill or stun a large fish immediately after it is tailed or gaffed. Strike the fish on the head just between and behind the eyes. Failure to use a priest can result in personal injury or equipment damage from a large fish thrashing about out of the water.

COMMON FLY-FISHING PROBLEMS AND SOLUTIONS

Problem: Scaring fish.
Solution: This is a problem most fly fishers encounter until they recognize that fish are frightened by their presence and noise as well as by the disturbance made in fly casting and presentation.

Stay low, move slowly and quietly, and wear clothes that do not contrast with the background. Try to cast so that your rod and line are not easily visible to the fish. Make your presentation softly, and keep your fly line and leader from splashing or floating over a fish.

Problem: Missing strikes.
Solution: Keep your fly hooks extremely sharp and stay *constantly alert.* Be ready the instant a fish takes the fly. Avoid excessive slack line. Practice striking quickly. Also regularly check to see if your hook point is dulled or broken from striking stones on your backcast. Polarized sunglasses are a great aid in seeing strikes and fish. Most students miss strikes simply because they do not react promptly and set the hook when they see or feel the fish seize the fly.

Problem: Breaking off fish on the strike.
Solution: Use less force when you strike, and make sure your hooks are very sharp. Do not strike harder on a large fish than is needed to set the hook on a similar but smaller fish. It's human nature to overreact to the sight of a big fish with a big strike. Try to stay calm. If breakoffs persist, you might increase the strength of your leader tippet. Tie your knots very carefully, and test them before fishing the fly. Check your tippet for wind knots regu-

larly. Wind knots can weaken your leader by 50 percent. Also, a longer tippet will have more "give," and will absorb mistakes better than a short one. Some fly fishers now put about 6 inches of shockgum into the butt of their leader to prevent such breakoffs.

Problem: Hooks breaking.
Solution: This is a common problem for beginners and experts alike. It occurs when the fly is allowed to drop and strike stones on the backcast.

Keep your up-and-back power stroke higher, and use a bit more power to keep the cast up. Sometimes the hooks will break on hooked fish; this happens because of poor hook quality or, more likely, because of improper placement and excessive tightening in a fly-tying vise when it was made.

Problem: Dry flies float poorly or sink.
Solution: If dry flies are properly constructed and waterproofed, they should float well. You may be presenting the fly too forcefully and thus dunking it on impact. Make sure the fly is well waterproofed with dry-fly spray or paste. Present the fly about 2 feet above the water so it will alight softly. When you pick it up, make one or two quick, brisk false casts to shake the water out of it. This tactic does not necessarily dry it completely but reduces its weight so it will alight softly again on the next presentation. After you catch a fish on the fly, blot off the slime and water with a soft paper towel, a chamois, or a tissue before casting it again. Check also to see if your fly-line tip may be sinking. This can cause your fly to go under, too. Add paste line flotant to the line tip to help it float.

Problem: Dry flies dragging and scaring rising fish.
Solution: When a dry fly moves across, up, or down the current unnaturally, it is *dragging* and will often scare a rising fish. Make your presentation with more slack leader, and learn to mend a surface line that is moving faster or slower than the fly to gain a natural drift speed.

Problem: Line and fly won't come off the water easily. This results from your floating line sinking. It may not be straight because of reel memory, or it may have become coated with particles of dirt.

Tips on Terminal Fly Tackle

One of the most frequent mistakes new fly fishers make is not regularly checking their tackle for possible problems. Here are some things to look for.

- Check the fly regularly, especially if it is not drawing strikes or you are missing strikes. Check for a broken hook, a dull or bent hook point, moss or weeds on the fly, a tangle with the leader, or fly parts wrapped around the hook bend. Also look for any damage that might affect the fly's looks or action.
- Check your knots, particularly your fly-to-tippet and tippet-to-tip knots, after landing several small or large fish or after extended casting periods. Knots weaken or slip when wet, from overtightening, and from abrasion.
- Check your leader for cuts, abrasions, or wind knots. Replace the tippet if it has a wind knot or an abrasion. Failure to do so will surely cause loss of fly or fly and fish.
- Check the leader for twists or curls, and straighten them by stroking the leader tight with your fingers and palm. Twists or curls cause the fly to cast poorly and land off target. If these will not straighten, replace them with a new leader or tippet.
- Check for fly-line tangles on or around the fly reel as well as around the rod between the guides.
- At least twice a day, check to see if the rod's ferrules are tight, if the guides are lined up, and if the reel is still tight on the handle.
- Look behind you! This is necessary to avoid poor up-and-back casts, hanging your fly in trees, or hooking people or animals that stand or walk behind you.

Solution: Clean your fly line with a damp cloth or soapy rag. Wipe the line dry and apply some fly-line flotant or polish. The fly line will float higher and pick up much more easily when it's kept clean and coated with flotant. You might also practice lifting the fly line out of the water more slowly and smoothly. (For straightening instructions see chapter 2, *Assembling Fly Tackle.*)

Problem: Fly goes too deep and hangs up on the bottom.
Solution: In still water, do not allow the fly to sink so long. Retrieve a bit faster. In flowing water, cast the fly with a little less angle upstream or start your retrieve sooner.

Problem: Sinking fly lines and heavily weighted flies are difficult to pick up.
Solution: Pull more of the line in past your rod's tip-top and use a short roll cast to lift the remainder. As the roll reaches the line's tip, initiate a regular pickup to begin your backcast. This procedure will work well for any type of fly that is difficult to pick up.

READING WATER

Reading water begins with the choice of what water to fish and when. All fish are cold-blooded and must live and feed according to season, weather, water temperature, and water volume. You should learn the seasonal requirements of fish in the water you plan to visit.

Once you are on the water, there are several ways you can read it. First, you must learn to recognize the overall *structure* of any area of a lake, stream, canal, bay, or ocean. Structure is what lies along the perimeter, lies on the bottom, or extends up from or down to the bottom. Structure may be rocks, moss beds, fallen trees, or other such natural or unnatural objects. It is around these structures that fish and their foods live. Food is more plentiful here, and the structure provides protection from predators.

Eddies and pools created by structures provide relief from strong currents. Spawning often takes place in these same fertile, protected areas. To find fish, learn to recognize

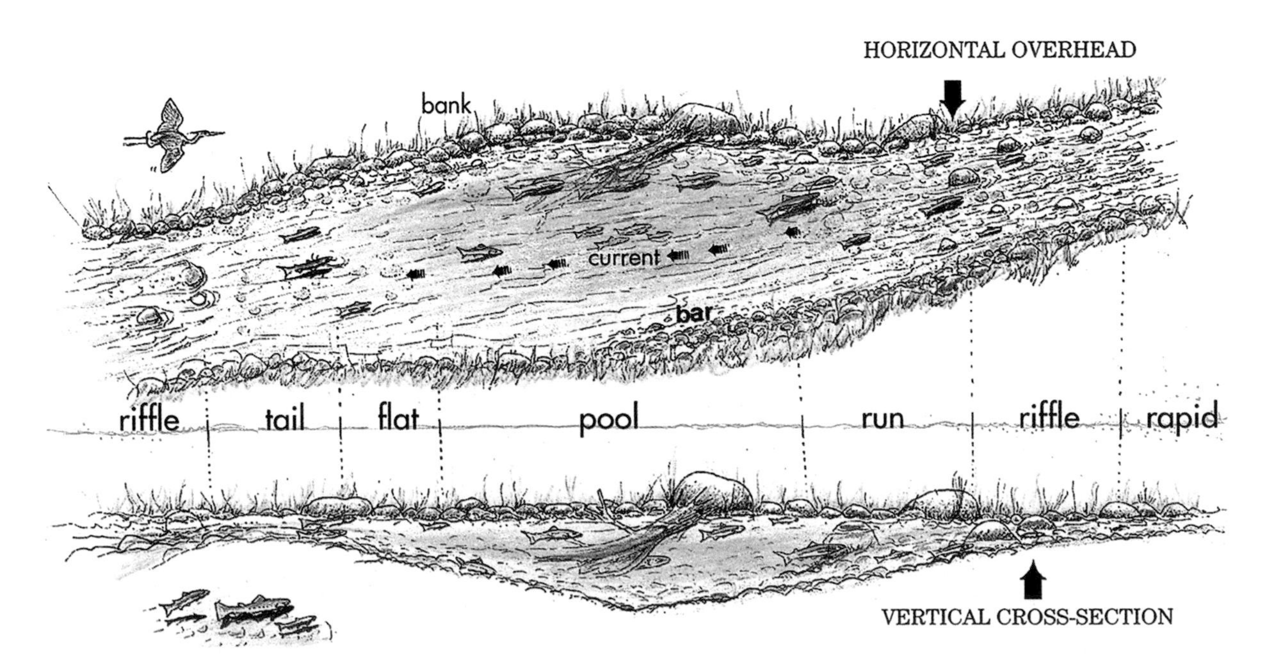

Freshwater Stream
Typical sections with structures that are probable fish locations.

major structure areas. Many anglers regularly use sonar units, or fish finders, to locate underwater structure and fish in waters too deep or murky to see well. The "sidefinder" units are most practical for fly fishing.

Clear water looks darker with an increase in depth. Water depth, bottom structures, and the fish's own color meet most of the protection and concealment needs of fish. Polarized sunglasses are a great aid to your seeing through the reflective water surface. If fish are not clearly visible at the surface or in the shallow water, they most likely will be hidden in the deeper, darker water. Since fish often have camouflage coloration, they will not be easy to see. The key to seeing fish is to watch for their movements and shadows on the bottom as much as (or more than) you watch for the actual fish.

In streams, the water's surface tells you how fast the water is moving and what structures might lie unseen in the murky or dark water. A large underwater boulder or log, for example, will cause surface irregularities. Flowing water usually moves fastest at the surface and slowest at the bottom. In streams, fish are usually found during feeding periods in moderate riffles, pocket waters, and runs; along the shoreline of pools; on flats; or in the pool tails. When they are resting or in nonfeeding periods, you may still entice strikes by fishing in deep pocket water, slower riffles, and runs, and down a pool's channel. Springwater inflows can attract fish in streams as it does in lakes.

Reading water, therefore, involves seeing fish or evidence of their presence, or identifying areas that are likely to hold fish. Good

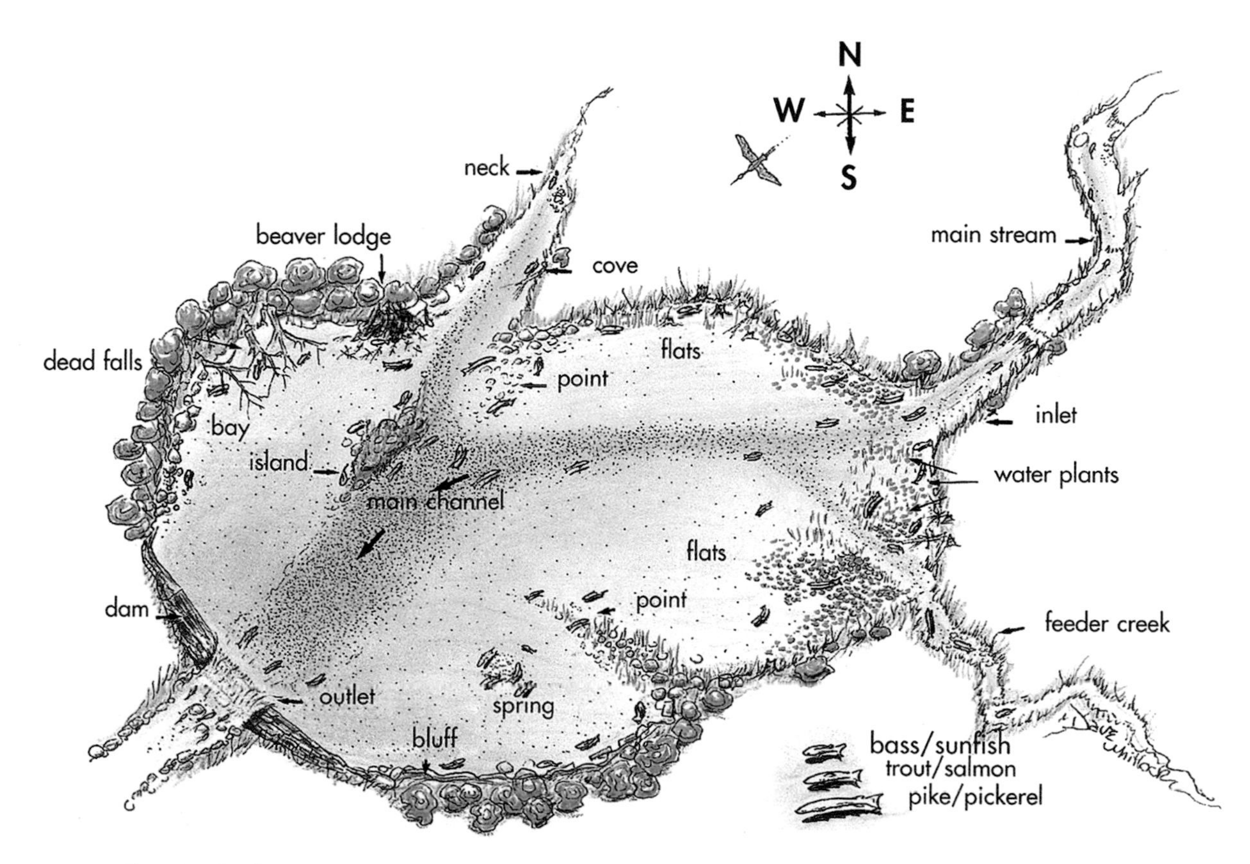

Freshwater Lake
Typical structures and fish locations.

water reading can save hours of unproductive fishing.

In lakes, fish are usually found feeding at inlets along weedy or rocky shorelines, over and around offshore weed beds, just off points, and up in coves. If the wind is blowing, they usually feed beneath the surface on the downwind side and on the surface on the upwind side. During nonfeeding periods, you catch fish in the deeper channels by fishing your fly deep or near the bottom. Natural springs seeping up from lake bottoms or flowing into lakes attract fish, especially during very cold and very hot weather. The nearly constant 45- to 55-degree F springwater provides most fish with a comfortable temperature. Fish finders are valuable tools for locating these areas and fish in large deep rivers, lakes, and oceans.

If fish do not strike your flies as quickly as you expect them to, have patience and keep your mind tuned to reading and studying the water. Change flies and methods, and try different areas. Fish do not feed constantly, and there will be periods each day when they seem asleep, and other times when they will be outright aggressive. Anglers often find their greatest satisfaction and pleasure in using their skill and wit to catch the fish that is the most reluctant to take the artificial fly.

5 The Biology of Fish

Fish are born, live, feed, and reproduce in a different medium than ours. To fly fish successfully for them you must understand their world of water and how they function in it.

Fish live as cold-blooded animals. Unlike us, their metabolism is continually affected by the temperature of the medium in which they live and breathe. As warm-blooded animals, we maintain a constant body temperature (98.6 degrees F). Our metabolism and activity can remain relatively constant over the four seasons. Because fish are cold-blooded and cannot keep their body temperature and metabolism constant, their level of activity is continually affected by the seasonal temperature variations of the water.

There is a temperature range of about 20 to 25 degrees F in which most fish metabolize well. When the water is colder or warmer than this range, they usually become sluggish or dormant, even dying if temperatures drop too low or rise too high above their ideal. To catch these fish as they are feeding actively and full of fighting energy, you must choose the right season and water temperatures for the species you wish to catch. There are four general groups of fish classified as to their temperature comfort zones.

- Cold-water fish, 40 to 65 degrees F.
- Cool-water fish, 50 to 75 degrees F.
- Warm-water fish, 60 to 85 degrees F.
- Tropical fish, 65 to 90 degrees F.

Water with temperatures in the middle ranges of each of these groups is where you will usually find the species you wish to fish for most actively feeding. When the water temperature dips lower than these ranges, fish tend to slow down in activity and feeding, and are likely to stay in deeper (warmer) water as surface temperatures get colder.

Surface feeding is most likely when water temperatures are in the upper ranges of these comfort zones; fish will also tend to stay in shallower water at these times. When water temperatures become significantly warmer than the comfort zones, fish usually become more or less inactive or lethargic. This is because warmer water contains less oxygen.

At lower temperatures, water holds more oxygen, so at the upper temperature limits fish often swim to deeper, colder water or to sources of colder water, such as springs and cooler tributary creeks. If these are unavailable, fish move to areas of maximum aeration, such as waterfalls, rapids, riffles, or windy surface areas. If these are unavailable, fish will gulp air at the water's surface. This, however, is a last resort before a fish suffocates and dies.

WATER TEMPERATURE COMFORT ZONES

Following are the water-temperature zones in which fish are most active. These ranges may vary 5 to 10 degrees F due to adaptation of species in some borderline areas.

Cold Water	
Trout	45 to 65°F
Char	40 to 60°F
Salmon	45 to 65°F
Grayling	40 to 60°F
Whitefish	50 to 70°F

Cool Water	
Pike	50 to 70°F
Muskie	50 to 70°F
Pickerel	55 to 75°F
Walleye	55 to 75°F
Yellow perch	55 to 75°F
Striped bass	50 to 70°F
Bluefish	50 to 70°F
Smallmouth bass	55 to 75°F

Warm and Tropical	
Largemouth bass	60 to 80°F
Crappie	60 to 80°F
White bass	55 to 75°F
Sunfishes	55 to 80°F
Catfish	55 to 80°F
Carp	55 to 80°F
Redfish	55 to 75°F
Tarpon	60 to 85°F
Snook	60 to 85°F
Bonefish	70 to 85°F

SEASONS

The four seasons affect a fish's activity in a number of ways. Winter usually is the period of least activity. Summer may also be a less active time because the water is often too warm. In the spring or fall, when water temperatures are closest to ideal for them, most fish have a mating, and spawning, season. Just before and during spawning season, fish are most easily located and caught on flies.

Each season, various species of fish move and search for the most comfortable water temperature. Water is much denser than air, so it changes temperature much more slowly than air. Fish may seek shallow, sunlit water in cold seasons or swim deep to escape the chill of a cold storm or intense heat of a long hot, dry spell. As they do this, they also try to find those areas where food and oxygen are plentiful—just as you would in your own comfort zone.

Fish also need shelter and protection: places to rest and hide from their enemies. These may be water structures, such as aquatic plants, boulders, holes, deeper water, and the like. Many fish species use these same areas to locate and gather or ambush live foods.

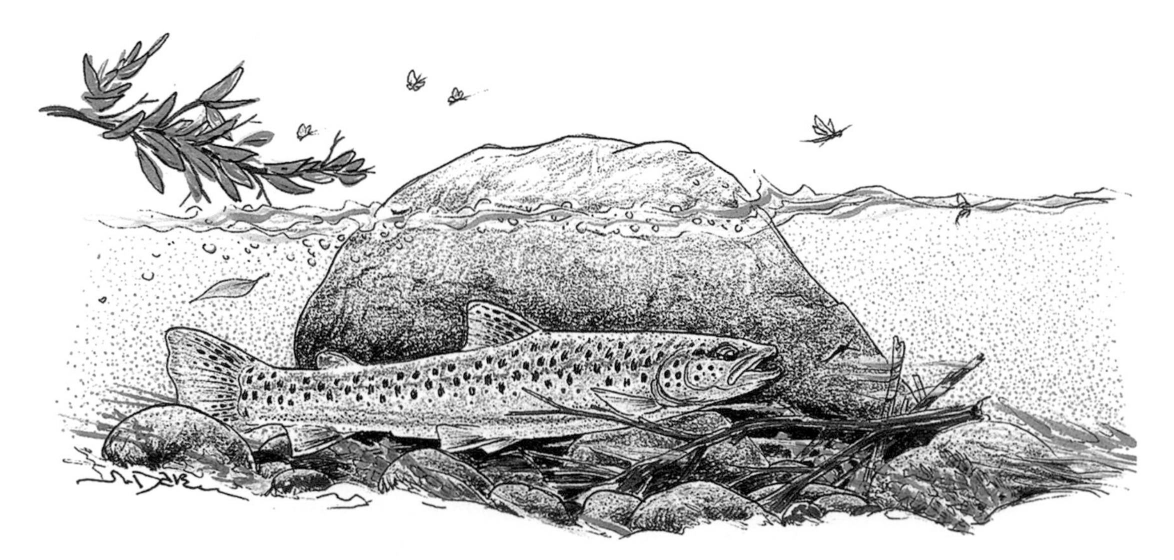

STREAM-WATER STRUCTURES

Aquatic vegetation, large boulders, rubble, tree limbs, roots, and overhead trees make ideal hiding and feeding structures for fish such as trout and smallmouth bass.

To find and catch fish consistently, you must locate areas where the right temperature and oxygen conditions combine with good structural environment to hide the fish and hold ample amounts of their food. Each species of fish has a specific pattern of requirements you should know and watch for. The challenge is to pick the right food imitation and skillfully present it in these "holding" areas to make the fish think it is alive and easy to catch.

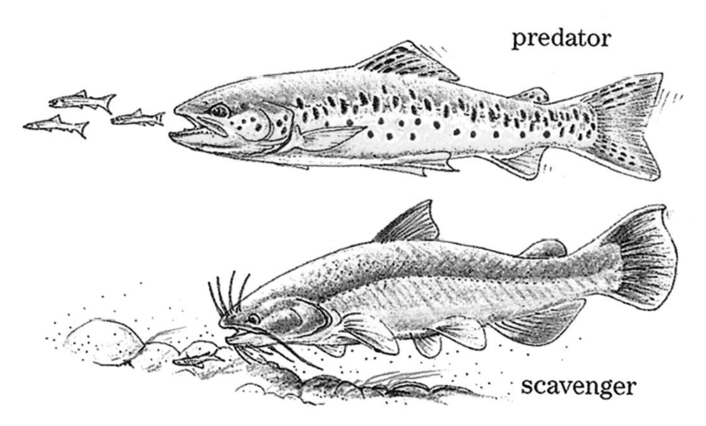

Predator fish feed primarily on live animal food. Scavenger fish feed primarily on dead animal forms and vegetation.

FISH SENSES: THE KEY TO GOOD IMITATIONS

Fish locate, inspect, and eat natural foods using their senses of sight, hearing, smell, and taste/touch. There are two major types of fish: **predators** and **scavengers.** Predators catch most of their food alive, while scavengers usually eat inanimate or dead foods. Each type uses a highly developed set of senses to locate foods and avoid or escape their predators. Both types can be caught on flies that correctly imitate these preferred foods.

Sight

Sight is a well-developed sense in most fish, especially those that are predators. Fish see either binocularly (with both eyes forward) or monocularly (one on each side of their heads), and have good close vision. Because of water clarity restrictions, fish have no need to see more than 20 or 30 feet away. They have good color vision as well, and most species have excellent night vision. Predators rely

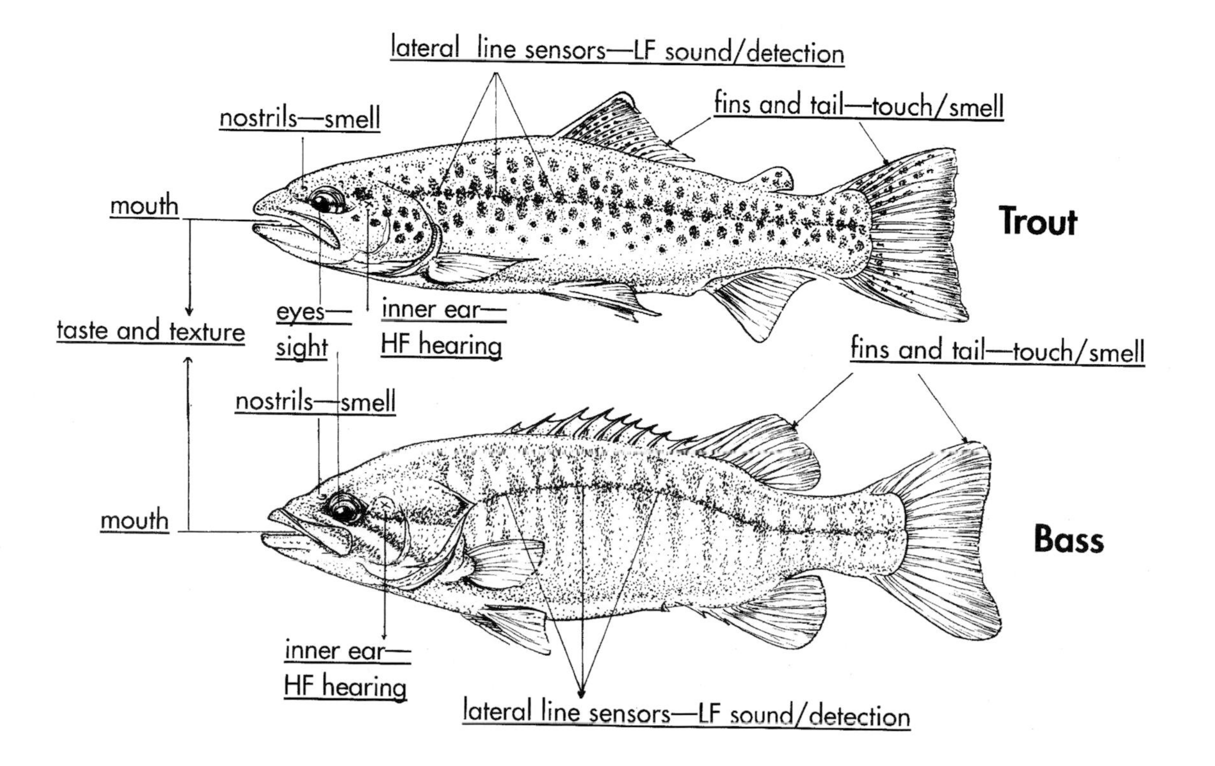

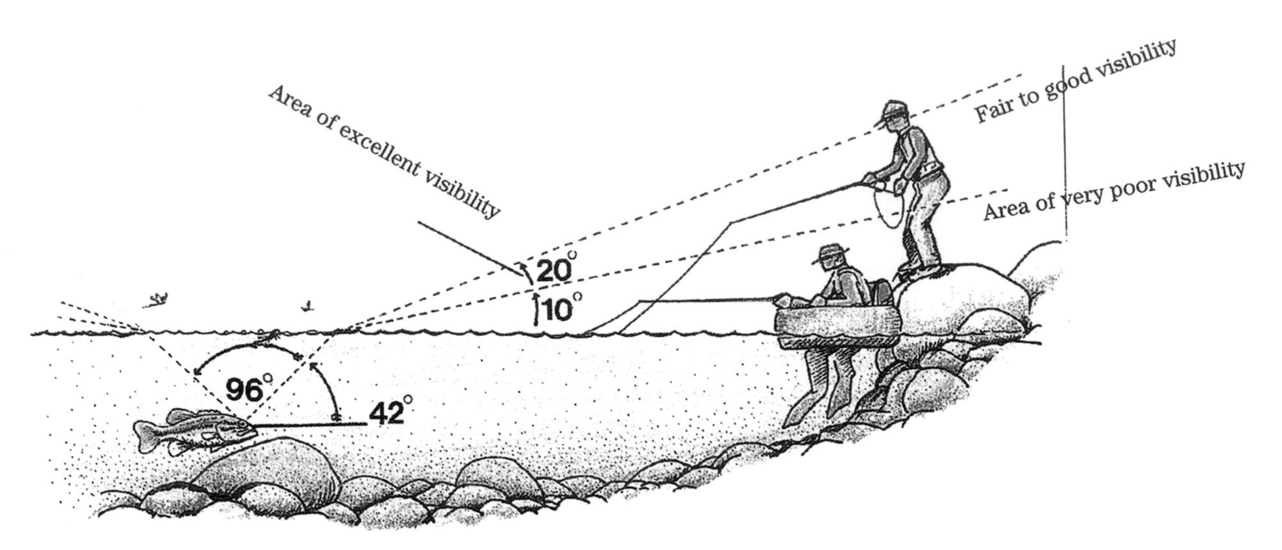

This diagram shows how fish see above the surface at various light-ray refractions. At 10 degrees off horizontal, fish see very poorly, especially on dark or very windy days. At 20 degrees off horizontal, fish vision is fair if light is good and the surface is calm. At over 20 degrees, fish see very well under most conditions.

mostly on sight while scavengers use it as a secondary sense for locating foods.

Hearing

Fish have highly developed dual hearing systems. The ears in their heads intercept high-frequency vibrations (200 to 800 cycles per second), and some can hear from 30 to 2,000 CPS. This form of hearing is much like our own except not as wide in range.

Fish also have a lateral-line hearing organ on each side of their bodies that picks up low-frequency vibrations, 200 to 15 CPS. This lateral line, which runs from behind the head to the base of the tail, is a series of tiny drumlike membranes with nerve ends that run from each to the spinal cord. With the lateral line fish can detect the size, speed, and direction of movement in the water of an object—such as another fish, a snake, a mink, or a fisherman. They use this line to detect food as well as enemies.

Since sound travels faster and more efficiently in water, fish rely on this dual hearing system almost as much as or sometimes even more than on sight to detect food and escape dangers, especially at times of low visibility.

Smell

Fish have a highly developed sense of smell that is much better than ours and surpasses even that of a bird dog or bloodhound. Both predator and scavenger fish identify foods by odor, but the scavengers use smell as their primary sense to detect and locate food. Predators, on the other hand, use smell more to confirm food they have located by sight or hearing.

Taste/Touch

On the surfaces of their bodies, fins, and mouths, fish have sensors that can taste and feel their foods. These are more or less secondary senses used after the potential food is located or captured. For instance, a fish might locate your fly and rub its body across it or bite it to determine if it is real food or fake.

Often, when a fish uses these senses, it appears that the fish has missed the fly when, in reality, it has touched and tasted it and in an instant rejected it because it did not feel or taste right. This is why you must react to a strike quickly, before the fish can recognize your fly as a fake and reject it. An effective imitation must look, sound, feel, and taste like real food to a fish. This is the fascinating challenge of fly fishing.

Predator fish are the most aggressive eaters and thus usually easier to catch on flies than are the less aggressive scavengers. Scavengers, on the other hand, are more easily spooked than most predators. They are also often more selective feeders, and so there is quite a challenge in finding (or creating) a fly that smells and tastes almost natural and then precisely presenting that fly to the fish. Because of this selectivity and their shy nature, most scavenger fish, once hooked, quickly panic and try to flee and escape in a fury of fast, strong runs. In our opinion scavenger fish are worthy sportfish, truly as much fun for fly fishing as predator fish.

Natural Foods for Fish

Wherever fish live, there is a natural food chain. Knowing food sources, imitating them with flies, and fishing them to fool and catch fish are the marks of a good fly fisher. A basic knowledge of streams, lakes, marshes, estuaries, oceans, and the fish foods they hold is important.

Unpolluted freshwater streams and lakes usually produce abundant fish foods. The major fish foods are aquatic insects, small fish, crustaceans, aquatic invertebrates, terrestrial insects, small mammals, small reptiles and other invertebrates, and aquatic plants.

AQUATIC INSECTS

Aquatic insects live a major part of their life cycles underwater. Their life cycles are generally one year, but in some groups life cycles are as short as two months or as long as four years. These insects provide fish with convenient year-round opportunities to feed on the immature nymph forms and the adults. Because of their abundance and vulnerability, they are often favored by fish such as trout, bass, or panfish, and so are important for the fly fisher to imitate. They are seldom important in saltwater fishing.

The most abundant aquatic insects are mayflies, stoneflies, caddisflies, midges, damselflies, and dragonflies. The life cycles for these insects include an aquatic nymph stage, which eventually emerges onto the water's surface and hatches into a winged adult insect stage. These adults, which live only a few hours, days, or weeks, mate and lay their eggs on the water (egg stage) and then die.

It was the desire to imitate these aquatic insects that initially stimulated the sport of fly fishing. A large number of standard fly designs are imitations of aquatic insects. Matching and fishing aquatic insects is still the most captivating method of fly fishing for trout, grayling, char, bass, and panfish.

Mayflies (Ephemeroptera) are a large, very important group of delicate, harmless aquatic insects that live in streams and lakes. The life cycle consists of egg, nymph, and adult stages. The nymph, which feeds and grows beneath the surface from periods of a few months to a year or two years, swims to the surface when mature and hatches into the first adult stage, the dun. The winged dun, an air breather, flies off the water's surface, leaving its nymphal skin behind. It conceals itself in the waterside terrestrial structures (trees, weeds, rocks, or bushes). The dun, after a short period—minutes to a day or so—sheds another skin and changes into the more vividly colored, sexually mature adult stage called the **spinner.** Spinners form a swarm

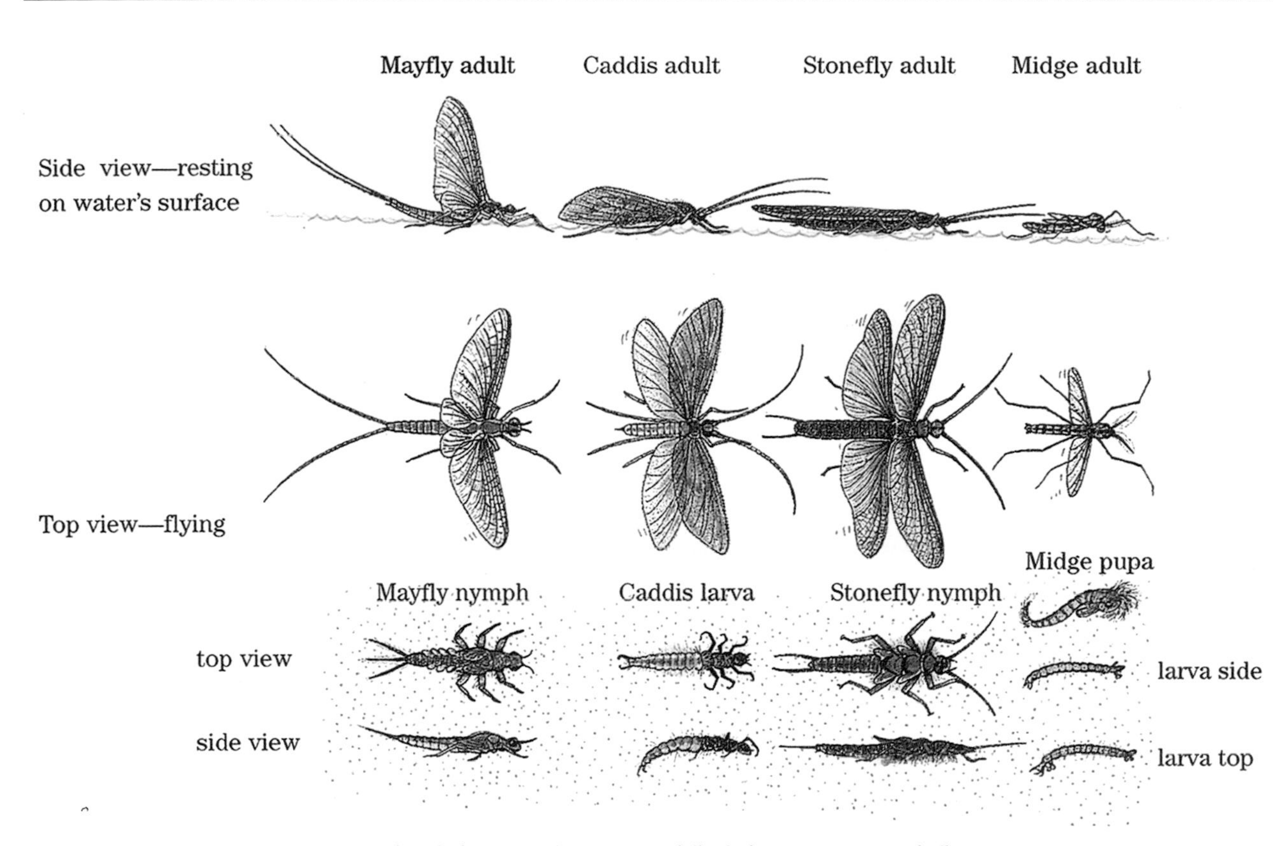

Four major aquatic insects that fish most often eat and fly fishers imitate with flies.

and fly near or over the water and mate in the air. The females immediately fly down to the water's surface and lay their eggs on or below the surface. Both males and females die shortly after this activity.

An adult is most recognizable by its large, upright, sail-shaped wings (at rest); long, round, slender, tapering body; and two or three tails. Nymphs have sets of gills on the sides and top of the abdominal segments and one pair of wing pads on their thorax.

Stoneflies (Plecoptera) are harmless aquatic insects that are generally large and live in very pure, well-aerated streams. They have a life cycle very similar to that of mayflies. The adult is best identified by two large pairs of wings, which at rest are folded or rolled around the top sides of the body, giving the insect an almost sticklike appearance. It has two distinctive large antennae and two distinctive tails, very widely separated.

Stonefly nymphs vary widely in size, color, and shape, according to species and age. Nymphs are best identified by their two distinctive wing cases (pads), two tails and antennae, and

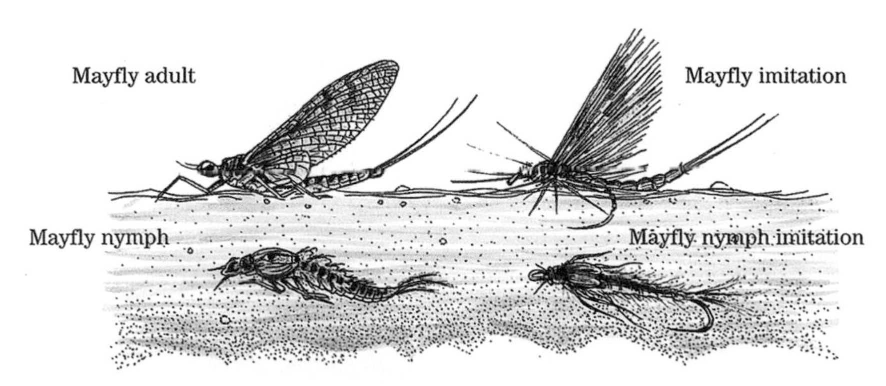

The mayfly is the hallmark of the origin of fly fishing.

Insect Size and Season, Northern Hemisphere

Aquatic Insects

January to March: Small sizes (18 to 26) of midges, mayflies, caddisflies, and stoneflies.

March to June: Small to medium sizes (12 to 18) of mayflies, caddisflies, midges, and stoneflies.

June to August: Large and small sizes (4 to 24) of caddisflies, mayflies, damselflies, stoneflies, midges, and dragonflies.

August to October: Small and medium sizes (16 to 24) of mayflies, caddisflies, and midges.

October to December: Small sizes (18 to 26) of midges, mayflies, and caddisflies.

Terrestrial Insects

Generally in small sizes (16 to 18) beginning around April, increasing in a variety of sizes steadily to early September, then decreasing in number but not size until fall and winter freezes. The crawling ants and beetles are first to appear in spring. Crawling and flying ants, moths, bees, flies, small and large beetles, inchworms, spiders, small crickets, and grasshoppers appear from late spring to midsummer. Flying and crawling ants, small beetles, various sizes of grasshoppers and crickets, leafhoppers, bees, wasps, caterpillars, and spiders appear from late summer until the first frost of fall.

Note: Aquatic adult insects and immature and adult terrestrial insects are most frequently imitated with floating flies. Immature aquatic insects (nymphs, larvae, pupae) are generally imitated with sinking flies.

fuzzy, light-colored gill filaments under and between their six legs.

Most stonefly nymphs emerge by crawling out of the water onto the stream shoreline. Smaller stoneflies, sizes 12 to 16 (½ to ¾ inch), often swim to the water's surface to emerge.

Caddisflies (Trichoptera) are a very widely distributed group of harmless, mothlike, lake and stream insects. They have a four-stage life

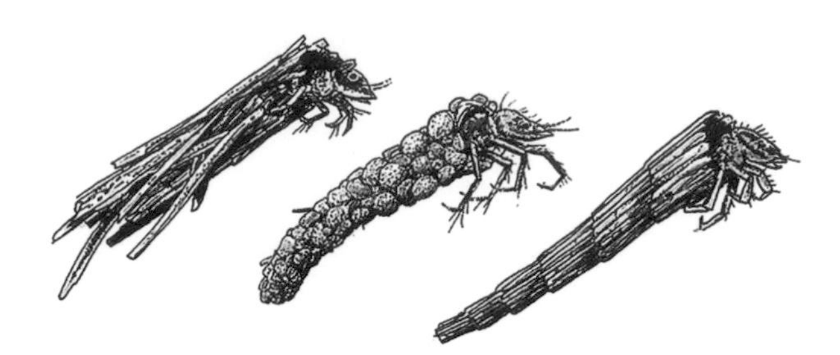

Three common forms of cased caddis larvae.

cycle: egg, larva, pupa, and adult. The life cycle generally lasts one year. From the **egg,** a **larva** is produced. This grubwormlike larva lives at the bottom of the water. Many species of caddisfly larvae construct a case in which they live. These cases are made uniquely according to species from glue and silklike filaments in combination with aquatic plant pieces, sand grains, or terrestrial plant parts. The cases are for protection and camouflage. Along the bottom, they resemble short, sticklike structures.

The larva develops into the third stage, the **pupa,** which is very similar to the cocoon of a butterfly or moth. The larva seals its case to begin pupation. This stage generally lasts a few weeks. Then the pupa, now very different physically from the larva, cuts out of its case; swims, rises, or crawls to the surface; and hatches into the **adult** caddisfly.

Adults live several days to several weeks, during which time they mate and lay eggs on or below the water's surface.

Adults are best distinguished from the three other major aquatic insects discussed by their tentlike or mothlike wing shape when at rest. Many appear opaque, fuzzy, mottled, and heavily weighted. Caddisflies have two

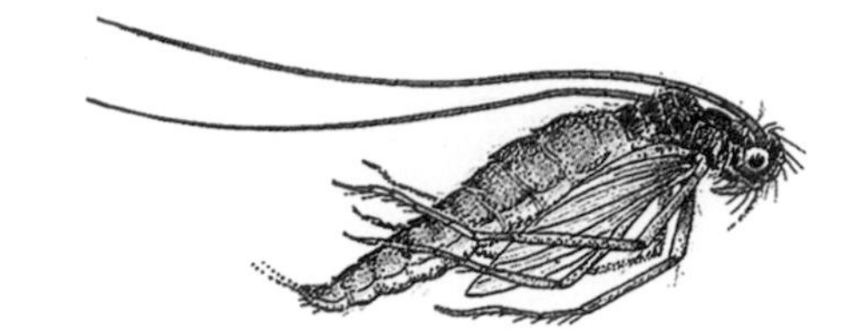

Emergent caddis pupa.

very long antennae and no distinctive tails on a modestly sized body.

The larva has a rather bare, light-colored abdomen with considerable gill filaments on its lower side. It has no visible wing pads on its darker thorax and no easily visible antennae or tails.

The pupa has six long, skinny legs, wing pads at the side or lower part of its midsection (thorax), and two very distinctive antennae. A good way to study pupae is to pick their sealed cases off the bottom structures and carefully open them to remove the delicate developing insects.

Midges (Diptera) are a very widely distributed and immensely abundant group of aquatic insects. Some members of the Diptera family, such as mosquitoes, blackflies, and deerflies, are biting bloodsuckers in their adult form. Midges have a very similar but usually shorter life cycle than caddisflies. They are generally very small insects, seldom exceeding ¼ inch in length.

The very important, harmless, mosquito-like midge adult is identified by its one pair of wings, which are smaller than its body and positioned flat on top and to each side of the body at rest. It has three pairs of very long, skinny legs. Males have two very large, plume-like antennae, but no tails.

The larvae are very simple, slender, segmented worms with no distinctively clear head, body, or tail. The pupae are similar in color to the larvae but have a much fatter head-thorax section. Close magnification will show gill plumes on the head and tail and folded legs and wings under the head-thorax section.

TERRESTRIAL INSECTS

Terrestrial insects—those insects that are born and spend their immature and mature stages on land—are a second major insect food source for many freshwater fish. This is especially so in warmer latitudes and, through the summer months, in colder parts of North America.

Fish feed on terrestrial insects that accidentally fall on the water during flight, during mating swarms, or from overhanging plants. Wind, rain, cold snaps, floods, drought, crop harvesting, and similar activities often create conditions that force terrestrial insects to become water-trapped. Some sink slowly, but most will float low in the water's surface film.

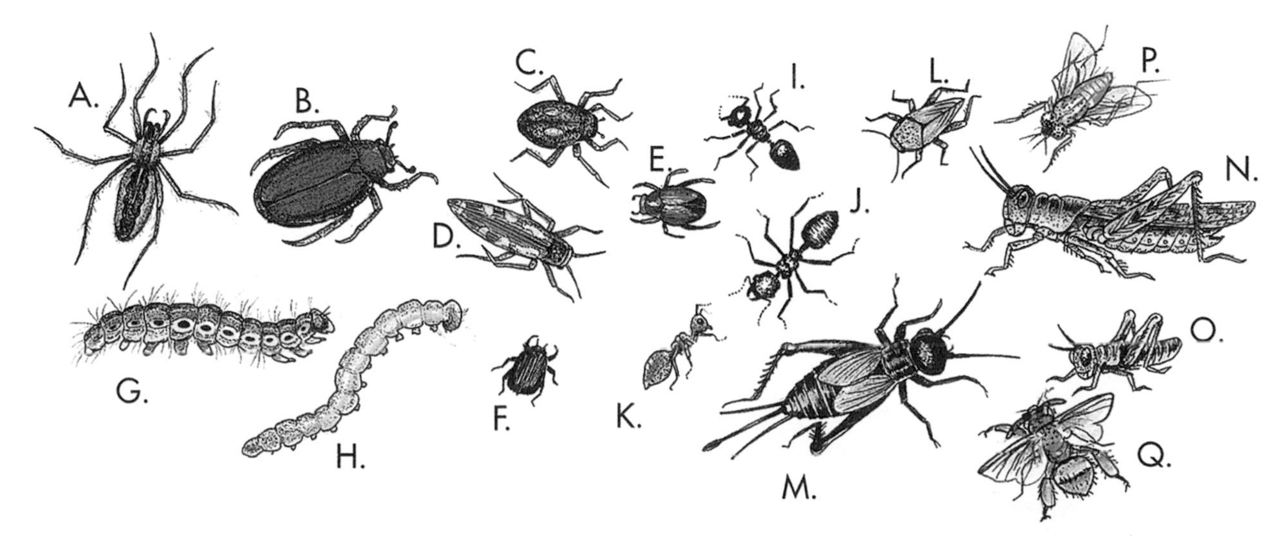

These are the terrestrial insects most important to imitate:
A. Spiders. B, C, D, E, F. Beetles. G. Caterpillars. H. Inchworms. I, J, K. Ants. L. Leafhoppers (jassids). M. Crickets. N. Grasshoppers (mature). O. Grasshoppers (immature). P. Houseflies. Q. Bees.

Most terrestrial fly imitations are low-floating designs.

The important terrestrial insects to imitate are ants, beetles, grasshoppers, leafhoppers, crickets, caterpillars (worms), wasps, moths, bees, and spiders. Terrestrial insects usually become more abundant and larger after aquatic insects decline in numbers and slow down in activity, around midsummer and into the fall months. Terrestrial insect activity slows or ceases with freezing water.

CRUSTACEANS

This is an important large group of natural aquatic fish foods that are similar to both aquatic insects and fish in their movements, shapes, and habits. They are widely distributed. The most important crustaceans for the freshwater fly fisher to imitate are scuds (freshwater shrimp), sow bugs, and crayfish. All three of these crawl along the bottom structures of lakes and streams. The scud and crayfish can swim erratically and rapidly backward if fleeing from a fish. Sow bugs, however, crawl along the bottom and are feeble swimmers at best.

Saltwater crustaceans important to imitate are various crabs, shrimp, and crayfish. Each of these can crawl and swim.

All species have a simple life cycle lasting one to several years, in which they seasonally increase in size. Like most other cold-blooded creatures, crustaceans are most active and abundant during the milder seasons. They are imitated by using wet flies and modified streamer designs. In still water, cast the imitation, allow it to sink nearly to the bottom, and strip it back toward you. In flowing water, strip it across and downstream.

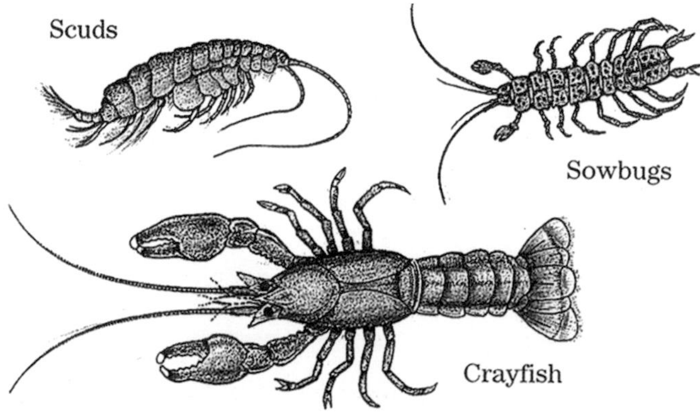

These are important crustaceans to imitate.

OTHER INVERTEBRATES

Earthworms and aquatic worms, aquatic leeches, and snails make up an assortment of fish foods that varies in importance depending on their abundance compared to the other major foods already described. Knowledge of their existence, life cycles, actions, sizes, and colors will—if used to properly create and fish imitations—enable the fly fisher to make good catches.

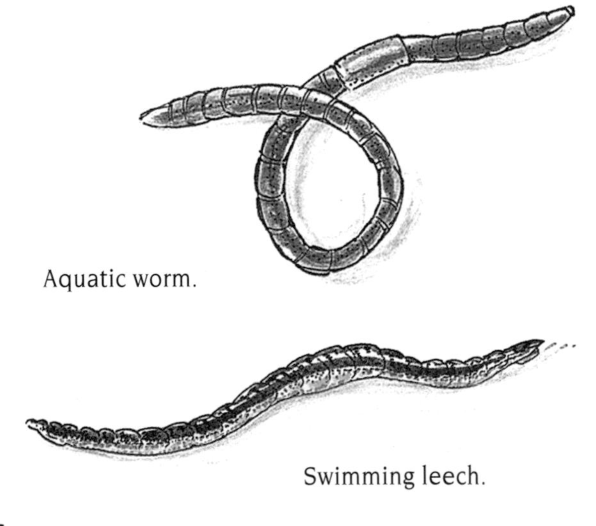

Aquatic worm.

Swimming leech.

MINNOWS

Minnow is the name anglers use to indicate mature small fish or immature large fish that other fish feed on. Minnows are sometimes called forage or baitfish. Like aquatic insects, they are important and abundant fish foods in fresh water. Min-

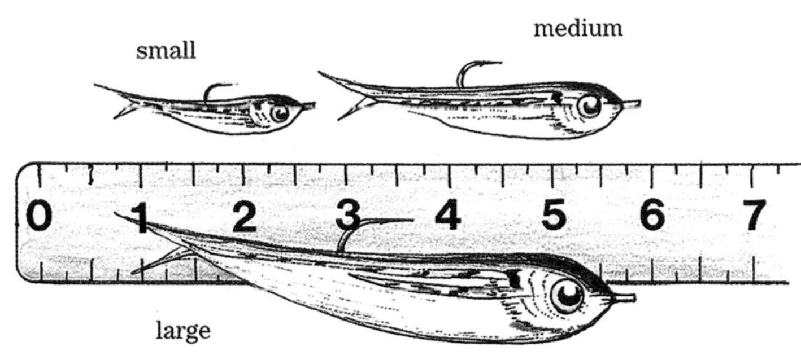

Most minnow species are 1 to 6 inches in length and can be imitated with three streamer-fly sizes.

nows are extremely important in salt water, as well.

Their life cycles, usually several years long, expose them daily to predator fish that ambush, chase, and eat them. Minnows are imitated by streamers and wet flies.

Fish eat a wide range of minnows. Generally, practical fly-fishing sizes are ½ inch to 8 inches long. They vary from natural colors to bright attractor colors. Minnows are found in all water areas from top to bottom, but usually choose an area specific to their species. For example, shad and shiners live in clear, open water, chub and dace near underwater structures, and sculpin and suckers on the bottom.

Minnow imitations are usually fished to imitate panic or distress. This action suggests vulnerability and stimulates attack by predator fish.

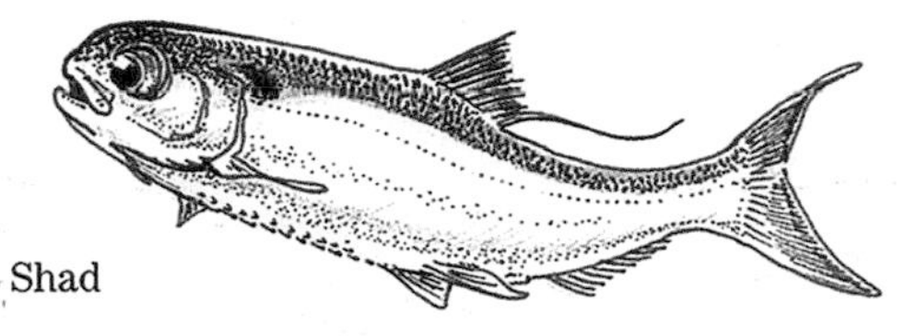

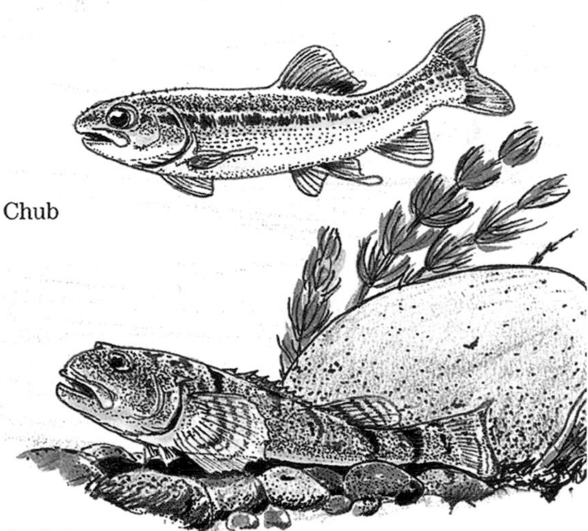

Three major minnow types: Shad, found in open water; Chub, found near underwater structures; Sculpin, are bottom-dwelling.

To sample most fish foods that swim, crawl, or burrow in a stream, use a fine-screened seine to capture them.

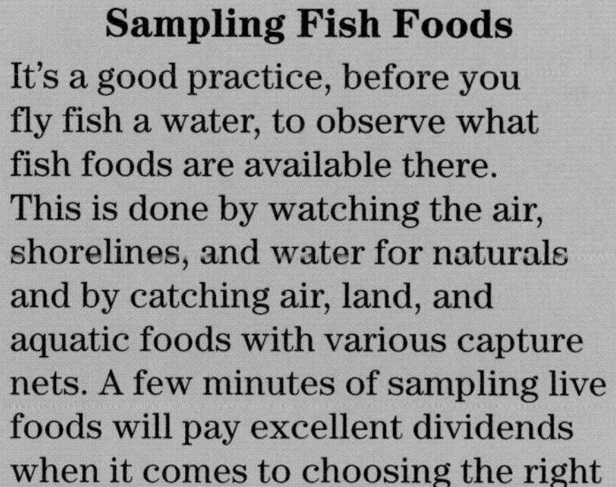

Sampling Fish Foods

It's a good practice, before you fly fish a water, to observe what fish foods are available there. This is done by watching the air, shorelines, and water for naturals and by catching air, land, and aquatic foods with various capture nets. A few minutes of sampling live foods will pay excellent dividends when it comes to choosing the right imitations.

THE ECOLOGY OF FISHERIES

Food chain is the term used to describe the sequence of feeding from the simple plants and animals through the most complex forms. Each more complex form feeds upon the lesser forms. The least complex forms feed on the decomposing matter of the higher forms, thus completing the endless food chain. The experienced fly fisher recognizes an excellent fishery by the food chain. Water lacking a good food chain provides poor fishing or no fishing. If fishing is poor or changes from excellent to poor, it is a strong indication of larger problems in the environment.

As a sportsman, you have an obligation to look after the environment. You may do so in many ways, such as by picking up litter, taking care not to damage the shore or bottom, reporting pollution and game violations, cooperating with landowners, writing letters to support important wildlife management projects, donating to wildlife, conservation, and preservation causes, volunteering to work on conservation projects, or releasing fish. Such investments will bring great dividends to you and future generations.

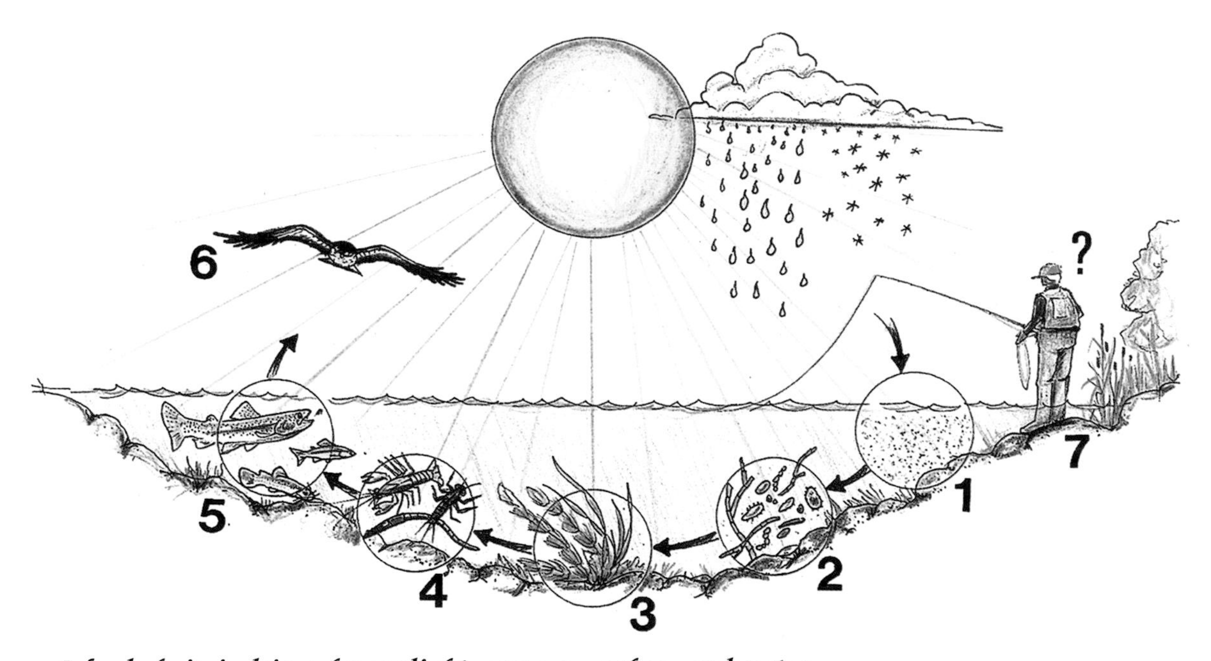

A *food chain is driven by sunlight, oxygen, carbon, and water.*
1. Dissolved nutrients. 2. Algae and diatoms. 3. Aquatic plants. 4. Invertebrates. 5. Fish. 6. Air and land predators. 7. Humans: What role are we playing in the conservative use and preservation of a successful food chain on the waters? We are just as dependent on clean water as the other food-chain members.

Fish Made for Fly Fishing

Fly fishing, especially when complemented by innovative and creative fly tying, is a fascinating method that provides almost limitless opportunity to catch almost any species of fish. You must be able to identify the fish; determine what it eats or will strike, and where, how, and when it will strike; and then tempt the fish into accepting your chosen fly.

Some fish, such as trout, salmon, bass, and bonefish, are classic fly-fishing quarry called **gamefish.** Others are thought to be of lesser sport. This is an arbitrary classification, however, and you will be better off making your own judgments here. You might be pleasantly surprised. We feel that any fish is more fun to catch fly fishing than with any other fishing method. Actually, we enjoy catching them all . . . and we predict you will also.

FRESHWATER FISH

Trout (Trout Family)

Trout are widely distributed cold-water stream and lake fish, and are the most traditional and popular fly-fishing quarry. In fact, trout probably are the main reason fly fishing was first conceived, and they have been the fish most sought after by fly fishers. The most common and widely fished species are rainbow trout, brown trout, cutthroat trout, and (more rare) golden trout. (The brook trout is actually a char, and is dealt with in the next section.)

In the Northern Hemisphere, most unpolluted freshwater streams and lakes that have average summertime temperatures of 50 to 60 degrees F and that seldom reach 70 degrees F will likely have trout living in them. Trout are sleek, strong, fast, and beautifully colored fish. They feed aggressively on a wide variety of natural foods, and can be enticed to strike many natural or attractor-patterned flies. Trout feed most actively in rising or stable water temperatures of 50 to 60 degrees F. They feed principally by sight, either on or below the surface. Most prefer to eat live small insects, crustaceans, and minnows. There are many popular fly designs to imitate these foods.

Trout average 8 to 12 inches (½ pound) but 15- to 28-inch or larger (2 to 8-plus pounds) fish are regularly caught on flies. Take great

Top: Brown trout.
Bottom: Rainbow.

care to release trout properly so that they may live to be caught again, or to spawn and provide the valuable breeding stock necessary to ensure future fishing.

Char (Trout Family)

Char are a widely distributed group of troutlike fish that inhabit cold and very cold waters of North America. Even more so than trout, they require very clean, clear, and cold lake or stream environments. Char are beautiful, vividly colored, strong, aggressive, and active fish. They feed on aquatic insects, minnows, fish eggs, aquatic worms, leeches, and crustaceans, and are generally thought to be more gullible than trout. Char prefer to feed in water of 40 to 55 degrees F.

The most popular species of true char are brook trout, arctic char, Dolly Varden, lake trout, and Sunapee trout. The splake is a hybrid char of brook and lake trout parentage. Brook trout are much more like true trout in their ranges and habits than other char. The other char are larger-water, deeper-feeding minnow eaters in general, so minnow imitations work best. Char that will hit flies range widely in size from 8 inches to 20 pounds. The deep, cold-water-living lake trout often run larger in size. They are not, however, the best char for fly fishing, because they are usually found very deep in a lake and are hard to reach by casting flies. Char, like trout, should be harvested sparingly.

Grayling (Trout Family)

A beautiful, delicate, relatively rare, troutlike cold-water fish that is highly prized by North American fly fishers, the grayling has a distinctive, large, sailfish-like dorsal fin. It requires very pure, cold, clear, lake or stream water. Most good grayling fishing is found in the Montana and Wyoming Rockies and in northwestern Canada and Alaska. Grayling feed predominantly on active insects but will also feed on crustaceans and small minnows. Smaller flies, especially dry flies, are most effective.

Brook trout (char).

Grayling.

and aquatic insects and are aggressive surface and subsurface fly strikers.

Grayling average 8 to 14 inches but grow as large as 4 pounds, especially in Alaska. They prefer to feed in water of 45 to 55 degrees F. Grayling are very active but not powerful fighters.

Landlocked Salmon (Trout Family)

Landlocks are believed by many authorities to have evolved from Atlantic salmon that were landlocked, perhaps thousands of years ago. They are somewhat smaller than Atlantic ocean salmon but every bit as beautiful, streamlined, fast, and hard fighting. Landlocks occur naturally in the rivers and lakes of Maine and southeastern Canada and have been successfully introduced to a few other northeastern states and other sections of Canada, as well as South America. They feed principally on minnows

A landlocked salmon taking a wet fly.

Atlantic Salmon (Trout Family)

On the Atlantic Coast, only the Atlantic salmon is native, and it is second only to trout in traditional popularity with fly fishers. In fact, in North American rivers, sportfishing is limited to using flies to catch these magnificent fish as they enter the rivers from May to October for their spawning runs.

Atlantic salmon often jump completely out of the water when hooked.

Although Atlantic salmon are thought not to feed once they return to fresh water to spawn, they strike wet, dry, and streamer salmon flies very well. When Atlantic salmon make their return journey to the ocean the following spring, they are known as black salmon or kelts. These fish feed voraciously on spring-spawning smelt and other minnows and aggressively strike large, colorful streamer flies. Salmon range from 3 to 8 pounds (grilse) and 9 to 40 pounds for mature fish. Good conservation practices should always be used with these beautiful fish, for their stocks are threatened.

Pacific Salmon (Trout Family)

There are five abundant species of Pacific salmon: chinook (or king), coho, silver, sockeye, pink, and chum. They are fine gamefish, but less popular with the traditional coldwater fly fisher than trout, Atlantic salmon, or char. Pacific salmon spawn once and die, whereas the Atlantic salmon may spawn more than once during its lifetime. Neither type of salmon eats once it returns to fresh water to spawn but will strike a wide variety of surface and subsurface attractor flies. All salmon are strong fighters. They average from 3 to 10 pounds for chum and sockeye, 8 to 20 pounds

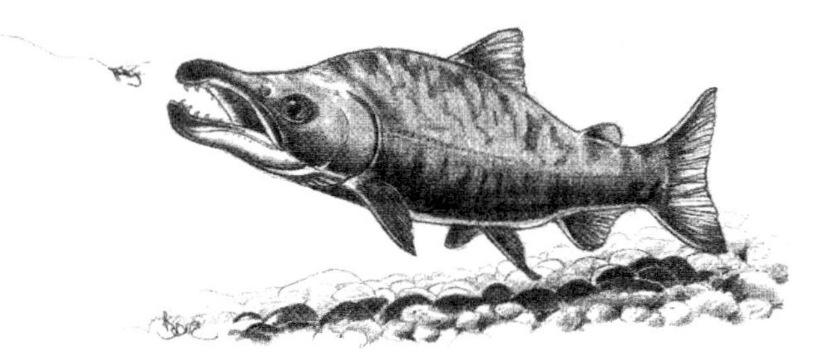

Pacific salmon take attractor wet flies best.

for coho, and 12 to 40 for chinook. Some chinook exceed 60 pounds. In the past few decades, many Pacific salmon and some Atlantic salmon have been successfully introduced to larger freshwater lake systems, such as the Great Lakes in the United States and Canada, as well as limited areas in the Southern Hemisphere including Argentina, Chile, and New Zealand.

Steelhead (Trout Family)

The steelhead is a unique rainbow trout that has adapted to a sea or large lake residence like salmon, and requires a temporary spawning run into connecting rivers. After spawning, steelhead return to the ocean or lake. Many feel that steelhead are equaled only by Atlantic salmon in their desirability as a large, strong, high-leaping, long-running freshwater fish to catch on a fly rod. They are most abun-

Steelhead.

dant in the coastal rivers from California to Alaska and in the Great Lakes. Steelhead average 4 to 8 pounds and often exceed 20 pounds in these areas. They do feed a little during their upstream and downstream migrations and will strike both natural and attractor surface and subsurface flies.

Sea Trout (Trout Family)

Sea trout and *coasters* are names often used for trout that live in the sea and, like salmon and steelhead, swim up connecting rivers to spawn. Most common are brown trout, cutthroat, rainbow, and char (brook trout and Dolly Varden). Because of their sea vitality, all are usually larger and significantly stronger than their resident freshwater counterparts.

Largemouth, Smallmouth, and Spotted (Kentucky) Bass (Sunfish Family)

Bass are found in warm and cool water. They are strong, handsome, amazingly adaptive, aggressive, and almost always willing

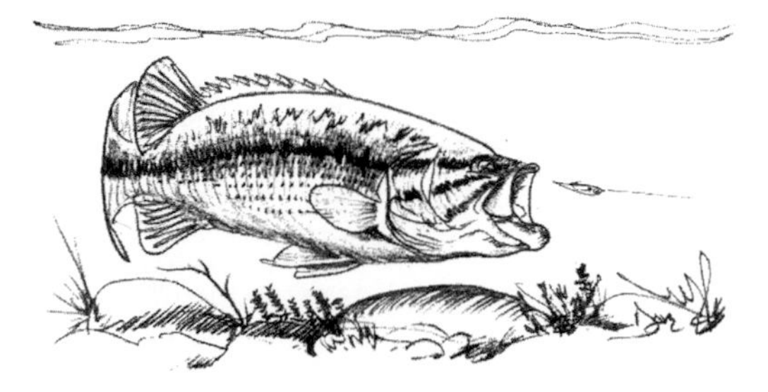

Streamer flies that imitate shad are effective for largemouth bass.

to take a fly. They prefer freshwater and brackish-water lakes and slower streams that are relatively unpolluted and have an average summer temperature range of 65 to 80 degrees F. Most North American fresh waters that are not trout fisheries will be bass fisheries.

Bass are opportunistic and feed aggressively on all types of insects, crustaceans, minnows, amphibians, reptiles, and mammals. They are less selective and generally prefer larger foods than do trout. Bass can be solitary or found in small, loose schools. They prefer to ambush live surface and subsurface foods along shorelines or near open-water structures such as large boulders, aquatic plants, fallen trees, or boat docks. They feed most actively in rising or stable water temperatures of 55 to 80 degrees F.

There are three popular species of bass: **smallmouth, largemouth,** and **spotted (Kentucky)** bass. They average about 1 pound or 12 inches, but it is not unusual to catch 2- to 10-pound bass on flies.

Smallmouth bass are closer to trout in their habitat preference, often inhabiting cool water. They are generally more popular with fly fishers because they are such tenacious fighters. The spotted and largemouth bass, however, are also fine fly-rod fish. All three strike hard, jump frequently, and fight a strong close-quarters battle.

Smallmouth bass are spectacular jumpers when hooked on surface floating flies.

Bluegill (Sunfish Family)

Bluegill are the most popular and abundant panfish in North America's cool and warm waters. They normally inhabit the same waters as bass, but in far greater numbers. Bluegill

Bluegill will eagerly strike small surface flies.

are sassy, quick, strong, and very aggressive. They feed on or below the surface on live or dead insects, crustaceans, and minnows. They are sight feeders. Their small size and tiny mouths make it necessary for them to feed mostly on small foods. Flies from size 6 to 16, or 1 to ½ inch long, are best.

Similar sunfish, such as common sunfish, long ear, yellow-breasted sunfish, red ear, green sunfish, rock bass, and pumpkinseed usually inhabit the same waters as bluegill and bass. All will strike similar types of flies and, like bluegill, they are usually very abundant. Most sunfish average 5 to 6 inches in length and occasionally grow to 1 pound or more. They are wonderful sport and convenient fish for practicing fly fishing.

Crappie (Sunfish Family)

A very abundant and widely distributed cool- and warm-water panfish, the crappie is usually present in the same waters as bass and bluegill, but generally prefers deeper, calmer water. Crappie are school fish that feed aggressively subsurface on small minnows, aquatic insects, and some crustaceans. They are usually found hiding and feeding beside and under various submerged structures, such as weed beds, reeds, dead trees, boat docks, or rock ledges. Crappie are both daytime and nighttime feeders.

There are two crappie species: white and black. The white crappie is generally more abundant in the South and Midwest and is a bit larger than the black. Blacks strike a fly more aggressively, fight a bit more, and do not form such large schools. Crappie average about 8 inches long and weigh between ½ pound and 1 pound. But specimens are regularly caught, especially during shallow-water spawning, that may weigh 2½ pounds or more.

White Bass (Bass Family)

White bass are an extremely abundant school panfish found in warm, cool, and cold waters. They prefer larger lakes and rivers rich with minnows and insects. White bass move almost constantly, feeding at all depths. They are aggressive and will strike streamers, nymphs, and topwater bugs. They fight extremely hard for their size, which averages about ¾ pound to 2½ pounds. They also have a short life span of only three to four years.

White Perch (Temperate Bass Family)

White perch are abundant schooling fish that average ¾ to 1 pound. They inhabit mostly northeastern and eastern seaboard state lakes and larger rivers that are classed as cool- or warm-water environments. Like their black-striped cousins, the white bass and yellow bass, they can be caught on small subsurface flies that imitate favorite foods such as minnows, aquatic worms, and aquatic insects. They are aggressive fly strikers and fight well. White perch, like white bass, make midspring spawning runs up rivers and lake inlet streams. At this time they are easiest to locate and reach with flies. During the summer and fall they school and stay off reefs and deep lake points, feeding most aggressively early and late each day.

Yellow Perch (Perch Family)

A relatively abundant cool-water panfish, the yellow perch prefers lakes but also inhabits some streams that usually are considered bass or marginal trout waters. They prefer to feed on subsurface and bottom aquatic insects, crustaceans, worms, and small minnows. They strike best on small flies fished slow and deep. Perch average about 10 inches (½ pound); some run as large as 2 pounds. They are fun to catch but are not particularly spectacular fighters.

Yellow perch prefer subsurface flies that imitate minnows and aquatic insects.

Walleye and Sauger (Perch Family)

Other common names for these fish are *walleye pike*, *jack fish*, and *pickerel*. Walleye and sauger are very popular cool- to cold-water schooling fish. They are widely distributed, living in clean, hard-bottomed, deep lakes and streams. Much like crappie, they make up in beauty what they lack in hard-fighting character. Most are nocturnal, subsurface feeders.

Walleye are predominantly minnow and leech feeders but occasionally feed on aquatic insects, amphibians, crustaceans, and worms. They average about 1 pound, but 3- to 7-pound fly-caught walleye are not uncommon.

Northern Pike (Pike Family)

Pike are fairly widely distributed cool- and cold-water lake and stream fish that are found mostly in the northern United States, Canada,

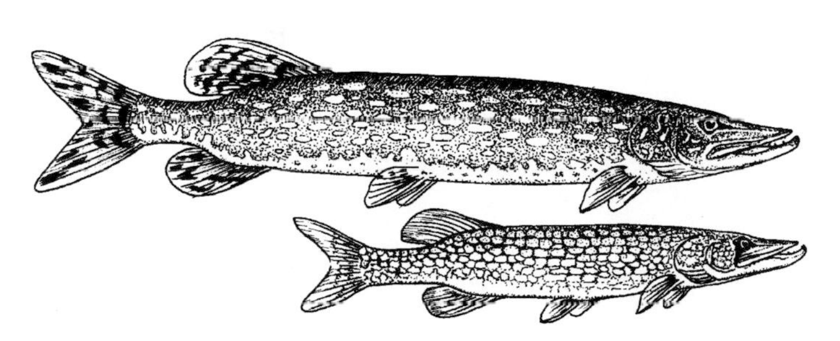

The northern pike is larger, but the pickerel hits a fly faster, harder, and fights more.

and southern Alaska. They are strong, very aggressive fish that prefer to ambush their food from near shore and bottom structures. They feed mostly on other fish, amphibians, crustaceans, mammals, and birds in water of 45 to 65 degrees F. As fly-rod fish, there has not been nearly enough said—they are truly as exciting as or more so than bass or trout.

Pike are alligatorlike in appearance, and that may discourage some fly fishers from appreciating them. They are frequently caught accidentally on bass flies or large trout flies. They average 20 inches and about 3 pounds, but often weigh as much as 15 to 30 pounds.

Muskellunge (Muskie) (Pike Family)

Muskie are large, somewhat rare, beautifully and vividly colored pikelike fish that are less widely distributed than northern pike but live in the same lake or stream conditions. Muskie are rarely caught on flies. However, they present a great challenge to the fly fisher because of their very large size (8 to 25 pounds), high intelligence, and wonderful fighting qualities. They make long runs and jump much more than pike. A stream muskie over 30 inches caught on a topwater fly is probably a rarer and more highly prized fly-rod trophy than any other freshwater gamefish.

A muskie, the tiger of freshwater fish, are outstanding to catch on a fly.

Chain Pickerel (Pike Family)

This is a smaller pikelike fish in the same family as pike and muskie. Chain pickerel are much more widespread in streams and lakes of the East and South, and they are lightning-fast, vicious, hard-striking, surface and subsurface ambush feeders. Their surface strike is something to be experienced! They are strong fighters that frequently "tail-walk" the surface when hooked. They feed on minnows, crayfish, leeches, large insects, amphibians, and small mammals. They average 12 to 18 inches, and occasionally 2- to 6-pounders are caught on flies. Most bass flies work equally well for pickerel.

Note: These three pike family fish have rows of long, needle-sharp teeth. Fly fishers should use a heavy nylon monofilament bite tippet of 40- to 80-pound test or a wire tippet to prevent them from biting off the fly. Avoid any hand or finger contact with the insides of their mouths or their gill rakers or you'll probably suffer painful cuts and abrasions. There are several tools available made to remove flies safely from a pike's mouth.

Shad (Herring Family)

A group of abundant, delicate, silver, deep-bodied school fish, shad principally prefer cool-to-warm, fresh, brackish, and salt waters. Most of these fish, including hickory shad, gizzard shad, American shad, skipjack, and golden eye, will strike small, flashy,

American shad.

brightly colored attractor flies during their spring spawning runs up streams that flow into larger rivers, lakes, and oceans.

These fish are fast, strong fighters, and generally willing leapers. They average from 1 to 3 pounds, with some species running up to 5 or 6 pounds.

Carp (Minnow Family)

Carp are abundant, incredibly hardy, golden-colored scavenger fish that live in warm, cool, or cold waters. They will readily take flies that closely imitate their preferred natural foods of aquatic insects, aquatic worms, terrestrial plants, tree seeds or fruits, and aquatic vegetation. Taking them consistently on flies requires as high a degree of fly-fishing skill as does any fish you will encounter. Carp average 3 to 8 pounds and often exceed 20 pounds. Their careful, slow foraging on the surface and on the shallow bottom of clear lakes and slow-moving streams, with their small, sensitive mouths, makes them a real test for the fly fisher. Sight casting to individual fish is the most consistent and fun way to catch carp on flies. Once hooked, they are beastly strong and stubborn fighters. Fly fishers discovering carp for the first time often compare them to bonefish, hence their affectionate name, the "poor man's bonefish."

Carp.

Catfish (Catfish Family)

Principally warm- and cool-water scavenger fish, catfish are abundant in most slow-moving streams, ponds, and lakes. They feed mainly by smell and touch at night or in murky waters, and by sight in some situations. They can be caught on flies that imitate their favorite natural foods, such as minnows, crayfish, aquatic worms, larger aquatic and terrestrial insects, and terrestrial plant seeds and fruits. The channel, blue, and bullhead catfish are most easily caught on scented, slow, deep-fished flies during the day or on or near the surface at night. They average from 1 to 3 pounds, but several species grow to 20 or even 50 pounds. Catfish, especially the channel cat, are often hooked by fly fishers while fishing for bass and trout, convincing lucky fly fishers that they've hooked the biggest bass or trout in the fishery!

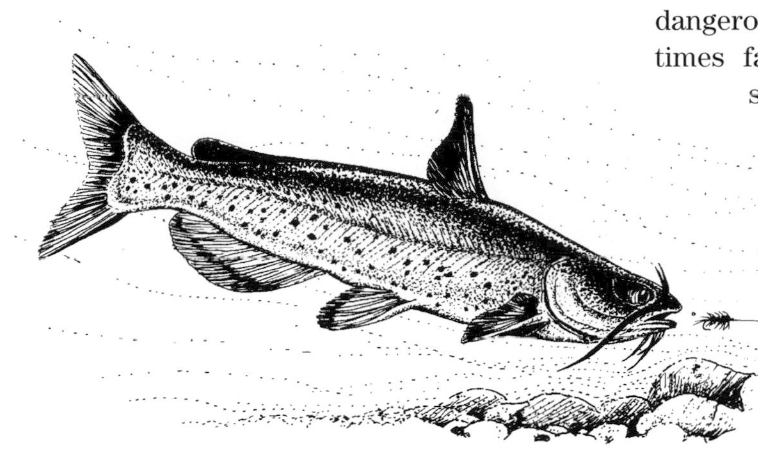

Channel catfish will strike flies that swim deep and slow and have a natural food odor.

Gar (Gar Family)

An armor-plated, cool- and warm-water prehistoric fish with fiercely toothed jaws that would shame a pike or alligator, the gar is abundant in most lakes and streams of the Mississippi and Ohio River systems as well as all the southern states west to Texas. All three major species—short-nosed, long-nosed, and alligator gar—are aggressive minnow predators and will strike most flies that imitate them. But because of their excessive rows of teeth set in iron-hard jaws, it's nearly impossible to *hook* them. They are best caught on nylon-floss hookless streamers. The fine nylon floss tangles in their rows of teeth. Gar are fun to catch, but take extreme care not to touch their mouths or you will surely be cut or bitten.

SALTWATER FISH

In recent years, saltwater fly fishing has become very popular, especially for certain species that frequent coastlines, tidal rivers, and shallow bays or flats. Although saltwater fish exceeding 150 pounds have been taken on fly tackle, most saltwater fly fishing is for species weighing 2 to 25 pounds. Because living conditions in oceans are demanding and dangerous, most saltwater fish are several times faster and stronger than freshwater species of equal weight.

Bonefish (Bonefish Family)

The bonefish, also called the gray ghost and the silver fox, is a silvery, sleek, torpedo-shaped, long-winded sprinter of shallow tropical flats. Extremely popular with saltwater fly fishers, bones average about 3 or 4 pounds and occasionally exceed 10 pounds. Hooked on a fly, they speed away and fight like a fish three times their weight! Bonefish can be caught on small subsurface flies that imitate favorite foods such as shrimp, crab, shellfish, worms, and minnows. Bonefish are hunted and eaten constantly by sharks, barracuda, and birds of prey so they are nervous, very cautious fish, having only their hearing, eyesight, color, and swimming speed to protect themselves. They are hard to see and approach, and proper fly presentation is difficult. But when hooked, exciting, high-speed dashes make bonefish worth the effort. Bonefish are usually carefully released by sport anglers.

Tarpon (Tarpon Family)

The tarpon, the uncontested king of saltwater fly fishing, is one of the world's most beautiful and spectacular gamefish. The silver king is a tropical to subtropical fish, and prefers water temperatures above 70 degrees F.

Tarpon migrate north up the Atlantic Coast and Gulf of Mexico each spring and summer and back south to Central and South America in the fall and winter. Tarpon vary in weight from 1 to over 200 pounds; all sizes, when hooked, make wonderful high jumps and strong runs. They will hit almost any fly that imitates minnows, squid, crab, sea worms, or shrimp.

Tarpon.

Tarpon have rough-lipped jaws, so you must use a heavy nylon bite tippet to prevent their wearing through the leader and escaping.

Because they are so special as gamefish, most tarpon are carefully released by sport anglers.

Ladyfish (Tarpon Family)

The ladyfish is a slender, silver, airborne flash of lightning when caught on light fly tackle, fighting far harder than its size would indicate—literally ripping the water with frequent leaps and long tail-walks. Ladyfish are quite common along the southern Atlantic Coast states, especially in Florida and along the western Gulf Coast. Ladyfish average about ½ to 1 pound and grow to 5 or 6 pounds. They strike small, fast-retrieved surface and subsurface swimming flies that imitate minnows and shrimp. They are especially active at night around lights over the water in places where tidal flows are strong, such as boat and fishing docks, jetties, bridges, and tidal creek channels.

Redfish (Drum Family)

Redfish, or channel bass, are becoming very popular as a poor man's bonefish. They are both more abundant and more widely distributed than bonefish, ranging along the Atlantic Coast from Virginia to the Florida Keys to southern Texas and Mexico. Redfish prefer to cruise and feed along shallow coastal beaches, bays, flats, channel cuts, islands, keys, trawl ramps, and brackish-water lagoons and channels. Although they are splendid fly-fishing targets and are on average larger than bonefish—about 4 to 10 pounds, up to 30 pounds or more—they are not as spooky, selective, or hard fighting as bonefish. What they lack in sophistication, they make up for in abundance, aggressiveness, size, and brute strength.

Redfish will aggressively and repeatedly strike surface and subsurface flies that imitate their favorite foods—crabs, shrimp, shellfish, minnows, and aquatic worms. Because redfish were almost wiped out not long ago by commercial and sportfishing and by environmental damage, most states have aggressive programs to restore them, with fishing restrictions such

Redfish.

as closed seasons and strict limits; some areas even have stocking programs. Today redfish are becoming much more abundant as a result of this concern. Most fly-caught redfish are released so that they will have an opportunity to spawn and increase the chances of restoring the fantastic redfishing of the past.

Weakfish (Drum Family)

Weakfish range from Massachusetts to Mexico along the Atlantic Coast. The two important species are the common weakfish and the better-known spotted weakfish or sea trout, so called because they have black spots similar to trout. The name *weakfish* refers to their tender mouths, which often tear when hooked.

Weakfish are great fly-rod fish. They are plentiful in shallow coastal waters, and eagerly strike surface and subsurface flies that imitate their favorite food, shrimp or minnows.

Sea trout like to feed in cool- and warm-water temperatures—60 to 85 degrees F—over grassy flats, jetties, beach lines, tidal channels, and river mouths.

The weakfish population has suffered a fate similar to those of the redfish and snook, with commercial netting and sportfishing pressure causing their numbers and size to dwindle in many areas. As more coastal states stop netting and restrict sportfishing, the weakfish should rebound, as have the striper, redfish, and snook.

Bluefish (Bluefish Family)

Bluefish are ravenous school fish that terrorize baitfish along the Atlantic Coast from

Bluefish.

Maine to Argentina. Their bloody feeding frenzies along surf lines, in bays, and at the mouths of tidal rivers have earned them the nickname "choppers"; they slash and devour any baitfish unlucky enough to get in their paths. Because they feed and move almost constantly in salt water, they are extremely strong, fast fighters and excellent fly-rod fish.

Blues run from 2 to 20 pounds, and usually travel in age-group schools as they migrate north in the summer and south in the fall and winter. They prefer fast-moving surface and subsurface flies that imitate frightened schooling baitfish, shrimp, and squid.

Their rows of sharp cutting teeth make a wire bite tippet almost mandatory. Also, take care not to put your fingers inside a blue's mouth; the fish will bite you severely.

Striped Bass (Temperate Bass Family)

Striped bass are native to the Atlantic Coast of North America, but also have been successfully introduced to the West Coast from northern California to Washington State, and into many large inland freshwater lakes and rivers.

Striped bass are an exciting, strong, beautiful schooling fish that usually weigh from 2 to 30 pounds and can exceed 50 to 70 pounds. Their name, *striped bass*, or *stripers*, comes from the vivid horizontal rows of black stripes on their backs and sides, running from head to tail against a silvery background. Striped bass occur naturally in salt water, but to spawn they must swim up freshwater rivers, similar to salmon. Stripers also can live very well in large landlocked freshwater systems. Stripers readily strike subsurface and surface flies that imitate their favorite foods, such as sand eels, American eel, menhaden, smelt, shad, porgies, sculpin, aquatic worms, crabs, and shrimp. Because stripers are very tolerant of water temperatures—38 to 80 degrees F—they can be caught almost all year where they live.

In the last couple of decades stripers have made a remarkable comeback along the Atlantic Coast and tidal rivers due to strict seasons and limits on lengths and amounts anglers can harvest. Stripers are considered

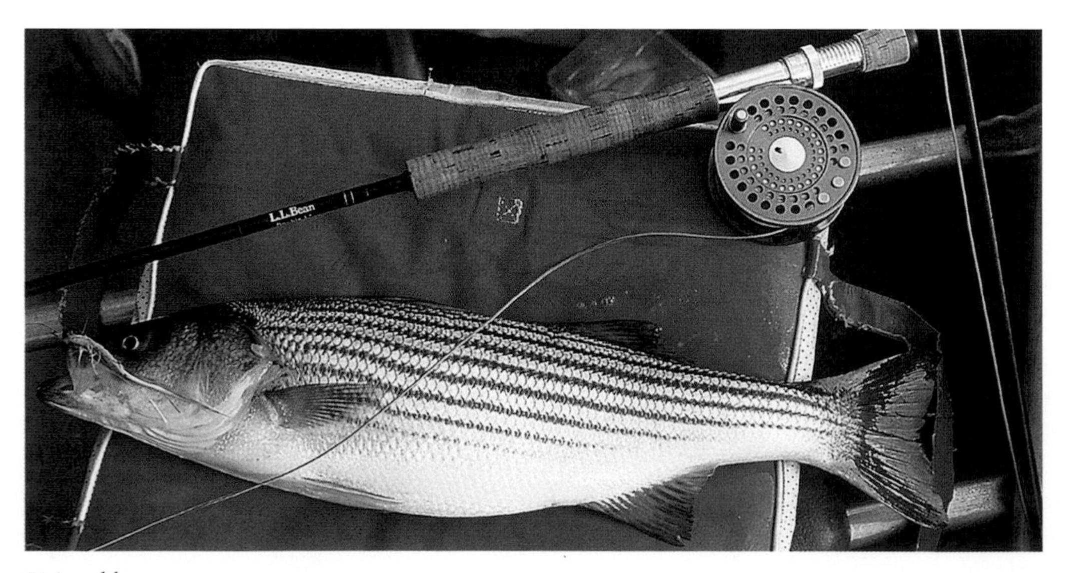

Striped bass.

one of the finest fresh- and saltwater gamefish you can catch on a fly.

Mackerel (Tuna Family)

Mackerel are a group of streamlined, swift-swimming, razor-toothed, eating machines that travel in schools. They are found off both the Atlantic and Pacific Coasts of North America from Canada to Mexico. Most species of mackerel will strike any small subsurface fly that even remotely resembles minnows, squid, aquatic worms, shrimp, and so on. When the 1- to 2-pound fish are in a feeding school, it's often possible to catch two, three, or four at a time if you use that many flies on your leader.

Two larger mackerel species—the Sierra mackerel of Pacific Central America and the king mackerel, or kingfish, an Atlantic Coast species—grow considerably larger (5 to 30 pounds) than the more common and abundant smaller mackerel.

Snook (Snook Family)

Many feel that snook are second only to tarpon as the most perfect saltwater fish for the fly rodder. Snook are beautifully shaped and colored, extremely strong fighters and jumpers, and intelligent feeders. They average about 3 pounds and 18 inches, but frequently are caught from 5 to 20 pounds and occasionally to 30 pounds or more.

Snook range mostly from Florida's Atlantic waters to the Gulf of Mexico and south into Central America. They prefer to live around shallow-water structures such as oyster bars, mangroves, jetties, bridges, lagoons, tidal creeks, canals, and flats. Snook also will move into brackish- and freshwater bays to feed. They will strike surface and subsurface flies that imitate baitfish, shrimp, eels, swimming crabs, squid, and aquatic worms. The more skillful you are with accurate fly casts and precise retrieving, the more success you will have getting snook to strike. Snook are staging a comeback in Florida, with commercial netting now banned and with strict limitations on seasons, sizes, and amounts for sport anglers.

Barracuda (Barracuda Family)

Barracuda are a much underrated fly-fishing quarry—truly electrifying when hooked on a fly. They are lightning-bolt strikers, fast-swimming, long-jumping flashes of silver predator. Barracuda average about 3 to 10 pounds and frequently exceed 20 to 30 pounds. Their range is mostly along the Atlantic and Gulf Coasts of Florida south to Central America. While most barracuda are probably caught by trolling in deep water or over wrecks using live bait, they are frequently found along beaches, islands, flats, channels, and mangroves. In these shallow areas they will strike fast-moving surface and subsurface flies that imitate baitfish, especially long, slender ones that resemble the needlefish, their favorite food.

Barracuda have a set of teeth that would make any wolf envious. They can cut a fish in half with one bite, so take great care to keep your hands and legs safe when you are landing or unhooking a fish. You will need wire bite tippets to land these razor-toothed gamefish.

This rundown of fish that are favored by fly fishers is a list of only some of the popular and abundant fish that will strike flies. There are several dozen more freshwater species and at least 100 more saltwater species targeted by fly fishers. A lot of the adventure, fun, and excitement of fly fishing is in catching unconventional as well as traditional fly-rod fish. To learn more about these fish and how to identify them, refer to A. J. McClane's *Field Guide to Freshwater Fishes of North America* and its companion book, *Guide to Saltwater Fishes of North America*.

SELECTING MATCHED FLY TACKLE FOR SPECIFIC SPECIES

TROUT: Light, small streams

Rod	7 to 8 feet, 3- to 5-weight, medium-fast action
Reel	Lightweight click-drag single action. Capacity: Up to DT 5F and 50 yards of backing
Backing	50 yards of 20-pound braided Dacron
Fly line	Matched to rod (3, 4, or 5) Double-taper floating
Leader	7½- or 9-foot all-purpose knotless taper with 3X or 4X tip
Tippets	3X, 4X, 5X, 6X, 7X
Flies	Sizes 18 to 6

TROUT: Light, spring creeks

Rod	7 to 9 feet, 1- to 4-weight, slow to medium action
Reel	Lightweight click-drag single action. Capacity: Up to DT 4F and 50 yards of backing
Backing	50 yards of 20-pound braided Dacron
Fly lines	Matched to rod (1, 2, 3, or 4) 1. Double-taper floating 2. Weight-forward floating
Leader	10-, 12-, or 16-foot knotless spring creek or midge-nymph taper with 4X, 5X, 6X, or 7X tip
Tippets	4X, 5X, 6X, 7X, 8X
Flies	Sizes 28 to 14

TROUT: Medium, small to medium-sized streams, beaver ponds, and small lakes

Rod	8½ to 9 feet, 4-, 5-, or 6-weight, medium to medium-fast action
Reel	Single action, with click or disc drag. Capacity: Up to WF 6F and 100 yards of backing
Backing	100 yards of 20-pound braided Dacron
Fly lines	Matched to rod (4, 5, or 6) 1. Weight-forward floating 2. Weight-forward sinking-tip
Leaders	Floating line: 9- to 12-foot all-purpose knotless taper Sinking line: 6-foot knotless sinking-line taper with 2X tip
Tippets	1X, 2X, 3X, 4X, 5X, 6X
Flies	Sizes 18 to 4

TROUT and STEELHEAD: Heavy, for medium and large rivers, large ponds, and lakes

Rod	9 to 9½ feet, 7-, 8-, or 9-weight, medium-fast action with short extension butt on handle
Reel	Single action with disc drag. Capacity: Up to WF 9F and up to 150 yards backing. Extra spools
Backing	100 to 150 yards of 20-pound braided Dacron
Fly lines	Matched to rod (7, 8, or 9) 1. Weight-forward floating 2. Weight-forward sinking tip 3. Weight-forward full sinking
Leaders	Floating line: 9-foot knotless taper with 0X tip Sinking lines: 6-foot knotless sinking-tip taper, 0X to 2X tip
Tippets	0X, 1X, 2X, 3X
Flies	Sizes 6 to 2/0

PANFISH: Medium, streams, ponds, rivers, and lakes

Rod	7½ to 8½ feet, 4-, 5-, or 6-weight, medium action
Reel	Single action with click drag and extra spool. Capacity: Up to WF 6F and 50 feet of backing
Backing	50 feet of 20-pound braided Dacron
Fly lines	Matched to rod (4, 5, or 6) 1. Double-taper floating 2. Weight-forward floating 3. Weight-forward sinking tip
Leaders	Floating lines: 7½- or 9-foot all-purpose knotless taper with 3X tip Sinking line: 6-foot knotless sinking-line taper with 3X tip
Tippets	3X, 4X, 5X
Flies	Sizes 14 to 6

BASS: Light to medium, streams, ponds, and lakes

Rod	8½ to 9 feet, 6- or 7-weight, medium-fast action
Reel	Single action or multiplier with click drag. Capacity: Up to WF 7F and 100 yards of backing. Extra spools
Backing	50 to 100 yards of 30-pound braided Dacron
Fly lines	Matched to rod (6 or 7) 1. Weight-forward floating bass-bug taper 2. Weight-forward sinking tip
Leaders	Floating lines: 9½-foot medium bass knotless taper with 1X tip Sinking line: 6-foot knotless sinking-line taper with 1X tip
Tippets	1X, 2X, 3X, 4X
Flies	Sizes 10 to 2

BASS: Heavy, large rivers, lakes, swamps, canals, bayous

Rod	9 or 9½ feet, 8-, 9-, or 10-weight, fast action with a powerful, stiff butt
Reel	Large single action or multiplier with click drag. Capacity: Up to WF 10F and 150 yards of backing. Extra spools
Backing	100 to 150 yards of 30-pound braided Dacron
Fly lines	Matched to rod (8, 9, or 10) 1. Weight-forward floating bass-bug taper 2. Weight-forward sinking tip 3. Weight-forward full sinking
Leaders	Floating line: 9½-foot heavy bass knotless taper with 0/2X to 0X tip Sinking line: 6-foot knotless sinking-line taper with 0/2X or 0X tip
Tippet	0/2X, 0/1X, 0X, 1X, and 2X
Flies	Sizes 4 to 5/0

SALMON: Heavy Atlantic salmon and Pacific salmon from 8 to 25 pounds

Rod	9, 9½, or 10 feet, 8-, 9-, or 10-weight, medium-fast action with short extension butt on handle
Reel	Quality single action with disc drag. Capacity: Up to WF 10F and 250 yards of backing
Backing	150 to 250 yards of 30-pound braided Dacron
Fly lines	Matched to rod (8, 9, or 10) 1. Double-tapered floating 2. Weight-forward long-belly floating 3. Weight-forward sinking tip 4. Uniform sink 5. Shooting head
Leaders	Floating lines: 9-foot all-purpose knotless taper with 2X to 0X tip Shooting head–sinking lines: 6-foot knotless sinking-line taper with 2X to 0X tip
Tippets	0X, 1X, and 2X
Flies	Sizes 8 to 1/0

PIKE AND MUSKIE: Heavy, lakes and large rivers

Rod	9½ to 10 feet, 9-, 10-, 11-, or 12-weight, fast action with stiff butt and extension butt on handle
Reel	Large single action with disc drag; two extra spools recommended. Capacity: Up to WF 12F and 200 yards of backing
Backing	150 to 200 yards of 30-pound braided Dacron
Fly lines	Matched to rod (9, 10, 11, or 12) 1. Weight-forward floating, saltwater, bass, or pike tapers 2. Weight-forward sinking tip 3. Weight-forward uniform full sinking
Leaders	Floating line: 9-foot heavy-butt bass, knotless tapered leader with 0/4X to 0X tip Sinking-tip and full-sinking lines: 6-foot knotless sinking-line taper with 0/4X to 0X tip
Tippets	0/5X, 0/4X, 0/2X, 0X
Bite tippet	12-inch bite or shock tippet of stiff hard nylon in 40- to 80-pound test, or plastic-coating braided wire in 15- to 50-pound test
Flies	Sizes 1/0 to 6/0, 3 to 8 inches long

GENERAL SALTWATER: Coastal tidal rivers, bays, and surf for striped bass, bluefish, drum, and channel bass

Rod	9 to 10 feet, 9- or 10-weight, fast action with powerful butt section; special saltwater models with extension butt
Reel	Large single-action saltwater resistant with disc drag
Capacity	Up to WF 10F and 200 yards of backing
Fly lines	Matched to rod (9 or 10) 1. Weight-forward floating saltwater taper 2. Weight-forward sinking tip 3. Sinking shooting-head system, sink rates of I, II, III, IV, V line densities
Leaders	Floating line: 9-foot knotless saltwater taper with 0/4X to 0X tip Sinking lines: 6-foot knotless sinking-line taper with 0/4X to 0X tip
Tippets	Fluorocarbon tippet, 12- to 20-pound test
Bite tippet (for bluefish)	12 inches of 15- to 30-pound wire attached to leader tip
Flies	Sizes 6 to 3/0

BONEFISH: Medium to heavy; also good for other shallow-water casting to 2- to 15-pound saltwater fish such as redfish, sea trout (spotted weakfish), bonito, permit, snook, snapper, and ladyfish

Rod	9 feet, 7-, 8-, or 9-weight, medium-fast action with small extension butt on handle
Reel	Single action, smooth disc drag, saltwater resistant
Capacity	Up to WF 9F and 200 yards of backing
Backing	150 to 200 yards of 20-pound braided Dacron
Fly lines	Matched to rod (7, 8, or 9) 1. Weight-forward floating long-belly, special bonefish taper 2. Weight-forward intermediate monocore bonefish taper 3. Weight-forward sinking tip
Leaders	Floating and intermediate lines: 9- to 12-foot knotless nylon or knotted fluorocarbon saltwater taper with 2X, 1X, or 0X tip Sinking tip: 6-foot knotless sinking-line taper with 0X, 1X, or 2X tip

Note: A bite tippet is not usually needed for bonefish and the other species listed. However, other fish such as sharks, barracuda, snook, and tarpon may sometimes take bonefish flies and bite through the leader. Sharp coral heads and branches can also shear the tippet. This outfit can be easily used to fish for these additional abrasive-mouthed species by using a bite tippet of hard nylon or wire.

LARGE TARPON and SNOOK: Heavy, from 30 to 100 pounds plus	
Rod	9 or 9½ feet, 10-, 11-, or 12-weight, extra-fast action with extra-stiff butt and extension butt on handle
Reel	Large single-action saltwater resistant with strong, smooth disc-drag system. Capacity: Up to WF 12F and 250 yards of backing
Backing	200 to 250 yards of 30-pound braided Dacron
Fly lines	Matched to rod (10, 11, or 12)
	1. Weight-forward floating saltwater or tarpon taper
	2. Weight-forward intermediate
	3. Weight-forward intermediate monocore tarpon taper
	4. Weight-forward sinking tip
Leader	9- to 12-foot saltwater taper with special 100 percent knot tip section design; 12- to 20-pound-test class tippet
Bite tippet	12 inches of hard Mason nylon in 40- to 100-pound test

8 Tying Flies

Fly tying, the hand manufacture of fish food imitations for fly fishing, is a major facet of the sport. We consider it to be the *other half* of fly fishing. Anyone who can fly fish can learn to tie flies—and we believe would really enjoy it.

Tying flies is an utterly fascinating and relaxing pastime that may very well double your pleasure and success at the sport of fly fishing. It is a perfect off-season indoor complement to fly fishing, and can provide just-the-right flies during fishing season. Imitating natural fish foods or creating attractor flies, then catching fish on your own handmade flies, is a unique pleasure, and it gives a great sense of pride. There is no limit to the fish foods you can imitate by tying flies.

Most fly fishers discover that tying your own flies is easily as much fun and rewarding as fly fishing . . . I consider it to be the other half of fly fishing!

Fly tying is merely wrapping a thread around a hook shank, binding to the hook various tying materials (hair, feathers, rubber, yarns, wools, plastics, and tinsel, to name a few) to simulate a fish food. With a basic set of simple tools, tying materials, and a few tying instructions, you can learn how to tie flies in a few hours. You will be amazed at how well fish will strike your own hand-tied flies. Over 10 years at the L.L. Bean Fly-Fishing Schools, three-quarters of our students caught fish on the first fly they tied.

Getting started fly tying is not expensive if you keep your involvement simple and basic, gradually expanding as your interest, skill, and finances allow. Since the cost of most commercial flies reflects the hand labor more than the materials, tying your own may cost you only a few cents each. Almost without exception, amateur fly tyers produce more flies than they can use, so the excess make wonderful gifts or create extra income to cover the expense of the sport.

This chapter can provide only a glimpse at fly tying; for a thorough discussion, read part 3, *Fly Tying*.

FLY-TYING MATERIALS

Natural materials, such as domestic and wild bird feathers, wild animal hair, and metallic tinsel, have been the traditional pillars of fly tying. In recent decades, however, fly tyers have come to accept a much greater range of materials, such as man-made synthetics, certain plant parts, and pen-raised domesticated birds and animals. There is ever-growing evidence that both hybrid natural materials and synthetic materials, if properly selected for

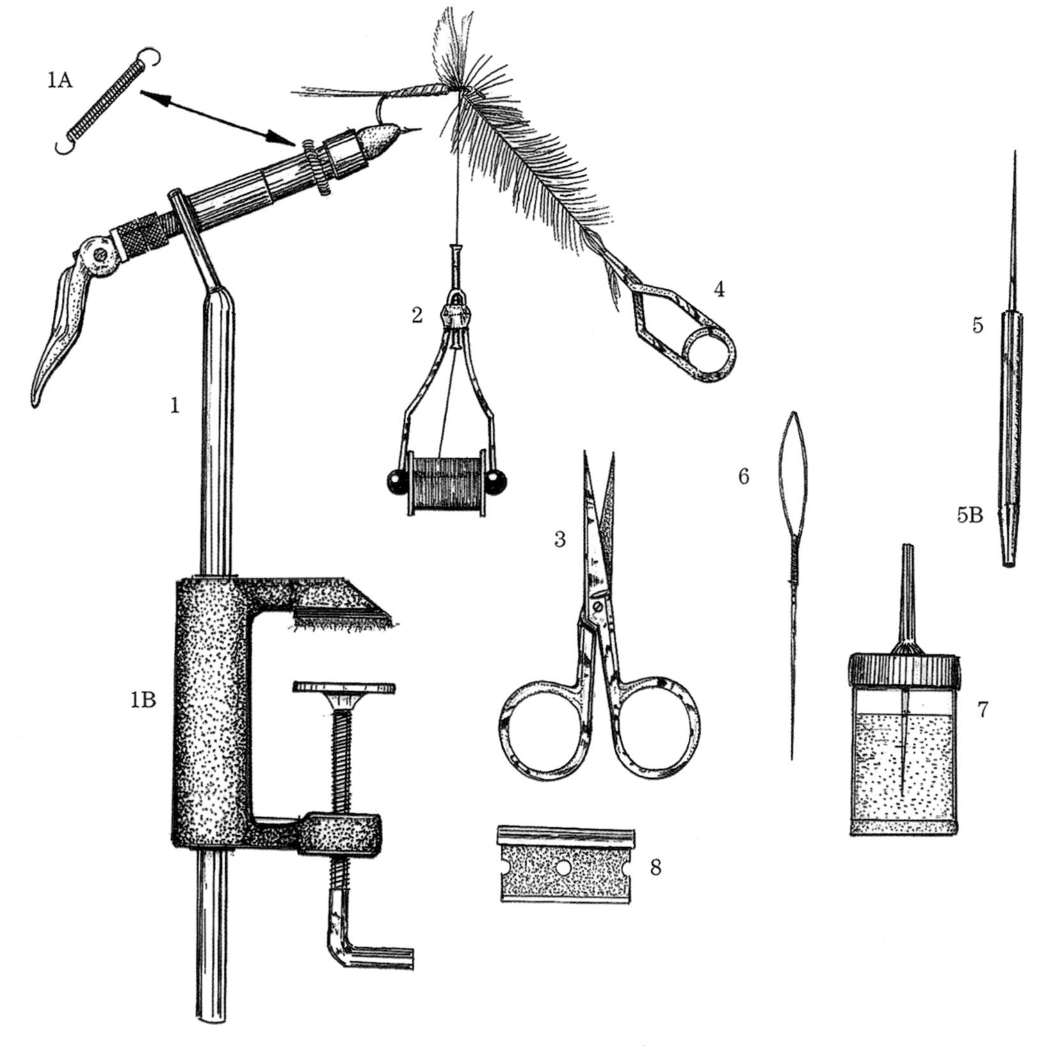

The Basic Fly-Tying Tools (*approximate cost*: $50 *to* $100)

1. Vise: Holds hook during tying.
1A. Spring materials clip: Fits on the vise cam and holds materials ready for use.
1B. Vise clamp attaches rise to table or desktops.
2. Bobbin: Holds thread during tying.
3. Needle-point scissors: Cuts and trims tying materials.
4. Hackle pliers: Holds small or delicate feathers.
5. Bodkin and half-hitch tool: Bodkin point (5A) picks and separates materials. Half-hitch tool (5B) helps form the half-hitch knot.
6. Simple nylon-loop whip-finish tool: Helps form whip-finish knot.
7. Fly-tying cement with applicator top: Glues, coats, and adds finish.
8. Single-edge razor blade for cutting or trimming thread and materials.

texture, color, and size, perform equally well as or can even surpass the traditional natural materials for making quality, functional flies. Remember that most traditional and modern fly designs and their color patterns are simply products of fly tyers choosing from among the suitable materials that are locally available to them. There is practically no limit to the materials that can be used.

Tying tools, materials, hooks, instruction books, and videos are readily available from retail stores and catalogs. Helpful fly-tying classes may be found at local tying clinics, community colleges, fly-tying clubs, and sporting-good stores. As you become more familiar with the tools and materials of fly tying, you will most likely enjoy making certain tools and gathering materials from hunting trips or excursions to garage sales, taxidermists, or sewing and craft-material stores. Discovering a new tool or material is a bonus adventure to the sport.

FLY-TYING HOOKS

Hooks are the foundation of all flies. They are available to accommodate almost any conceivable size, design, and imitation need of fly tyers. It is important to use the right hook for a fly's size, density, and intended performance.

Hook Parts

Eye: The looped opening at the end of the hook to which the leader's tip or tippet is attached. Types of hook eyes include the straight, ringed eye (R), turned-up eye (TU), turned-down eye (TD), ball-eye (B), and looped eye (L). Try to select hooks with eyes that are completely closed.

Shank: The hook's section between the eye and the bend that provides the length and

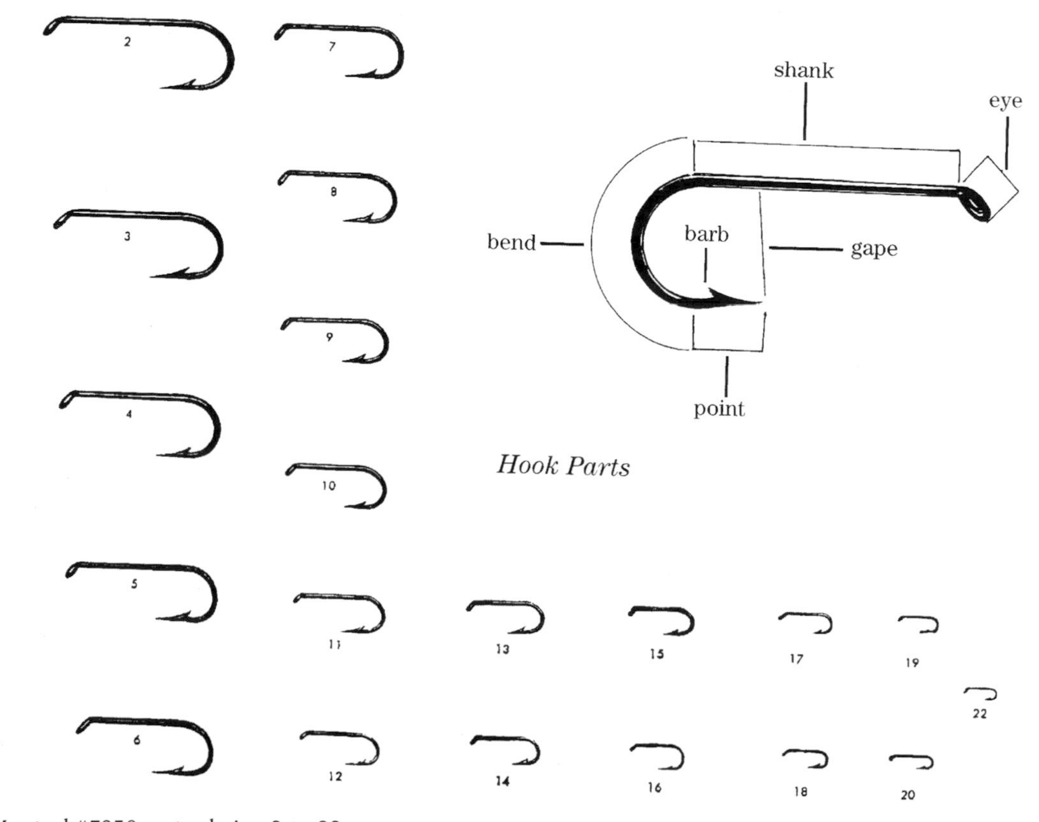

Hook Parts

Mustad #7958, actual size 2 to 22.

foundation for attaching the materials. Shank lengths vary from extra short (XS) to extra long (XL).

Bend: The curved portion that determines the hook shape. Some examples are round, Limerick, and Sproat bends.

Point: The sharp or spear-shaped lower end portion that penetrates the fish's mouth. Chemically sharpened points are usually superior in sharpness.

Barb: Just behind the point, the barb is designed to aid in keeping the hook lodged at the mouth tissue of the fish. Barbless hooks or those with microbarbs are best for fly fishing, since they allow fish to be released more easily.

Gap: The vertical distance between the point and the shank.

TYING A WOOLLY WORM WET FLY

The Woolly Worm wet fly is a simple fly to tie, yet it involves many of the basic fly-tying procedures. It is also a very effective fly design for taking almost all types of fish. Here are the materials you will need to create your own Woolly Worm. For another perspective on this fly, see page 121.

HOOK:	Tiemco #5263 or Mustad #9672, TDE 2XL, size 6.
THREAD:	Waxed monocord, black or yellow.
TAIL:	Tip of hackle (rooster feather).
BODY:	Medium black chenille.
BODY HACKLE:	3- to 4-inch-long neck or saddle hackle.
CEMENT:	Clear fly-tying cement (Dave's Flexament is recommended).

Tying Steps

Before you begin tying your first fly, carefully read over these instructions and study each illustration. Next, lay out all your tools and materials and seat yourself comfortably so that you can reach your vise and view it from the side and top. Make sure that you have a good light source angling from above and behind you toward the vise and table.

As you begin to tie the Woolly Worm or any other fly, strive to get the *proportions* correct. Use the hook to judge these, and study a sample fly or illustrations. If the proportions are correct, the fly will cast, swim, and hook properly.

The versatile Woolly Worm in various color combos and sizes.

Tying Steps

1A. Position the hook in the vise jaws so that the point and barb are not covered by the vise jaws and the shank is almost parallel to the tabletop. Tighten the jaws just enough to grip the hook firmly.

1B. Pull out about 3 inches of thread from the bobbin. Hold it tight against the middle shank with your left hand; hold the bobbin in your right hand. Now wrap the thread firmly with the bobbin (held in your right hand) over, down, under, and back over the hook (clockwise) shank, working toward the hook eye. Stop just short of the eye, and wrap back over the first wraps. This **jam knot** locks the thread on the hook shank. Now wrap the thread back to the hook bend and carefully trim away the excess thread tip with scissors. A thread-wrapped hook shank provides a better surface to attach and cement materials.

2A. The tail. With your scissors, cut the tip off the end of the hackle feather for the fly's tail. It should be *one-third* as long as the hook shank.

2B. With your left thumb and index finger, hold the hackle tip just over the junction of the hook shank and bend. With your thread bobbin, make about two or three loose wraps around the hook and the feather stem while still holding the feather tip exactly where you want it to be tied. Now tighten those wraps and make about six more over the hook and feather stem.

In most cases when attaching material to the hook shank with thread, making a few loose wraps first *and then* tightening will ensure that the material remains in position when the thread is tightened.

Release your hold on the feather, and check its position. If it seems a bit out of line, simply pull or twist it into position.

3. Attaching hackle. Just at the end of the hook shank, next to the tail, place the hackle tip end with your left thumb and index finger. Wrap thread closely around it three or four times, and then tighten the wraps. Now make about six more tight wraps over the tied-down hackle end to secure it. Place the hackle butt in the materials clip.

4A. Attaching body chenille. Cut a strand of chenille about four or five times the length of the hook shank. On one end, pull away some of the fuzzy fibers to expose about ⅛ inch or more of the chenille's thread core.

4B. Now place this chenille thread tip just beside the tail and hackle tie-down area (at the shank and bend junction) and wrap it down.

4C. Body cementing. Lightly overcoat the entire hook shank with fly-tying cement. This glues the attached materials and seals the hook shank and thread wraps against water damage. It also provides additional adhesion for the body material that is next to be wrapped over the shank.

5A. Body. *Important:* Advance the thread now to just behind the hook eye.

5B. Wrap the chenille around the hook shank. Begin at the hook bend. Using a right-to-left-hand exchange, wrap the chenille in the same direction that the thread is wrapped. Space the wraps so that they just touch each other.

5C. *Important:* Stop wrapping just before you get to the hook eye—about one

Tying Steps

hook-eye length away. Wrap thread across the chenille to tie it down to the hook shank. Make about six to eight firm thread wraps, and clip away the excess chenille with the tips of your scissors, *taking care not to cut the tying thread.*

6. Body hackle. Grasp the hackle butt with your right hand and wrap the feather around the body from the hook bend to just behind the hook eye. Make a forward spiral wrap of between three and five turns. Try to position the wraps between the chenille wraps.

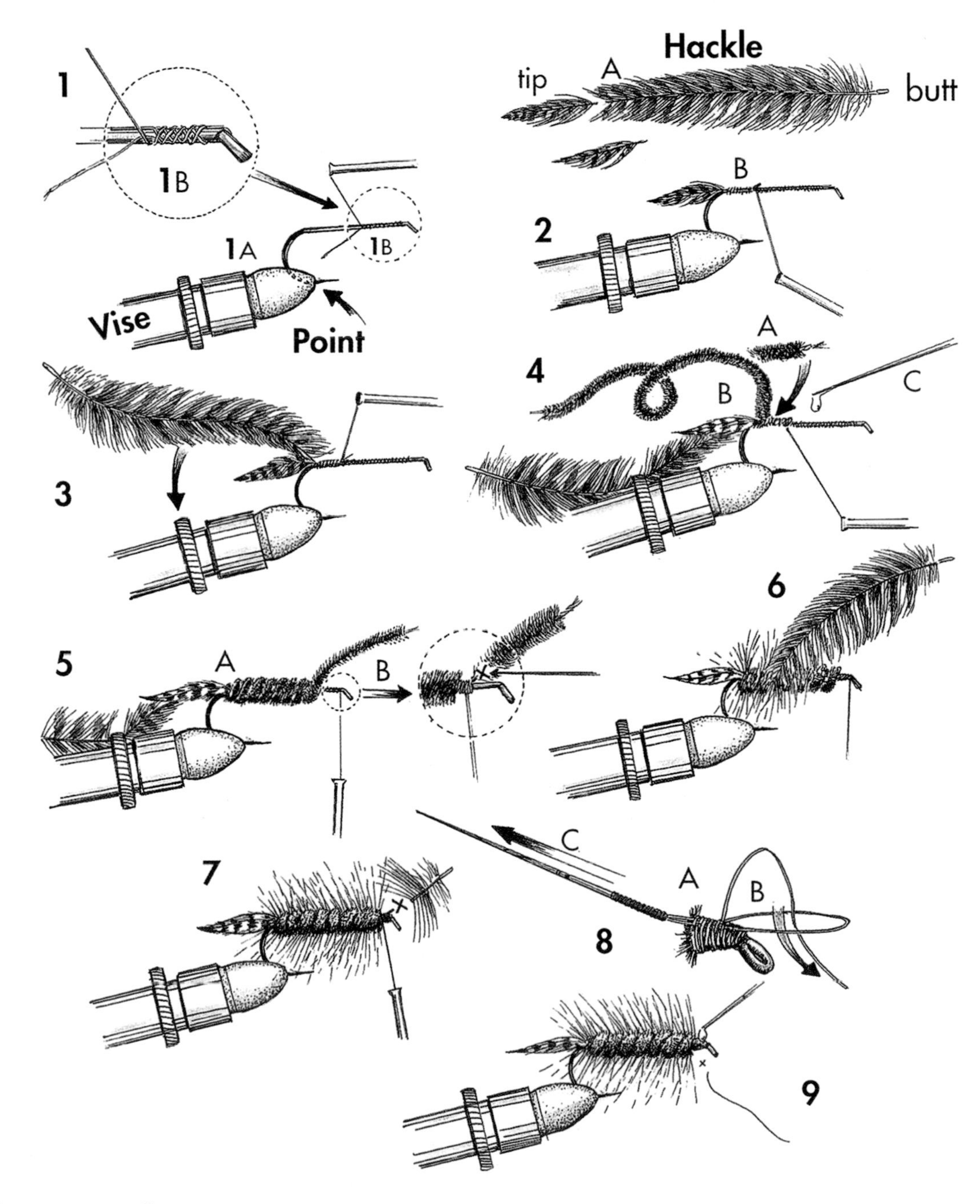

Steps for tying a Woolly Worm.

Tying Steps

7. When the hackle has been wrapped to behind the hook eye, make one full wrap around the shank and then tie down the stem with your thread. Carefully trim away the excess stem and butt with your scissor tips.

   Do not crowd the hook eye with the hackle wrap or there will not be enough space to make the fly head and finish knot. Study the illustrations closely to avoid this and other possible problems with proportions and shaping.

8A. With tying thread, wrap over the chenille and hackle tie-down area to cover them and to form a neat, small thread head. The head wraps should be just up to the hook eye but not over it. Make sure the wraps are smoothly placed and tight.

8B. Head whip-finish. Place the whip-finish tool's nylon loop over the fly's head. Make about 6 to 10 firm (but *not tight*) wraps over the loop and head, advancing from the back of the head toward the hook eye and loop end.

8C. Pull about 6 inches of thread off the bobbin spool. While holding the thread tight with your left-hand fingers, cut the thread so it is about 3 or 4 inches long. Now place the cut thread end through the nylon loop. Keep tension on the thread so the wraps will not loosen or unwind.

8D. Grasp the whip-finisher handle, keeping the loop *above* the hook eye, and pull back so that the loop slides under the wraps until it pulls free, pulling the thread end with it. Next, tighten the thread wraps of the whip-finish by pulling on the thread end. Trim away the excess thread with scissors as close as possible to the head.

9. Head finish. Paint the thread wraps carefully with one or two coats of fly-tying cement. Take care not to plug the hook's eye with cement or allow any to get on the body or hackle. If this happens, blot the excess out of the hook eye before it can harden. A small feather or toothpick works nicely for this cleaning.

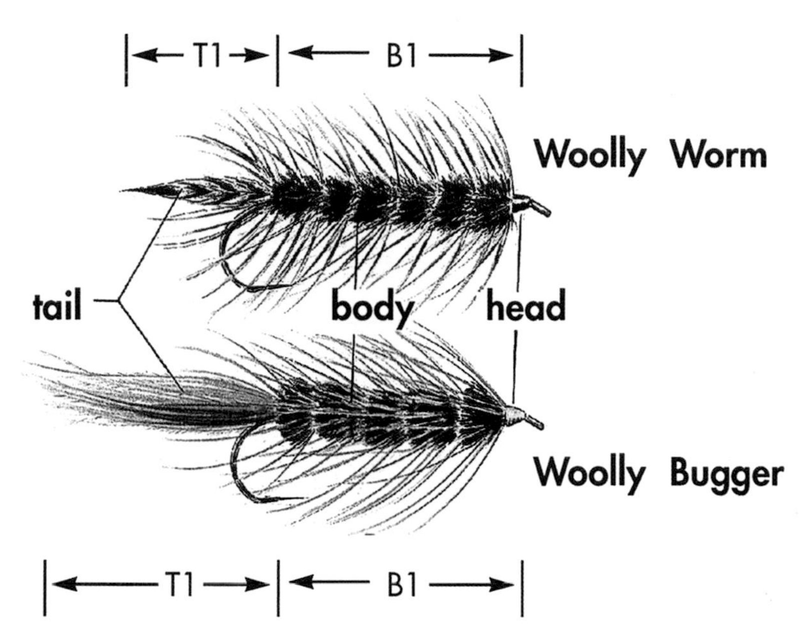

Proportions for the Woolly Worm and the Woolly Bugger: A Woolly Worm's tail is half the length of its body; a Woolly Bugger's tail is the same length as its body.

You have just accomplished many of the most important techniques and steps in fly tying. Repeat tying this fly several times at least, allowing time to relax and let your skill and dexterity develop. Each time, the tying will become more fun and you'll do much better, too.

By simply substituting a marabou feather tip for the hackle tip, you can make a second important fly, the Woolly Bugger. Make the marabou tip tail equal to the hook-shank length. You can also vary the fly's size and the colors of chenille, hackle, or marabou to create a wide selection of effective Woolly Buggers and Woolly Worms.

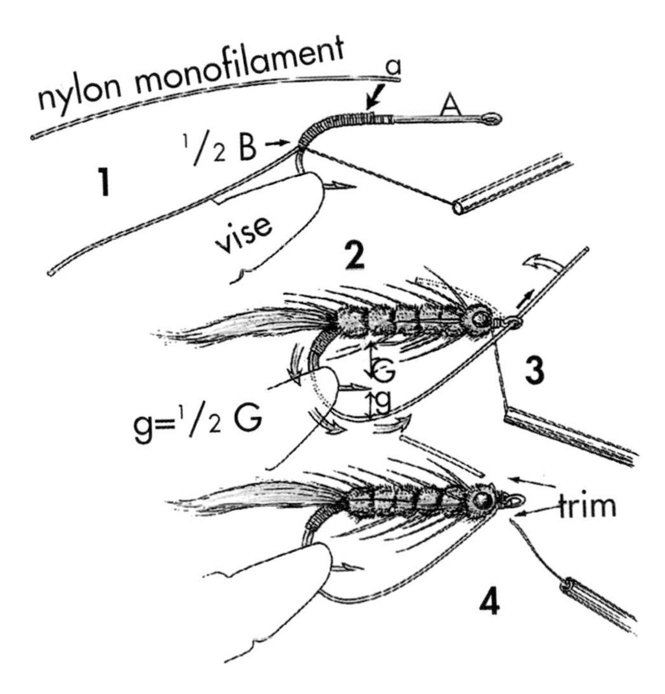

Snag Guards

Most flies can be tied with a simple, flexible nylon monofilament loop to prevent many of the hang-ups on water structures.

1. Attach a mono strand that is three-quarters the diameter of the hook wire (A) to the rear portion of the hook shank and half of the upper bend (B).
2. Tie the fly as you normally would.
3. Bend the nylon strand down under the hook and pass it through the underside of the hook eye. The loop formed (g) should extend half of the hook gap (G) below the hook point.
4. Using tying thread, wrap the nylon strand to the bottom of the hook behind the eye, then bend the upper part of the strand down and wrap it to the upper hook shank behind the hook eye. Whip-finish, trim the excess strand away, and cut away the thread. Coat the wraps with fly head cement.

Fly-Fishing Safety

Fly fishing is an outdoor sport that requires attention to safety to avoid accidents. In addition to the constant threat of sunburn, the most common accidents experienced while fly fishing are falling, hooking yourself or another person, and being bitten or cut on hands or fingers by a fish. All are easily avoided or made less likely when you take a few basic precautions.

AVOIDING FALLING

Most falls occur while you are approaching or leaving the water or while wading fast-flowing, irregular-bottom streams. Loss of balance happens most frequently when you are in water from an inch deep to just above your knees. In such shallow water you have lots of confidence, and you tend to step or walk quickly and without caution. In deeper water you step more slowly and cautiously, and the deeper water helps hold you erect.

To avoid falls, be sure to wear a wading boot or shoe with a sole and heel made to grip the type of bottom you're on. Rubber-cleat soles are best for soft bottoms—sand, fine gravel, silt, or mud. Felt soles are best for hard bottoms made up of large, irregular-sized rocks and flat bedrock covered by slick algae. The felt actually scrubs the algae away and grips the rough rock surface. Take great care in walking up or down wet dirt, clay, or leaf-laden banks while wearing felt-soled shoes, however. These surfaces may be as slippery as ice against the wet, smooth felt.

In swift water over hard, slick rock bottoms, use soles that have felt and soft-metal stud or cleat combinations. The metal cuts slightly into the rock's surface. Take care with this combination while walking over dry rocks, because you lose some traction.

No sole material can compensate for careless footwork while wading. Learn to slowly shuffle and feel your footing from step to step. Do not pick up one foot until the other is firmly in place. Whenever possible, watch for bottom pitfalls using polarized sunglasses. Large boulders, flat, slick rocks, depressions, tree limbs, roots, mucky bottoms, loose rocks, and drop-offs can put you down quickly if you do not see, feel, or suspect them.

You will have an easier time wading if you use a wading staff as your searching "foot" or foundation as you take each step. You can select a stout streamside stick or buy a special wading staff. I recommend the Folstaff, which folds conveniently when not in use and immediately unfolds and automatically stiffens when you need it for wading or hiking to or from the stream.

Wade Carefully!

Try not to wade against the current. Wherever possible, cross by going with the current. If you begin to lose your footing or balance, you can slap your fly rod down on the water to regain balance without harming the fly rod. If you do fall or wade over your head, do not fight the current. Relax and go with it. Keep your feet downstream and your head upstream until the water or a friend helps you to safety. If you are fly fishing with a companion, help each other wade safely across bad stretches. One way is to place your hand on the other's shoulder or lock arms. Another way is to hold hands. Four legs are twice as safe as two—any dog, cat, or horse can tell you that!

Hip Boots

Hip boots are one of the most convenient ways to wade water, but they can also be the most dangerous if you fall or step into swift or deep water. Never wade in above your knees while wearing hip-high waders. Do not wear them in a boat or where you might step or fall into water over your head. Hip boots quickly fill and handicap your ability to swim.

Chest-High Waders

When wearing chest-high waders, *always* wear a belt snugly around their outside to prevent them from filling with water if you wade too deep or fall. It is a good idea to experiment by going too deep in waders or hippers in a swimming pool, with a friend standing by, just to get a sense of what would happen should you fall down or go too deep while fishing. The experience may well save your or another's life. Your clothing and waders will hold air and remain buoyant to a certain extent. This will keep you floating if you do not struggle or swim violently with your legs. Use your arms and fly rod to keep upright, and for swimming.

FISH BITES

Bites, cuts, or punctures from fish's sharp teeth, sharp gill-plate edges, and spined fins are common hand injuries. Some of these wounds are very painful, and occasionally infectious and even poisonous. So it pays to use certain precautions when landing and handling any fish. A dip net, a tailer, a gaff, and various mouth-opening and hook-removal tools will, if used properly, almost entirely eliminate these dangers. Protective gloves are also useful for handling and unhooking some fish, as well as when dressing a fish to eat.

First, do not get so excited when you land or unhook a fish that you forget to keep your hands and fingers away from its mouth, gill plates, and fins. Learn which fish can hurt, and how. For instance, all trout, char, and salmon have sharp teeth, but none have cutting gill plates or sharp, spined fins. A snook has a harmless mouth but razor-sharp gill plates and needle-sharp dorsal-fin spines.

So keep the fish out of your hands by using a net or by beaching it. Keep your fingers out of its mouth or off gill plates by using a hemostat, needle-nose pliers, or a hook disgorger to unhook it.

HOOKING ACCIDENTS

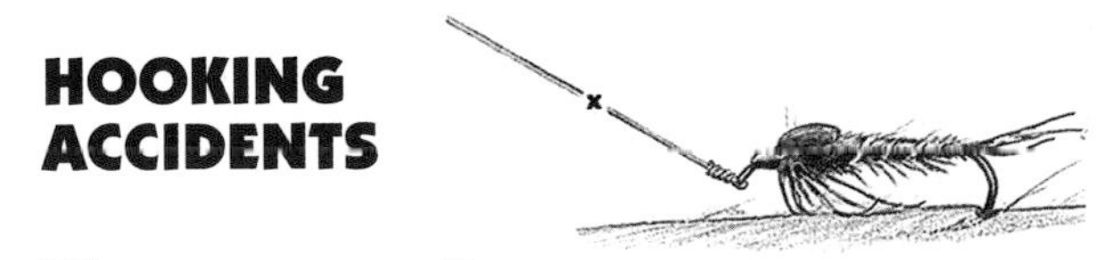

When you practice fly casting on the lawn or over water, use a hookless practice fly or cut the hook off an ordinary fly. Wear a brimmed or billed hat, glasses, a tight-weave

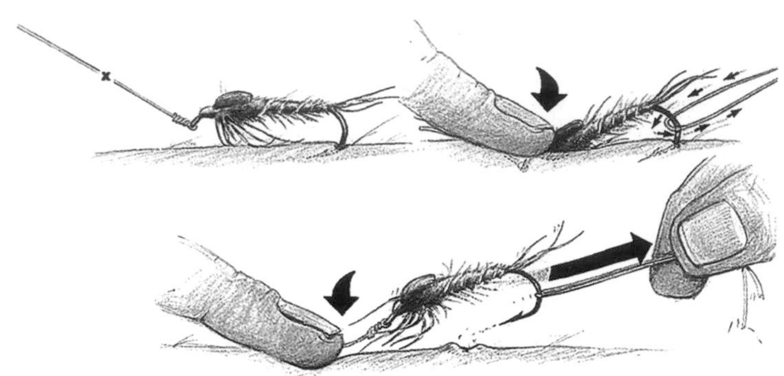

How to remove a hook that has penetrated into the skin beyond the barb:

1. Cut the leader.
2. Place a loop of monofilament around the hook bend and press the fly head down.
3. Press down on the leader directly before the fly and make a quick, straight pull back with the loop.

long-sleeved shirt, and long trousers for protection. Such apparel almost completely protects you from the most common hooking accidents.

Watch where you and everyone else are located, and do not get in each other's casting paths. On windy days, be particularly careful about where your fly goes on the backcast. When your fly strikes and holds to an unseen object behind you, do not attempt to free it with more pulls until you know what it has caught on. It might be another person, your pet, or even yourself. Also, never try to jerk a hooked fly loose from hang-ups on backward or forward casts without taking care that it will not snap back and hit you.

When you wade, keep a good distance away from other anglers and watch the wind's effect on the fly. In a boat, be very careful of the other occupants, and try to keep the boat angled so you do not allow your backcast to travel over the boat. If you are right-handed and you cast from the bow to the shoreline, keep the boat moving parallel to the *left* shoreline. Then your backcast will be ahead of the boat. The opposite is best for the left-handed caster.

If you should hook yourself or someone else, there are several actions you might take for safe hook removal. First, it is essential to relax the hooked person with assurances, then remove the hook as promptly and painlessly as possible (or get to an emergency room quickly) in order to avoid the person going into shock.

If it is a barbless hook, just grasp the fly and remove it by reversing the entry path. If the hook has a barb and it has penetrated past the barb, the situation may be a bit more serious. First, do not panic. After all, the hook has done very little tissue damage, so just relax. Ninety-nine percent of all hooks can be painlessly and quickly removed.

If you have hooked yourself and someone is with you, let your companion remove the hook; if you are alone, you can remove the hook if you can easily reach it with both hands. If you cannot, cut the leader tip off the fly and seek help elsewhere.

Should the fly be lodged in the eye socket area, or buried in the skull bones or in the throat or neck, *go immediately to the emergency room of the nearest hospital!*

Here are steps to follow when the situation is one in which you decide that you or a companion should remove the hook: First, cut off the leader at or near the fly eye, and put your fly rod aside. Then determine if the hook is just buried or has turned and exited the skin. Most hooks will be buried. If it is only buried to or just past the bend, follow Procedure A. Follow Procedure B if it is turned back out.

Hook Removal: Procedure A (for a hook buried to or just past the bend): Take a section of heavy nylon monofilament, or other fishing line or fly line, long enough to secure a firm handhold on when it is doubled. Pass it through the hook bend and back toward the direction opposite where the hook entered. With one hand, take a firm grip on the doubled section of line, just a few inches from the hook bend. With the other hand, press down the hook eye (fly-head area) with your index finger or thumb against the skin.

While pressing down on the hook eye, make a straight, smooth, quick, firm pull on the doubled line *away from or opposite the direction the hook entered.* The fly will pop out immediately without much pain or tissue damage. Some bleeding may occur, but that's okay—it will help flush the wound. Encourage the bleeding for a while, then stop it by applying direct pressure.

Hook Removal: Procedure B (for a hook that is turned back out): This removal method can only be attempted if you have a pair of side-cutting diagonals (dikes) or pliers. If you do not, do not attempt removal but go to a hospital emergency room or to a physician for assistance. Check the hook to see if the barb has cleared the skin. If it has not, push it on out with the pliers. Cut off the point and barb with side-cutting pliers and remove the debarbed hook by backing it out along the same path by which it entered. Allow the wound to bleed, then stop it with direct pressure.

In either case, treat the wound with antiseptic and cover it temporarily with a sterile bandage. As soon as convenient, consult a physician about the need for a tetanus shot.

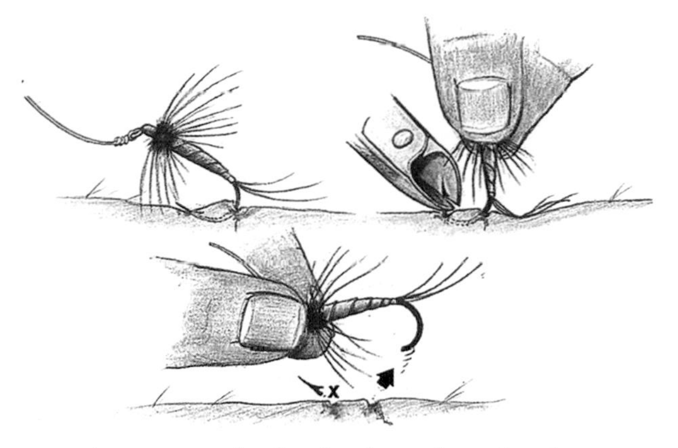

How to remove the hook when the point has penetrated skin and emerged:

1. Cut the leader.
2. Rotate and push the hook point up until the barb emerges. Cut off the point and barb.
3. Back the hook out of the entrance.

My golden rule is never to fly fish with a barbed hook or with a companion or student who doesn't have on a barbless fly. If all fly fishers would observe this, being hooked would seldom be painful or dangerous.

10 Fly-Fishing Apparel and Accessories

Fly fishing, being an on-the-water, all-season outdoor sport, requires certain apparel and accessories to provide comfort, efficiency, and safety.

Clothing: No matter what season or weather you fly fish in, you will function best if your clothes are as light as conditions allow: loose, comfortable, breathable, and nonbinding. They should be functional, not impractically stylish or fancy. Choose layered clothes that breathe and give you protection against sun, wind, dampness, and insects. For practicality, avoid nonwashable fabrics. To avoid being seen by fish and biting insects, choose subtle, natural colors.

Fishing hats: The ideal hat for fly fishing should have a good visor and brim to give your head and neck protection from sun, glare, wind, and insects. It should be reasonably rainproof and fit snugly enough so that the wind will not blow it off; a chin or safety strap is handy in high winds. Under certain conditions, you may want a hat that will accommodate a bug net. A fringe benefit of wearing a hat is that it protects you from getting hooked in the head.

Rain and wind jackets: A good jacket must be rainproof. The most practical jacket for wading folds into a small bundle and fits inside your fishing-vest back pocket or your wader pouch. For wading, it should not go below your waist. It should have a hood that will comfortably fit over your head and hat. Drawstrings at the hood and waist and snug wristbands help keep out rain, insects, and wind. Be sure your jacket will fit over your normal outerwear, including a fishing vest. Don't waste your money on jackets that are made from plastic that hardens or stiffens in cold weather.

If you intend to fish without waders from shore or from a boat, your jacket should extend at least below your hips for ample protection.

Fishing vests and chest packs: For fly fishing on foot, a fishing vest or chest pack is extremely useful. It should contain enough well-designed pockets to carry what you will need for an entire day's fishing. This includes fly boxes, rain jacket, sunglasses, film, and so on. Choose a lightweight model without too many pockets. Shorty-style vests are most practical for the fly fisher who wades fairly deep. If you are a nonswimmer or you regularly wade treacherous deep water, a flotation fishing vest is strongly recommended. I prefer a model with built-in flotation over the gas inflatables. When fishing from shore or a boat, you may choose to use a tackle box or kit tackle bag instead of a vest or chest pack.

Chest packs are an increasingly popular alternative for carrying fly boxes and small accessories. Access to these items is somewhat more convenient than with a vest, but some fly fishers find them a bit more bulky and in the way. I recommend that you try both and decide for yourself.

USEFUL FLY-FISHING ACCESSORIES

Polarized sunglasses—a must for fly fishing
Wading staff
Creel
Clippers
Hook sharpener
Scissors/pliers
Leader wallet
Fly boxes
Fly flotant
Fly-line dressing
Paper towels
Leader-tippet spools
High-energy bar
10-foot cord
Compass
Band-Aids
Matches (waterproof) or butane lighter
Small whistle
Folding cup
Insect repellent
Small knife
Patch kit
Lip balm
Hemostat
Thermometer
Small aquarium net
Sunblock
Small bottle of water

Waders: For cold-water wading, chest-high waders are a necessity. There are two designs: the stocking-foot wader and the boot-foot wader.

Stocking-foot waders are more portable and lightweight, and allow more freedom of movement. They are better for getting in and out of boats and floatplanes, for backpacking, and for float-tube fishing. You must wear thick socks or gravel guards and good, sturdy wading shoes over the feet of stocking-foot waders.

Boot-foot waders are generally more durable, heavier, and warmer but can restrict leg movement more. These waders are faster and easier to put on and take off, because the shoe or boot is part of them. When the fishing is easily accessible, boot-foot waders are a better overall choice for the fly fisher.

If you plan to fish in colder weather and wade deep, cold water, and you have no weight-load problems, then insulated waders are ideal, especially those made from neoprene. Insulated boot-foot waders are best for extreme cold. Lightweight waders are less durable but more portable and less tiring to wear. They are more practical in warmer conditions. In very cold conditions, extra underwear and stocking insulation can be worn.

For hot weather, cold-water wading, or tubing, choose lightweight stocking-foot waders. The breathable lightweight waders made from Gore-Tex or similar fabrics are ideal for avoiding excessive condensation inside your waders. It's important to avoid abrasive surfaces or kneeling with lightweight waders to prevent leaks. If Gore-Tex waders seem to seep water, usually washing them cleans the fabric so it can function correctly.

For extremely warm conditions, you might want to just wade wet. Shorts or jeans, with good wading shoes and heavy socks, will work nicely. Long pants with polypropylene long underwear work nicely for cold-water wet wading. Always wear long pants and high-top wading shoes with thick soles when wading saltwater flats, bars, and bays. This is important to avoid injuries resulting from encounters with barnacles, corals, stinging creatures, and other hazards.

Wader boots, like hiking boots, should give you protection against ankle, foot, and toe bruises and sprains. More importantly, they should give good bottom traction. There are three general types of boot soles:

Rubber cleats are best for soft mud, clay, and sand bottoms, but very dangerous on slick bedrock or rubble-rock bottoms.

Felt soles are good for hard bedrock and rubble-rock bottoms where there is moderately swift water or very slick algae. Felt soles are poor for mud, sand, or clay bottoms.

Soft-metal cleat or stud soles are ideal for hard bedrock or large-rubble bottoms that are very slick, or in very swift water. They are fair to good for soft-bottom wading. Metal cleats are impractical, however, for wearing in boats or rafts or on dry rock.

Felt or metal-cleat wading sandals, which fit over either wading shoes or the boots of waders, are very convenient when you want to convert quickly and simply from one sole to another.

Wader suspenders, belts, and patch kits are absolutely necessary accessories for waist- and chest-high waders.

Hip-high wading boots are a popular, convenient, comfortable means of fishing from shorelines and wading shallow water. Do not use them for boat wear or wading areas over your knees. If you go in too deep, they quickly fill with water and will disable your legs for swimming and balance.

Wader belts and wading staffs are two important safety items. The snug wader belt will take part of the wader weight off your shoulders, but more importantly, it will keep your waders from filling with water if you fall or go into water that's too deep. The wading staff can serve as a third leg while you wade slick or swift water, or assist in testing the depth ahead of you. It also helps you negotiate stream shorelines or steep trails.

11 The Present and Years Ahead: Ethics and Manners

Once you've learned the basics of fly fishing, you're ready to reap the rewards. You'll find that fly fishing will greatly multiply your pleasure on the water; you'll enjoy the process of casting itself, and you'll enjoy the special thrill of tempting a really difficult fish to your fly—perhaps one you've tied yourself.

It won't all be easy. You can't learn all of fly fishing in a week or from any book. Skill takes motivation and regular practice. You'll have to be patient with your flaws and try steadily to correct them. There will be frustrations—wind knots, sloppy casts, the inability to match a specific hatch of insects when fish are rising to them everywhere in sight, times when you're fly tying and you seem to have nine thumbs. You must *want* to perfect your techniques, and you must practice constantly. Believe me, it's worth the effort. This sport has given me over 50 years of pleasure.

Fly fishing can provide you a lifetime of pleasure, too—and part of that pleasure lies in improving your skills, becoming more adept at the various arts of fly fishing, and gaining more and more experience on the water.

Of course, the future of *your* fly fishing depends in part upon the future of everyone's fly fishing, and that depends upon the protection of our quarry and of the waters in which they live. More and more people are coming to love the *quality* of their fishing. They want to fish for wild fish in clean, natural surroundings. Fewer people are killing their fish today. They realize that tempting a fish to the fly and playing it on sensitive fly tackle is often the best part of fishing, and that releasing them provides fish to tempt another day. Sections of many rivers are now under catch-and-release restrictions, and the quality of the fishing they provide has improved immensely.

I began to fish actively at age six. My parents and grandparents were all anglers, and they were wonderful role models. They taught me not only how to catch fish, but also how to respect fish, other anglers, and the outdoors. The longer I live, the more I realize how fortunate I was to have such good early guidance. Today, many new anglers are entering the sport without parental role models or mentors, and must learn about outdoor behavior and respect from other anglers or teachers.

The first rule to follow is, as always, the Golden Rule: "Do unto others as you would have them do unto you." Be considerate, in other words, and try to avoid distracting or interfering with other anglers. Here is a list of good fishing manners:

- Do not crowd other anglers. Let them fish an entire pool if they get there first. Give them space.
- Do not rush ahead of another angler. Either fish a good distance behind or walk on shore past a long stretch of water past, at least into the next pool or bend in the river.
- If the water is already crowded, do not make matters worse by squeezing in, too.
- Ask other anglers in the area if you may share the water. If they say okay, do so carefully and don't get in their way, put down (scare) their fish, or make excessive conversation while they try to concentrate on their fishing.
- If you have a good spot and you notice other anglers waiting for a chance to fish it, either give up the spot after you have fished it a while or invite them to share the water with you.
- When you pass other anglers on foot, wading, or in a boat, make a circle around them as widely and quietly as it takes to not disturb them or the fish. Avoid loud greetings and remarks as others fish.
- If you are in a powerboat, be very careful not to throw a high wake when you are near bank anglers, waders, or people in small boats, tubes, or kick boats.
- Some public salmon rivers have rules about rotating through the pools, giving each angler a reasonable time to fish through. Follow this system strictly. This is an excellent way to share any trout or bass stream as well.
- Do not litter, especially with cigarette butts. They are offensive for others to see and harm fish and birds that eat them.
- When you hook or lose a fish, refrain from loud speech, profanity, screaming, or other noises that interfere with other anglers' serenity.
- When going to fish private land or water, ask permission first and take care where you park, walk, eat, clean fish, and toilet. Walk on paths; go under fences, or use styles or gates; always close gates; avoid frightening livestock; and do not litter.
- Pick up other people's litter (cans, strike indicators, cigarette butts, gum wrappers, and so on). Litter tends to attract more litter.
- Respect the rights of any legal angler. All sportfishing methods are just as worthy as fly fishing. Don't give other anglers a hard time if they choose other methods.
- Even if you release most fish you hook, don't become a numbers hog. Be conservative about how many fish you fight and handle on any given day. Catching alone puts a burden on the fish—and the fishery. I have a Texas friend, Paul, who after we catch 8 or 10 bass each will say, "Dave, I'm not mad at these bass, so let's stop and give them a break."
- Don't walk up to and peer over a high bank where others are fishing; your profile can put down rising fish and scare them away.
- As you travel to and from fishing waters and while you fish, endeavor to inflict as little foot damage as you can. Take care not to wade over fish nests, break down soft banks, or otherwise disturb the fishery. Never throw sticks or stones into a trout river.

One of the nicest common veins fly fishers seem to share is an unselfish attitude toward other fly fishers, especially those needing help with tackle, flies, casting, or techniques. I have always been proud of us for being that way. Be sure to take advantage of it now; and later, when you are thus skilled, help those who are as you were once yourself.

Because a lot of serious anglers have worked hard to protect our waters, the future of fly fishing is bright today. But you'll have to help if it's to remain so. Keep improving your skills; keep trying to catch more species of fish on the fly; help protect our fisheries—and have lots of fun fly fishing!

Postscript: Fly Assortments

STARTER TROUT ASSORTMENT

Parachute Adams, #14 (dry fly)
Royal Wulff, #10 (dry fly)
Elk-Hair Caddis, #12 (dry fly)

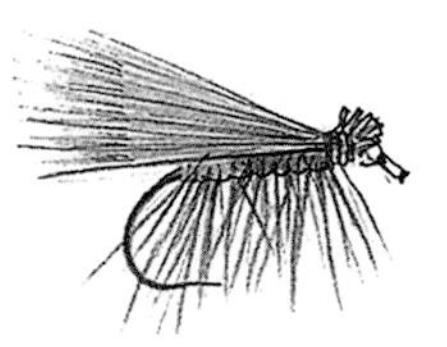

Elk-Hair Caddis dry fly—tan/olive

Dave's Hopper, #10 (terrestrial)
Black Ant, #14 (terrestrial)
Gold-Ribbed Hare's Ear, #14 (nymph)
Red Fox Squirrel Nymph, #10 (nymph)
Zug Bug, #12 (nymph)
Muddler Minnow, #8 (streamer)
Woolly Bugger, black and olive, #8 (streamer)
Clouser Minnow, #6 (streamer)

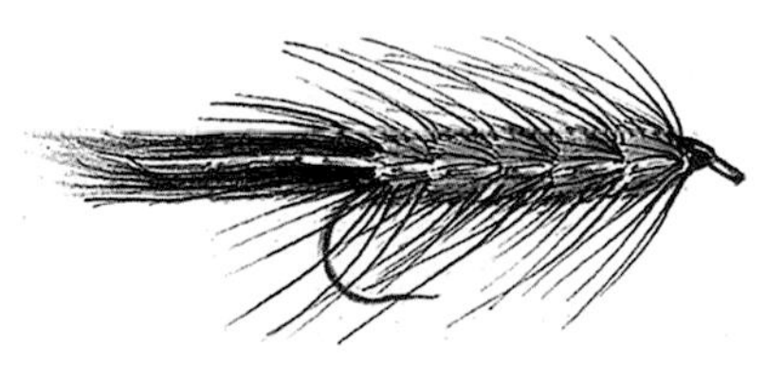

Woolly Bugger—olive-and-black Bugger

Near Nuff Sculpin, tan and olive, #8 (streamer)

STARTER PANFISH ASSORTMENT

Sneaky Pete, black and chartreuse, #10
Sponge Spider, black and yellow, #10
Most Whit Hair Bug, yellow, #10
Humpy, orange belly, #12
Dave's Hopper, #8
Tellico Nymph, #12
Red Fox Squirrel Nymph, #10
Woolly Bugger, yellow or black, #8
Clouser Minnow, chartreuse and white, #8
Black Marabou Minjig, #10

STARTER BASS ASSORTMENT

Most Whit Hair Bug, Fruit Cocktail, #6
Near Nuff Frog, #10
Popper, yellow or black, #4
Pencil Popper, white and pearl, #4
Sheep Streamer, shad, #6
Lectric Leech, black, #4
Near Nuff Crayfish, brown, #6
Clouser Minnow, brown and white, #4
Woolly Bugger, olive or black, #4
Eelworm Streamer, purple or black, #2
Dahlberg Strip Diver, chartreuse or white, #2

Dahlberg Strip Diver—chartreuse

Frog Diver, orange belly, #6

STANDARD DRY-FLY SELECTION FOR TROUT

Adams, #14, #16, #18
Light Cahill, #12, #16, #18
Quill Gordon, #12, #14, #16
Black Gnat, #14, #16, #18

Blue-Winged Olive, #14, #16, #18
Hendrickson, #10, #12, #14
March Brown, #10, #12, #14

Special Dry Flies

Gray Fox Variant, #12, #14
Brown Spider, #10, #12
Dun Variant, #14, #16
Brown Bivisible, #10, #12
Parachute Adams, #12, #14, #16
Irresistible, #12, #14, #16
Royal Wulff, #10, #14
Henryville Caddis, #12, #14, #16

Dry-Fly Terrestrials

Black ant, #12, #14, #16
Cinnamon ant, #14, #16, #18
Beetle, black, #10, #14, #18
Dave's Hopper, #8, #10, #12
Jassid, #16, #18, #20
Green inchworm, #10, #12, #14
Cricket, black, #10, #12, #14

Match-the-Hatch Dry-Fly Series

No Hackles or Comparaduns

Dun gray wing, yellow body, #16, #18, #20

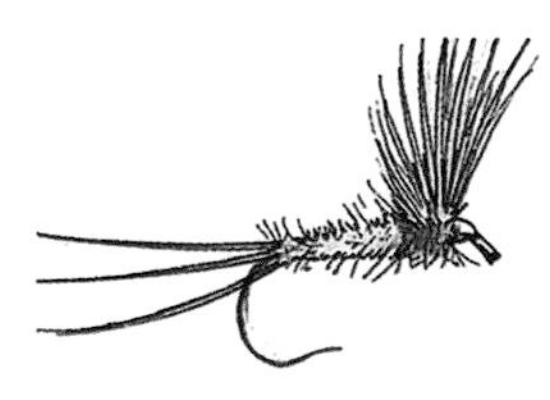

Comparadun dry fly—E. *dorothea*

Slate gray wing, olive body, #14, #16, #18, #20
Slate gray wing, tan body, #12, #14, #18, #20

No Hackle Hen or Poly Spinners

White wing, black body, #18, #20, #22
Light gray wing, yellow body, #16, #18, #20
Light gray wing, reddish brown body, #14, #16, #18
Light gray wing, gray-olive body, #12, #14, #16

Paraduns

Dun gray wing, tan body, #8, #10, #12
Slate gray wing, olive body, #8, #10, #12
Cream wing, yellow body, #6, #8, #10

Elk-Hair Caddis or Borger Poly Caddis (Dry Flies)

Tan wing, brown body, #12, #14, #16, #18
Tan wing, olive body, #14, #16, #18
Tan wing, gray body, #12, #14, #16
Tan wing, orange body, #6, #8, #10

STANDARD WET FLIES

Leadwing Coachman, #10, #12, #14
Royal Coachman, #10, #12, #14
Light Cahill, #12, #14
Parmachene Belle, #8, #10, #12
Black Gnat, #12, #14, #16
Iron Blue Dun, #12, #14, #16
Gray Hackle Yellow, #10, #12, #14
Gray Hackle Peacock, #10, #12, #14
Black and Grizzly Woolly Worm, #6, #8, #10

Nymphs

Gold-Ribbed Hare's Ear, #10, #12, #14, #16
Tellico, #10, #12
Zug Bug, #10, #12, #14
Darkstone, #2, #4, #6
Brownstone, #4, #6, #8
Goldenstone, #6, #8, #10
Dave's Shrimp, #12, #14, #16

Dave's Shrimp

Gray Nymph, #8, #10, #12
Red Squirrel Nymph, #8, #10, #12, #14
Damsel Nymph, #8, #10

STANDARD STREAMER ASSORTMENT

Clouser Minnow, #2, #6, #10
Near Nuff Sculpin, #6, #8, #10
Woolly Bugger, #6, #8, #10
Deep Sheep Streamer, #2, #4, #6
Gray Ghost, #2, #6, #10
Black-Nose Dace, #4, #6, #8
Mickey Finn, #6, #8, #10
Muddler Minnow, #2, #6, #10
Black Ghost, #4, #6, #8
White Marabou, #2, #4, #6
Yellow Marabou, #6, #8, #10
Dark Spruce, golden, #2, #4, #6, #8
Light Spruce, silver, #4, #6, #8, #10
Hornberg, #2, #4

SALMON FLIES (WET)

Silver Gray, #2, #6, #8
Blue Charm, #2, #6, #8, #10
Rusty Rat, #4, #6, #8, #10
Black Dose, #4, #6, #8, #10
Cosseboom, #2, #4, #6, #8
Jock Scott, #2, #4, #6
Muddler, #2, #4, #6, #8
Butterfly, #4, #6, #8

SALMON FLIES (DRY)

Bomber, #1/0, #4, #8
White Wulff, #4, #6, #8
Rat-Faced McDougal, #4, #6, #8
Mackintosh, #2, #4, #6
Salmon Skater, #8
Dave's Adult Stonefly, #2, #4, #6

BASS- AND PIKE-BUG ASSORTMENT (TOPWATER)

Dave's Diving Frog, yellow and orange belly, #2, #6
Dahlberg Strip Diver, chartreuse and black, #2, #4
Sneaky Pete, chartreuse and black, #2, #8
Umpqua Trophy Baitfish, red and yellow, yellow perch, #2, #2/0
Most Whit Hair Bug, yellow, black, red, and white, #2, #6, #10
Near Nuff Hair Frog, #2, #6, #10
Hula Popper, yellow, frog, black, #1/0, #4
Pencil Popper, yellow, white, black, #1/0, #4
Slider Bug, yellow, black, white, #1/0, #4
Sneaky Pete, chartreuse and black, #4, #8
Muddler Minnow, natural, black, white, yellow, #1/0, #4, #8
Dalberg Diver, frog, yellow, black, grizzly, silver minnow, and perch, #2, #6, #10

FLATS ASSORTMENT (BONEFISH, REDFISH, PERMIT)

Chico's Bonefish Special, #4, #6, #8
Dave's Salt Shrimp, #4, #6, #8

Dave's Hopper

Crazy Charlie, white, tan, #4, #6, #8
Clouser Minnow, chartreuse and white, #1/0, #4, #6
Snapping Shrimp, brown, #4, #6, #8
McCrab, tan or blue, #4, #1/0
Puff, tan or white, #4, #1/0
Swimming Crab, tan or brown, #2, #4, #6
Baited Breath, white, #6, #8, #10
Flats Popper, red and white, #4, #1/0
Horror, brown, #6, #8, #10

SALTWATER ASSORTMENT (TARPON, STRIPER, JACK, BARRACUDA, BLUEFISH, MACKEREL, DRUM, SNOOK)

Eelworm streamer, black, yellow, white, #1/0, #4
Grass Shrimp, gray, pink, tan, gold, #1/0, #4, #8, #10
Glass Minnow, white, blue and white, brown and white, #1/0, #4, #6, #8
Sea Ducer, red and yellow, red and white, #2/0, #4
Lefty's Deceiver, white, yellow, roach, red and white, black, blue and white, #2/0, #2, #6
Tarpon Special, yellow grizzly, blue grizzly, cockroach, orange grizzly, #3/0, #1/0
Skipping Popper, red and white, yellow, blue and white, #3/0, #1/0
Pencil Popper, yellow, white, silver, black, #3/0, #1/0, #4
Muddler Minnow, #3/0, #1/0, #4, #8

PART
2
Fly Casting

Preface

Any fish worth catching is worth catching well. That's what draws us to fly fishing. We use the tiniest, most delicate lures imaginable. Many are little more than pieces of fine fluff. We cast them with one of the most graceful motions found in all of sport. And we fight most of our fish in a starkly primitive manner, by holding on to the line and manually pulling the fish to us. But flies and fighting fish are for the other parts of this book: this one is about that graceful motion, the cast, fly fishing's poem.

There are few things as beautiful as casting a fly. When done properly, a cast can be sublime—simple physics translated into aerial ballet. On the greatest days, we forget that we are even using a fly rod; we look at a place on the water and our fly just seems to land there. There are also times, usually when the fishing is slow and our minds are wandering, when the rod takes over, demanding our full attention. It becomes almost a magic wand, one that we cast and cast, trying to make that one perfect cast. Just for the joy of it. Just to see that loop of line unfurl in the sky above our heads. Just so, on the way home from the water, we might think, "I made some great casts today. The loops had symmetry, but the bottom had a tiny bounce in it. Maybe next time I can throw a cast that's even better."

I wrote this book to take you closer to the perfect cast, the cast that seems to make itself while you stand by and watch in awe. Physicists speak of an elegant theory, one that is precise, neat, simple. That is what I hope for your casting: that, though falling short of perfection, it may be precise, neat, and simple, without excess motion. The elegant cast is the simple cast, the one that quiets the body and the mind, making room for reverence of fish and waters.

These pages reflect my bias as a fly-fishing generalist. Few self-respecting trout specialists would teach the double haul before the reach cast. But the double haul is more fun and, unlike the reach, is used in the pursuit of nearly all types of fish.

Whether this is your first day or 20th year of fly fishing, the methods in these pages will help you become a better caster. They are based on two decades of collective casting wisdom refined at the L.L. Bean Fly-Fishing Schools, and on the teaching of the leading casting instructors of our time. You'll learn how to make a simple four-part cast and to progress step by step through roll-casting, false-casting, shooting, and coping with wind. You'll learn advanced techniques such as double hauling and slack-line casts. You'll learn why heavy flies require imperfect, almost ugly, casts. You'll also learn some tricks that will help you when things go wrong. Along the way, there are strange offerings such as the belly cast and the inverted reel cast. We'll kick a few dogmas, too: like the ones that say you are supposed to watch your backcast, wait for the tug at the end of the backcast, and land the fly before the line.

The truth is that absolute perfection in casting is unattainable. But think of all the fun you'll have trying! One day in 1978, I was fishing Slough Creek in Yellowstone National Park when the fish were practically begging me to put my grasshopper imitation on the water. Instead, I put the fly in the tall grass behind me—dozens of times, it seemed, under a hot sun and hounded by mosquitoes. It was driving me crazy to have to repeatedly unhook my fly from that grass. I was a long way from perfection in those days.

Back home, I replaced my fiberglass rod with a longer, stiffer graphite model and practiced making more vertical backcast stops. By the time I was able to take another trip to Yellowstone, my casting was much improved. Fishing that stream the second time was like a dream from which I have never awakened. All day long, I put the fly on the water and all day long the fish ate it. I've since caught more fish and bigger fish in one day, but that was my first day of trout-fishing heaven. The memory inspires me to this day.

Whether you are practicing on your lawn or fishing the water of your dreams, you will always have the luxury of making the elegant cast. But there will be many times when you are unhappy with your results. I've been there countless times; I'm always amused when I make a casting mistake at the fly-fishing school, and the students think I did it on purpose.

You will find that your casting errors diminish over time. Your loops will become streamlined, the line above will seem to float, your rod will not even whisper during the backcast, and the fly will land out where the fish are. You'll notice that the fish will come easier. You'll get that sound in your voice, that lift in your spirit that I've heard and seen in so many of my L.L. Bean casting students when they say, "This is *great!*"

I admit that I have cast for hours on end over dewy lawns and fishless waters. I've been enthralled by that feeling of casting well, that quality of motion that I want to teach you. Like me, you may discover that you can wander out into the backyard and be hypnotized watching that loop of line leap from your rod tip as you false cast into the air, where large fish levitate in your imagination and the fishing never ends.

While I've never made that perfect cast, I'm still trying.

HOW TO USE THIS SECTION

If you are new to fly fishing, read these chapters in order. You'll get an approximation of what a student at the L.L. Bean Fly-Fishing Schools learns, but without the hands-on help. When you stumble, reread the descriptions of the steps you are learning. And remember that mistakes are one of your best teachers: To learn to cast is often to learn how not to cast. If reviewing the steps doesn't fix the problem, go to the *Troubleshooting* section at the end of the chapter.

The boxes in each chapter contain some casting wisdom, some fish stories, and some tangents. Most will deepen your understanding of the cast. The boxes at the beginning of each chapter will provide you with a context for what you are about to learn.

Take this book outside with you and study the photographs. Mimic them. Move your hand, arm, and rod into the positions you see in the book. This book assumes that you are right-handed. For example, when the book talks about forming a D during the roll cast, a left-hander will need to mentally reverse this analogy. Make sure that you understand each photograph and the text that accompanies it before moving ahead.

Other than a casting instructor, the most valuable companion to this book is a video camera. Using the pause button, freeze the tape of your casting at the various stop positions to make sure you are making the casting motions as shown in the illustrations. (There's more about how to videotape yourself in chapter 17.)

Even if you have been casting for a long time, you'll find some pearls in these pages. Students at the L.L. Bean school who come to us with years of experience marvel at how much there is still to learn, even about something such as a 45-foot cast that they may have taken for granted. If you just want to learn to cast farther, or with more ease, *check your fundamentals first.* Review chapter 13, *The Four-Part Cast on a Lawn.* Practice the pop/stop with your elbow close to your body, relaxed at your side. Try the casts at the end of that chapter in the *Playing Around* section. Then go to chapter 16, on *False-Casting*, and do the drills listed under *Tip Casting*, *Midsection Casting*, and *Playing Around.* Then go to chapter 6, *Lengthening Your Cast*, and study the section on *Shooting Beyond 45 Feet.* Be sure to try the *Playing Around* drills in that chapter. Then go on to chapter 19, *The Double Haul*, and chapter 20, *Special Casts.*

You have set a high bar for yourself: Learning to cast from a book is harder than learning from a live instructor. If you like what you read here and you want to learn more, attend the L.L. Bean Fly-Fishing Schools (1-800-FISH-LLB) or one of the other good casting programs around the country. Another option is to contact the Federation of Fly Fishers (FFF) in Bozeman, Montana, at 406-585-7592. As the governing body for casting instructors in the United States and Canada, they will gladly refer you to an FFF-Certified Casting Instructor or Master Casting Instructor in your area.

12 11 Habits of Highly Effective Casters

For skilled casters, most of the following are truly habitual, things they do without question. For example, they practice and often fish with a bright line so they can see what the line is doing. They use a small practice fly to keep it from dominating the line and leader. They clean the line so it shoots well. They wear a hat and sunglasses.

Get into the habit of doing these things and they will become second nature for you, too. You'll be happy if you do. Your casting and fishing will suffer if you don't.

USE THE RIGHT OUTFIT

An ideal outfit for many beginners to learn and fish with is an 8½- or 9-foot graphite rod designed for a 5- or 6-weight line. Few fly rodders are without a rod in this size and weight range. Most trout guides will tell you that they could spend their lifetimes happily fishing with one of these rods.

Grandpa's old bamboo rod should be kept on the mantelpiece. Bamboo rods are beautiful anachronisms: They're aesthetically superior but functionally inferior to graphite rods. To a lesser degree, the same is true of fiberglass rods: There are some pleasant-casting fiberglass rods, but a good graphite rod makes casting easier than a good fiberglass rod. When you are first learning, even if you are learning an advanced skill like the double haul, you owe it to yourself to have every advantage.

An outfit is properly matched when the line weight matches the line designation on the rod, and the reel is of the appropriate size to hold the correct line. If you are not sure whether your outfit is matched, call the L.L. Bean fly-fishing experts (1-800-FISH-LLB) to ask their opinion, or take your outfit to a fly-fishing specialty shop. As a general rule, buy your tackle from one of the firms that specializes in fly fishing. This is a complex sport, and an uninformed clerk or inappropriate purchase can make fly fishing too difficult.

If you are a small person, or if you think you may be somewhat lacking in hand and arm strength, you'll enjoy using an 8- or 8½-foot rod for a 4- or 5-weight line. This type of rod weighs less than a 9-footer and will make learning easier for you. After your hand and forearm get used to casting this rod, you may want to try casting a 9-foot 6-weight rod. The 9-foot rods have a number of subtle practical advantages over shorter rods, but they can be more tiring to cast for long periods, especially for people with untempered casting muscles.

Women and kids sometimes find the typical fly-rod grip to be a bit too thick to fit comfortably in their hands. If you are trying or buying a new rod, flex it back and forth with your thumb on top of the grip to see how it feels. No matter who you are, use a rod that feels comfortable in your hand, even if you don't know what you are doing yet.

USE THE RIGHT FLY LINE

When you are first learning to cast, your fly line should be a brightly colored floating line in either a weight forward or double taper. The weight forward is the more versatile of the two, but the double taper is just fine if that's what you happen to have. If you practice with a dull-colored line, it is harder to see your triumphs and errors. If you use a sinking line, its increased density can make the line unfurl abruptly and awkwardly, which will make learning harder for you. If you are using a line that is more than five years old, replace it with a new one. Fly lines degrade with age, just as windshield-wiper blades do.

WHAT IS A 6-WEIGHT LINE?

Fly lines are grouped according to how much they weigh in the front 30 feet, the part closest to the leader and tippet. A 6-weight line is slightly heavier than a 5-weight line and therefore requires a rod that is a tad stouter than a 5-weight rod needs to be. A 12-weight line is extremely heavy, requires a very stiff rod, and is used to cast heavy flies to huge fish. A 3-weight line is very light, requires a delicate rod, and is used to cast very small flies.

USE THE RIGHT LEADER

Your leader should be 7½-feet long, knotless, and taper to a 2X, 1X, or 0X tippet. (The X number is determined by subtracting the diameter of the tippet—in thousandths of an inch—from the number 11. So a 0X tippet is .011 inch thick and a 2X is .009 inch thick; 2X tippet is therefore thinner than 0X and thicker than 4X.) Unless you already have some casting experience, don't practice casting with: (1) a leader longer than 7½ feet, (2) a leader tapering to a tippet thinner than 2X, or (3) a knotted leader (its taper is achieved by knotting together many segments of progressively thinner monofilament).

An ideal matched outfit for most fly fishers is a 9-foot 6-weight rod with a weight-forward, floating 6-weight line.

Leaders longer than 7½ feet are harder for beginners to cast, and leaders thinner than 2X may tangle. A knotted leader can tangle mercilessly for a beginner. Once you become comfortable with your fly casts, you may have plenty of fishing opportunities that call for a 10-foot knotted leader tapering to a 6X tippet. Just don't practice with one.

MAINTAIN A HAPPY LEADER

Your leader may develop simple little overhand knots—wind knots—during casting (see the illustrations in chapter 17). They are a fact of life, more so for beginners than experts, and they weaken the leader. Cut out these knots if they are in the tippet (thin) end, or undo them if they are in the butt (thick) end. When you have to cut them out of the tippet, your leader will become shorter. When it shrinks to 6 feet, use a surgeon's knot to add 18 inches of the appropriate tippet. For consistency, if you started with a 0X leader, add 0X tippet, and so on. For more about leaders, tippets, and knots, see book 1, *L.L. Bean Fly-Fishing Handbook*.

USE THE RIGHT PRACTICE FLY

A leader without a practice fly is like a car without tires. To practice well, tie a piece of bright synthetic yarn onto the end of your leader using a clinch knot or a Duncan loop, also called a uniknot. (If you use the clinch knot when tying on a real fly, be sure to use the improved version.) Trim the short end of this knot as close as possible. The piece of yarn should then be trimmed to the size of a raisin or a pea. Then put fly flotant on it to make it float well. This practice fly is superior to and much cheaper than cutting the hook point off an actual fly. I wish someone had told me that when I started casting, because I neutered so many good Royal Wulffs and Elk-Hair Caddis.

Trim your practice fly to the size of a raisin or a pea.

MARK THE LINE

This tip has made a big difference in the learning curve of students at the L.L. Bean schools in the past few years. It may seem trivial, but once you do it, you'll be glad you did. Take a permanent waterproof marker and mark a 2-inch band around the line 37 feet from the tip of the line. Why 37 feet? Because holding the line at that mark will let you cast with most of the thick part of the line, called the head, outside the tip-top guide. That's the length of line that most rods are designed to cast optimally. If you add a 7½-foot leader to the line and you make a successful four-part cast (discussed in the next chapter), your fly will land 45 feet away. We call that a 45-foot cast, and that's long enough to catch a lot of different kinds of fish all over the world.

ALWAYS WEAR GLASSES OR SUNGLASSES AND A HAT

Wear them when you cast and fish. Even that innocuous-looking practice fly could seriously damage your eye. I've been hit in the face many times by errant casts, mostly on windy days, and my glasses have saved my sight. The hat has saved my skin.

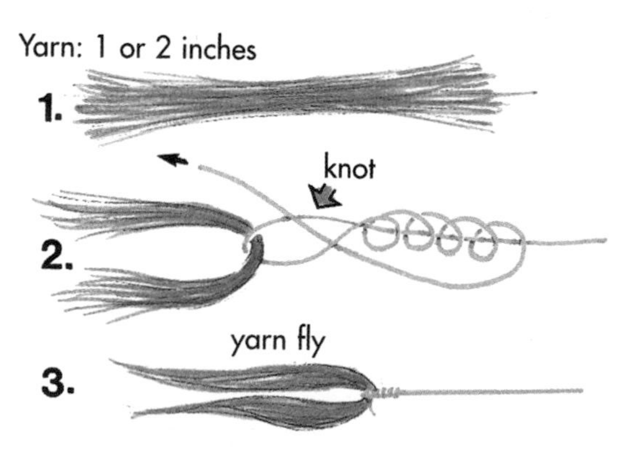

You can use a clinch knot for attaching yarn to make your practice fly.

Mark the line at a point 37 feet from the tip.

STRETCH THE LINE AND LEADER

Fly lines and leaders are made of sophisticated polymers, but they are not perfect. If you store them all curled up, as on a fly reel, they tend to remember the curls. It will help your casting and fishing if you get into the habit of stretching your line and leader to eliminate these curls each time you cast. The easiest way to stretch the line is to rig the rod (see chapter 13) and have a friend pull out about 50 feet of line. You hold on to the reel while your friend holds onto the tip of the line, and the two of you simply pull for a few seconds. You'll feel the line stretch quite a bit as you do. Just make sure the rod is not bent at all during this operation, to avoid damaging it.

You can also eliminate the line curls yourself by wrapping the line around a smooth object, or by just pulling and stretching a few feet at a time between your hands.

To stretch the leader, hold the butt, or thick, end and draw the leader through your tightly clenched hand *slowly* a few times. This warms the leader as you stretch it. When you are done, you should see the leader hanging nearly straight, without pronounced coiling. Don't use a leader straightener—usually a leather or rubber pad—as this can overheat the leader and weaken it.

CLEAN THE LINE

Like bare feet on a sidewalk, most lines pick up lots of dirt. Before doing anything involving shooting, described in chapter 17, clean your line by drawing it through a wet cloth. This will remove much of the dirt from the line and will make it float better. Next, draw it through another cloth treated with a fly-line dressing. This will make your line last longer and shoot through the guides more easily.

Stretch the line by wrapping it around a smooth object, making sure not to bend the rod.

TO PRACTICE IS TO CELEBRATE

Practice can bring beauty to your life. Take the late Jay Gammel, a retired junior-college professor in Baytown, Texas, who had spent his leisure time hunting, fly fishing, and fly casting. On a Texas-hot day in August 1995, he was 60 years old, his spine was badly degenerated, and he had terminal lung disease. He had just been discharged from the hospital, so he could go home to die. He loved to cast so much that despite his pain and afflictions, he insisted that he cast on the day he got home. With the temperature outside at 105 degrees F, his son helped him out to the worn place in the front yard where they had stood during their years of casting together. Jay sat down in a lawn chair and laboriously pulled the entire 90-foot fly line from the reel, followed by a few feet of backing. Unable to double haul because of his spine, he false-cast and made two presentations, both times draping the practice fly over the fence at the edge of their yard. From where he sat the fence was exactly 100 feet away. "That'll do," he said. Jay went back inside, happy with his two casts. They would be his last.

Jay Gammel knew that the best place to practice is wherever you can, whenever you can.

11 Habits of Highly Effective Casters

1. Practice with an 8½- or 9-foot rod designed for 5- or 6-weight line. If you lack strength in your forearm, use an 8- or 8½-foot 4- or 5-weight rod. Make sure the grip of the rod is comfortable in your hand.
2. Practice with a bright, floating line.
3. Your leader should be 7½ feet long, knotless, and tapered to a 2X, 1X, or 0X tippet.
4. Keep your leader free of knots; add tippet when it gets too short.
5. Tie synthetic yarn onto the end of your leader and trim it to the size of a pea.
6. Mark your line 37 feet from the tip.
7. Wear glasses and a hat.
8. Stretch your line and leader before you start practicing.
9. Clean the line, especially if you will be shooting line or fishing.
10. Practice wherever and whenever you can.
11. Be patient as you practice.

BE PATIENT—YOU ARE NOT AN IDIOT

You'll make lots of mistakes, so don't beat up on yourself when you do. Sometimes you'll regress. There will be dips in your learning curve but, with practice, the curve will trend upward. That's all part of the learning process; every skilled fly caster has been there.

The Four-Part Cast on a Lawn

This is the sweetest cast, the foundation of fly fishing. It is brief and almost crystalline in its simplicity. Although it is also called the overhead cast, it can be done sidearm and even underhanded.

Our goal in this chapter is to learn to count to four with a fly rod and to cast the practice fly 45 feet in the process.

At first, you should practice the four parts of this cast—pickup, backcast, forward cast, presentation—on a grassy lawn. It's easier to start on a lawn than on water. Of course, you can pantomime this cast anywhere. If you do this at work, people will think of you as someone who desperately needs a vacation.

Stand comfortably and stand up straight when you practice.

STANCE

Stand comfortably. If your feet are pointing in the general direction of your cast, that's good. Eventually, you will need to learn to cast no matter where your feet are pointing, because the stones in the river or the orientation of the boat will often dictate your stance.

Stand up straight; try not to hunch over like a great blue heron. Fishing may be life and death for the bird, but it's just fishing to you.

PANTOMIME THE CAST WITHOUT YOUR ROD

Mimic the positions you see in the photographs.

- Start with your elbow relaxed at your side, holding an imaginary rod pointing down at the water. Throughout the cast, your forearm and thumb should be aligned in a forward/backward plane, toward the fish, not off to the side.
- Mimic the pickup of the line from the water by slowly tilting your forearm toward vertical.
- As your imaginary rod passes through a position roughly 45 degrees above the water, accelerate it, first slowly, then briskly until your forearm snaps to a stop just short of vertical. Imagine your thumbnail pointing straight up, not back behind you. Freeze your arm there: you have just mimicked the backcast. Pause for the imaginary line to straighten in the air behind you.

Start with your elbow relaxed at your side, holding an imaginary rod.

Slowly tilt your forearm through the pickup, accelerating it until it snaps to a stop, just short of vertical. Your thumbnail should be pointing straight up.

- Begin the forward cast with your forearm simply reversing its course, starting slowly but accelerating to an abrupt stop at a position *above* the horizon.
- Once your arm has totally stopped, gently lower your forearm to the ground as your imaginary line unrolls in the air and falls. We call this the presentation, or delivery.
- Practice this at least 10 times.

Many casters prefer to lift their elbow slightly (no more than 3 or 4 inches) during the backcast, and to pull the elbow back down to their side during the forward cast. The longer the cast, the more you will need to raise your elbow. While it is not always necessary to do this during a 45-foot cast,

Starting slowly, accelerate the forward cast to an abrupt stop, with your forearm stopping at the 45-degree position.

Gently lower your forearm to the ground as your imaginary line unrolls in the air and falls.

You may prefer to lift your elbow slightly, no more than 3 or 4 inches, during the backcast.

Periodically look at your thumbnail. It should be pointing straight up at the backcast stop.

you will need to do so to make longer casts and crisp roll casts. In search of elegance and a quiet body when casting, I raise my elbow no more than I have to. Whether you choose this style during the short casts is something for you to decide. Try it both ways; choose the one that feels best.

Casting Is Counterintuitive

A good fly cast is counterintuitive. Our natural tendency is to wave the rod through a wide arc when casting. Perhaps the most challenging part of the cast is resisting the temptation to do this. In the beginning you'll have to "stop short," particularly during the backcast. In most casting, doing less with the rod usually means getting more from the cast.

As you'll see in the photographs in this book, casting is not robotic. Even a highly skilled caster displays some variation in style, even over the course of a few minutes. Casts are like snowflakes—no two are truly identical.

Do 10 more casts. Periodically, when you stop after your backcast, turn your head and *look at your thumbnail.* It should be pointing straight up. Look at your elbow. It should be either relaxed at your side or elevated slightly in front of you. When you stop after your forward cast, look at your thumbnail: you should see it pointing up at about a 45-degree angle in the sky, not straight at the horizon. You should also see your forearm and upper arm form about a 45- to a 90-degree angle. Do *not* straighten your arm during the forward cast. Doing so is labori-

At the forward-cast stop, you should see your thumbnail pointing up at about a 45-degree angle in the sky, not straight at the horizon. You should also see your forearm pointing above the horizon.

Don't do this. Straightening your arm during the forward cast is awkward, tiring, and will someday undermine your ability to make long casts someday.

ous, tiring, and will undermine your ability to make long casts.

By doing this pantomime, you are educating your muscles and giving them a memory of what the cast requires.

Now you're ready to pick up the rod.

What Is Muscle Memory?

Muscle memory is the ability of your muscles to repeat a motion without your thinking about it, because of many repetitions in the past. It's what allows you to walk while chewing gum, to ride a bicycle, or to serve a tennis ball. The pantomime will help you to do the casting motion correctly with enough repetition that your muscles will remember what to do, even when you are not paying attention. This will let you relax and even daydream as you fish, enriching your fishing experience and ensuring that, during your reverie, some of the big ones will get away.

HOLD THE ROD

Your thumb should be on the grip with your index finger opposite your thumb. Don't forget this or you'll have trouble stopping the rod on the backcast. Now squeeze the grip hard, very hard. Good. *Never do that again.* Your grip should be relaxed, something that you can do for hours on end with no strain.

Keep your thumb on the grip. This will let you accelerate the rod on the forward cast and stop the rod on the backcast.

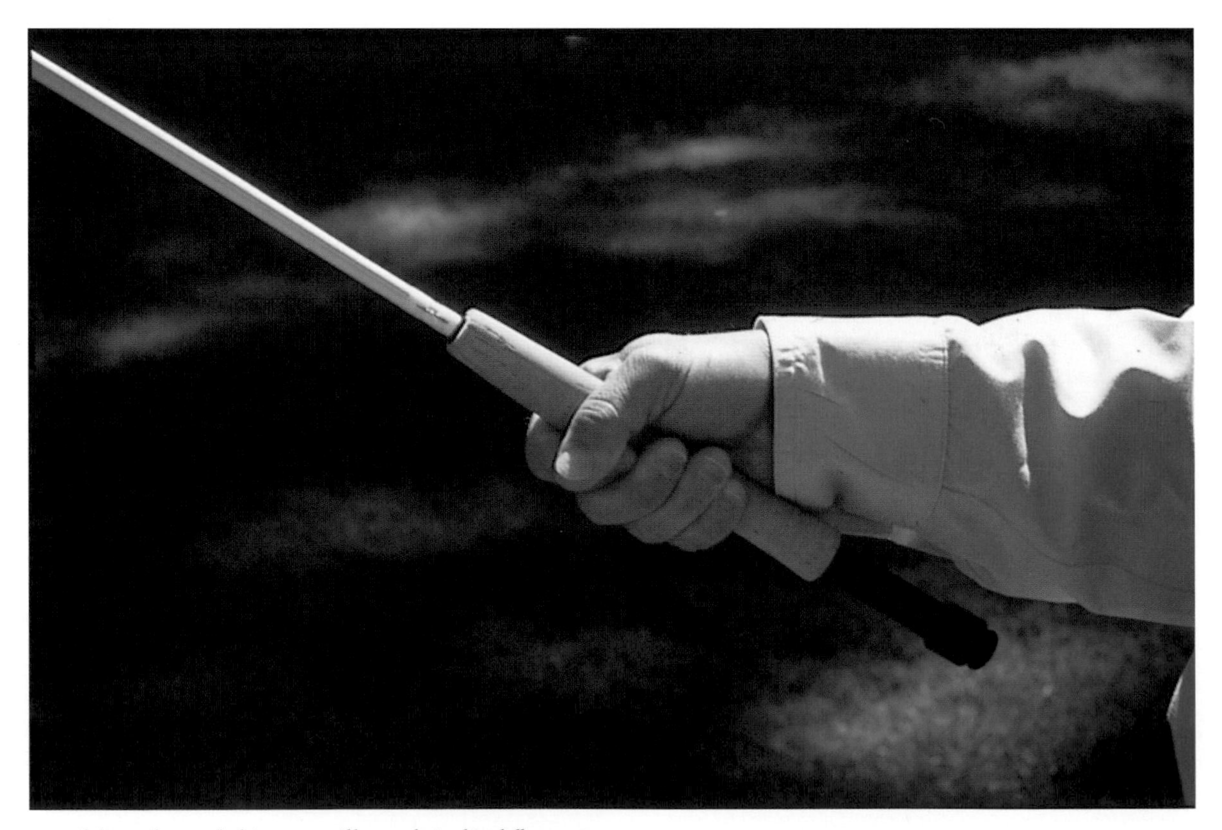

Holding the rod this way will result in bad fly casts.

TILT THE ROD

Tilt it slightly off to the side while pointing it up. This will usually keep the line from hitting the rod and will prevent the unsettling sight of the fly coming at your head at 60 miles per hour. If the line hits the rod often, or if you flinch each time the fly hurtles past you, tilt the rod even farther to the side.

Cast with the rod tilted slightly off vertical.

FLEX THE ROD

Flex it back and forth with no line. Move the handle very little while making the rest of the rod flex a lot. (It may help you to put your left hand on the end of the rod as an anchor point.) You can see how making a relatively compact motion with your hand and forearm can translate into a big motion in the rod.

Notice that it's easier to do this when your elbow is close to your side and your hand is slightly in front of you. Now hold the rod up in the Statue of Liberty position and try the same thing. That's harder, isn't it? *Casting is easier when you keep your rod hand and your elbow very close to your body.*

Do the four-part cast 10 more times while going through the same checklist you did earlier:

- Begin and end every cast with the rod tip nearly touching the water.
- Check your thumb position after the back-cast stop.

PANTOMIME WITH AN UNRIGGED ROD

Repeat the casting pantomime sequence you did earlier, but this time do it while holding the rod. Do this at least 10 times, carefully, deliberately:

1. Pick up slowly.
2. Transition smoothly into the backcast; pause.
3. Make the forward cast.
4. Lower the rod to the ground for the presentation.

Every cast begins and ends with the rod tip nearly touching the water.

At the backcast stop, be sure your elbow is either relaxed or slightly in front of you.

- Make sure your rod freezes as you wait for the would-be line to unroll behind you.
- Be sure your elbow is either relaxed or slightly in front of you during this time.

At the end of the forward cast, your rod and forearm should be pointing up.

- At the end of the forward cast, your rod should completely stop and should be pointing up in the sky; your forearm should be pointing above the horizon.
- Lower your rod gently after this stop as the imaginary line falls to the ground.

For the presentation, slowly lower your rod tip after the forward cast comes to a complete stop.

If you've noticed how short a distance the rod is moving, you're doing just fine. Remember, the less you move the rod, the more you'll get from the cast. Also, notice that your hand is lower after the forward-cast stop than after the backcast stop. This is as it should be.

Now do the cast 10 more times, making sure to start each cast slowly, but accelerating the rod to an abrupt stop at the end of the cast. This applies to both the forward and back-casts. *This acceleration to a stop is the single most important thing you do with a fly rod. Without it, the cast cannot happen.* It means that every backcast you make starts with a *whimper* and ends with a relative *bang*, and that every forward cast you make starts with a *whimper* and ends with a relative *bang*.

CASTING A LINE FOR THE FIRST TIME

- Pull line off the reel until you expose your 37-foot mark.
- String the line through the guides by doubling over the tip of the line. We call this a rigged rod. Now lay your rod down so it points in your casting direction.
- Pull all that line straight out through the guides and lay it down so it is still straight. Stretch the line and leader as described earlier.
- Pick up the rod, making sure to keep the tip pointed *down*, because most fly casts begin and end with the rod tip pointing at the water.

What Does Acceleration-to-a-Stop Feel Like?

With graphite fly rods, the acceleration-to-a-stop often feels more like a two-speed stroke—slow, then flick—than a gradual acceleration. Many casters describe a "twitch," "pop," or "snap" at the very end of the backcast and forward cast. Depending on the length of line you are casting and the weight of the rod, this will feel like anything from a twitch—a quick contraction of your hand and forearm muscles—to a thrust of energy. I think of the end of the acceleration as a **pop/stop: pop,** as the last tiny burst of acceleration; and **stop,** because the stroke must end. To do the right thing, try these analogies:

1. Still without a line on your rod, try to cast the tip section off the butt of the rod. Try to do it during the backcast and then during the forward cast. (The butt is the thick end of the rod.)
2. Put an inch of water in a cup. Hold it as though you are about to make a forward cast. Now mimic the cast, trying to cast the water as far forward as possible. If most of the water went out in front of you, you did the right thing. If most of the water went up in the air, you accelerated too abruptly. (Don't try this indoors.)

If you ease forward and pop/stop, most of the water will fly out in front of you.

If you pop too soon, most of the water will go up in the air.

String the line through the guides by doubling over the tip of the line.

- Pin your mark against the grip with your index finger, your middle finger, or both, leaving a 2-foot loop of line hanging down between your rod hand and the reel. We'll use this loop later when we begin to strip line. Your other hand, called the line hand, can just hang at your side.

IS THERE A BREEZE?

If so, position yourself accordingly. Just turn yourself so that your rod hand is on your *downwind* side, with the rod pointing perpendicular to the wind. This will prevent the wind from blowing the line into you or your rod during the backcast or forward cast.

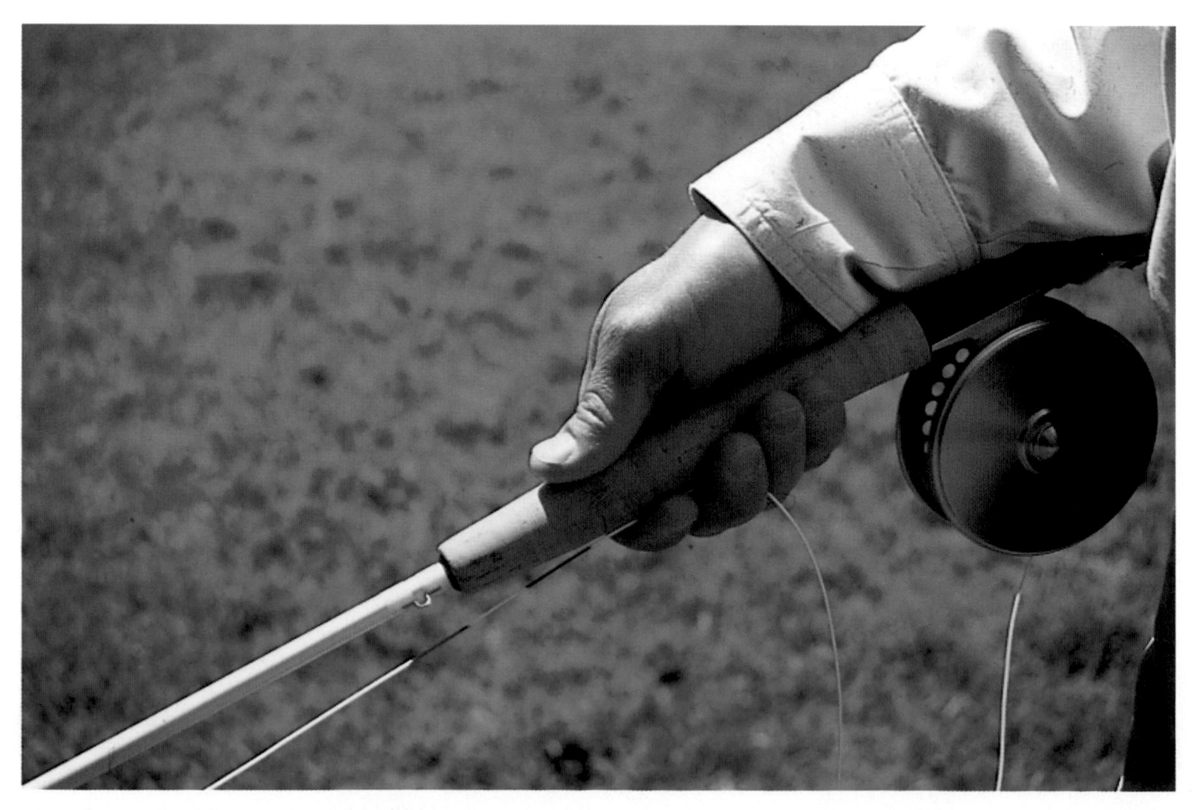
Pin the marked line against the grip.

If there is a breeze, position yourself so the wind is blowing perpendicular to the rod and the rod is on your downwind side.

PICKUP

Until you get to chapter 17, begin *every* cast with the line fully extended, straight out in front of you, with the rod tip practically touching the ground. Gently lift the rod tip by tilting your forearm upward, keeping your elbow close to your side. Increase the speed at which the rod tip sweeps up. When the rod passes through the 45-degree position, begin your backcast. The pickup and backcast are different phases of the cast, but they should feel to you like one smooth motion. There is no hesitation or "hitch" between the pickup and backcast.

Begin every cast with the line fully extended and the rod tip practically touching the ground.

As the rod passes through the 45-degree position, begin your backcast. There should be no hesitation or "hitch" between your pickup and backcast.

BACKCAST

The backcast flows smoothly from the pickup, with the rod accelerating from a whimper at 45 degrees to an abrupt pop/stop just beyond vertical.

PAUSE

Let the line straighten behind you. Try to anticipate when the line will completely straighten behind you, and start your forward cast just before. You should not feel a tug when the line straightens behind you. If you do, your fly is either too heavy for casting practice or you neglected to tie on a leader.

Accelerate the rod to a pop/stop.

Pause to allow the line time to fully straighten behind you.

FORWARD CAST

This is the exact opposite of the backcast. Start slowly, accelerating to an abrupt stop, with the rod stopping about 45 degrees above the horizon. Remember, *the forward cast has no more and no less energy than the backcast.* It should move at the same speed and acceleration as the backcast.

Accelerate the rod forward to a pop/stop.

Stop the rod completely at the end of the forward cast. The loop of line flying off the tip is described in chapter 16.

PRESENTATION

After the rod has completely stopped at the end of the forward cast, let gravity lower the rod tip along with the line as it falls to the water. This is a gentle motion. You are simply allowing the tip to drop with the line. At the end of the presentation, the rod tip should nearly touch the ground. If your line is nearly straight on the ground in front of you, that's great! Keep doing it.

As the line unfurls and is pulled to the ground by gravity, slowly lower your rod tip to the ground. The tip should fall as the line falls.

Among other things, you may notice that your hand is lower after stopping the forward cast than after stopping the backcast. Don't worry; this is the way it should be.

At this stage, try not to practice more than 20 minutes at a time. Without a casting instructor present, your concentration may flag and you may develop some bad habits.

During the forward cast, your hand should travel down.

Why Is the Acceleration-to-a-Stop so Important?

When your backcast or forward cast is viewed from the side, the tip of your rod should appear to move in a straight line. By starting slowly and accelerating to a pop/stop, your rod tip will move this way. If you don't accelerate at the end, or if you accelerate only in the beginning and slow down to a stop, the rod tip will move in a lazy, convex path and the cast will be ineffective.

The progressive acceleration to an abrupt stop over a short arc is what makes the rod tip travel in a straight line and makes the cast successful.

This caster never accelerated the rod, so the tip didn't bend. The line followed the tip through the convex arc, resulting in a poor cast.

How Does Your Arm Make the Acceleration-to-a-Stop Happen?

During the cast, two things happen sequentially. As your forearm accelerates toward the stop, your rod bends (or "loads") against the weight of fly line in the air. What causes the rod to pop to a stop is that your wrist kicks in just a *little* bit at the end of your forearm's journey while the forearm twitches. Even though your wrist moves during the pop, it stops the rod just beyond vertical (backcast) and at 45 degrees above the horizon (forward cast). During a typical 45-foot backcast or forward cast, this sequence takes less than one second and should feel like one continuous motion. If you feel as if you are drowning in details right now, just move the rod from the start to the stop, starting slowly and speeding up to a pop/stop.

This is a wristy cast. The angler's rod is at the backcast stop, but his forearm is at the forward-cast stop. This casting style will severely limit your fly-fishing horizons.

PLAYING AROUND

Close your eyes: For some reason, many people cast better with their eyes closed. There are no visual distractions. Give it a try!

The line slam: Make a backcast and forward cast in which you try to make the line slam into the rod. The line probably won't hit the rod, but you will make a successful cast. This can be helpful if you've had trouble conceptualizing the pop/stop.

The belly cast: This is not some cruel joke to get your neighbors to laugh at you. First, lie down with the line pinned against the grip and fully extended in front of you. While leaning on your elbows, make some four-part casts. As always, start with the rod tip low to the ground, and make several four-part casts: *pickup, backcast, forward cast, presentation.* Keeping your elbows on the ground, remember to bring your forearm almost to vertical while accelerating to a pop/stop; point your thumb straight up at the backcast stop; pause; accelerate to a pop/stop during the forward cast; allow your forearm and rod to return to horizontal during the presentation. Yes, it sounds weird, but it's a really fun way to learn to cast with a minimum of wasted motion. It also proves that casting is the same whether you are wading in a river or fishing from a canoe or float tube.

Keeping your elbow on the ground at all times, make a belly cast. The backcast is the same as during a conventional four-part cast . . .

. . . as are the stop positions.

TROUBLESHOOTING

Videotaping yourself can be very helpful if you are having some troubles. The tape can expose most of the following errors to your view:

Five Common Problems

1. Why isn't the line straightening out in front?

- You may have forgotten to start every cast with the line fully extended on the ground, straight in front of you.
- You may be popping the rod too far back during your backcast. This will cast the line down toward the ground behind you and, consequently, up on the next forward cast. To fix this, attempt to stop your rod nearly vertically during the backcast, still with the pop/stop. Your next forward cast will then have a much better chance of straightening out.
- You may be pausing too long before you start your forward cast, which allows your backcast to fall near the ground. This sends your forward cast up high, and makes it fall in a heap.
- You may not be accelerating to a pop/stop at all, causing the rod tip to move too slowly at the end of the cast.
- You may be accelerating to a pop/stop with too much force, causing the line to bounce back after it has fully extended in the air.
- You may be starting your forward cast with too much speed, which sends the line up high in the air, and then into another heap. Remember, start slowly.

2. You hear a noise like a snapping bullwhip during your forward cast. This happens when you start your forward cast too soon, before the backcast has had time to fully straighten. To correct this, pause a little longer between the backcast and forward cast.

3. The line keeps hitting you or the rod. This usually happens because there is a crosswind blowing the line into you or the rod on either the forward cast or backcast. To fix it, rotate your body so the rod is on the downwind side of your body. Be sure to cast with the rod tilted slightly off to the side, away from vertical.

4. You hear a whooshing noise during the backcast. You are probably accelerating the backcast quickly rather than slowly. Start *slowly.* Remember that the rod goes fast only at the end of the cast, not at the beginning. You may also be moving the rod through a very long arc. Keep the casting arc short by stopping your backcast just *barely* beyond vertical.

5. Your casting hand is getting tired. Take a break. Massage your casting hand with your line hand. This may be a good time to start living dangerously—try casting with your *other* hand. For more about this, see *Playing Around* in chapter 15.

14 The Roll Cast

All the casts in this book feel good, but a roll cast has a special feeling. When I first started teaching casting, this was one cast that still didn't feel right to me: It took a lot of energy but yielded little in return. With practice and some guidance from another instructor, I soon had my roll casts leaping off the rod tip and unfurling above the water.

The roll cast is really a modified forward cast without a backcast: It's a four-part cast without the first two parts. You'll use it when you can't make a backcast because of obstructions behind you, or when your line is in a heap on water in front of you. It can also be used to pick up line from the water in preparation for a backcast (described in chapter 18). Many beginners treat this as a baby cast, but it isn't. You will use the roll cast countless times during a typical fishing day.

GETTING LINE ON THE WATER

Roll casts must have resistance to work properly. Unless you use a clipboard to hold the fly, you can't practice this successfully on the lawn. To get started on the water, pull line off the reel until you get a couple of feet past your 37-foot mark. With the leader, fly, and a few feet of line on the water, point your rod down at the water and make quick, aggressive sweeps of the rod, back and forth with the rod tip barely above the water. This motion is the same one we used earlier (in chapter 13) when we flexed the rod back and forth with no line—we moved the grip very little, while making the rest of the rod flex a lot. With a little line on the water, this will cause all the

Allagash River, Northern Maine

You are picking your way along the rocky, wooded shore of Maine's remote Allagash River. There is no room behind you for a backcast. Small brook trout are rising splashily to caddisflies emerging on the surface. You make short roll casts to them with your size 14 Elk-Hair Caddis on 4X tippet. This is only a vague imitation of what the fish are eating, but they are unsophisticated and rise to your fly with abandon. Brook trout have been in this remote river since the last ice age, but they look as if they just came from an expressionist painting. They have brilliant orange bellies and creamy white edges on their delicate fins. Their vermiculated flanks look like an artist's brooding abstraction. You catch many of them, and you have only read as far as the *Roll Cast* chapter in this book.

rest of the line to swish out through the guides onto the surface. Once you get the leader and tip of the line on the water, the whole operation should take no more than five seconds. Now pin the mark against the grip, leaving a 2-foot loop to hang between your rod hand and the reel.

For roll-casting on a lawn, use a clipboard to hold your practice fly. Otherwise, your roll casts will fall in a heap.

To set up for a roll cast, slowly drag the line and fly into position.

To get the line onto the water, keep the rod tip barely above the water and make long, aggressive snaps of the rod, back and forth.

SETUP

This is done *very slowly.* You are not making a backcast; you are gently moving the rod into position behind you to make the roll cast. To do it, draw the rod to the backcast position, but in ultra-slow motion. Your rod should move in a single plane, tilted slightly off to the side, just as during the standard pickup and backcast. The leader and fly never leave the water; they just get dragged slowly along the surface as you move the rod into the setup position. If you notice that your setup is causing the leader and fly to lift off the water, slow down your setup. The roll cast is easier if you raise your elbow somewhat, so your upper arm generally points toward the fish.

Move the rod to the backcast stop position. Raise your upper arm and point it out toward the fish. The rod and line form a tilted D.

PAUSE

Wait with the rod motionless at the back-cast-stop position for about three seconds until the line has stopped moving behind you. Before you come forward, you should see your rod and line form a D. (Look for a reverse D if you are left-handed.)

ROLL CAST

- As with the four-part cast, the rod should travel in the same plane throughout the cast; it should not curve or sweep to the side.
- Start forward very slowly by pulling *down* with your elbow and hand. As you do this, your forearm and rod should tilt forward. As your rod moves through the vertical position, accelerate hard to a pop/stop, somewhere near 45 degrees above the horizon.
- Compared to the forward casts you did earlier, the roll cast starts more gently but ends even more emphatically, with a harder pop/stop. This is because, unlike the forward cast, you have to make the line over-

Start by slowly pulling down with your elbow and hand to tilt the rod forward.

As your rod moves through the vertical position, accelerate hard.

The roll-cast pop/stop is even more emphatic than it is in the forward snap of a four-part cast. In particular, the pop feels like an electric pulse, a spasm of the forearm. Your hand may only travel 3 or 4 inches during this pop, or burst.

come the drag of the water before it gets airborne.

- When you finish, you should once again see your rod and your forearm pointing somewhere above the horizon, with your elbow very close to your body. As in thc four-part cast, a loop of line will fly off your rod tip immediately after the abrupt stop.

PRESENTATION

You've been here before. As the roll cast unfurls and the line falls, lower your rod tip along with it.

PLAYING AROUND

Off-shoulder roll cast: Remember in chapter 13, when you positioned yourself so that the rod was on the downwind side of any crosswind? Well, now that you are on the

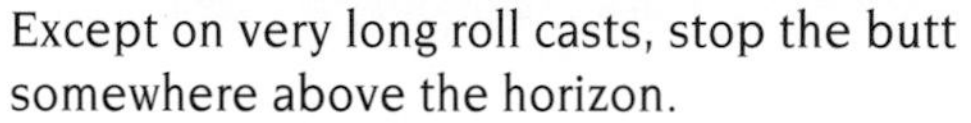
Except on very long roll casts, stop the butt somewhere above the horizon.

water, you don't have that luxury: The water is where it is. What you *can* change is where the tip of the rod travels. You can practice this even when there is no wind.

Imagine that you have a crosswind blowing from right to left. Tilt the rod over your head so the tip-top and the line travel on your downwind side. How? Instead of tilting your forearm

The end of the roll cast looks like the forward portion of a four-part cast because it is a forward cast, without a backcast.

For the off-shoulder roll cast, push your elbow out from your side and bring your hand in close to your ear. This will tilt your rod over the top of your head.

away from you while keeping your elbow in close to your side, do the opposite. Push your elbow out from your side and bring your hand in close to your ear. This will tilt your rod over the top of your head. This keeps your hand on your right side, where it is strongest, and puts the rod tip over your left shoulder. This position ensures that the wind will blow the line away from you instead of into you. Otherwise, the roll cast is done exactly as you did it before.

The two-handed roll cast turbocharges your roll cast. It's great when you're using a heavy outfit, when it's windy, or when you need a long cast.

Two-handed roll-casting: If you're struggling with the roll cast or your arm is just tired, you can use two hands to roll-cast. Simply put your left hand on the end of the rod and do the roll cast. You'll find it much easier to pop/stop the rod, and you may be dazzled by the results. I use two hands

Roll-Casting for Corporate CEOs and Other Overachievers

The Spey rod, named for a famous salmon river in Scotland, is a two-handed rod that enables skilled casters to roll-cast specialized lines beyond 80 feet! Done properly, it is beautiful to watch and enables its practitioners to reach distant salmon when fishing in front of a steep or wooded streambank. The physics are the same as with a typical roll cast, but the rod feels ungainly at first. The proper technique takes considerable patience to master. Like single-malt Scotch, Spey casting is an acquired taste.

Casting as Daydreaming

If all this casting detail seems mentally taxing, you're not alone. Except for the gifted few (I was not a member of this group), this is a lot to remember at first. But just like learning to drive a car, you'll notice that as you practice, you'll think less and less while you cast better and better. Eventually you'll find yourself daydreaming as you cast and fish, your mind drifting off into woods or up into sky. These times are often interrupted by the fish.

whenever I need to make a long roll cast. Also, this is a great technique for children, whose arms often lack the strength to accelerate and stop a rod properly during both the roll cast and the four-part cast.

TROUBLESHOOTING

Four Common Problems

1. The line piles in front of you. You either started the forward cast with too much acceleration before ending too slowly, or your pop came too late in the cast, driving the unfurling line down into the water instead of over the water.

2. Your line unrolls only partially. This probably means you need more energy throughout your forward stroke. Start the roll cast more forcefully, but remember that you need the abrupt pop at the end of the stroke.

3. It's windy. End your roll-cast stroke farther down, close to the horizon. This will help drive the cast under the wind, giving it less "sail area." When you do this, you'll need to make the first part of the stroke move a little faster than normal.

4. The line is hitting you or tangling on itself. Even if there is no wind, this can happen when the caster is positioned between the line and the path of the rod. For example, if you are trying to roll-cast the line straight out from your position while the line is to your left, a conventional roll cast will cause the line to hit you. Try it: You'll be kissed by a wet practice fly. To compensate, use the off-shoulder roll cast. Tilt your elbow out and your hand in, putting the rod tip over your left shoulder. Make the cast.

If you try to roll-cast the line straight out from your position while the line is to your left . . .

. . . the result will be ugly. Use the off-shoulder roll cast instead.

The Four-Part Cast on the Water

The four-part cast is the bread-and-butter cast, the one that trout guides pray their clients can make. As far as we can tell, the cast has not changed much since Dame Juliana Berners wrote the first fly-fishing book in 1496. It is, of course, easier to do this cast now, with modern rods and lines, than it was in her time. But learning it still requires patience and practice.

In this chapter, we build on what you have done in the previous three chapters. The only new twist is that you have to develop a smooth pickup from the water, one that transitions into a nearly vertical backcast.

STANCE

Imagine that you are at a party, talking to a 5-foot-tall fish. That's how you should stand.

PICKUP

Begin every pickup with the line fully extended, straight out in front of you, with the rod tip pointing down at the water. The pickup is much more important when you are lifting the line from the water than when you are lifting it from land. Water has surface tension that holds on to the line as you try to pick it up. The pickup requires you to *ease* the line *gently* from the water and transition smoothly into the backcast. Again, this will look and feel like one smooth motion. The

Yellowstone Lake, Northwestern Wyoming

You are standing on the shore of Yellowstone Lake in Yellowstone National Park. The surface of the huge lake is a boundless mirror, reflecting the volcanic mountains to the east. Large cutthroat trout cruise the shoreline searching and rising for *Callibaetis*, a speckled-wing mayfly. You are fishing with a size 16 Sparkle Dun and tiny 6X tippet. You make simple four-part casts of just 30 feet, then you watch your fly sit motionless on the mirror for a long time. You see rises here and there as you wait, watching your fly. You gaze up at the mountains in the distance. There is a noise, a disturbance where your fly was sitting, so you raise the rod tip to set the hook, but the fish is already gone. They will be rising for hours. It is a beautiful day.

Begin every pickup with the line fully extended and the rod tip nearly touching the water.

From a gentle pickup, transition smoothly into the backcast.

motion is just as it was on land except that your rod will now bend more against the drag of the water on the line. The pickup ends and the backcast begins the moment you see the end of the fly line lift off the water, usually when your rod is pointing about 45 degrees above the water.

The backcast, forward cast, and presentation are exactly the same over the water as they are over the lawn. Do as many repetitions of this four-part cast as you can.

Watch the practice fly land on the water with the line fully extended. If it's not fully extended, see *Troubleshooting*.

Accelerate the rod . . .

. . . to an abrupt stop. Pause to allow the line to unfurl behind you.

The Sound of Silence

Most good fly casts are virtually silent. If you hear a tearing sound during the pickup, a whooshing sound during the backcast, or a whistling sound during your forward cast, see *Troubleshooting* at the end of this chapter.

Accelerate the forward cast to a pop/stop about 45 degrees above the horizon.

Gently lower the rod tip, along with the falling line, to the water.

INVERT THE REEL

This is a test to make sure you are using your forearm in the cast. Simply invert the reel and make some casts with it butting up against the underside of your forearm. (Make sure the reel touches your forearm at the backcast stop.) Actually, you could have snuck this far into the learning process by casting mostly with your wrist. This would be fine if you never planned to fish anything heavier than a 5-weight and never planned to cast more than 45 feet. In short, it limits your fishing horizons. Casting with the inverted reel forces you to get in the habit of bending at the elbow and casting with your forearm.

What Do the Start and Stop Feel Like?

During the **backcast,** you'll pull against your index finger and push against the butt of your hand. When you make the **backcast stop,** your thumb enforces the stop. The backcast stop should look as if your rod has hit an invisible wall. Your thumb and two smallest fingers make that wall.

During the **forward cast,** you'll push with your thumb and pull with your two smallest fingers. At the **forward-cast stop,** stop the rod with your index finger and the butt of your hand. A good way to feel this is to pantomime with the unrigged rod again.

Your thumb and two smallest fingers enforce the backcast stop. They keep the rod from tipping back farther. The backcast stop should look as if your rod has hit an invisible wall.

Your index finger and the butt of your hand enforce the forward-cast stop.

The Power Snap or Pop/Stop

Fly rods have become stiffer over the years as a result of changing preferences and the advent of space-age materials, so the transition from slow to pop/stop has become more abrupt. When my students put their hands on mine to get the feel of how I cast, some of them say that the pop/stop feels like a jerk. If we were using the old bamboo rods, they would feel a more gradual final acceleration. They might then say, "It feels as if you're speeding up and then stopping." If you're curious about how this would feel, cast an 8-weight fly line on a 5-weight rod. The relatively heavy 8-weight line will cause the light 5-weight rod to bend more and react more slowly to your casting motion than a 5-weight line would.

> **What About Watching Your Backcast?**
>
> Advanced casters will sometimes watch their backcast to improve their casts. They are able to turn their heads to watch without being distracted. They know what they are looking for in their backcast and can use what they learn from seeing only one backcast to improve the next one. On the other hand, novice casters already have a lot on their minds and are unlikely to benefit from this yet. Among novices the practice can lead to the unconscious habit of repeatedly looking at some nebulous area up in the sky for the purpose of "watching the backcast." This complicates the cast. Once you have mastered the double haul and can comfortably cast beyond 60 feet, you can learn a lot from watching your backcast. Until then, avoid it.

PLAYING AROUND

Cast with your other hand: This is not only a good way to rest your casting arm but also a great way to learn.

Strange but true, most fly casters are better casters with their off hands than with their dominant hands. That is, they make more elegant casts than they do with their dominant hands. Why? Your off hand is a clean slate. It has no bad casting habits, no bad golf-swing habit, no tennis memory. It is a true novice. It usually learns to cast faster and better than your dominant arm. Once it does so, it trains the other side to do better. How? Only your cognitive psychologist knows for sure. But it is a joy to watch our fly-fishing school students cast beautifully with their off hand after protesting, "I can't do *anything* with my left hand." This may sound like New Age logic, but you *have* to try it!

Close your eyes: This is another New Age drill that works. Like casting with the other hand, it leads many novice casters to breakthroughs. It will let you fish with confidence at night, when big striped bass and brown trout are feeding heavily. Again, you just *have* to try this!

Use two hands: Pin the line against the grip, put your left hand on the butt end, and cast with two hands as you did with two-handed roll-casting. Notice how easy it is to accelerate the rod to a pop/stop.

To ensure that you are casting primarily with your forearm, try casting with the reel butting up against the underside of your forearm. Make sure the reel stays there at the backcast stop.

TROUBLESHOOTING

Six Common Problems

1. Your fly lands after the line has landed. So what? The fish don't notice and, more important, they don't care. The notion that the fly must land before the line does is folklore, probably invented by someone who wanted to exclude newcomers from the sport. (That said, it's *fun* to make the fly land before the line, and there is one very specialized fishing situation that calls for it. To learn how, see *Playing Around* in chapter 16.)

2. Your line isn't extending fully. This one is serious. See *Troubleshooting* in chapter 13.

3. Your leader looks as if it's been attacked by a cat. It's kinky and riddled with wind knots and your casts aren't straightening out. It's time to attach a new leader with either a nail knot or loop-to-loop connection. (The nail knot is better for casting and fishing, but the loop-to-loop is easier to do.) Or for more options, see part 1, *Fly Fishing*, beginning on page 30.

Differences in Casting Style

The more you cast and fish, the more you'll see fly fishers who don't cast the way you do. In fact, judging by what you've learned in these pages, you'll see many whose casting looks all wrong. They use too little forearm or they move their elbows or shoulders a lot. They may bring the rod back too far during the backcast or drive the rod down to the horizon during the forward cast. Many of them struggle to get the fly to the fish. But you'll notice that some of these people who cast "incorrectly" nonetheless get the line to lay out beautifully on the water. They have learned how to compensate for inefficiencies in their casting style. Or maybe they never liked the feel of the most efficient cast. Maybe they just like to move their bodies more than you or I do while they fish. The difference between what they do and what you do is just that you are more efficient than they are: You cast with less energy and less effort than they do. They have become comfortable with their casting style, even though their casts burn more calories than yours do. This doesn't mean that they are less effective than you, however. I've seen countless ugly casts yield beautiful fish. Most important, these anglers love fishing just as much as you do.

This is not the intended result.

An abrupt pickup has ripped line and water from the surface, making a hissing, tearing sound. If you hear this sound, ease the line up from the water and transition smoothly into the backcast. Wait until you see the tip of the fly line lift off the water before you start the backcast.

4. You hear a tearing or ripping sound during the pickup. It is common for beginners to try to yank or rip the line up off the water. A good test of whether your pickup is too fast is when you hear the line come off the water. An abrupt pickup makes a tearing or hissing sound as the line chaotically rips water from the surface. If you hear this sound, slow down your pickup. *Ease* the line up from the water, and transition smoothly into the backcast just as you see the tip of the fly line lift off the water. Practice overcompensation; pick up the line too slowly. Do it again and again. Get used to the sound of silence as you pick up the line.

5. You hear a whooshing noise during the backcast. You are probably beginning the backcast too abruptly. Start *slowly.* Remember that the rod goes fast only at the end of the cast, not at the beginning. You may also be moving the rod through a very long arc. Keep the casting arc short by stopping your backcast at a point barely past vertical.

6. You hear a whistling or hissing noise during the forward cast. This should only happen when you are casting ultra-long distances. If you hear a hiss during a 45-foot cast, you need to slow down your forward cast. Remember that it should travel at the same speed as your backcast. Practice overcompensation: Make a forward cast that has all the correct hand, arm, and rod positions and that has the pop/stop, but that moves *too* slowly. Make your forward cast so slow that the line coming off the rod tip can't fully unfurl in front. Practice this until your typical forward cast quiets down.

16 False-Casting

This is the beauty cast, the signature cast of our sport, appearing to nonanglers as a waving back and forth of the rod and line. In fact, *false cast* is a misnomer. This is a true cast, but it is made in the air and not presented to the fish. It is simply a backcast and forward cast repeated without interruption by a presentation.

We use a false cast to:

- Blow-dry a waterlogged fly.
- Perform an in-air change of our fishing direction.
- Lengthen the cast in the air (when combined with the shooting technique you'll learn in the next chapter).

A false cast can be performed anywhere: It is as lovely on a grassy lawn as on a rumbling river.

In this chapter you'll learn how to false-cast, and how to use that as a stepping-stone to longer casts. You'll also learn about the loop of line that you flick off the rod tip each time you stop the rod. (In false-casting you make a lot of these loops quickly.) Finally, you'll enjoy the hypnotic rhythm of false-casting: Time seems to be suspended while you are practicing it.

San Juan River, New Mexico

You are fishing the San Juan River in northern New Mexico. It holds 20,000 big, fat rainbow trout per mile, and it seems that most of them are rising right in front of you. Predictably, there is a steady emergence of tiny, size 20 *Baetis* mayflies on this snowy noon in January; your Sparkle Dun is a good imitation. Even though there is ice in your guides, your 8½-foot 3-weight rod, 11-foot leader, and 6X tippet allow you to rhythmically place your fly upstream of the rainbow snouts sipping insects in the surface film.

You've just caught your second fish; the fly has become waterlogged during the struggle. Your hands are too cold to tie on a new fly, one that's dry and buoyant. Instead, you false-cast a few times to shake some water off the fly, then place it in front of the feeding rainbows. The fly is barely floating. A fish takes it but you try to set the hook too quickly and miss. The fly starts to sink. A few more aggressive false casts dry out the fly just enough so you can get one more good drift and a shot at just one more fish. That's all you ask, just one more.

HOW TO FALSE-CAST

- Pin the line against the grip at the 37-foot mark.
- Keeping the rod tilted slightly off to the side, make your usual pickup; ease the

By slowly rotating your body as you make a series of three false casts, you can move the fly from the position in figure 1 to the position in figure 6, while preventing the fly and line from slapping the water.

line off the water and accelerate to your normal pop/stop backcast.

- After the stop, freeze your rod. (Do not let it creep forward during the pause.) Then make your forward cast—it is an exact reversal of the backcast.
- After the rod stops on the forward cast, freeze your rod in that position. Keep it motionless until you see the leader almost fully unfurl in front of you.
- Just before the leader is about to straighten, make your backcast, accelerating to your habitual pop/stop, making sure to stop your backcast *exactly* where you stop all your other backcasts.
- Continue this for a total of three false casts—three backcasts and three forward casts.
- As the third successive forward cast is unfurling, make the presentation, lowering

the rod tip to the water exactly as you have done many times before. Your fly should not have touched the water during the false casts.

Your last forward cast should stop exactly where your first forward cast did, just where it does during the four-part cast. Remember, all backcasts and forward casts during false-casting have the same amount of energy and acceleration as they do in your four-part casts. *All* your backcasts and forward casts should stop in the same place as they do in your four-part casts.

Some people freak out and seem to lose body control during false-casting. When the line is in the air, they feel like Atlas holding up the world. If this sounds like you:

- Relax and take a deep breath before you start.

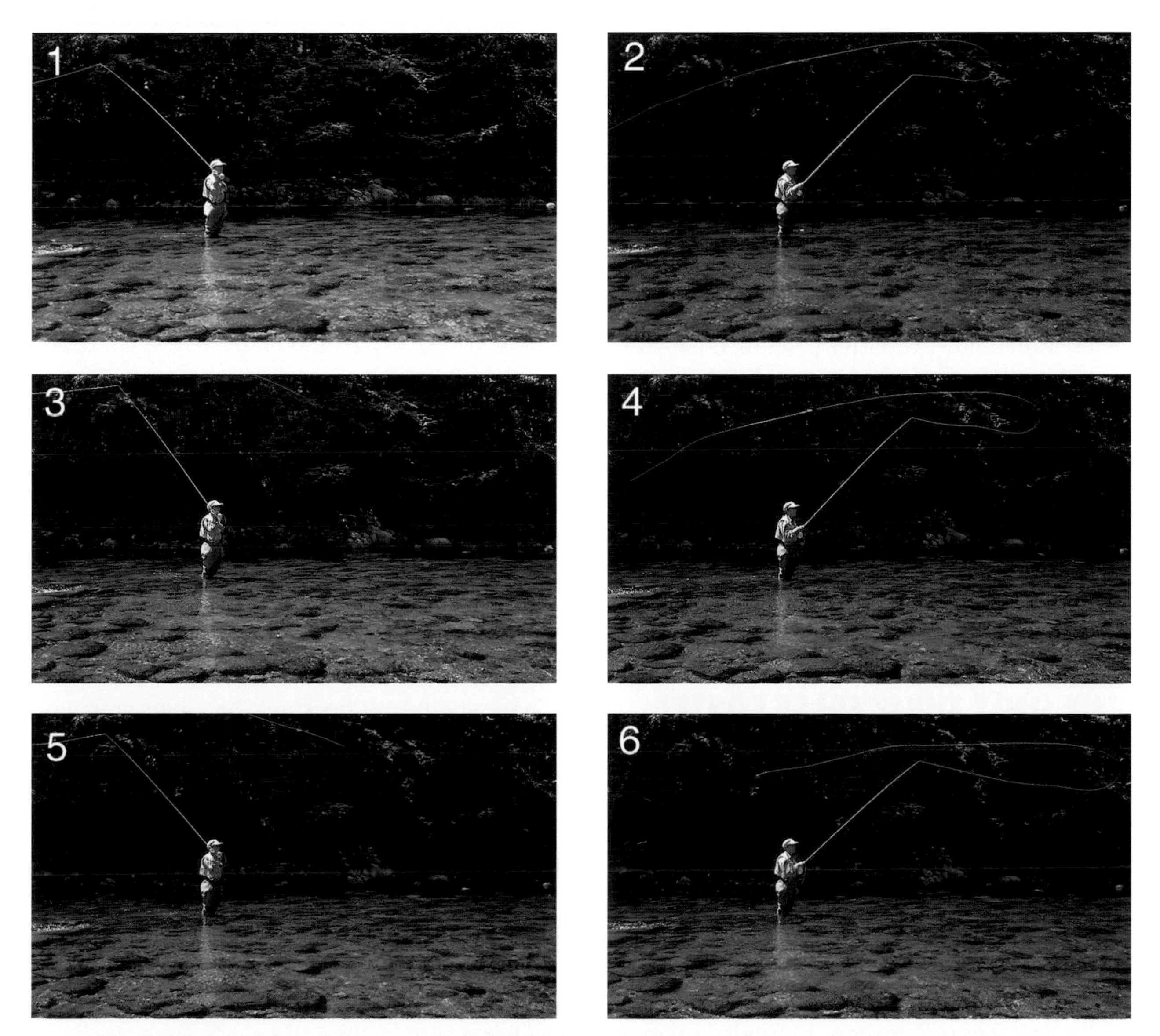

Here is a series of three false casts. Until you begin to shoot line in the next chapter, every backcast, as shown in figures 1, 3, and 5, should stop in the same place, as should every forward cast, as in figures 2, 4, and 6.

- As usual, keep the rod tilted slightly away from you.
- Concentrate on just making the next cast; don't worry about the line. Don't think about keeping the line up in the air. You just have to keep making the next cast.
- Freeze the rod after each stop to let the line unfurl, just as you did in the four-part cast.
- Just before the line fully straightens, make the next cast.
- If the cast blows up, that's okay. You're fly casting and entropy sometimes wins.

- You may find it easier to pantomime the false cast with only your hand before you try it again with a rigged rod.

Remember that learning means making lots of mistakes, so be patient when false-casting. Just keep at it, taking deep breaths or laughing when you get fouled up. Walk yourself through the instructions again if things aren't going well. Now may be a good time to set up the video camera to help analyze what you're doing, as discussed in the next chapter.

A Minimalist Goes Fly Casting

Minimalism is elegance. It is casting with a quiet body, one that wastes no motion on the cast. So teach your muscles to do the least possible to make each false cast. If you can teach them do very little now, they will have room to do much more when you learn to cast longer distances.

Why Only Three False Casts?

You should keep things simple, especially in the beginning. To false-cast incessantly is to invite entropy, the principle of physics that tells us things ultimately fall apart. It's like playing with fire: It can be alluring and mesmerizing but eventually you *will* get burned. The line may hit the rod, tangle on itself, or just self-destruct. When you are fishing with a real hook on the leader, there is an even greater chance of this happening. So in the beginning, limit yourself to three false casts.

There is another good reason to do this. When fishing, there is rarely a need to make more than three or four false casts. If you get into the habit of limiting your false casts on the water, you will be a more effective fly fisher, because your fly will spend less time in the air with the birds and more time in the water with the fish. When you learn to shoot line in the next chapter, your limit of three false casts will, paradoxically, help you achieve greater distance per cast: The fewer chances you give yourself to move the rod, the more line you will make yourself shoot on each cast to reach your target.

The Line Hand Debuts

You're about to make a leap here. Start holding the line in your left hand, not pinned against the grip. For obvious reasons, this is now called your *line hand*. Your hands should be separated by 12 to 18 inches, and there should be roughly an 18-inch belly of slack hanging between your line hand and the reel. There should be no slack between your line hand and the first stripping guide. Make some four-part casts and then some false casts while holding the line in this manner. Be sure to keep the same spacing between your hands throughout the cast; do not separate your hands during the backcast and reunite them during the forward cast. This will prevent the fly line from sliding up through the guides at the wrong time during the forward cast, which would reduce the cast's success. Prac-

Begin to cast with the line in your left hand, not pinned against the grip. Keep the same spacing between your hands throughout the cast.

tice holding the line through the entire cast. *Do not* let it slide through your fingers (that's for the next chapter). Get accustomed to this—it is what much of real trout fishing is all about.

TIP CASTING

If you need to cast your fly a mere 25 feet to a rising trout, you will need to learn to cast just by flexing the tip of the rod against the short section of fly line in the air. This will feel like just a little flick of the rod tip at the end of the backcast and forward cast. Hold the line in your line hand, not pinned against the grip. Make the pickup as usual, but make a very short backcast. You'll hardly need to move your forearm at all: You can use your wrist almost exclusively if that's comfortable. Practice these as four-part casts, and then as sets of three false casts. Practice minimalism. Do the least possible to flip the tip (pop the stop) and send the loop of line on its way. Practice doing *too little*, so little that even the 25-foot cast doesn't straighten out in front. Then increase the energy of your stroke so the line and leader just barely

In a tip cast, move the rod through a very short arc and just barely flip the rod tip. Do the least possible to flip the tip (pop the stop) and send the loop of line on its way. Notice how high the rod points at the stop.

What Is the Loop?

When you watch someone else cast, you'll see a bend or loop of line fly off the rod tip after each stop of the backcast, forward cast, and roll cast. This loop is the vehicle for the line's progress. Its unfurling is what straightens the line behind and in front. When you hear someone say, "You throw a nice loop," that is a high compliment. If they say, "You throw a tight loop," you've really arrived. The smaller the distance between the top and bottom of the loop, the tighter the loop is said to be. Other things being equal, the tighter your loop, the better able you will be to cast into the wind and to cast longer distances.

A tight-loop backcast.

A tight-loop forward cast. If you can make tight loops, you'll have a great fly-fishing life.

A wide-loop backcast.

A wide-loop forward cast. A loop like this makes fishing difficult.

unfurl. It will feel as if you are cheating, that casting *can't* require so little energy and motion in the rod.

MIDSECTION CASTING

This is what you've been practicing all this time. Hold the line in your line hand, not pinned against the grip. Make three false casts followed by a presentation. If your rod and line are properly matched, a 45-foot cast should load the rod into the midsection, and you'll feel it bending more than it did during the tip cast. You should notice that your arm, hand, and rod have to travel farther to successfully make the cast. *The longer the cast, the farther back the rod must travel during the backcast and the farther forward it must travel during the forward cast.*

A typical 45-foot cast requires that the rod move through a longer arc, bending into its midsection.

The loop from a midsection cast is wider than the loop from a tip cast.

CASTING A REAL FLY

Up until now you've been casting a practice fly made of yarn. A fly with a hook usually weighs more than the yarn. You'd think a heavier fly would be easier to cast than something nearly weightless, but the opposite is true. It is dramatically more difficult to cast a big fly or a "heavy" fly, such as one that incorporates lead to make it sink, than a small, light fly.

In fly casting, the weight of your line needs to be such that it "bosses around" your feather of a fly. If the feather is weighed down, it tends a have a mind of its own as the loop unfurls, and it tends to boss the line around instead. What does this mean to you? *When you first start fishing, use the smallest unweighted fly that is reasonable for the fish you will catch.* Unless you are breezing through the casts in this book, don't tie on a size 8 Woolly Bugger, because it will probably be unruly when you cast and fish it.

If you are after trout or panfish, try using a dry fly such as a size 14 Adams or Royal Wulff. In the next chapter you'll learn how to animate your fly, and you can start swimming a nymph such as a size 14 Gold-Ribbed Hare's Ear or Pheasant Tail. These flies will get you started safely. As your casting improves, you can move to the larger, weightier flies. (Casting seriously heavy flies is described in chapter 20.)

Even expert fly rodders cringe when the fish require them to cast heavy flies. Add wind to the mix, and these flies will eventually hit anybody in the vicinity. It feels like getting shot by a BB gun, and it's one reason you should always wear glasses and a hat while fly fishing. I once fished with a guide in breezy Belize who said he often worked in a thick wool sweater (despite the steamy-hot tropical climate). When I asked him why, he replied, simply, "Bad fly casters, mon." His clients weren't necessarily bad casters, but they were fishing weighted flies in windy conditions.

PLAYING AROUND

Make 20 or 30 consecutive false casts. Why not? Live dangerously. Once you have mastered the three-false-cast series, you have a license to practice perpetual false-casting. *This is perhaps the single fastest way to progress as a caster.* It builds muscle memory faster than the four-part cast, and it tends to expose any casting flaws. Yes, it can lead to bad fishing habits by keeping the fly out of reach of the fish. But it sure feels good, and if the fish have to wait for the fly because you like to cast it back and forth in the air, picturing yourself as the graceful caster in your own fly-fishing movie, so be it.

Shadow Casting

Near my house in Maine is a college whose great expanse of playing fields is surrounded by tall pines. Sometimes, when the sun is just peeking over the pines, a fly caster is seen there. Turning himself so the sun illuminates his left side, he false-casts, watching to the right his stop positions in shadows on the grass or snow. Unlike the videotape, the shadows show him instantly how he is casting. He likes the simplicity of it, thinking Thoreau would have preferred it this way.

Practice casting tight loops and wide loops. During your series of 20 or 30 false casts, make your loops as tight as you can, then widen them. To go from tight to wide, lengthen your casting arc—that is, make your rod stops occur farther apart. You can also do this by easing off or softening your pop/stops.

Experiment with your casting style. Now is a good time to play with the elbow lift. Remember in chapter 13, when you learned that you can elevate your elbow during the backcast? Maybe you chose to adopt that style over the elbow-at-your-side style for short to medium-length casts. Continuous false-casting is a great way to try the alternative to see if it suits you. Holding the mark in your line hand, make a few false casts with your elbow relaxed at your side. Then make some with your elbow rising and falling 3 or 4 inches with each casting stroke. Keep doing the one that feels and works best.

Make the presentations at random. This is a fun exercise! Have a friend watch you false-cast and periodically say "Now" during a forward cast. At that time, complete the forward cast as usual with the abrupt stop and the rod pointing at the usual 45 degrees above the horizon. Then make the presentation. This forces you to make every forward cast identical to the preceding one, because you never know when it will be your last. It's a great cure for "last-cast-itis," the disease that makes casters think the last forward cast must be more powerful than the ones that preceded it.

Make the fly land before the line. Trout fishers sometimes use this cast when fishing eddies in fast water. It allows the fly to get the longest possible natural drift in the eddy before the fast water drags the line and fly away. It's also just plain fun. Cast in a vertical plane and stop your backcast nearly straight up. Then make your forward cast a little more powerful than normal and stop the rod a little closer to vertical than normal. Done correctly, this will cause your fly to touch the water just as the leader unfurls. The fly therefore gets to the water before the line has had time to fully descend. It works best with heavier flies or with short, stout leaders and short casts. Again, be patient. This technique is best practiced without presentations, during continuous false-casting. Try to make the fly kiss the surface at the end of each forward cast. Later, you'll learn the curve cast, which is this same cast made in a horizontal plane.

TROUBLESHOOTING

Two Common Problems

1. The line seems to be flying right at your face during the backcast. Keep the rod tilted off to the side and make sure that you are properly positioned in any crosswind, as you learned in chapter 13.

2. It's just not working—your forward cast isn't extending fully. This usually happens for one of four reasons:

- You forgot to pop/stop on your forward cast, your backcast, or both.
- Your backcast stopped progressively farther and farther beyond vertical. It should stop in the same spot every time.
- You didn't wait for the line to straighten behind you or in front of you before starting your next cast. Make a longer pause before you start the next cast.
- Your last forward cast is too strong, stronger than the preceding ones. Make every forward cast a clone of the previous one; each one should have the same amount of energy.

To land the fly first, before the line, make your forward cast a little more powerful than normal and stop the rod a little closer to vertical than normal.

17 Lengthening Your Cast (Stripping + Shooting + False-Casting)

Stop here if you have no predatory instincts, because the next technique is going to cause *a lot* of fish to bite your fly. Most fish bite things that move. A little pseudo-animal (your fly) moving through the water looks like lunch to trout, bass, pike, walleye, striped bass, bonefish, tuna, you name it. If you can move your fly through the water for 20 feet and repeatedly cast it back to where you started, you can go almost anywhere on this earth and catch fish. If you can move it through 30 or 40 feet of water, over and over again, hundreds of times a day, you'll be positively dangerous.

So far, you have learned to cast the fly onto the water with the roll cast and the four-part cast, to pick it up, cast it again, and to false-cast it. In this chapter you are going to learn how to animate your fly, to make it come alive, by stripping (pulling) it toward you. This is a critical, but easy, stage in your evolution as a fly fisher. Once you strip line in, you'll need to extend it back out. This is done in the air by allowing line to shoot through the guides after each forward-cast stop. Shooting is not difficult; it just takes practice. Along with double hauling, it will be the great leap forward in your fly fishing.

Some Words About Distance

It is fun, but not practical, to cast an entire 80- or 90-foot fly line with a fly on the end. It is rarely necessary to cast more than 60 feet. Still, being able to do so gives you the tools you need to fish in some pretty difficult conditions. If you want to make casts longer than 50 feet, be sure to use a line with a weight-forward taper. Because of its extra weight and thickness beyond 50 feet, a double taper is not suitable for long casts.

CLEAN YOUR LINE. NOW!

It is imperative that you have a clean fly line when you learn to shoot. A clean line will run freely through the guides and out toward the fish. A dirty line will drag through the guides and simply won't shoot well. This is just as frustrating for an advanced fly fisher as it is for a novice. At the L.L. Bean Fly-Fishing Schools, we used to clean the lines

Blue River, Indiana

You are in a kick boat, in stocking-foot waders with fins on your feet, floating the Blue River in southern Indiana. You've heard that people fish here for things like red ear sunfish, smallmouth bass, and rock bass. Live crayfish are the bait of choice among local anglers. You are fishing your trusty black Woolly Bugger on your 9-foot 6-weight rod. You are making 50-foot casts to submerged logs and rocks, and to places where the water is a deep green and has cut away the banks beneath the sycamore trees. You are animating the fly back toward your boat with 1-foot strips, bringing it in about 25 feet with each retrieve. Then you make your pickup and three successive false casts, shooting some line with each forward stroke so that the fly extends back to about 50 feet. You do this for hours, shooting line on each false cast and stripping the fly back toward you. Every few minutes a goggle-eyed rock bass, with its oversized red eyes, bites your fly. And if it's not a rock bass, it's a pumpkinseed, with its brilliant orange and blue hues. Occasionally a feisty little smallmouth attacks your fly. The fishing is good and you think about how many waters there are to fish and how you'll never live long enough to fish them all.

Float tubing is a great way to fish waters too small for a powerboat or too windy for a canoe. Notice that the backcast stop is the same in a float tube as it is when you are standing.

every day before we taught shooting. We now use lines with a coating that all but eliminates the need to clean the line. If your line lacks this technology, you should clean it often.

ESTABLISH TWO-POINT CONTROL

Start by holding the 37-foot mark in your line hand, with the line straight on the water. Bring your line hand directly to your rod hand and transfer the line to your rod hand. Pin the line loosely against the grip while continuing to hold line with your other hand. This is called two-point control, because you have control of the line with both hands. When you are fishing and the line is on the water, you should *always* have two-point control. This will enable you to retrieve the fly, and to begin to retrieve the fish once you hook it.

When you are about to cast, release the line from the grip and hold it in your line hand for the cast. You should not have two-point control during any part of the cast. Once the cast is back on the water, reestablish two-point control. Yes, this conflicts with what you learned in earlier chapters, but pinning the line against the grip was recommended initially to make learning as easy as possible. Now you'll need to unlearn that technique to cast and fish in the real world.

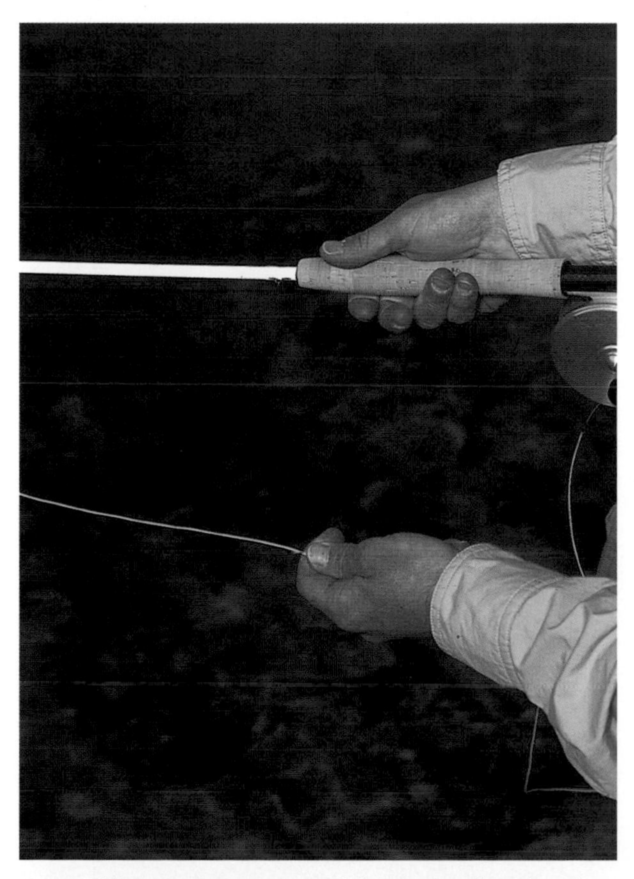

To establish two-point control, bring your line hand directly to your rod hand . . .

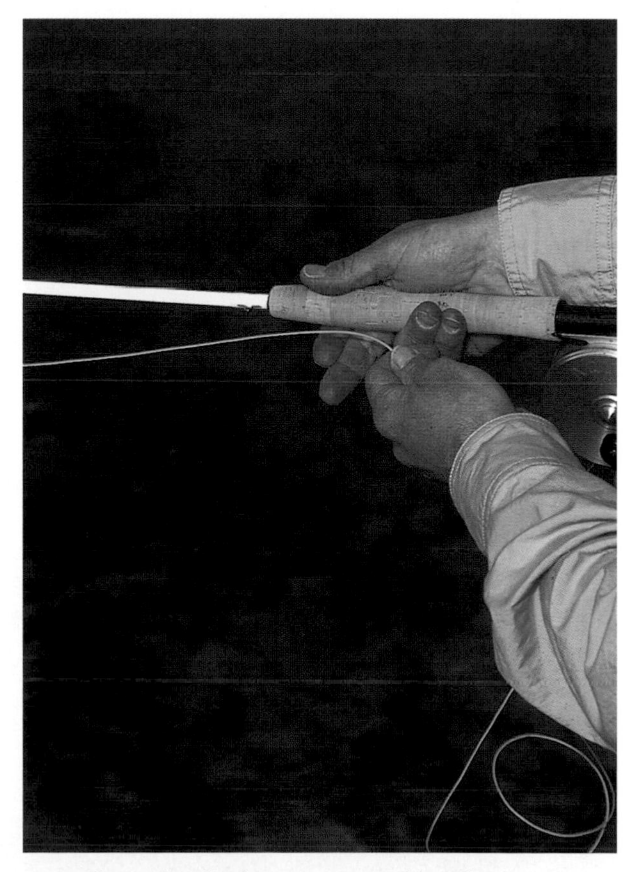

. . . and transfer the line to your rod hand.

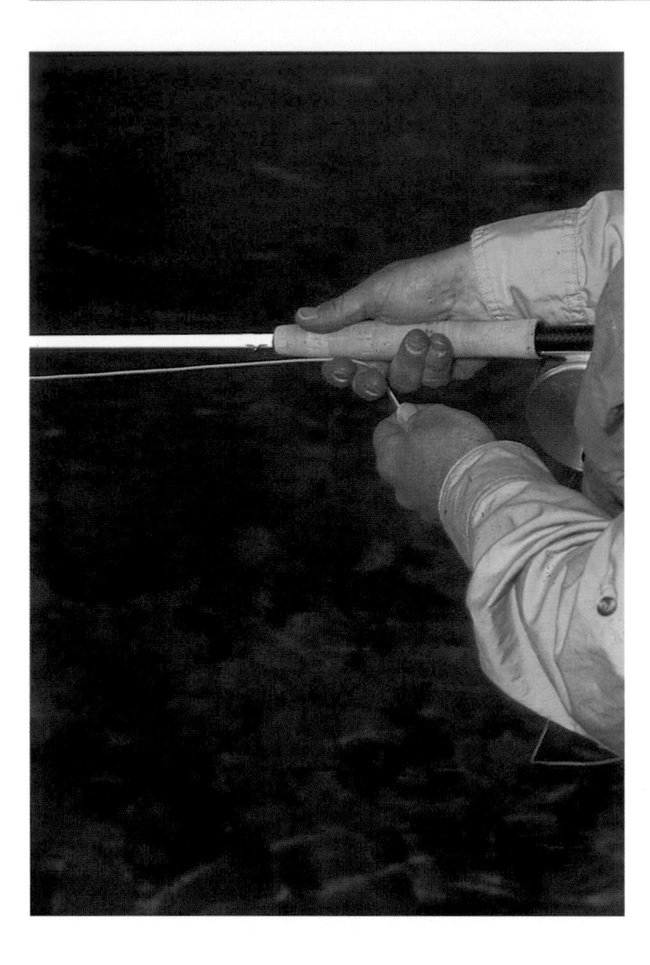

You should establish two-point control whenever the line is on the water. It gives you control of the line with both hands.

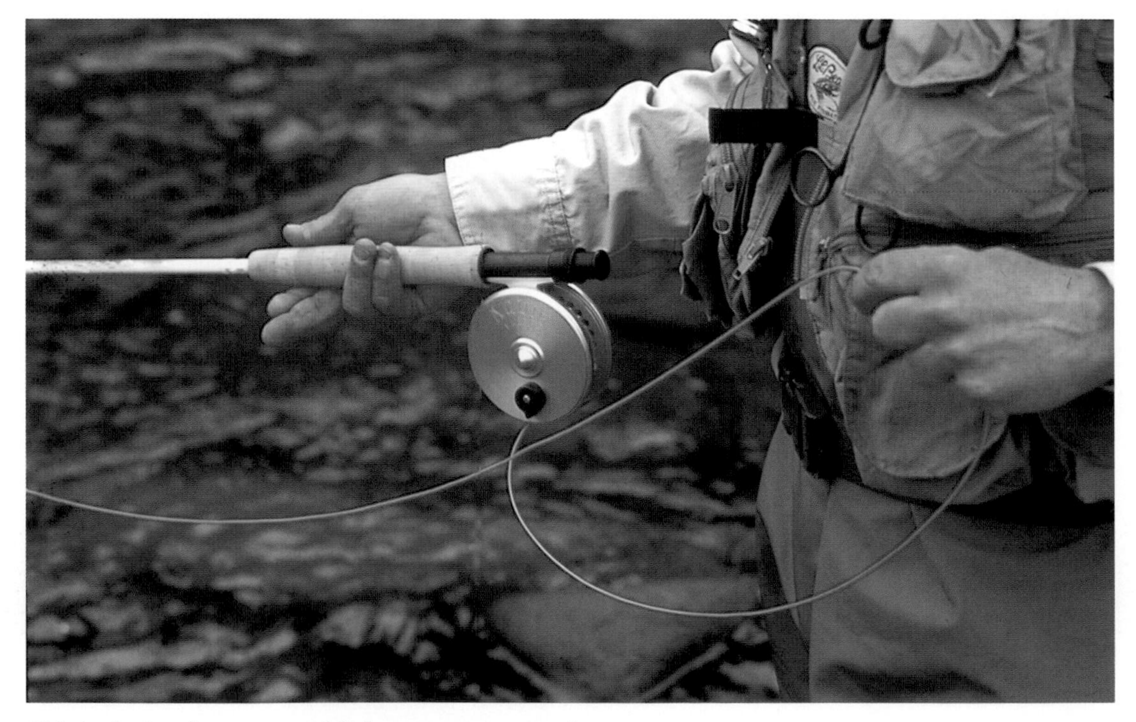

This is the hard way to establish two-point control.

STRIPPING WITH TWO-POINT CONTROL

Make sure your rod is pointing *down* at the water when you do this. (Many advanced fly fishers actually put the tip in the water while stripping line.) In your practice so far, when you've pinned the line against the grip, you've had a 2-foot length of line hanging down between your rod hand and the reel. Start this sequence from that position.

- Using your line hand, grasp the line hanging just below your rod hand (you now have two-point control) and pull 18 inches of line through the space between the fingers of your rod hand and the grip. (Don't use more than two fingers on your rod hand for this.) Allow the line to slide freely through your rod hand. This is called stripping.
- Drop the 18 inches of line you just stripped with your line hand and pick it up again just below the fingers of your rod hand. Pull another 18 inches of line through the fingers of your rod hand.
- Repeat this over and over again until you have pulled in most of the line.

Again, point your rod *down* at the water when you do this. You can see that if you keep doing this, you will pull any slack out of the line and your fly will "swim" toward you. Stripping with a low rod tip is how a fly should be animated, not by pumping or twitching the rod as a spin fisher would. This is also the best position from which to detect a fish biting a subsurface, out-of-sight fly, and from which to then set the hook.

Practice stripping by pulling the line straight back and away from your line hand versus pulling the line straight down from your rod hand. This will protect the fingers of your rod hand from getting line burns. In saltwater fly fishing, for example, you may strip

Stripping straight down is comfortable for most fishing . . .

. . . but to prevent line burns when stripping fast, pull the line back rather than down from your line hand.

Why Should the Rod Tip Be so Close to the Water?

There's a good casting reason: When you start the pickup with the rod tip by the water, you have more potential distance in which to make a smooth pickup and good backcast. On the other hand, a good trout-fishing position when you want your fly to drift naturally ("dead drift") in the current is with the rod up in the air. But this compresses the arc in which the rod can make the pickup and backcast, making those parts of a cast more difficult for a beginner.

Trout fishing from the dead-drift position. With practice, you will be able to make a pickup from this position.

There's a good fishing reason for keeping the tip low: When you are stripping your fly through the water with the rod tip low, there is no slack to diminish your retrieve, so every twitch of your line hand translates directly into the swimming of your fly. Also, when a fish strikes, the absence of slack lets you make the strongest possible hook-set, if needed.

Keeping the rod tip low helps you achieve not only a good pickup but also good fly response to stripping, sensitive strike detection, and solid hook-sets.

the fly with fast, 3-foot-long pulls through many hundreds of yards of water in a day. This technique of pulling straight back can help you avoid some real pain. You usually don't make such long or fast strips in trout or bass fishing, so it's less painful to strip down instead of back in those types of fishing.

PREPARING TO SHOOT

- Starting with the mark in your line hand and the line straight on the water, establish two-point control, and strip in 3 feet of line.
- From your line hand, drop the portion you just stripped; then grasp the line again just below the fingers of your rod hand.
- Holding the line in your line hand, release the line from the grip *before* you make the pickup. From now on, *always release the line from the grip before you make a pickup* (thereby releasing two-point control). This will help you immensely with shooting and, eventually, with double hauling (see chapter 19).

HOW TO SHOOT

Begin your usual four-part cast. The pickup and backcast are unchanged. When shooting, however, the forward cast requires a tiny bit more energy in the pop/stop than usual. (Most casters overpower their casts unknowingly, even when they aren't shooting.) The *instant after* you stop your forward cast, release your hold on the line and let it slide through your fingers and up through the guides. The momentum of the unfurling loop will pull the slack between your line hand and reel out through the guides. The presentation is as always—while the line falls to the water, allow the rod tip to fall with it.

If you started by stripping in 3 feet from your mark, all 3 feet of line should have shot out through the guides. In the beginning, practice shooting line only at the end of the forward cast. Later, as you progress, you'll find that you can also shoot line at the end of the backcast.

Many casters mistakenly try to help the shooting of line by overpowering the forward

The instant after you stop your forward cast, release your hold on the line and let it slide through your fingers and up through the guides.

False Casting + Shooting = The Road to Bliss

I was once fishing a small lake in Wyoming that had a well-deserved reputation for large rainbows and cutthroats. There were a few other anglers on the water who, like me, were in float tubes. I was having outstanding fishing with my good old black Woolly Bugger, casting it out 50 feet and retrieving it erratically to within a few feet of the rod tip. In the pellucid mountain water, I could see the fish following it and being antagonized into striking by the long, stuttering retrieve.

The other anglers around me seemed unable to false-cast and shoot line, so they couldn't cast the fly back out after such a retrieve. They were either making four-part casts or trolling. They didn't catch much. If they could only have done what you are about to do here, they could have had much better fishing that day.

cast, by moving the rod in a longer arc toward the horizontal, or by trying to push the line up through the guides with their line hand. The only extra things you should do are:

- Use a *slightly* more emphatic pop/stop.
- Release the line the instant after the rod stops on the forward cast.

Where should the rod be pointing after this stop? Right where it has always stopped: at 45 degrees above the horizon.

Practice this sequence many times over. Start at the mark; establish two-point control; strip in 3 feet of line; release the line from the grip; make a pickup, backcast, and forward cast; release the line to shoot; then lower the rod tip to the water as the line falls. Only after you can comfortably shoot the 3 feet of line out to the mark should you progress to False-Casting + Shooting.

FALSE-CASTING + SHOOTING

This is a watershed in your development as a fly fisher, not just as a caster. A four-part cast puts the fly 45 feet away. Stripping in 3 feet and shooting it back out lets you fish the area only from 42 to 45 feet away. Being able to shoot line on three or four successive forward casts will let you extend your fishing beyond 45 feet, and it will let you fish the water within 42 feet. This will open a whole world to you.

Except for certain types of trout fishing, this is the technique that you will use every time you go fly fishing, for the rest of your life. *When combined with stripping, it is the single most important sequence in this book.* When you master it, all fly-fishing doors will be open to you—whether you're fishing streamers for trout, poppers for bass, or shrimp imitations for bonefish on the Florida flats.

Make sure the area at your feet is clear of things that can catch the line. A lawn is ideal for this. You are going to make your habitual three false casts, allowing some line to shoot at the end of each forward cast.

- Begin by stripping in 10 feet of line from the mark and allowing it to pile at your feet.
- Make the pickup, and firmly hold the line in your line hand during the backcast and forward cast.
- Immediately *after* the forward-cast stop, release it and allow it to shoot perhaps 2 feet. Pinch it firmly with your line hand just as the leader unfurls at the end of the forward cast.
- Make the second backcast and forward cast, releasing line *after* the second forward-cast stop, to shoot roughly 3 feet.
- Firmly pinch and hold the line through the third backcast and forward cast, shooting the last 3 feet of line *after* the forward cast stop.
- Make your presentation, returning the rod tip to the water.
- Do this many times over until it is comfortable.

You'll notice that your first false cast, with only 20 feet of fly line in the air, may not shoot well. This is because there is less line weight for the rod to load against, so the rod consequently bends and unbends less when you stop. To counteract this, make quicker casting strokes over shorter casting arcs with short lengths of line. Your first one or two strokes should be aggressive tip casts. As the line lengthens with each forward-cast shoot, your stroke must become slightly longer in both time and distance, loading the rod into the midsection.

Like so much of what you learned earlier, this process takes concentration and practice. Your brain must coordinate the pinching and releasing motion of your line hand with your backcast and forward casts. This is a time when you must be patient. Laugh when things go wrong and celebrate when they don't. Once your muscles remember what to do, you'll return to daydreaming as you false cast, shoot, and retrieve your practice fly. As you learned earlier, don't tie on a heavy fly such as a Woolly Bugger or Clouser Minnow. Make sure that you can do this well with a practice fly before you advance to something heavier.

Again, if you have trouble with this sequence, unrig your rod and pantomime it. When you can make this series of casts successfully, you are truly ready to fish the world.

SHOOTING BEYOND 45 FEET

You may be ready now to make longer casts, beyond 45 feet. As the cast lengthens, your stroke must become slightly longer in both time and distance, loading the rod deeper into the midsection. Remember: *The longer your cast, the farther back the rod must travel during the backcast and the farther forward it must travel during the forward cast.* This means your thumbnail will point well beyond vertical at the backcast stop. And because there is more line to unfurl in the air, your pauses must be longer, too.

Five Reasons Why You Should Learn to Cast 90 Feet

1. Why else are fly lines so long?
2. It's a good way to lose weight.
3. It'll look great on your résumé.
4. Fly casting may someday be an Olympic event.
5. It will enhance your love life.

- Pull more line off the reel, 10 feet past the 37-foot mark, and let it fall.
- Hold the mark and, with the line straight on the water, make a pickup.
- Make just two false casts, shooting 5 feet of line after each forward-cast stop.

If your line is clean and your casts are true, you should see that extra 10 feet of line shoot out through the guides. That's a 55-foot cast! Do that over and over again.

Up to a point (casting does have limits), the more line you are carrying in the air at the beginning of the cast, the more you can shoot at the end of the cast. You will eventually get to the stage where you'll shoot all of those extra 10 feet in just one forward stroke.

PICKUP FROM THE DEAD-DRIFT POSITION

When fishing your fly dead drift (without dragging it through the water), you'll have your rod tip up in the air when the fly is on the water. It would be tedious to lower your rod tip and pull in slack so you can make the smooth pickup you've learned every time you cast. Instead, practice the pickup and four-part cast beginning from the dead-drift position. Having mastered the smooth pickup from the low-rod position, you'll be surprised by how easy it is to now make both the pickup and backcast in such a short arc of rod, from the dead-drift position.

> **Videotape: Your Virtual Casting Instructor**
>
> You've come this far, patiently reading, studying the photographs, and practicing. You owe it to yourself to see yourself cast. Tape yourself. Other than having a live casting instructor to help you improve, this is the most effective learning tool you can use.
>
> Set up your camera on a tripod and point it perpendicular to your casting direction. It should be on the same side of your body as your rod hand. At first, make sure the lens setting is just wide enough to include the rod on both the forward and backcast. Do a series of four-part casts and false casts. Then set the lens to a wider angle to capture the shape of the loops as they come off the rod tip on both the forward cast and backcast. Repeat the casts you did earlier. When you play the tape of your casting, use the pause button so you can compare your hand, arm, and rod positions to the ones you see in this book. Your forward and backcast loops should be the same size and shape, like mirror images. Finally, cast directly at the camera. On tape, you should see the rod travel in the same plane on the forward and backcasts.

Playing Around

Shoot line on the roll cast. Make a roll cast that has a particularly aggressive pop/stop, one that has a tight loop and lots of power. Shoot some line immediately after the stop of the roll cast. You'll get the best results if you do it with the two-handed roll cast you learned earlier. You'll have to shoot line from its pinned-against-the-grip position. This is a good technique to use when you are fishing in front of a high bank or a lot of vegetation. Practice this one, because it's another one that will impress your friends and catch more fish.

Shoot line on your forward cast *and* your backcast. You're skilled enough now to do this, and you already know how. In addition to shooting after the forward-cast stop, do it after your backcast stop, too. It will double the rate at which you pinch and release the line. It may feel awkward at first, but you will get used to it and it will pay off

For better shooting from your backcast, pivot the reel to the side.

By popping the rod too early in the cast, you may cause a tailing loop. This will often tangle your leader.

in fewer false casts and more time with your fly in the water. (There is a technique that will make line shoot more readily on your backcast—pivot the reel to the side during the backcast. This is unorthodox, but it really works.)

Get the most from the least. Practice shooting as much line as possible on each false cast. Make a 55-foot cast and strip your fly 30 feet toward you. See how few false casts it takes to get the fly back out to 55 feet. This getting-the-most-from-the-least is the path to elegance.

TROUBLESHOOTING

Three Common Problems

1. The line is hardly shooting through the guides. Make sure that:

- Your line is clean.
- Your four-part cast is unchanged from what you were doing in earlier chapters.
- Your forward cast pop/stops at the 45-degrees-above-horizontal position.
- You release the line the instant (one nanosecond) after the forward-cast stop.
- You put a slightly more emphatic pop/stop at the end of each forward cast.

2. The line slides through the guides during instead of after the forward cast and ends up in a heap in front of you. You'll know this is happening because you can hear your line hissing as it slides through the guides during the forward cast. To cure this, hold the line firmly without slippage until the nanosecond *after the forward cast has stopped.* It may be easier if you first make some four-part casts in which you just hold the line in your line hand without shooting. Once you are confident that you can hold the line during the cast, try releasing it again after the stop. If you still struggle with this, that's okay. It happens to a lot of casters. Put the rod down and pantomime, in slow motion, the entire cast. Be sure to hold the imaginary line firmly until just after the rod has stopped.

3. The last forward cast is getting tangled on itself. This is called a tailing loop. It occurs when the pop is made in the beginning or middle of the forward cast instead of immediately before the stop. It causes the rod tip to dip low, then spring back up, and that's what fouls up the line. Many casters do it by making the last in a series of false casts different in style than the previous casts: They try to pop the cast too early in the stroke, long before the stop. One sneaky way to fix this is: Just don't make the last cast! Instead, present the fly on your second-to-last cast. This will cause you to make the last stroke just like the previous ones, albeit with the wee bit more energy you add on each successive forward stroke. Remember, no matter how long or energetic your cast, the pop must occur at the very end of your casting stroke, immediately before the stop.

Tailing loops often cause wind knots to form in your leader. They significantly weaken your leader and should be cut out.

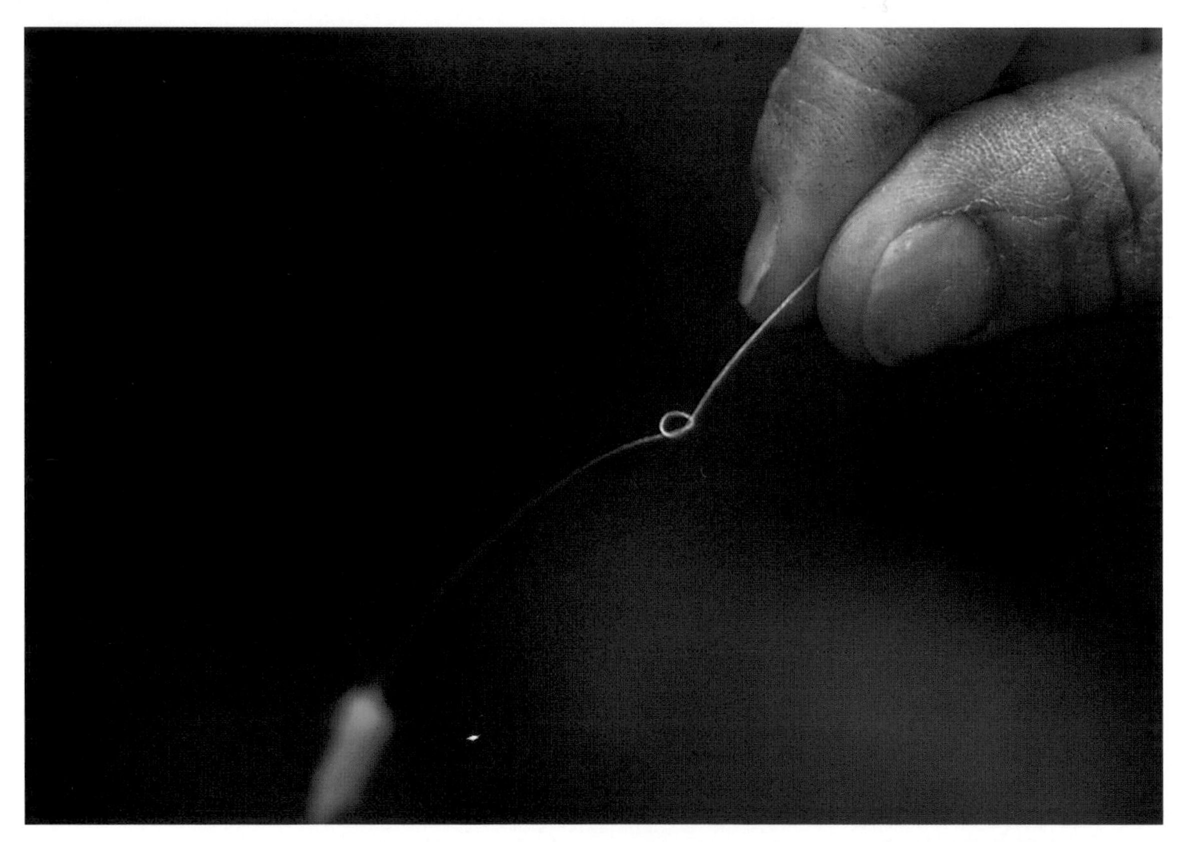

A wind knot, usually in the tippet, often results from a tailing loop. This one has not yet tightened.

This is a tightened wind knot, which will weaken the leader dramatically. It should be cut out and the fly retied.

18 Wind Casting

We may as well get used to it: Wind is nature's way of distributing heat around the globe. Much of this activity seems to happen in places that have great fly fishing—places like western Montana, with its wealth of rainbows and indigenous cutthroats; southern Chile, with its huge European brown trout; the Florida Keys, with their silver-bullet bonefish. With practice and patience, you may be able to fly cast successfully in 20-mile-per-hour winds. It's not easy, but it will keep you on the water after others have gone home. In this chapter you'll learn skills to let you fish in some pretty difficult conditions.

CASTING IN CROSSWINDS

These are the easiest to cope with. A crosswind from your left side enables you to use the standard four-part cast, roll cast, or false cast on your right side. If the wind is particularly strong, cast in a sidearm plane. This is just a fly cast tilted completely on its side with the rod moving in a horizontal plane throughout the cast. Be careful to keep your tight casting arc and to use your usual disciplined stop positions.

If the wind is coming from your right side, do what you did earlier in the off-shoulder roll cast: Tilt the rod over your head so the tip-top travels on your downwind side. Push your elbow slightly out to the side and bring your hand in close so your hand and forearm point to the top of your head. This keeps your hand on your right side, where it is strongest, and puts the rod tip over your left shoulder. The

Beartooth Plateau, Southwestern Montana

You are standing on the shore of an unnamed lake 10,000 feet high on Montana's Beartooth Plateau. It is stormy. The wind is howling down the lake, right into your face, bringing all the fish food from the surface with it. There are 15-inch brook trout that have never seen a fly before, feeding indiscriminately just a few rod lengths out. The wind is pushing you away from the water. The experts would say that your leader is too short and stubby for your size 10 black Woolly Bugger, but it's too much trouble to add tippet right now. You make a vertical backcast and drive your forward cast down hard to the water. Your fly slams the surface and a brookie smashes it instantly. You set the hook and silently scoff at the leader mavens. It's a nice fish. You are no longer mad at the weather.

A sidearm cast is helpful in crosswinds. Tilt the rod nearly to the horizon.

wind will now blow the line away from you instead of into you. Otherwise, the cast itself is done exactly as you did it before. Most important is to keep the rod moving in the same plane forward and backward, not in a curving motion.

If the crosswind from the right is gentle, a sidearm cast may work for you, although I still prefer the off-shoulder under these conditions.

Why not cast left-handed if there's a crosswind from the right? This may sound appealing, but the fact is that fishing with your off hand will feel as if you are trapped in someone else's body. The casting itself doesn't feel so odd—you practiced it earlier—but stripping your fly and setting the hook feel, well, strange. And when you actually hook a fish, you'll want to put the rod back into your dominant hand anyway. But try it. You may like it.

During the sidearm cast, keep your casting arc small to make your loops tight.

If the wind is coming from your rod side, cast off-shoulder and the wind wil! blow the line and fly to your downwind side

CASTING INTO A HEADWIND

The most effective way to make short to medium-length casts into a headwind is keep your loop tight. Keep the length of your casting arc and of your pop/stop as short as possible. Yes, this limits your distance, but you're up against what lawyers call an act of God, so relax. The more you grit your teeth and try to punch the cast into the wind, the more trouble you'll have. This often causes tailing loops and the resulting wind knots. No, wind doesn't cause the knots, but it can induce you to make the tailing-loop error that causes them.

Another strategy in a headwind is to make a sidearm cast. Because wind speed is slowest just above the ground (or water), this lets you cast your line underneath the strongest winds.

You can also make your backcast more vertical and your forward cast farther down than usual. Casting forward and downward makes the line straighten when the fly is just inches, instead of feet, above the water, so it won't be blown back at you.

If you need to make longer casts into the wind, learn to double haul, as shown in the next chapter.

CASTING WITH A TAILWIND

If you're using a floating line and you don't need lots of distance, make a roll cast. A tailwind can really boost the power of this cast, and can make an anemic roll cast look as if it's on steroids. If the tailwind is strong, you may have some difficulty with your setup, because the wind may keep blowing it forward. Try setting up with your rod tilted farther back toward the rear than usual.

You can also make a more downward backcast and a more upward forward cast than usual. This keeps the backcast a bit lower—under the strongest winds—than it would normally be. The forward cast is then lofted upward, where it is caught by the wind and sailed out over the water. Also try the sidearm backcast. This keeps the backcast close to the ground, where the wind is slowest.

THE ROLL-CAST PICKUP

Sometimes it can be awkward to make a straight-line, low-rod-tip pickup. This can occur when there's a tailwind. It happens more commonly when you're fishing dead drift (rod tip up) upstream, and your fly has drifted back close to your position. (There is often a lot of slack on the water when the fly has drifted close to you.) You've practiced making a pickup from this position, but it can be difficult to do well with all that slack. Instead, try something else: a roll-cast pickup. Your high-rod-tip position requires you to move the tip back only a few feet into your setup position. Make the usual forward-stroke portion of the roll cast. After the line has fully extended in the air, but before it has hit the water, make a backcast. You have just substituted a roll cast for a conventional pickup. This may seem inconsequential, but you'll find more and more situations in which to apply it. It is another one of those casts that is inexplicably satisfying.

In a strong headwind, you can make a nearly vertical backcast . . .

. . . and a slightly more emphatic, more downward forward cast than usual.

You can then violate the rules and allow your forward cast to swing upward somewhat, lofting the line up into the carrying winds.

In a strong tailwind, fish your backcast; make the forward cast into the wind.

FISH YOUR BACKCAST

Face backward, into the wind, and make a forward cast into the wind. Once the forward cast has unfurled, turn and direct your forward cast toward the fish. The wind should then help your backcast extend fully. As the backcast falls toward the water, turn around and fish the cast. Because it is easier for most of us to make a tight-loop forward cast than backcast, you'll have a better chance of fully extending the line into the wind with this technique. This may sound like some kind of trick, but saltwater anglers frequently use it when fishing from a boat in windy conditions. You can also use it when your backcast must be carefully placed to avoid snagging in the trees: Make a forward cast into a space in the trees, then turn around and fish the backcast.

As the backcast falls, turn around.

Fish your backcast.

PLAYING AROUND

Don't play around when it's windy or you will displease the fish gods. If you insist, try this drill, but only when it's calm. It is a fascinating mind/body game to play.

Deliberately Cast Tailing Loops

Having spent all this time willing your body to do the right thing, you are now going to teach it to do the wrong thing. Sounds crazy? Yep, this is another one of those counterintuitive ideas that works. Like careening Dad's car around an icy vacant parking lot, it's a great way to learn how not to do something. Learning to deliberately cast tailing loops makes you much less likely to throw them accidentally when it's windy, when they most often occur.

Start by making some of your usual false casts. Now make some in which you pop the forward cast too early. Pop long before you stop. In other words, make the burst of acceleration come at the beginning or in the middle of the cast instead of at the end. If you see tailing loops, you win! Just don't make a habit of this.

TROUBLESHOOTING

Expect occasional wreckage when it's windy. You may cast tailing loops and wind knots; you may get hit by the fly or stung by the line, you may end up with your line tangled in a macramé project. As always, be patient. The more train wrecks you have, the more you will learn how to avoid them. If you're like me, you'll suffer through the lesson many, many times before you get it right. Yes, fly fishing is hard work, but you're just the right person for the job.

Why Few Instructors Can Deliberately Cast Tailing Loops

I serve on a board at the Federation of Fly Fishers that trains and certifies fly-casting instructors. One of the requirements for certification is that instructors be able to make all the "bad" casts—from wide-open loops to tailing loops. To be effective, good instructors must be able to demonstrate to their students what they are doing wrong, requiring the instructor to make the same kind of faulty cast that the student is making. An inability to cast a tailing loop on demand is probably the biggest stumbling block for prospective instructors. Why? Because they have to override their muscle memory of the good cast. So how do they learn to throw bad casts? The same way they established their muscle memory. Practice.

The Double Haul

If you are coordinated enough to ride a bicycle or drive a car, you can learn to double haul. When you do, your overall fishing success will make a quantum leap. The double haul turbocharges your fly cast by increasing the speed at which the loop travels and unrolls. It turns *less* into *more.* It actually lets you cast a tighter loop and a faster line, over more distance, all while doing less work with your rod hand. Simply put, it makes your fly get out there faster and makes long casts less work and more fun. And I mean fun!

Done correctly, a double haul is nearly as exciting as that first time you rode your bike without training wheels. Most double haulers can tell you exactly when and where they first learned to do it.

This technique requires the line hand to tug on the line during the forward cast and again during the backcast, repositioning itself between each cast in preparation for the next one. The tug is called a single haul. The resetting or rebounding of the hand makes it a double haul. When fishing, the double haul is usually combined with shooting to lengthen the cast. Proper double hauling looks exactly like the casting you've done up to this point, with the addition of a well-timed haul and rebound of the line hand.

Turneffe Atoll, Belize, Central America

On the second largest barrier reef in the world, you are wading an immense expanse of coral sand and marl that teems with tiny crabs, grass shrimp, and other bonefish foods. The wind is blowing, as it almost always does in the Tropics. You are using a 9-foot 8-weight rod with a 12-foot 0X leader. Your fly is a size 6 Crazy Charlie, and it looks like some cheap piece of costume jewelry. Even at high tide the water is rarely more than 4 feet deep. Any fish you hook here has only one place to go—away—and only one speed at which to swim—Mach 1. Your guide sees a school of dozens of 3-pound bonefish feeding together, with their dorsal fins exposed like silvery sickles glinting in the sun. The bonefish are 80 feet away, swimming toward you in 8 inches of water, and they are hyper-wary of barracuda and good fly casters. Your guide tells you to cast 10 feet in front of them. You double haul, making a couple of false casts off to the side of the school to avoid spooking them. You redirect your last cast in front of the school and your fly drops 60 feet away. The fish are now at 70 feet and closing. They keep coming. Your guide says, "Strip it," and you retrieve the fly 18 inches. A fish breaks for your fly and your guide quietly says, "He's coming." Your heart starts to hammer. Then . . . the alarm rings, you wake up, you smell coffee.

Even if you only trout fish with dry flies within 45 feet, you should learn this cast. No, it probably won't help you in this kind of fishing. It just feels good! Synchronizing the tug on the line with the stroke of the rod, and feeling the resulting synergy, is perhaps the greatest pleasure in casting.

The double haul is mostly used when:

- Casting longer distances, beyond 45 or 50 feet.
- Fishing with rods heavier than 6-weights.
- Casting into a headwind.
- Showing off.

In slow motion, pantomime the double haul without a rod. This is your start position for the backcast double haul.

GETTING STARTED

Pull 10 feet of line off the reel past the 37-foot mark and stretch it out at your feet. *Clean the line* (this is essential). Holding the line at the mark, warm up with an easy series of three false casts. Good. Now put the rod down, because you are going to learn this by pantomiming.

PANTOMIME THE DOUBLE HAUL WITH YOUR HANDS

Carefully do this step by step, in *very* slow motion at first:

1. Start with your rod hand in the forward-cast stop position, with your elbow down, forearm at a right angle to your upper arm, and the imaginary rod pointed up at 45 degrees.
2. Position your line hand just 2 inches below your rod hand. This is the position from which you'll start the double haul.
3. Pantomime your usual backcast. *During* the backcast, pull your line hand and imaginary line directly down and away from your rod hand, so that your hands are separated by approximately 2 feet at

As the rod hand backcasts, the line hand hauls. This is a single haul.

With the rod hand frozen in place, the line hand returns to the rod hand to prepare for the forward-cast haul.

As the rod hand makes the forward cast, the line hand hauls.

the end of the backcast. You just made a single haul.

4. The haul begins slowly as the stroke begins slowly, it accelerates as the rod accelerates, it pop/stops as the rod pop/stops.
5. Pause for the backcast to unfurl. Freeze your rod exactly as you usually do during the pause. With your rod motionless, bring your line hand back to meet your rod hand, again with the 2 inches of separation. This is a new position for your line hand, with your left arm crossing in front of you.
6. After the pause, pantomime your usual forward cast. As you do, tug your linc hand directly away from your rod hand, so there is again about 2 feet of separation. The timing of your haul coincides exactly with the timing of your forward stroke—you are simply accelerating the separation of your hands.

As the imaginary forward cast unfurls, the line hand resets to permit the next backcast haul.

The Hardest Parts of the Double Haul

For most people there are three challenges in the double haul. You must:

- Make the line hand bounce back up to meet the rod hand.
- Make sure the rod hand *stays still* while the line hand comes to meet it. (Only very advanced casters can cheat on this one.)
- Tug with the line hand *during* instead of slightly before or after the forward and backcasts. Try to haul *against* the bending of the rod.

7. As you did after the backcast stop, freeze the rod in the forward-cast stop position and bring your line hand up to within 2 inches of your motionless rod hand.
8. You have just pantomimed a backcast double haul and a forward-cast double haul.
9. Repeat this sequence until you turn blue.

You should do this pantomime dozens of times until the rebounding of your line hand during the rod pauses is a simple reflex action, a down-up motion. As you gradually speed up to a real-time pantomime, you'll see that this rebounding must happen the instant the line hand reaches the bottom of its travel.

PANTOMIME THE DOUBLE HAUL WITH YOUR UNRIGGED ROD

Once you are confident that your pantomime is correct, pick up your unrigged rod and pantomime with that. Use your normal casting stroke with your usual amount of energy. Practice this continuously until:

- Your rod hand moves exactly as it would during false casting with a line.
- Your line hand pulls at the same time your rod hand casts.

Try pantomiming the double haul with an unrigged rod. This is the start position for your backcast double haul.

As the rod hand backcasts, the line hand hauls.

With the rod hand frozen in place, the line hand has returned to the rod hand to prepare for the forward-cast haul.

The rod hand makes the forward cast as the line hand hauls.

The hand has reset to permit a haul on the next backcast.

Timing and Length of the Haul

The easiest way to haul is to do it throughout the casting stroke. The speed of the haul should be synchronized with the speed of the cast. That is, the haul begins slowly as the stroke begins slowly, it accelerates as the rod accelerates, it pop/stops as the rod pop/stops.

The length of the haul varies with the length of the casting stroke. As you remember, to cast a longish line—say, 55 feet—you need to move your arm through a longish stroke. Your haul will be correspondingly longer on the 55-foot cast than it is on the preceding 47-foot cast.

- Your line hand rebounds instantly after the haul, and the rod hand freezes the rod as it does so.

THE DOUBLE HAUL WITH YOUR RIGGED ROD

- Warm up by holding the line at the mark and making repetitive false casts without shooting. Just keep the line pinched in your line hand for now.
- Keeping the line pinched (don't shoot yet), start double hauling. Feel the extra bend in your rod as your haul against it. Your hauls should be timed so that it feels as if you are pulling the line against the bend of the rod. (You are.)
- *Don't change your casting stroke at all.*
- During each pause, you should feel the line being pulled up through the guides (it's technically *shooting*) as your line hand rebounds the 2 feet or so to your rod hand. If you are impatient to see results, let the line shoot after one of your forward stops.

To make the line shoot better behind you, swing the reel off to the side during the backcast, as you did when you first learned to shoot. If this seems to foul you up instead, forget that you ever heard of it.

The backcast begins.

The line hand hauls during and in opposition to the backcast.

This is a backcast with a single haul. The line hand must now reset to prepare for a haul on the next forward cast.

The line hand resets to the motionless rod hand, enabling a haul on the forward cast.

As the rod begins the forward cast, the line hand begins to haul.

The forward cast and forward haul have stopped at the same instant.

The line hand resets, as it does on every double haul.

HAULING AND SHOOTING IN THE REAL WORLD

Practice continuous no-shoot double hauling while false-casting: It's a great way to become proficient with the double haul.

- Once you are comfortable with this and you think it's going well, release (shoot) line on the last of your forward false casts. During real fishing, double hauling is usually done in conjunction with shooting.
- You'll know you've made a huge step when you can make a pickup, double haul and shoot some line on the backcast, then double haul and shoot again on the forward cast.
- One test of mastery is that you will make a series of two or three false casts during which you double haul and shoot on every backcast and forward cast. That's what much of real-world tarpon fishing and bonefishing is like.

Videotape Your Double Haul

You'll be amazed by how much you can learn from this. This time, the camera should be on the rod-hand side of your body, slightly forward of perpendicular to your casting direction. This will let you view both the line hand and rod hand together. Watch the tape for any signs that you are doing something other than what you've read. In particular, look for these no-nos:

- Your rod hand comes forward to meet your line hand after the backcast stop. This is called *creep*, and only very advanced casters can get away with it.
- You are not hauling simultaneously with your casting stroke.
- Your forward-cast haul looks like it's only about 3 inches long relative to your rod hand.

This caster couldn't freeze his rod at the backcast while he reset his line hand. Instead, he has brought his rod hand forward to meet his line hand. With so little arc in which to make a forward cast and a forward haul, this cast is doomed.

MELTDOWN

Be prepared for plenty of wreckage and mental meltdown. *It's common to crash and burn a lot as you learn this.* Stay with it. You have to make your brain conquer your body's natural impulses. You will be successful: Follow these instructions carefully, don't get discouraged, and you will be double hauling soon. I promise.

When you foul up, go back to each step of the instructions and make sure you understand it.

IF ALL ELSE FAILS

- Return to the pantomime and *close your eyes.*
- Move through each step, first with just your hands, then with the unrigged rod.

Most important, videotape yourself if it's not working, compare the tape to the instructions, and you'll see your error. There may be more than one error, but that does not make you a klutz, just a caster.

PLAYING AROUND

Try double hauling with your other hand. You're pretty hot stuff, being the only person on your block who knows how to double haul. Now it's time for an ego check. Try casting with your left hand and hauling with your right hand. As usual, when you first try it, be ready to laugh at yourself. It is really fun and feels like some strange out-of-body experience. It will definitely make you smile, win friends, and influence people. It will probably amuse a few fish, too. But stay with it. Practice! You can do this!

Double haul with your eyes closed. This is another one of those New Age techniques that really works. It is a great way to concentrate on only the task at hand, and makes you focus on the nuances (we won't call them faults) of your double hauling.

Try hauling with your leg! Here, the leg is reset for the next forward-cast haul. Don't try this after a couple of beers.

Double haul with your leg! If this guy can do it with his leg, you can do it with your arm.

TROUBLESHOOTING

The best way to troubleshoot is to videotape yourself and compare what you see on the tape to what you see in these instructions and photographs. It will be worth it.

20 Long Casts, Aerial Mends, Special Casts

LONG CASTS

Don't forget to clean, dress, and stretch your line and leader before questing for the far horizon.

The Butt Cast

So far you've shot casts to about 55 feet with nothing more than the midsection cast, where you made the rod bend into its middle. With the double haul, you added perhaps 10 or 15 feet. An elegant caster can use exactly the same motion that you have been using throughout this book to cast out to 80 feet. But it's easier to do this if you start raising your elbow during the backcast *and* moving the rod through a longer arc. Your stop positions must move farther apart as you make the long cast, and your pauses must be longer. On extremely long casts your backcast and forward stops may be nearly parallel to the ground!

A very long cast requires that the rod bend down into its butt. During the forward cast, try to pull the rod down as you accelerate. Imagine that you are pulling down with your elbow. Here, the pop/stop becomes more of a

Used for very long casts, the butt cast bends the rod nearly to the handle.

pull/stop. That is, the motion just before the stop takes longer than a "pop." It's because of the weight of that long line you have suspended in the air. Your little graphite rod doesn't have enough stiffness to let you simply "pop" the tip of the rod to a stop.

When attempting long casts, it may help to hold the trailing end of the grip (just ahead of the reel) and, during the backcast, to swing the reel off to the side. If these things seem to make casting harder, however, don't do them.

Carry a Long Line

This drill is used by the top distance casters in the world, but it works for everybody. What is the longest cast you can make without shooting or double hauling? At that length, pin the line against the grip, then false-cast continuously for many repetitions, trying to make a smooth stroke ended by an acceleration/stop. Use the butt cast. Do this until you think you've mastered it. Now let out 1 more foot of line, pin it, and repeat the drill. Remember that the more line you cast, the longer your casting stroke is and the farther your hand, forearm, and elbow must travel. It may take you quite a while before you are ready to lengthen again, but that's okay. This is a very effective exercise, but only if you are patient.

The more line you carry, the longer your casting stroke is and the farther your hand, forearm, and elbow must travel.

Add the Double Haul

Once you become comfortable carrying a long line using the method I've described, add the double haul. This may seem simplistic, but it's no less than what the best casters in the world do to cast farther.

AERIAL MENDS

These are used mostly when trout fishing. By placing slack line upstream, you enable the fly to drift farther downstream before the current tightens the line and unnaturally drags the fly.

Once you're comfortable carrying a long line, add the double haul.

The placing of slack line upstream of the fly before the line hits the water is called an aerial mend. The reach cast is just one of many aerial mends, but it is the easiest and most common.

Reach Cast

In chapter 17 you learned why the low rod tip is such a good position for animating your fly, setting the hook, and ensuring a smooth pickup. You also learned that, when dead drifting a fly, you should fish with the rod tip elevated. You'll get an even longer dead drift if you make a reach cast. This is a slack-line cast that positions slack fly line upstream of the fly.

To make a reach cast, do the first three parts of the usual four-part cast. Immediately after the forward-cast stop, point the rod about 45 degrees upstream of your stop position and reach upstream with your rod hand as you do. Do this as the line is beginning to fall toward the water. You need to complete the reach before the line lands. Otherwise, the movement of the rod upstream will drag the line across the water, which will drag the fly.

The reach cast is virtually the same whether the current flows left to right or right to left. If it is flowing left to right, the reach is simply made across your body. If you are facing directly across the river, for example, your rod should finish the reach cast facing 45 degrees upstream.

To make a reach cast, make a conventional forward cast . . .

. . . and reach upstream with the rod instead of making your usual presentation.

Another view of the reach cast. Stop the forward cast . . .

. . . and reach upstream.

Your upstream reach should be completed before the line lands.

Shoot Line During the Reach

Try it; it's just like shooting line at any other time except you are reaching the rod to one side as you do.

S-Cast

The S-cast is another aerial mend, used mainly when you are fishing downstream to selective trout. Immediately after your forward stop, move the rod tip from side to side in tight oscillations. This will cause S's to form in your line as it falls onto the water. The slack S's enable a longer dead drift before the current straightens the line and drags the fly. It is a fun cast with a pretty result.

To make the S-cast, move the rod tip side to side in tight oscillations just after the forward stop.

Curve Cast

There are two purposes for a curve cast: First, you want to cast around a corner; second, you want to make an aerial mend by casting some slack upstream of the fly. When I learned the first version, it looked like another magic trick. The idea is to use a sidearm cast with an overpowered forward cast that is then stopped too short. It causes the fly to curve around to the left of the line and is called a positive curve cast.

The fly can be made to lay out to the right of the line by underpowering the sidearm cast so that the line falls to the water with the loop intact. This is sometimes called a negative curve. Properly executed, the curve cast literally casts the fly around a corner.

Unlike the other casts in this book, however, it is extraordinarily difficult to present a curve cast accurately on the first cast. On the lawn, nailing the latter two out of three practice casts is fine, but not on the water. In my years as a bassaholic, the curve cast has probably landed me a couple of fish that I wouldn't have otherwise caught.

Despite the above disclaimer, this cast is really fun to practice. You'll have an easier time if you practice with a relatively heavy fly and a 7½-foot stout leader and make short casts. Make a sidearm stroke so the loop travels in a horizontal plane, overpower the forward stroke, and stop the forward cast just a little sooner than you normally would. You may recognize this as just a sidearm version of the fly-first cast in chapter 16.

Anglers for selective trout use the curve frequently to lengthen the dead drift of their flies. They're often willing to sacrifice accuracy for a long, natural drift. Because of the nature of dead-drift fishing, the slack-line version is usually done with a small fly and a long, thin leader. You simply can't make this curve as much as you can with a heavy fly and short, stout leader. You are fighting physics, so don't be disheartened when you encounter this. With practice you can get your cast to curve some, and that's a good outcome.

To curve the line, overpower your sidearm cast, stopping the forward stroke prematurely.

SPECIAL CASTS

Some of these, such as casting heavy flies and fishing your backcast, are quite practical. Skip-casting is sometimes handy to have in your arsenal. Sky-casting is whimsical. Hand-casting is the ultimate trick cast. If you can hand-cast, you're good.

When casting heavy flies, make a wide, lethargic loop. Use a longer, slower stroke than usual.

Casting Heavy Flies or Split Shot

This requires what looks like bad casting technique. You'll have to trust me on this. When casting heavy flies or a leader burdened with split shot and a strike indicator, you should cast a *wide* loop. You know how to do this: Use a longer, slower stroke than usual. Your backcast should tip farther back than usual, and your forward cast should lean farther forward. End with an anemic pop/stop or even a SLOP/stop. Imagine that you've taken Valium and you've got the *slows*. That's how to cast weight.

Don't try to make long casts with heavily weighted flies unless you are using a specialized shooting-head line. If you want to learn why (make sure you are wearing a protective hat and glasses before you do this), pinch two pieces of split shot right above your practice fly. Then try to make a long cast or some tight loops. It's a disaster, isn't it? You'll never do *that* again. Shorten up your line and try it again with the slow, sleepy, Valium cast. That's the way to do it.

Double hauling works with heavy flies but, again, slow down and lengthen your stroke. Remember the *Playing Around* drill in chapter 16, *False-Casting*, when you tried to cast with so little energy that the loop barely got out there? In that drill you used a tight-loop, tip cast. This time, use a slow butt cast. Try that same approach when casting weight. Try to cast *too* slowly, too lethargically, and your cast should turn out just right.

Fishing Your Backcast

You did this earlier, when fishing with a tailwind. When you are fishing in a wooded area with some gaps in the trees, turn around and make a forward cast into one of the gaps.

Then allow your backcast to simply fall onto the water. Of course, you can just use the roll cast if there are no gaps, but that can limit your distance.

Skip-Casting

While practicing the curve cast, try to make the fly skip off the water (it won't work on land) during the forward cast. It's easier to make it skip if you double haul while making continuous false casts, using a sidearm cast. Together, this may sound like a lot, but you know all these techniques. At the beginning of the forward stroke, dip the rod down *slightly*. As the cast progresses, tip the rod up slightly. This makes the fly kiss the water on each forward cast. This dipping/tipping is very subtle. Success comes after lots of practice.

What earthly reason would prompt anyone to do this? Some of the world's great trout, bass, and snook fishing lies beneath overhanging vegetation, where a conventional fly cast would land your fly in the trees. While the skip cast is inaccurate and prone to blow up, it's a blast when you skip the fly under some greenery and a fish nails it!

To skip-cast, make a sidearm stroke. Dip the rod tip down slightly during the beginning of the stroke and up slightly as the cast progresses.

Sky-Casting

This is just what it sounds like. It has no real practical application, but it feels good. Like the skip cast, it's easiest to do a sky cast while making continuous false casts with double hauls. Just direct your backcast down into the grass behind you, and the forward cast way up in the air in front of you. This will require your forward cast to stop about 15 degrees short of vertical. You'll be surprised by how high you can launch the practice fly. Don't be surprised if you cast some tailing loops while doing this, because you will have a tendency to move the rod tip in a concave path during the forward stroke. Don't do this if there are rocks behind you, or you'll thrash your line and lose your fly!

Hand-Casting

You may have heard about or seen some casting guru casting a fly line with only bare hands. Well, it's surprisingly easy to do this. Why should you try it?

Because it's another one of those casts that's just fun to do! Hand-casting is also a fine way to improve the timing of your double haul. It can be practiced on land or water but is easier on land. Here's how it goes:

- Use a weight-forward line, not a double taper.
- You *must* clean and lubricate your line. Otherwise, you will burn the skin right off your fingers.
- To reduce drag, make your practice fly no larger than a pea and use either a nail knot or a superglue connection, not a loop-to-loop, for your leader-to-line junction. Both are illustrated in part 1, *Fly Fishing;* see pages 31 and 30.
- Start with about 35 feet of line out straight in front of you and some slack at your feet.
- Stand with your left foot well in front of your right foot.
- Lean forward, toward the line. Grasp the line as though you are going to double haul. (You are.)

- Pull the line for the pickup, then accelerate into the backcast. Haul while doing this, just as you would if you were using a rod.
- As you accelerate the haul with your line hand, thrust your rod hand back, pivoting your body to face backward. *Your elbow should brush right past your ribs* and the backcast should fly past them shortly thereafter. *The closer you keep your rod hand and elbow to your body, the easier this cast is.*

- Rebound your line hand to your rod hand as soon as you have finished the haul.
- At this point you should be facing behind you, with most of your weight on your right foot, your rod hand pointing straight back, and your line hand in position to make the forward haul.

- You *must* let the line land on the ground behind you. Trust me.

- Now simply reverse the sequence for the forward cast. While hauling, bring your rod hand right past your ribs and forward as if you were shoving a sword at the fish. As with the backcast, start slowly and accelerate to a stop. Then let her fly.

The faster and farther apart your hands move during the backcast and forward cast, the longer your hand cast will be. This means that your hauls will seem almost violent compared to the sedate hauls you've made while using a rod.

Postscript: Just One More Cast

If you happen down a certain back road in Freeport, Maine, on a warm summer evening, you may see something wonderful. The L.L. Bean Fly-Fishing Schools students have left for the day, and now the casting instructors are at play. We are in the company of those who taught before us on that same lawn and casting pool, and of those who taught them. We remember our teachers as we cast: "Joan taught me this way." "Mel teaches it this way." "Lefty describes it this way." We are infatuated with loops of line in the air, with the talk of it, with the teaching of it.

Ellen and Brian are trying out a new technique for teaching the roll cast. Harvey and Joe are going smallmouth bass fishing next week, and they are humorously discussing the best way to cast a big bass bug. For the sheer fun of it, Craig and I are sky-casting. After teaching casts for 14 years, Pat is on the casting pool, quietly making four-part casts: pickup, backcast, forward cast, presentation. Time and again they are beautiful, elegant casts, yet perfection eludes him, as it does all of us. But on this soft summer evening, he moves a little closer.

PART 3

Fly Tying

21 Getting Started

Fly tying is really not very difficult, but it can seem that way to the beginner. It was considerably harder for those of us who began many years ago, because we didn't have the learning aids that are available today. Not that many people tied flies back then, either, and few of those who did were willing to share.

I saw a fly tied for the first time when I showed up for my first lesson. It was a Mickey Finn streamer, a pattern that's included in this book. I managed to struggle through a couple of them, with my instructor coaching me through each step. Things would have gone much better if I'd had a bit of orientation first. I would suggest this to all beginners. If you can watch someone with adequate basic skills tie a few flies, your fledgling attempts will be much easier.

While I've tried to be as explicit and detailed as possible in this book, both in text and photographs, no book is quite as helpful as a good teacher. You *can* learn to tie flies by following the instructions in these chapters, but you'll progress more easily and quickly with a tutor at hand, and the book serving as a text.

As your tying skills and interests develop, you will need and want some additional tools and instruments. I'll describe many of these in the rest of this chapter. In the beginning, however, a few basic tools will suffice. They are:

1. Fly-tying vise.
2. Fly-tying scissors.
3. Bobbin.
4. Hackle pliers.
5. Bodkin or dubbing needle.

THE VISE

The fly-tying vise is a specialized instrument of which there are a number of types. The most common, and the one I recommend for beginners, is the simple **lever/cam** design. The jaws, or chuck, of the vise are tightened around the hook by pushing down a lever at the rear. The spread of the jaws is easily adjusted to accommodate hooks of larger and smaller wire diameters, or thicknesses.

Most lever/cam vises are in proper adjustment for the hook at hand when the lever is at approximately the five-thirty position. Each, however, has its own idiosyncrasies. If your vise comes with an instruction sheet that provides information about this adjustment and other important details, please refer to it before you insert your first hook. Lacking this, follow the six o'clock rule, and play with the adjustment until the hook is held firmly. *But* (and this is a big but) don't force the jaws to close by exerting extreme pressure.

There are lots of really heavy-wire hooks out there, and eventually you may encounter them. Atlantic and Pacific salmon flies often use such hooks, as do many saltwater patterns. It's important to avoid trying to mount a hook into the jaws of your vise that's heavier—meaning thicker—than the vise was designed for. If you can't close the jaws with ease when they are at their maximum width adjustment, don't force it, as damage will almost surely result.

There are two schools of thought on how a hook should be mounted in a vise. One school advocates burying the barb and point, thus avoiding having your tying thread get cut by the point. The other school advocates gripping the hook by the lower part of its bend and allowing the barb and point to be exposed, which optimizes access to the hook from the rear. I use both methods, depending on the type and size of hook. This will be explained in the forthcoming pages.

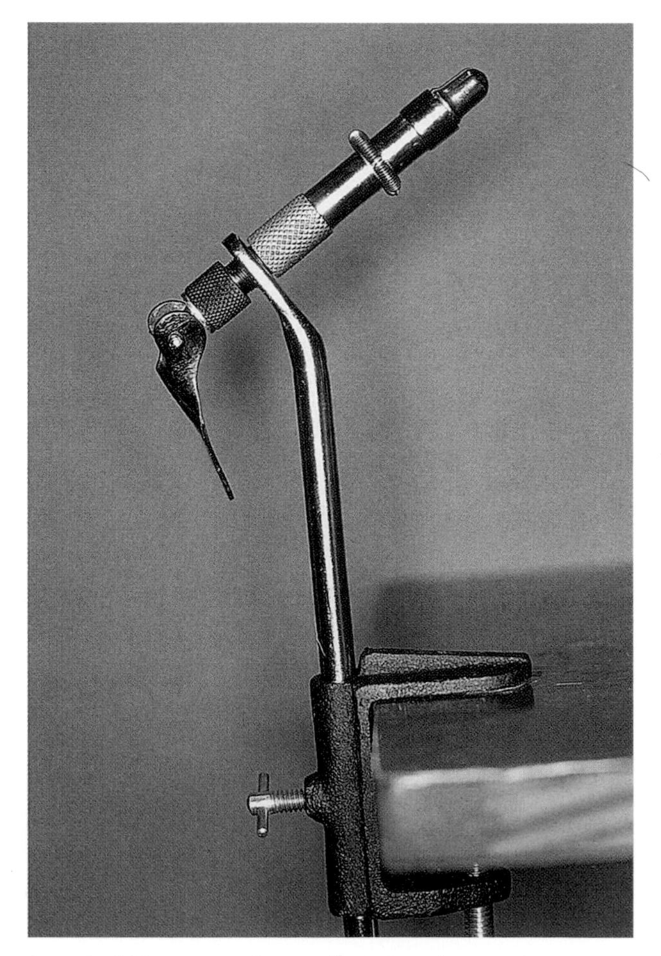

A typical Thompson A-type fly-tying vise.

In the costlier types of vises, other features are incorporated. One that can be quite helpful is angle adjustment, which enables you to make the attitude of the collet tube that holds the jaws either steeper or flatter. This attitude is also related to hook size and type. For example, it's much easier to work on smaller hooks with the collet tube at a steep angle.

Another useful feature is the ability to revolve, or rotate, the jaws—and concurrently, of course, the hook. This works best with vises that have the angle-adjustment feature, so that the tube and jaws can be set at level, allowing you to look at and work on both sides of the fly. This is not the same as a full-rotating vise, which is a more sophisticated instrument that uses a special design to enhance rotating capability.

Vises come with either a **C-clamp** or **pedestal** mounting arrangement. The clamp offers the advantage of adjustable height and is considerably lighter in weight—an asset when traveling. The pedestal offers the flexibility of being able to work on any flat surface without regard to thickness or overhang. Also, it does not interfere with a lap drawer, such as might be found in a typical fly-tying desk.

Keeping your vise at the proper height is an important factor in your tying efficiency and comfort. There being no way to change the height of a pedestal vise, you may have to put something under its base if it needs to be raised, or heighten your chair seat if the vise needs to be relatively lower. Some kind of office chair that is height adjustable is ideal; however, such a major purchase is usually not necessary, because vises today are designed with the typical tying setup in mind.

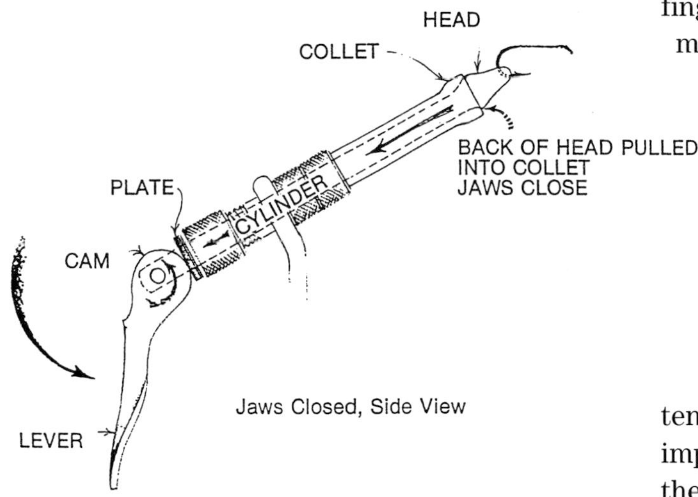

A functional drawing of the vise.

SCISSORS

If you have only one pair of scissors, they should be fine enough for close work. This means that the tips should come to a sharp point and be precisely matched. There's a liability, however, to such scissors—the cutting of heavy or tough materials. At the very least, you must avoid cutting such materials with the tips of the scissors; instead work well down into the blades. Better to have a second, sturdier pair at hand. They need not be expensive. Nail clippers are useful for cutting thick quills, oval tinsel, plastic wraps, and similar materials.

There is a wide variety of scissors on the market. In addition to the sharpness and fineness factors, there's the matter of fit. This applies to the size of the finger loop and to the overall length of the scissors. Many tyers, myself included, keep their scissors in their right hand at all times, with the fourth finger through one of the loops. In order for you to do this without getting stabbed, the scissors must be long enough to extend beyond the palm of your hand. For those with small hands, 3½ inches (90 mm) may suffice. I find that 4 inches (100 mm) works better.

The size of the finger loops is also a matter of personal fit. Some people like oversized finger loops. I like a closer fit, as I feel it gives me more precise control. Try several, and see what feels good.

BOBBIN

The fly-tying bobbin is a most useful tool: It replaces several tedious operations formerly done by hand, eliminates a lot of knot tying, and maintains tension on the thread. Far and away the most important consideration with a bobbin is that the tip of the tube be perfectly smooth; otherwise, it will cut the thread, which is a nightmare. Certain bobbins have been known to develop sharp-edged tubes over time simply through wear—that is, the action of the thread. Some bobbin manufacturers have switched to ceramic tubes or inserts to prevent this.

If you find yourself constantly breaking thread when you're using only moderate tension, or if you notice thread fraying all the time, suspect your bobbin. Try to borrow one that's known to be nonlethal; get an experienced tyer to help, if possible. You may find that it's not you, it's your tool—in which case you return it, of course.

Most bobbins need to be adjusted for proper tension. The idea is that the bobbin should hang in suspension without feeding out thread by virtue of its own weight. The thread should feed out readily and smoothly, but under a modicum of tension. This is achieved by mounting a spool of thread in the tool and adjusting, or bending, the limbs of the wishbone until you like the feel.

BOBBIN THREADER

This tool is truly a "one-trick pony," so to speak. It's used to draw the tying thread through the tube of the bobbin. Generally, it consists of a sharply pointed loop of fine wire. Lacking this, you can get by with a piece of fairly stiff monofilament, doubled over. The dental floss threaders that are sold in drugstores make great bobbin threaders.

HACKLE PLIERS

Hackle pliers are also a special-purpose instrument. Their main purpose is to grip a feather while you wrap it to form a hackle. There are a number of designs on the market today, some of which are quite a departure from the basic or conventional. While I'm very much in favor of innovation, I believe that it must stop short of gimmickry. Therefore, I strongly advocate simple hackle pliers that embody these features: a firm yet gentle grip, a comfortable size and shape for handling, and a sufficient weight to hold a feather in position when hanging suspended. The latter is important because quills have a certain stiffness and will try to unwrap themselves unless tension is maintained.

After 35 years of tying, I still prefer what are called English hackle pliers, which meet these criteria. The grip can be improved by adding a small piece of heat-shrink tubing to one of the jaws; this also lessens the possibility of breaking feathers. A word of caution: Don't get one of those miniature pliers that look so cute in the store. These are harder to handle and lack sufficient weight. Small flies can be worked on just as easily with normal-sized pliers; it's the jaws that count, not the overall size of the tool.

Some people use those little spring-loaded electronics clips as hackle pliers. I don't approve of them for general work, because they are too light and the wrong shape. Still, they are very useful for certain operations. One of these is the twisting and wrapping of peacock herl, which we'll be doing later in the book. They don't cost much, and are very handy.

HACKLE GAUGE

In dry-fly tying, the proper sizing of hackle is very important. Eventually, you'll be able to flex a feather, look at the barb length, and tell what size it is. In the beginning, though, you may need the assistance of a hackle gauge. I suggest a model that has a small peg, pin, or something around which you can bend the feather to simulate its being wrapped around the hook. There are several that can be attached to the post of the vise—a most convenient feature.

BODKIN

Also called a **dubbing needle,** this tool is simply a sharp-pointed instrument that is used for such tasks as picking out fur bodies and applying head cement. My favorite bodkin is a hardware store item called a pin vise. It enables you to change points anytime you choose. What more need be said?

There's another method for picking out and fuzzing up fly bodies, using a little piece of "male" Velcro—that is, the side with the tiny hooks. It works great and never cuts the thread.

HAIR EVENER

This device is also called a **stacker.** Its function is to enable you to quickly and effectively align the tips of bundles of hair that are to be used in making wings and such. Here again, a number of designs are available. The most important consideration is that the tool be of adequate size; those with narrow tubes will only work with small bunches of hair and are quite ineffective for evening up bundles of calf tail hair, which is crinkly and requires a generously sized tube. Remember, you can operate on smaller bunches with a wide-tubed stacker, but not vice versa.

HAIR PACKER

This is a very specialized instrument that is used when spinning deer or similar hair. As the bunches are tied in place, the packer is

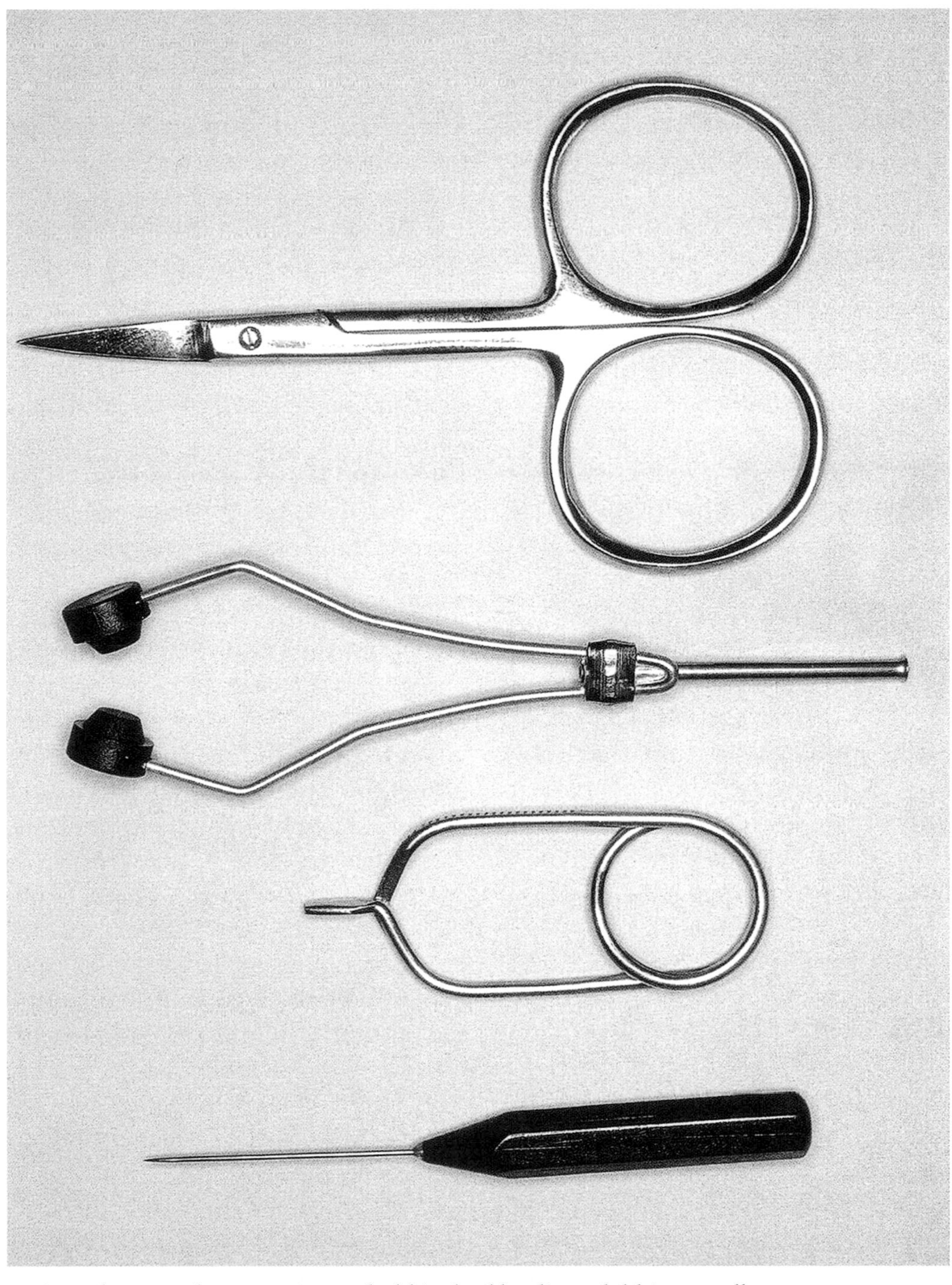

Basic tools. From the top: scissors, bobbin, hackle pliers, dubbing needle.

used to compress the hairs, which improves the results. It's a low-cost item in fly shops. You can also make a serviceable one yourself by disassembling a typical ballpoint pen and using the housing.

WHIP-FINISHER

The most effective knot for tying off the thread after you complete a fly is the whip-finish. It is sometimes used during intermediate steps as well. It is easily done by hand, but even more easily and quickly done with a good tool. I particularly like the Matarelli whip-finisher. Here again, it's advisable to buy the larger model, which is much more versatile.

HALF-HITCH TOOL

In the next chapter, you'll learn the basic knots. While I can assure you that making half-hitches by hand is very simple, you should be aware that there is a tool for doing it. Unless you're one of those people who just love tools, I see no need for this one.

MATERIALS CLIP

This is an adjunct to the vise that holds on to certain types of materials while you perform subsequent operations. The best example is securing ribbing tinsel while tying the body of a fly. Many vises come equipped with a materials clip. In any case, it's a useful and low-cost add-on.

There are other devices that serve specialized purposes in fly tying. You'll undoubtedly find out about them as you go along, and it's your decision as to which, if any, will be helpful. As I stated earlier, I'm all for innovation, but only in the interest of progress. Essentially, my rule is not to use a tool for any task that I can do just as well by hand.

CHEMISTRY

Fly tying has its own chemicals—substances that are used to finish off heads, protect vulnerable components, and enhance certain materials. Perhaps the first question that needs to be addressed is: Why use a head finish in the first place? The answer may seem obvious—but not so fast. Actually, I believe that, given modern synthetic waxed threads and well-tied whip-finish knots, fly heads could be left unfinished with minimal danger of their coming apart. After all, how long does the average fly last, anyway?

But then, with unfinished heads, you have to be careful not to damage the thread with forceps or some other tool when you unhook fish. Also, flies simply don't look as pretty without a nicely finished head. So I vote for lacquer or cement of some type. In fact, I use two coats on larger flies with more prominent heads.

There are quite a few **head cements** and **lacquers** available today. In most cases, they use a solvent of some type. These include acetone, methyl ethyl ketone (MEK), toluol, and lacquer thinner. Pretty potent stuff. Usually, the stores carry the thinners, so that you can buy the right one for whatever lacquer or cement you prefer, in modest quantities. This is important. While a general lacquer thinner may seem to work on a particular product, it may actually be changing the formula. So while some coatings may respond well to a general-purpose thinner, it's best to use the one that's recommended.

Most head finishes are of the hard variety. There are, however, a few that are described as "flexible." These are clear compounds that dry to a tough, rubbery finish, rather than a hard, brittle one. They have adhesive qualities and are useful in keeping stuff together. They can also be used to perform repair jobs, such as mending splits in jungle cock feathers.

It may be that a common clear head lacquer is all you will ever require. However, many tyers find other substances to be of considerable value. Among these are the so-called superglues of the cyanoacrylate type. They are extremely strong and fast drying and can be used to protect quill bodies and other delicate components. At this writing, Zap-A-Gap seems to be the most popular.

Epoxy is sometimes used to finish off heads on larger flies, especially those with eyes on them. Certainly, there is nothing stronger or more durable. The process is a bit tedious, however, what with the mixing and drying time. Even the five-minute variety requires a number of hours before the fly can go fishing. The main thing is to get the mix right, because if the proportions aren't very close to being exactly equal, it will never thoroughly cure. If that should happen, try to remove the first coat with a little acetone and stir up a new batch. Also keep in mind that epoxy won't set up properly in an overly cold environment.

When you buy epoxy, make sure it's the clear type. Either the regular or the five-minute will work; the only problem with the latter is that it doesn't allow you much working time. I suggest that you avoid those two-part finishes intended for coating and wrappings, if you want a thick, protective head; they are very low in viscosity.

There's a little problem with applying epoxy over waxed thread, because it doesn't penetrate the way solvent-based thinners do. For security's sake, you might first apply a coat of well-thinned clear lacquer and allow it to dry completely.

We are now seeing products that are described as being, shall we say, "environmentally considerate and responsible." Most recently, we've begun to see lacquers with water-based finishes. They are truly solvent-free and can be thinned and cleaned up with plain water. They come in various colors, and there are two types of clear: hard and flexible. (More about these in chapter 28.)

THREADS

There is an amazing variety of threads on the market today. It makes sense to use the type and size (thickness) of thread that's best suited to the task at hand. This doesn't mean that larger flies are always best tied with heavier threads, however. It's a matter of function and style.

Generally speaking, finer threads work better than thicker ones. You get better gripping power with more wraps of fine thread than you do with fewer wraps of thick thread, and a much neater effect to boot. This is especially true when finishing off heads. I do most of my tying with 8/0 Uni-Thread, except where extra-strength hook coverage is required.

There's the question of plain versus waxed thread. Back when silk was the only game in town, proper waxing was a necessity, for several good reasons. With synthetics, most of these reasons have disappeared. However, a little wax can still be helpful when you're working with certain types of materials.

One consideration with waxed threads is the penetration and adhesion of head finishes. With solvent-based lacquers, this problem is minimized, as the solvent abets penetration and bonding. With epoxy and the new water-based finishes, there can be a problem. For this reason, I do one of two things when using these latter finishes: Either I avoid using waxed thread, or I apply a coat of solvent-based lacquer before I apply the final finish coat.

22 The Basics

Practically all operations in fly tying involve thread. Thus, you need to know how to load the thread into the bobbin, attach it to the hook, wrap it around the hook, and, later, secure and detach it. This requires mastering one simple wrapping technique and two basic knots: the half-hitch and the whip-finish. In fact, if you are reasonably competent with the whip-finish, you may never want to resort to the half-hitch.

LOADING AND TYING ON THREAD

First, let's load the thread into the bobbin. You might want to refer to the comments on bobbin adjustment in chapter 21. If you are satisfied that your bobbin is properly adjusted, proceed as follows:

1. Seat the spool in the bobbin.
2. Run out 6 to 7 inches (150 to 175 mm) of thread.
3. Run the bobbin threader of your choice through the tube and out the other end.
4. Run the thread through the loop of the threader and pull it through the tube.

No problem with this, right? Check to see that the thread feeds smoothly. If further bobbin adjustment is needed, do so at this time.

Now you're ready to tie the thread onto the hook. This is simply a matter of wrapping the thread over itself along the hook shank. First, be aware that the thread—and, in fact, almost everything in fly tying—is wrapped over and away from the tyer. In other words, if you were looking at the process from the eye end of the hook, the wraps would be going clockwise.

I realize that a certain percentage of the world's population is left-handed. No problem; it's absolutely okay to face the vise the other way and do things as nature programmed you. The rules and instructions still apply; just reverse the right-hand/left-hand commands.

Here's the procedure for tying on:

1. Hold the bobbin in your right hand and the end of the tying thread with your left hand.
2. Position the thread against the far side of the hook.
3. While maintaining tension, wrap the thread around the hook five or six times, working rearward, so the wraps cross over themselves.
4. Release the bobbin and let it hang. Hold the tag end (the excess) of the thread tight

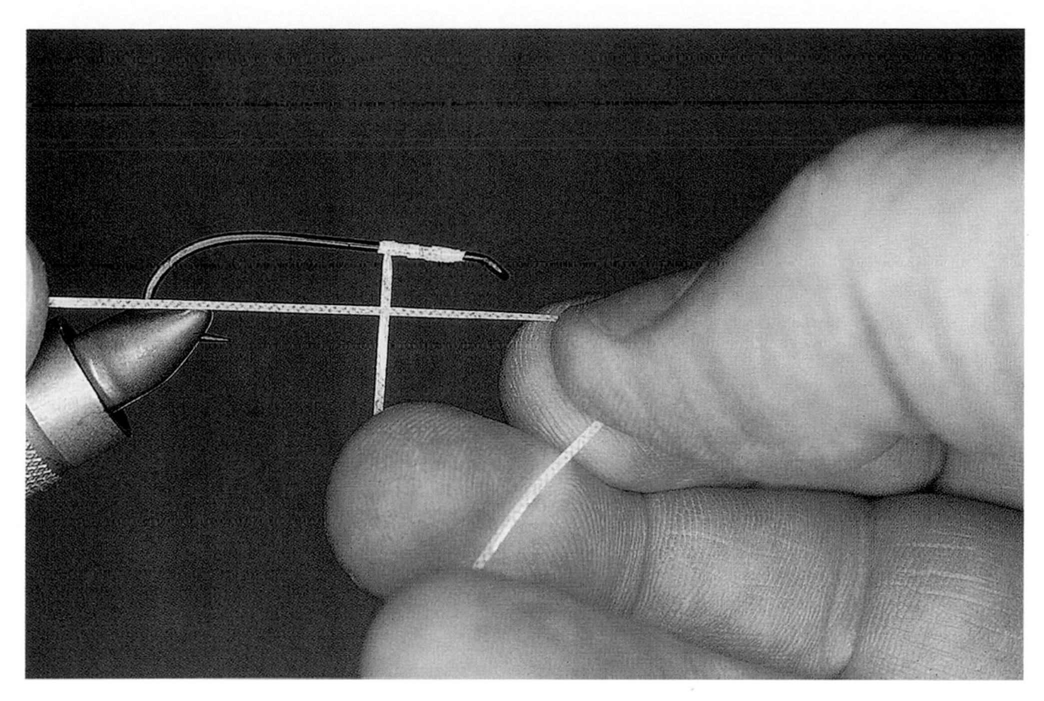

The beginning of a half-hitch.

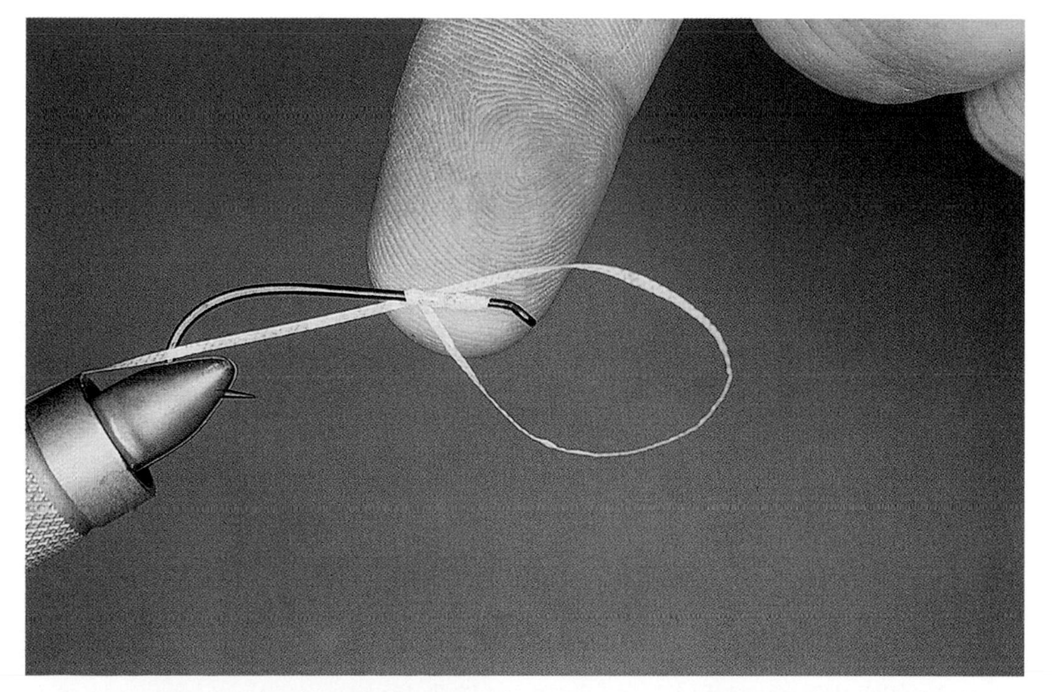

To complete the half-hitch, pass the thread loop over the eye of the hook, anchor it against the backside of the hook with a finger, and tighten, nooselike.

with your left hand, applying tension, and trim it off flush with the hook, using your scissors as a lance. This is better than cutting the thread in the normal manner, because no little stub is left.

As I mentioned, there are only a couple of knots that have application in fly tying: the half-hitch and the whip-finish. The **half-hitch knot,** or usually a series of several of them, is used to secure a tying operation at some point in the construction of a fly. It is sometimes used by beginners in lieu of the whip-finish to tie off at the completion of a fly, but the whip-finish is a much more secure knot and should be mastered. Here's how the half-hitch goes:

1. With your right hand, twist the thread to form a triangular loop, with the thread crossing in front of itself, and the bobbin off to the rear.
2. Pass the thread around the front of the hook in such a manner that the eye protrudes through the triangular loop.
3. With a finger of your left hand, press the thread against the back of the hook, to keep it from coming undone.
4. Pull the thread from the rear to tighten the loop.

> **Important!** As a beginner, you'll be breaking or accidentally cutting the tying thread now and then. In fact, this will happen occasionally even after you've become a master tyer. It's very important to know what to do when this happens. I call this Disaster-Avoidance Technique Number One.
>
> Always have your hackle pliers at hand. If you should break or cut the thread, immediately seize the tag end that's hanging from the hook and maintain tension. Then attach your hackle pliers to it, and let them hang. Now simply tie on again, bind down the hanging tag, release the hackle pliers, trim off both the old and new tag ends, and go about your business.

The **whip finish** can be done with one or two hands. The single-handed method is a bit tricky, so I'll teach you the two-handed one here.

1. Pull out enough thread so that the bobbin may be laid aside—it is not, and should not be, involved in this procedure.
2. Make a triangular loop as you would with the half-hitch, but somewhat larger.
3. With your left hand, hold under tension the side of the loop that passes around the hook, while the other side of the loop—the thread coming from the bobbin—hangs straight out in front of the hook eye.
4. Wrap the thread that you've been holding in your left hand around the front of the hook, passing it back and forth between your two hands as you go. What you are doing is binding the other thread to the hook in nooselike fashion. Make five or six wraps.
5. With your right hand, insert something like a dubbing needle or toothpick into the loop and use it to maintain tension, while holding the other end of the thread with your left hand.
6. Tighten by pulling with your left hand. As the loop becomes tight behind the eye of the hook, withdraw the needle or toothpick and tighten securely.
7. Using your scissors like a lance, cut off the thread.

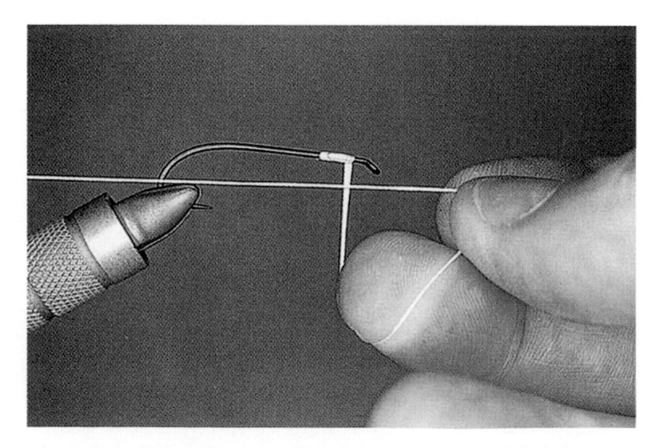

The whip-finish begins the same as the half-hitch.

Before you tie an actual fly, I suggest that you practice these procedures until you are comfortable with them. Once you can execute them with a reasonable degree of skill, you're ready for your first adventure in fly tying.

The part of the thread that's coming off the hook is wrapped around the hook five or six times. The part of the thread that goes back to the bobbin forms a standing loop in front. Using both hands, pass the thread under and around the hook, binding the thread that goes back to the bobbin to the hook shank.

HOOKS AND POSSIBLE SUBSTITUTIONS

It is my unpleasant duty to inform you that there is virtually no standardization in hook descriptions. You will see specifications such as **4X long, 3X fine, Model Perfect bend,** and so forth. They are quite arbitrary, and the various manufacturers take considerable liberties in the application of them. Thus, hooks listed as having, for example, a 3X-long shank or 3X-fine wire may differ remarkably among manufacturers. You can expect to find variations in shank length, wire weight, shape of bend, and other criteria. This can result in variations (usually small) in the tying process and in the appearance and proportions of the finished fly.

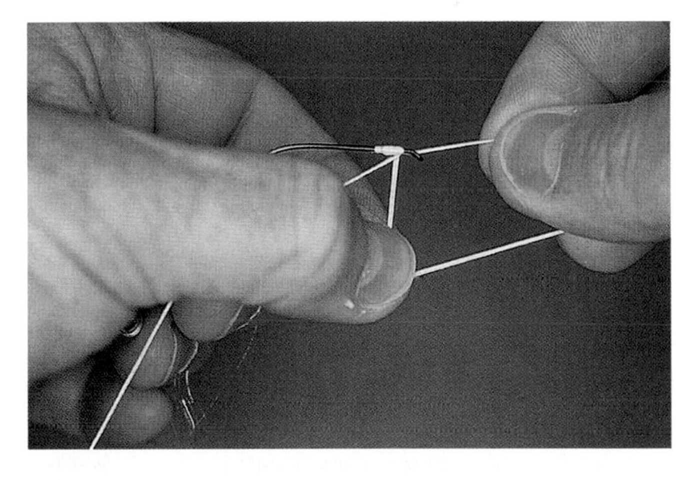

Even though it constitutes an imperfect system for describing the characteristics of hooks, you'll be encountering such nomenclature frequently, so let's see what it all means. The term *X* means "extra." Thus, if you see a hook designated as being a size 12, 2X long (2XL), it means that its shank is two hook sizes longer than that of a standard-shanked size 12; in other words, it has the gap (*gape* is the old British term) of a 12 and the shank of an 8.

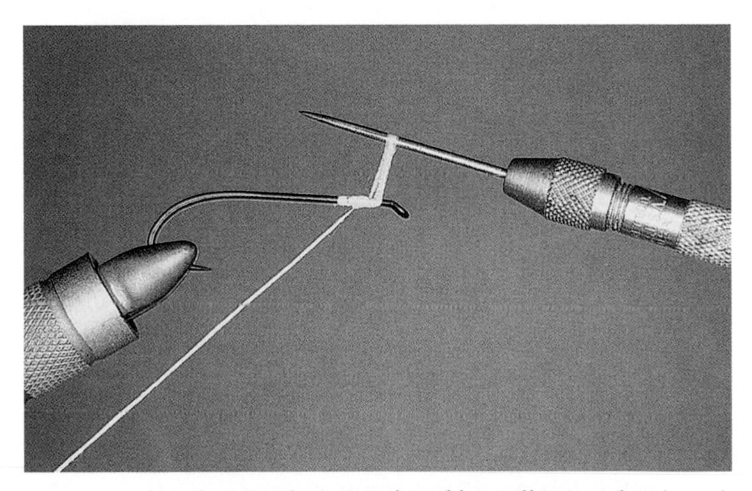

The whip-finish is completed by pulling on the thread from the bobbin end, tightening nooselike. Apply tension with a needle or something similar, as shown.

Since the X system deals in relatives, there must be a benchmark, or starting point. It is generally accepted that a standard-length shank is two times the gap of the hook. As I mentioned, there are variations among manufacturers, but they are usually modest enough not to be a source of trouble. The hooks are sufficiently interchangeable that the same proportions will result in the finished fly.

This is not always the case with wire diameter, which is also defined using the X system. For example, *3X-fine wire* is meant to describe a very fine-wire dry-fly hook. However, the variation among manufacturers is greater in this application, and there doesn't seem to be an agreed-upon benchmark. For example, some years ago, one hook maker put out a dry-fly hook designated 4X fine. It didn't seem all that fine to me. After the judicious application of a micrometer to this hook and another from a different company marked 1X fine, I found the 4X hook to be a hair thicker of shank than the 1X, which is considered standard dry-fly wire. Such discrepancies exist in wet-fly and streamer hooks as well.

The best that I can suggest is that you learn about the various hooks and apply that knowledge to the selection of them. This is of particular importance with dry-fly hooks, where relatively small differences can be meaningful. You might try interrogating the personnel of the store you frequent, to see if they are aware of the idiosyncrasies of the hooks they carry. But don't be shocked if they are not.

As you progress in fly tying, you'll learn more about hooks through your personal experiences and observations. I'm not going to belabor the matter here, but I do think that you should be generally acquainted with hook nomenclature and the fact that it's not entirely accurate. There may well come a time when you'll want to carefully examine the hooks you intend to purchase to be sure they will enable you to successfully tie the shape, style, and weight of fly that you want.

At the risk of dating this book, I provide herewith a listing of the more popular hooks used in fly tying today. It is not a complete listing. New hooks come onto the market fairly frequently these days, and it's really difficult to stay current. However, I think this list provides some valuable orientation. Note that some hooks are listed in two categories; that's because they are in-betweeners.

Typical Wet Fly	Daiichi #1550; Mustad #3906; Partridge #G3A; Tiemco #3769[1]
1XL Wet Fly/ Nymph	Daiichi #1560; Mustad #3906B or #7957B; Tiemco #3761
2XL Nymph	Daiichi #1710; Mustad #9671; Partridge #D4A; Tiemco #5262
3XL Nymph	Daiichi #1720; Mustad #9672; Partridge #H1A or #D3ST; Tiemco #5263
4XL Nymph/ Streamer	Daiichi #1750; Mustad #79580; Partridge #CS17; Tiemco #300
Streamer	Daiichi #2340 or #2370; Mustad #9575 or #3665A; Partridge #CS17; Tiemco #300
Standard Dry Fly	Daiichi #1180 or #1100; Mustad #94840; Partridge #E1A or #L3A; Tiemco #100 or #5210[2]
Long Dry Fly	Daiichi #1280; Mustad #94831; Partridge #H1A[3]

[1]Tiemco #3769 has slightly heavier wire.
[2]While all of these hooks are suitable for tying dry flies, there are slight variations in wire diameter, shape, size, and design.
[3]These hooks are represented as being adaptable for tying longer dry flies, such as hopper and stonefly patterns. However, wire thicknesses vary a little, the Mustad being the finest in diameter at this writing.

Some final thoughts on hooks. Today, we return our gamefish to the water, hopefully unharmed. Debarbing the hook is an important part of this process. Still, I do believe there are a few exceptions.

Some of today's fly-tying hooks have very small barbs and can be used as is. I don't like to debarb my salmon hooks, because landing an Atlantic salmon, especially a sizable one, is a rare experience and usually a difficult one. Thus, I use hooks with very conservatively sized barbs, such as the Daiichi #2421 and #2441. I feel that with due care and hooks of this type, I can release my salmon with assurance of survival.

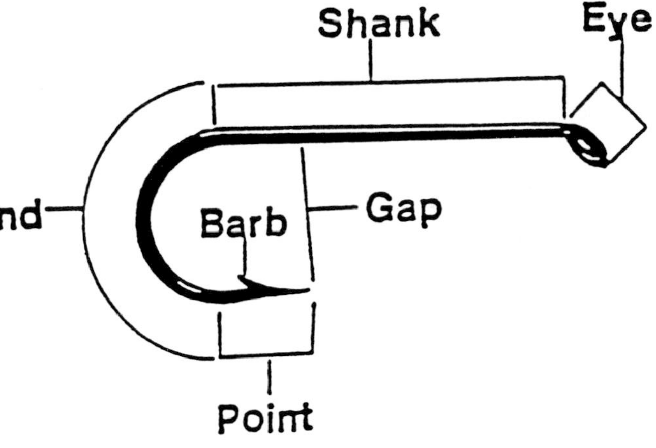

The parts of a hook.

It's always best to debarb a hook before tying a fly on it, for the simple reason that the hook might break during the debarbing process. Small pliers or forceps with smooth jaws work fine. Larger, stronger hooks can be debarbed by using the jaws of the tying vise—carefully, of course. I don't suggest this for fine-wire dry-fly hooks; they should be handled more gently.

The idea is to flatten out the barb or cause it to break off. Some hooks, dry-fly models in particular, use a more brittle type of steel, and the barb will usually break off under moderate pressure, leaving a small bump in its place. You'll feel it happen. Don't try to flatten this bump any further; you've done enough.

23 The Woolly Worm

I can think of no better type of fly for a starter than the Woolly Worm. It is very easy to tie, yet it's very effective on trout, panfish, and even the occasional bass. It can be tied in practically any size and color combination, and it requires very inexpensive materials.

You'll recall that I mentioned in chapter 21 that the hook can be mounted either with the point exposed or with it hidden in the vise jaws. Since we're using a fairly large, strong hook here, I recommend burying the hook point in the jaws. This will effectively prevent you from accidentally catching the thread on the point and cutting it.

With this type of fly, a long feather is required. I advocate tying it in by the tip end, so that its barbs are progressively a little longer as the feather is wrapped forward. This results in a good-looking tapered effect and, I firmly believe, enhances the effectiveness of the fly.

In this lesson, you'll learn three very important techniques, specifically:

1. The thread pinch wrap, which is probably the most important technique in fly tying.
2. Wrapping a hackle that is tied in by the tip.
3. Tying off materials.

You'll also learn about **chenille,** a most user-friendly tying material. This stuff looks like a caterpillar, and well it should, because its name is derived from the French word for that insect.

I should mention that the proportions of materials are relative to the size of the hook. For larger or smaller hooks, you should use thicker or narrower chenille and larger and smaller feathers, respectively, in order to maintain proportions.

Woolly Worm Dressing

HOOK:	Medium shank length, 2X to 4X long, fairly heavy wire; see the hook chart in chapter 22 (page 240). Usually tied in sizes 4 to 10.
THREAD:	Black 6/0 or 8/0.
HACKLE:	Black, long, and fairly soft.
BODY:	Medium-thickness black chenille.

Tying Steps

1. Tie the thread on up front just to the rear of the hook eye, trim off the tag end of the thread, and wrap to the rear of the hook, where the bend begins.

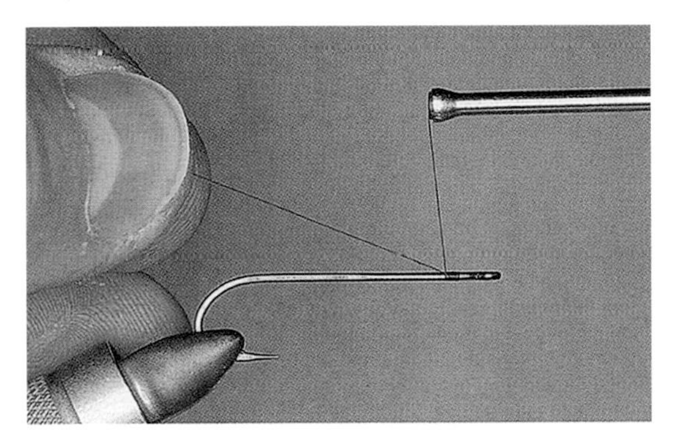

Tying on (step 1).

2. Cut off a piece of chenille about 5 inches (125 mm) in length. With your thumbnail, scrape off a little of the fuzz at one end, exposing a bit of the thread core.

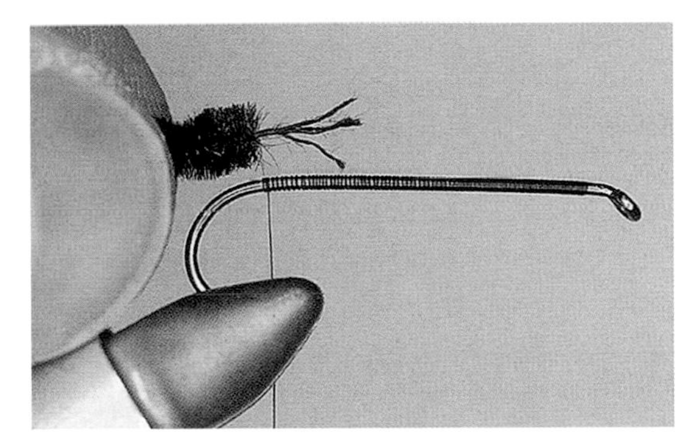

Thread at bend of hook, chenille prepared to be tied in (steps 1–2).

3. With your left thumb and forefinger, hold the chenille on top of the hook in the position shown.

4. Bring the thread up between your left thumb and forefinger. Pinch together the thread, the exposed core of the chenille, and the hook itself.

5. While maintaining the pinch, sneak the thread downward between your fingers on the far side of the hook, catching the chenille core against the hook shank.

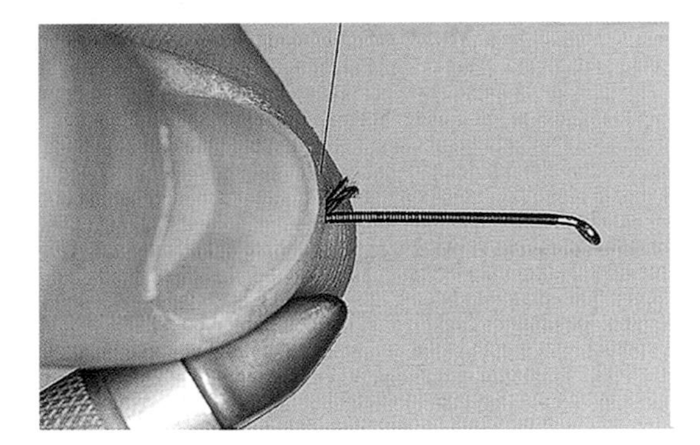

Tying on the chenille with a pinch wrap (steps 3–5).

6. Repeat this move several times. Then release the pinch, trim off any excess core material, and take a few firm thread wraps, moving forward by about the thickness of the chenille.

Chenille tied in, thread positioned for tying in the hackle feather (step 6).

7. Select a hackle feather and prepare it by carefully stripping off the fluffy material around the butt end. Starting at the butt end, gently stroke the fibers, which are called **barbs,** so that they stick out at approximately a right angle to the quill. Don't break off or cut off the quill,

Tying Steps

because you'll need this for a "handle" when you wrap the hackle.

A typical Woolly Worm hackle feather, prepared to be tied in (step 7).

8. Near the tip end, stroke back the barbs on both sides, thus exposing the quill. Hold the feather against the bottom of the hook with the good, or shiny, side facing you, and bind the quill to the hook at this spot. The idea is that during wrapping, the shiny side is facing forward.

9. Secure the tie-in by binding down the tip of the feather as you work forward with the thread. Cut off any excess well before you get to the eye area. The thread should now be positioned a little way behind the eye. Leave yourself some space there for tying down the chenille, which is a bit bulkier than most materials.

The hackle feather tied in, thread wrapped to front (steps 8–9).

10. Pick up the chenille and begin wrapping it around the hook. Remember: Always wrap away from yourself. Take one turn behind the tie-in point of the feather, then come in front of it and continue. This protects the quill from the rear, and better positions the feather for wrapping.

Wrapping the chenille (step 10).

11. When you reach the spot where the thread is hanging, proceed as follows: Hold the chenille with your right hand, maintaining tension. Pick up the bobbin with your left hand and lift it over the chenille and the hook several times. Then transfer the bobbin to your right hand and take several more firm wraps. When you're sure the chenille is securely tied down, cut off the excess and bury the end with a few more wraps. Don't crowd the eye!

The chenille body completed (step 11).

Tying Steps

12. Pick up the hackle and begin to wrap it, shiny-side forward, in spiral fashion, following the wraps of chenille. Ideally, the quill should sink between the wraps of chenille. Also, it is most helpful to stroke back the barbs with your left hand as you wrap. This helps keep them from getting tangled with the quill, results in a more attractive hackle, and streamlines the shape of the fly overall.

Wrapping the hackle (step 12).

13. This step is optional but, in my opinion, desirable. When you've reached the front of the chenille body, providing you have enough feather left, take two or three additional wraps of hackle, one against the other, stroking back the barbs as you wrap. This puts a good-looking finish at the front of the fly.

14. The hackle feather is tied off in the same manner as was the chenille. Hold the end of the quill with your right hand and perform several or more "lift-over" bobbin moves under firm tension. Transfer the bobbin to your right hand and take a few more firm wraps. When you're sure you've secured the feather, cut off the excess and bind down the stub of the butt.

The completed Woolly Worm (steps 13–14).

Now you're ready to execute the whip-finish, per the instructions in chapter 22. Afterward, apply at least one coat of head lacquer, allowing for thorough drying between coats.

A little hint: If you plan on tying several Woolly Worms at one sitting, you can conserve on chenille by cutting pieces that are long enough for three or four flies. This reduces the loss that would accrue from waste tag ends with each fly.

Now you've tied your first fly. Admire it, cherish it, fish with it, and save it. I sorely wish that I'd saved my beginning flies; they would make great keepsakes today, almost forty years later.

It is very common in fly tying and fishing to embellish simple flies with little additions, in the interests of diversity and enhanced attractiveness. We hope, of course, that the fish see it this way. Frequently, a small tag of yarn is added to the Woolly Worm. It could be red, hot orange, bright green, or whatever. The tag is tied in place before the tying of the fly. Here's how it's done:

1. Tie on up front and wrap the thread about 25 percent of the shank length to the rear.
2. Cut a piece of yarn perhaps 1½ inches (40 mm) in length. Tie it in with pinch wraps on the top of the hook. Trim off the excess.
3. Take hold of the tag with your left hand and apply tension. Then wrap the thread to the rear, binding down the yarn as you go. It is helpful to hold the yarn slightly toward yourself, in order to counteract the torque effect of the thread.
4. When you reach the bend, stop, and trim the tag to the desired length. I would suggest that it be rather short, as shown.
5. Proceed with the Woolly Worm.

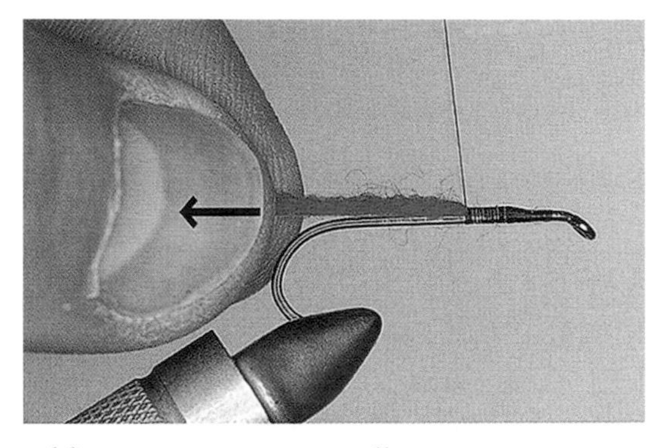

Adding a yarn tag to a Woolly Worm (steps 1–4).

Adding a yarn tag to a Woolly Worm (steps 1–4).

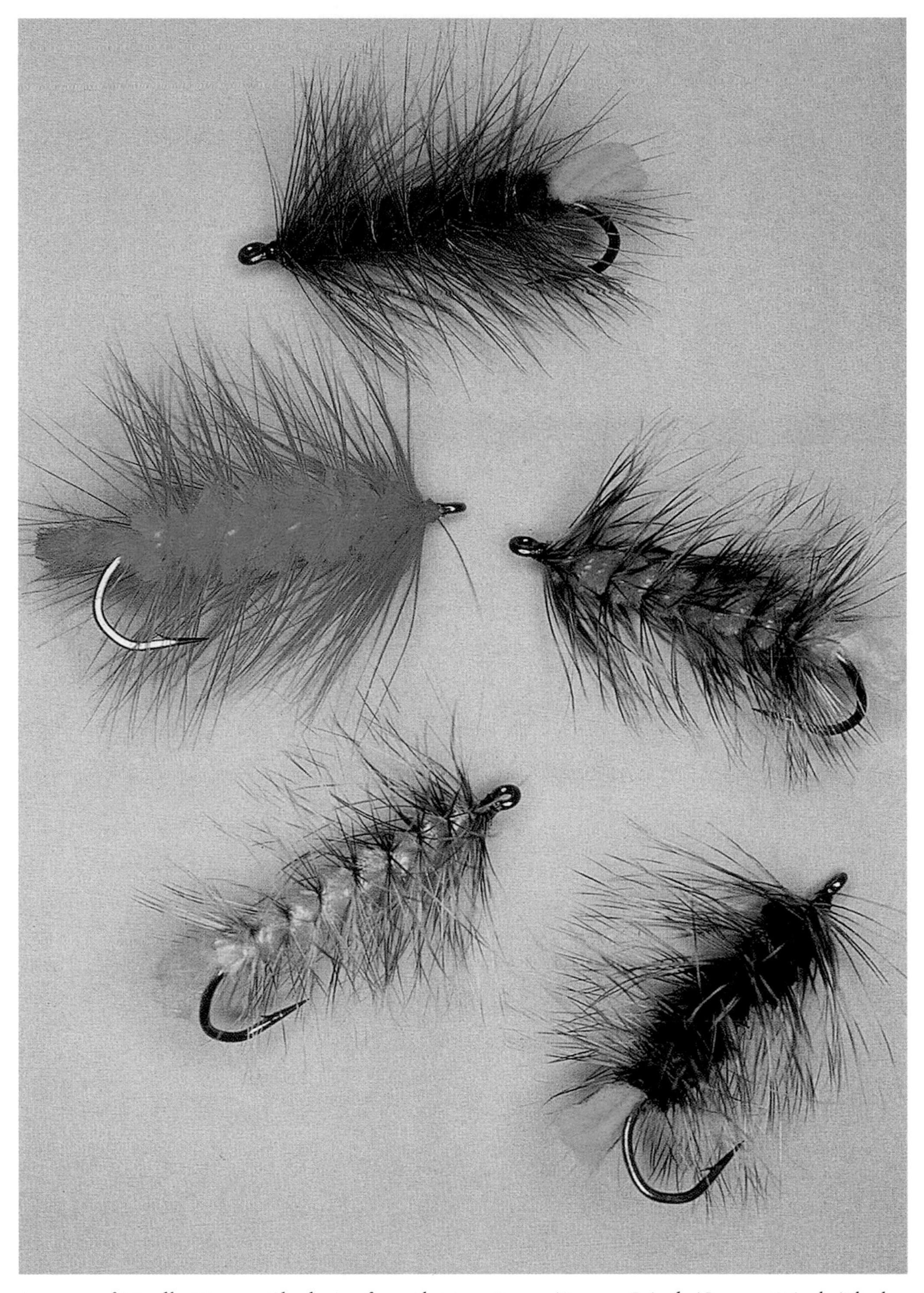

A group of Woolly Worms. Clockwise from the top: Brown/Brown, Grizzly/Green, Grizzly/Black, Grizzly/Yellow, Hot Orange/Hot Orange.

Some Woolly Worm Patterns

Note: The hooks for these flies are the same as for the one in the tying lesson. If you wish to vary the thread color to better match and complement the colors of the flies, feel free to do so.

1. **Grizzly/Black**

   TAG: (optional) Red or green yarn.
   BODY: Black chenille.
   HACKLE: Long, soft grizzly (barred rock) rooster feather.

2. **Grizzly/Green**

   TAG: (optional) Chartreuse yarn.
   BODY: Bright green chenille.
   HACKLE: Long, soft grizzly rooster feather.

3. **Grizzly/Yellow**

   TAG: (optional) Yellow yarn.
   BODY: Yellow chenille.
   HACKLE: Long, soft grizzly rooster feather.

4. **Brown/Brown**

   TAG: (optional) Red or green yarn.
   BODY: Brown chenille.
   HACKLE: Long, soft brown rooster feather.

5. **Hot Orange/Hot Orange**

   TAG: (optional) Orange yarn.
   BODY: Orange chenille.
   HACKLE: Long, soft orange-dyed rooster feather.

The Woolly Bugger

Let's build on what was learned in the Woolly Worm lesson by tying its successor, the Woolly Bugger. Essentially, this is nothing more than a Woolly Worm with a tail. The tail is usually made out of a material called **marabou,** which is a fancy name for turkey body feathers, dyed whatever color. Soft fur from the arctic fox also makes a great tail.

Two new techniques will be demonstrated:

1. Tailing the Woolly Bugger.
2. Weighting a fly.

As with the Woolly Worm, the proportions of materials should be matched up with the size of hook you're using. For this type of fly, I like a hook 3X or 4X in shank length. The size might range from 1/0 to 10. Here, I'm using a size 6.

Woolly Bugger Dressing

HOOK:	Medium shank length (3XL to 4XL), typically sizes 2 to 10.
THREAD:	Black 6/0 or 8/0.
TAIL:	Black marabou feather.
UNDERBODY:	Soft wire, fine to medium thickness.
HACKLE:	Barred rock (grizzly), long and fairly soft.
BODY:	Medium-thickness olive chenille.

Typing Steps

1. As was done with the Woolly Worm, tie on up front just to the rear of the hook eye, trim off the tag end of the thread, and wrap to the rear of the hook. Then create a smooth thread base right ahead of where the bend begins to slope off. Just a couple of layers is sufficient.
2. Select a marabou plume that has soft, fairly straight barbs. If you see that the quill extends out into the part you'll use for the tail, go in with the very tips of your scissors and snip it out below the tie-in point, keeping in mind that the tail will be about the same length as the hook shank. Then strip off the very fuzzy material around the butt end. Be careful, however, not to discard too much material.
3. Stroke the fibers toward the tips with your left hand, bringing them together and neatening them. It is helpful to slightly moisten the feather while performing this operation.
4. Measure the marabou plume against the hook shank. As stated, they should be of equal length. Then set the feather atop the hook and tie it on with a few pinch wraps. Secure it with a series of firm wraps in that area; then trim off the excess as closely as you can.

Turkey marabou plume before and after center quill is snipped out (step 2).

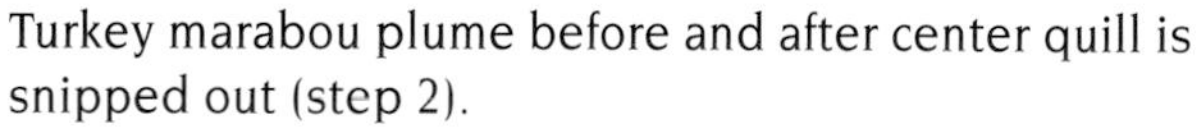

Turkey marabou plume before and after center quill is snipped out (step 2).

Tying in and trimming the marabou (steps 3–4).

Tying in and trimming the marabou (steps 3–4).

Tying Steps

5. Cut off a piece of wire about 6 inches (150 mm) in length. Remember the little hint at the end of the last chapter about conserving materials when tying several flies at a sitting? It applies here to both the wire and the chenille.

6. Note that the thread is not involved in affixing the wire; it simply molds itself to the hook as it is wrapped. Abut the wire against the chopped-off tail butts, thus effecting a smooth transition. Wrap it neatly forward, with the turns abutting one another. Stop well short of the eye. You should allow for one full turn of chenille ahead of the wire. Trim off the excess at both ends.

7. This is optional, but important. Spread a coating of adhesive, such as head lacquer or, better yet, Zap-A-Gap, over the top of the wire, and allow it to penetrate between the wraps. This helps secure the underbody.

8. The remaining steps are exactly the same as for the Woolly Worm. Cut off a piece of chenille about 5 inches (125 mm) in length. With your thumbnail, scrape off a little of the fuzz at one end, exposing a bit of the thread core.

9. Tie in the chenille with pinch wraps, secure it, and trim off the tag of the core.

10. Select a hackle feather and prepare it by carefully stripping off the fluffy material around the butt end and stroking the barbs to a right angle to the quill, per steps 2 and 3. Tie it in by the tip end with the good, or shiny, side facing you, secure, and trim.

Wrapping on the wire (steps 5–7).

Chenille and hackle feather tied in (steps 8–10).

Typing Steps

11. Wrap the chenille, taking the last turn just ahead of the wire. Tie it off, secure it, and trim off the excess.

12. Wrap the feather as instructed for the Woolly Worm—shiny-side forward, in spiral fashion, following the wraps of chenille, stroking back the barbs as you go. At the front, take two or three additional wraps of hackle, one against the other, stroking back the barbs as you wrap. This puts a good-looking finish at the front of the fly. Tie off as previously instructed, do a whip-finish, apply lacquer, and head for the water.

The completed Woolly Bugger (steps 11–12).

Some Woolly Bugger Patterns

Note: The hooks for these flies are the same as for the one in the tying lesson. If you wish to vary the thread color to better match and complement the colors of the flies, feel free to do so. A weighted underbody is generally used on Woolly Buggers.

1. **Black/Grizzly/Peacock**
   TAIL: Black turkey or fur marabou.
   BODY: Peacock herl.
   HACKLE: Long, soft grizzly rooster feather.

2. **Pale Olive/Brown/Pale Olive**
   TAIL: Pale olive turkey or fur marabou.
   BODY: Pale olive chenille.
   HACKLE: Long, soft brown rooster feather.

3. **Pink/White/Pink**
   TAIL: Pink turkey or fur marabou.
   BODY: Pink chenille.
   HACKLE: Long, soft white rooster feather.

4. **Purple Flasher**
   TAIL, BODY, & HACKLE: All purple; materials as per usual.
   FLASH: Purple Krystal Flash or similar; a few strands mixed into the tail.

5. **Black Psychedelic**
   TAIL: Black turkey or fur marabou.
   BODY: Iridescent dubbing: a mix of rainbow Lite Brite and black fur.
   HACKLE: Long, soft black rooster feather.

Woolly Buggers are tied in many different color combinations. My all-around favorite is the same as the one we just tied, except with a peacock herl body.

Another popular embellishment to this fly is a bit of glitz in the tail. This could take the form of a few strands of Krystal Flash, Glimmer, Flashabou, or any of such shiny materials. Just don't overdo it; too much flash has an adverse effect on fish.

A flock of Woolly Buggers. From the top: Purple Flasher, Brown/Olive, Black Psychedelic, Hot Pink/White, Black/Grizzly/Peacock.

25 The Soft-Hackle Wet Fly

The so-called soft-hackle wet fly has been with us for centuries. The oldest of the British angling books describe patterns that are, in essence, soft-hackles. They would surely work just fine today in their original dressings.

This type of fly is suggestive, in a general but apparently convincing manner, of emerging insect life. It serves as a very good imitation of emerging caddisflies as they transform from what is known as the pupal to the adult stage. Soft-hackles are also suggestive of emerging mayflies, small crustaceans, and other forms of aquatic life.

The list of dressings for soft-hackles is practically endless. Entire books have been written about them, and many magazine articles. To my way of thinking, the patterns that will become your favorites are those that work where you fish. Thus, it's helpful to learn as much as possible about the insects in your fishing area.

In this lesson, we'll tie a peacock-bodied soft-hackle and add a bit of **tinsel** for a highlight. This is not the same as Christmas tree tinsel; it's made especially for fly tying. There are several types, the most common being flat and oval; we'll use the latter here. The two most popular colors are gold and silver. With today's flat tinsel, which is usually made of Mylar, you'll find gold on one side and silver on the other. Both types come in several widths or thicknesses. Here, we'll use fairly fine oval.

Peacock herl is a wonderful material that appears in so many of our historic "killer" flies. It can be purchased either in bundles or by the tail. For most applications, the bundled stuff works just fine. If you get into streamer tying, however, in which peacock fronds are frequently used in a different manner, you'd be better advised to buy the tails.

The techniques we'll examine in this chapter are:

1. The peacock herl body.
2. The oval tinsel rib.
3. The soft-hackle collar.

In chapter 21 you'll recall that I mentioned the spring-loaded electronics clip as being very helpful in working with peacock herl. The reason is that peacock herl quills are often quite flat and resist being twisted together with thread, which is necessary for reasons of durability. The electronics clip is the ideal tool for gripping and twisting them. I think this more than justifies the couple of bucks it costs.

Peacock Soft-Hackle Dressing

HOOK:	Wet fly, regular shank length, typically sizes 8 to 16. Refer to the hook chart in chapter 22 (page 240).
THREAD:	Black 6/0 or 8/0.
RIBBING:	Oval gold tinsel.
BODY:	Peacock herl.
HACKLE:	Grizzly (barred rock) hen feather.

Tying Steps

1. Tie on near the front of the hook, leaving a fairly long tag of thread—about 5 inches (125 mm)—which is not to be cut off, because you will use it subsequently.

2. Cut a piece of tinsel a few inches in length and tie it in on the bottom of the hook. Then hold both the tinsel and the thread tag with your left hand and, while applying tension, bind them down along the bottom of the hook shank, stopping at the bend. This is similar to the procedure described in chapter 23 for adding a yarn tag to a Woolly Worm (see page 246).

3. Select a few pieces of peacock—let's use five here—and cut back the tips a little, in order to do away with the most brittle part. Tie them in as a bunch by the trimmed tip ends at the rear of the hook, where the bend begins to slope off. Then wrap the thread forward to where you'll want the body to end, leaving plenty of space for tying off the peacock and the tinsel, wrapping the hackle, and doing the whip-finish.

   The reason for tying in the peacock herl by the tips is twofold: to reduce bulk and to maximize herl. The quills are much thicker at the butt ends, and the herl is sparser.

4. Be sure that both the peacock and the thread that was left hanging are located together at the bend of the hook and that there is no space between the two; otherwise, the thread will come across the peacock and may cut it. Pick up the tag end of thread and start twisting it together with the peacock, in effect forming a virtual chenille. Don't take too many twists at first, because the thread might sever the herl.

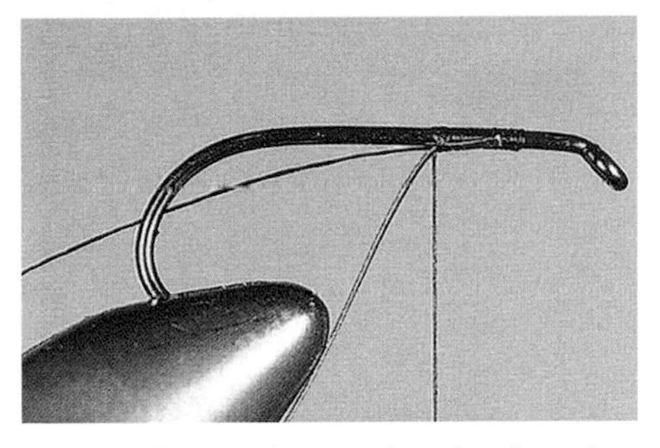

Tying in the tinsel. Note that the thread tag is not trimmed off (steps 1–2).

Note: If by some chance you've forgotten and have cut off the thread tag, no sweat. You can either tie in another piece of thread or form a long loop and cut off one side of it, whichever you find more convenient.

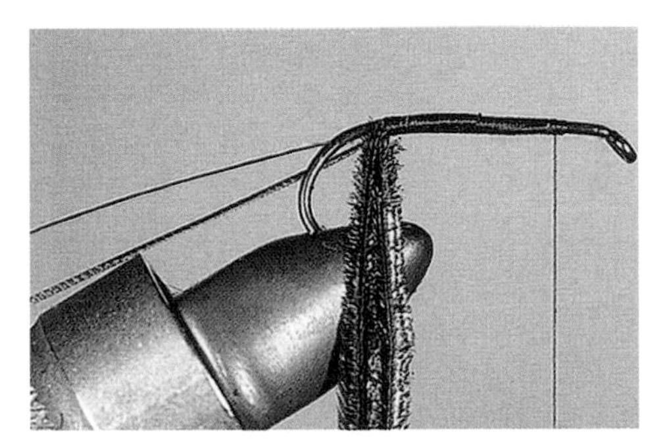

Peacock tied in, thread advanced to the front (steps 3–4).

Tying Steps

5. Begin wrapping the herl and thread "chenille" around the hook, working forward with each wrap abutting the one before it. Continue twisting the thread and herl as you go. If you run into difficulty with twisting, you can resort to the electronics clip or regular hackle pliers.

Wrapping the peacock and thread combination (step 5).

6. When you reach the spot where the thread or bobbin was left hanging, tie off and trim the peacock as you would chenille.

The peacock body completed (step 6).

7. Pick up the tinsel and spiral-wrap it forward over the herl. Here, you have the option of reverse-wrapping, as I'm doing here, so as to further reinforce the peacock. This simply involves wrapping toward yourself instead of away. You'll get four or five turns. Try to keep them as evenly spaced as possible. Secure and trim the tinsel tag end.

Reverse-wrapping the tinsel ribbing (step 7).

The completed ribbing (step 7).

8. The soft hackle is done in a somewhat similar manner as the large hackles of the Woollies, with a couple of departures. Select a hackle feather whose barbs will extend about 1½ times the gap of the hook, give or take a little. Prepare it by carefully stripping off the fluffy material around the butt end and stroking the barbs to a right angle to the quill, per previous instructions. Tie it in by the tip end with the good, or shiny, side facing you, secure, and trim.

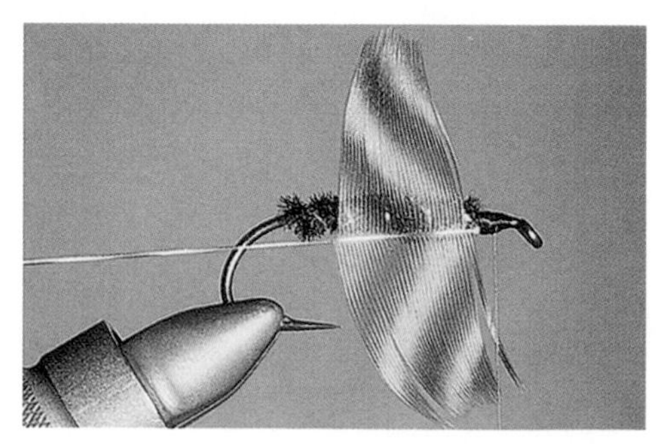

The hackle feather tied in place (step 8).

Tying Steps

9. For working with this smaller feather, I'd suggest using your hackle pliers. Wrap the feather as instructed for the front end of the Woollies, shiny-side forward, stroking back the barbs as you go, so that the hackle forms a graceful cornucopia around the fly body. Two wraps should be sufficient—at the very most, three. You don't want to overdress your soft-hackle wets. In some cases, one turn is all you'll want.

10. Whip-finish, lacquer the head, and you're done.

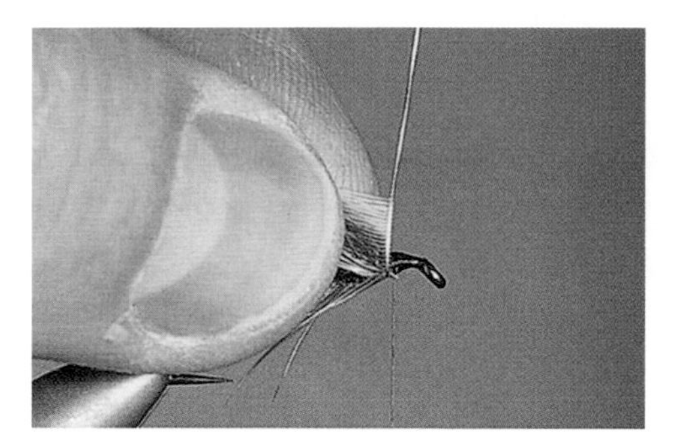

Stroking back the barbs while wrapping (step 9).

The completed fly (step 10).

If you wish, you can perform an operation known as **folding the feather** ahead of time. This makes forming the cornucopia somewhat easier. Here's the drill:

1. After preparing the feather, take hold of it by the butt end with your hackle pliers.
2. Grip the pliers with the fourth and fifth fingers of your right hand, leaving your thumb and forefinger free for action.
3. Hold the tip of the feather with your left hand. With the quill under tension, use your right thumb and forefinger to stroke the barbs to whichever side of the quill they naturally belong. The feather is now ready to be tied in and wrapped.

I urge you to master this technique, because it's used in several important fly-tying operations. We'll revisit it several times throughout the book.

I might mention that many soft-hackle dressings call for bodies made of a stranded material called **floss.** Again, this is fly-tying floss, not the stuff your dentist yells at you for not using properly. It comes in many colors and a variety of thicknesses. A thin skein of floss is preferable for the relatively small hook sizes usually used for these flies. Tyers of Atlantic salmon flies use floss a great deal. A few of them even insist on floss made of silk, which was and is the traditional raw material.

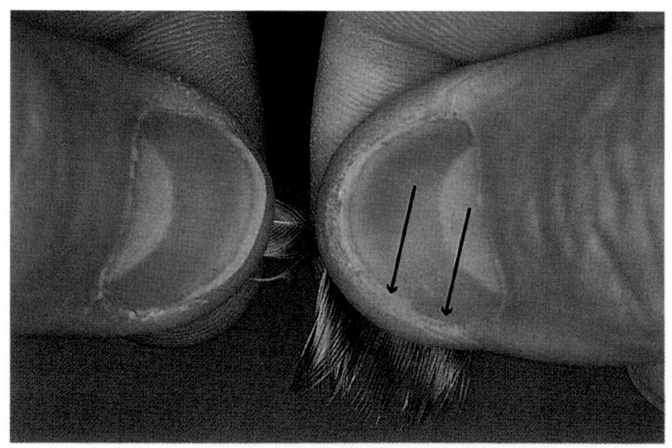

How to fold a feather and gather barbs (supplemental steps 1–3).

THE BEAD-HEAD ENHANCEMENT

A fairly recent addition to the fly tyer's arsenal is the introduction of beads with holes drilled through them. The addition of these beads to standard patterns has imbued these flies with a remarkably different sort of action or behavior in the water, more like a miniature jig. They also, of course, add weight.

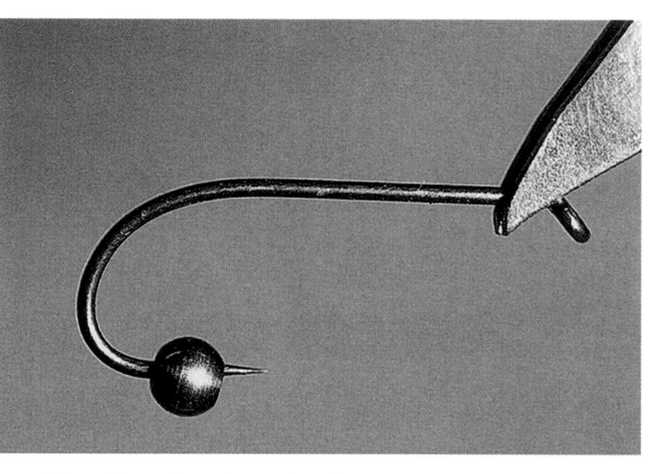

Mounting a bead on a hook.

At this writing, beads are available in several metallic colors, including silver, gold, brass, and black, and also in a range of sizes. Glass beads are available as well; I haven't tried them yet. Typically, the beads are drilled in such a manner that the hole is larger at one end than the other. It's important to be aware of this, because it governs how you mount the bead on the hook.

With bead-head flies, the bead goes on first, before you mount the hook in the vise. This is done by inserting the point of the hook into the bead's smaller hole, so that the larger one faces to the rear once the bead has been slid into position. Debarbing abets this process.

Let's briefly revisit our soft-hackle wet fly and add a bead. You simply mount the bead ahead of time and slide it forward to the eye of the hook. Then tie the fly in the usual manner. At the end, you have the choice of wrapping the hackle behind the bead or of tying off, sliding the bead back over

Two versions of a bead-head soft-hackle: the bead behind and in front of the hackle.

the tie-off wraps, then tying back on again, making the hackle, and completing the fly. Of course, you'll need to leave some space up front if you opt for the latter method.

In either case, it becomes self-evident why the bead was mounted with the wide end rearward: It enables you to cover the thread wraps that immediately precede it. I suggest that you build up the thread a bit before tying off, so that the bead fits fairly snugly and is stabilized. When the bead is situated ahead of the hackle, I advocate tying on again at the eye and wrapping some thread back against the front of the bead, in order to immobilize it. You might also consider putting a small droplet of Zap-A-Gap or the like on the thread wraps before you slide the bead back over them.

Some Soft-Hackle Patterns

Note: The hooks for these flies are the same as for those in the pattern lesson. If you wish to go slightly longer on the beaded patterns (1XL), that's fine. Please refer to the hook chart in chapter 22 for specifics (see page 240).

1. ***Peacock/Brown***

BODY:	Peacock herl.
RIBBING:	(optional) Oval tinsel, either gold or silver.
HACKLE:	Soft brown feather.

2. ***Pheasant/Hun/Bead***

HEAD OR THORAX:	Copper bead.
BODY:	Cock ring-necked pheasant tail fibers.
HACKLE:	Hungarian partridge feather, preferably brown phase.

3. ***Ellis***

THORAX:	Black dubbing or bead.
TAIL:	(optional) Hungarian partridge, preferably gray phase.
BODY:	Stripped quill from the eye of a peacock tail.
HACKLE:	Hungarian partridge, preferably gray phase.

4. ***Orange Fishawk***

BODY:	Orange floss or substitute.
RIBBING:	Fine gold tinsel, either flat or oval.
HACKLE:	Soft badger feather (cream with dark center).

5. ***Grouse & Green***

BODY:	Green floss or substitute.
RIBBING:	Fine gold tinsel, either flat or oval.
HACKLE:	Hungarian partridge, ruffed grouse, speckled hen, or similar feather.

Bead-head flies are amazingly effective. You can add beads to just about any soft-hackle and to nymphs and streamers as well. For example, the Hare's Ear Nymph that we'll be tying in the next chapter makes a superb bead head. I usually use a gold bead for that dressing.

A bunch of soft-hackles. Clockwise from top right: Ellis, Grouse & Green, Pheasant/Hun/Bead, Peacock/Brown, Orange Fishawk.

26 The Nymph

You may already be aware that trout take most of their food underwater, and a very large percentage of it consists of nymph life. Technically, **nymphs** are the larval forms of mayflies and stoneflies. Caddisflies—and, in fact, all aquatic insect life-forms that eventually become winged—have larval forms, but in entomological terminology, they are not properly called nymphs.

For the moment, let's consider mayfly nymphs only. According to my observations, these are less distinctive than the winged forms—or at least I've found the trout to be less selective of nymphal life than with the imago, or subadult, forms. I believe this has to do with their drab coloration, the diffusion of the currents, and the fact that light diminishes with the depth of the water, which of course affects visibility.

The bottom line is that general nymph patterns have always been, and continue to be, very successful. And none has accounted for the deception of more trout than the redoubtable Hare's Ear. This is an ancient British pattern. Literature going back two centuries and more describes the scraping of the poll (hair and fur) from the mask of a hare and using it as **dubbing.**

Now there's a new term: *dubbing.* That's the modern American version; in the traditional British, it's *dubbin.* On this side of the pond, we use the word as both a noun and a verb. In other words, it's the fur, and it's also the act of applying the fur to the thread, and then to the hook.

My first encounter with the Hare's Ear was in the form of a winged wet fly. That style of tying has pretty much given way to the more contemporary, and probably more entomologically accurate, nymph and emerger schools. The decline was also influenced by the relative difficulty of tying the wings. In my fledgling days, we never thought about the difficulty. It was an integral part of one's fly-tying education, and we just did it.

I still love winged wet flies and consider them a useful addition to my arsenal. It's often necessary to show the fish something different, and they don't see this sort of fly very often these days. And from a teaching standpoint, there's no better exercise in mastering the all-important pinch wrap than that of tying wet-fly wings. So we'll have a go at them in the next chapter.

But back to the Hare's Ear Nymph. We no longer have to scrape our own dubbing off the bunnies; we now buy it prepackaged in fly shops. Quite a variety of shades and textures are available. Here, we'll stay pretty close to the traditional, which consists of a mottled, tweedy mixture of hair and fur in tans, grays, and rusts.

Having stated that it's now an over-the-counter product, I still should tell you that Hare's Ear dubbing is very easy to make—and you don't even need a bona fide English hare's mask. Common American rabbit will do, provided you have something to mix in as an additive that will imbue it with the spikiness (there's an esoteric fly-tying word) that characterizes the original. The guard hairs found along the backbone of a gray squirrel or, better still, a fox squirrel are ideal. Just cut them off and mix them with the material cut from the mask of the bunny.

Serious fur mixers usually use a coffee mill—one of those little machines that grinds up coffee beans, nuts, and such. However, the same effect can be achieved as follows:

1. In a small bowl, mix some lukewarm water with a few drops of liquid dish detergent.
2. Cut off the various furs and hairs and place them in the bowl.
3. Stir the stuff around until it is well mixed.
4. Pour the mixture into a sieve and rinse until the detergent is washed out.
5. Squeeze out as much water as you can, then lay the dubbing on a paper towel to dry.

This method works for all kinds of furs and hairs, and even for combining synthetics with natural materials. This is not always feasible in a blender, because some of the synthetics are plastic and will get gooey when zapped by the blades. Incidentally, don't try to use a conventional bottom-bladed blender; not only won't it do the job, but the material will quite possibly get bound up in the blades as well, which will destroy the motor.

The Use of Wax

Some dubbings spin onto the thread very easily and smoothly, whereas others present more difficulty. For this reason, we sometimes resort to the use of a little wax. Personally, I'm not crazy about wax and seldom use it. I recognize, however, that some people have very dry skin, and a touch of wax is most helpful for them. I counsel you to choose a nonsticking wax and to use it very sparingly. Sticky, or tacky, waxes tend to cause the material to adhere more to your fingers than to the thread.

Wax can be applied to the thread itself, the fingers, or both. Remember that you are probably tying with prewaxed thread; it's the norm these days. By applying plenty of finger pressure as you spin on the dubbing material, you can create a little heat and activate the wax in the thread. If this doesn't seem to do the job, then dab a very thin coating of nontacky wax onto the forefinger of your right hand.

The nymph we are about to tie is of typical construction, and if you can tie this one, you can tie all similar dressings. A word about the **wing case:** This is the part of the nymph's anatomy that protects the immature wings until the insect is ready to hatch out. We are going to use a narrow strip of leather from a goose or duck wing, treated with an adhesive, to emulate this component. There are other materials that also make great wing cases. Bugskin, which is actually very thin leather, is one of them. Another is Thin Skin, an interesting synthetic product from the Wapsi Company. Both are available in quite a wide range of shades and markings. As your knowledge of aquatic life develops, you'll find yourself making associations between the fly-tying materials you see and the insects you encounter astream, and these products will help you emulate what you see.

This version of the Hare's Ear Nymph is very basic and simplistic. There are a number of embellishments commonly employed by fly tyers; I'll describe a few at the end of the chapter. Incidentally, this pattern is tied both with and without gold tinsel ribbing. Here, I've included it. If you prefer to omit it, that's okay. I've also listed the wire underbody as optional, but personally, I prefer integrating weight in the tying process to having to add weight to the leader in order to get my nymphs down to fishing depths.

Before we begin, a few words about the dubbing process. There are two basic methods: single thread and double thread, or spinning loop. Here, we'll use the former. Afterward, I'll show you how the spinning-loop process goes, so you also have that method in your arsenal.

Hare's Ear Nymph Dressing

HOOK:	1X or 2X long, medium-gauge wire, typically sizes 8 to 16.
THREAD:	Preferably brown 6/0 or 8/0, but black is allowable.
TAIL:	A small bunch of the dubbing with guard hairs included.
UNDERBODY:	(optional) Fine lead wire or substitute.
RIBBING:	(optional) Fine oval gold tinsel.
BODY/ THORAX:	Hare's Ear dubbing.
WING CASE:	A narrow strip from a gray goose or duck wing feather (see the note below).
LEGS:	The dubbing, picked out a bit around the thorax.

NOTES ON SINGLE-THREAD DUBBING

Please read this message before going farther. Common dubbing mistakes made by beginning tyers are:

1. Trying to apply the material in clumps, rather than wisps.
2. Uneven distribution.
3. Failing to pinch tightly enough while spinning.
4. Using too much dubbing overall.

While great dissimilarities exist between them, certain rules apply to all sorts of dubbings:

1. Tease out the material in tiny wisps.
2. Try to lay the fibers parallel to the thread.
3. Build up the "worm" of dubbing slowly, gradually, and smoothly, using small amounts.
4. While wrapping the dubbing onto the hook, if you find that you need a little more, don't wait until you've run out. Apply it while you still have a couple of wraps left on the thread, so as to effect a smooth integration. Back off a couple of turns, if necessary.
5. Conversely, if you find that you've applied too much material to the thread, back off a wrap or two, remove the excess, re-spin, and rewrap.

As you develop dubbing skill, you'll be able to shape the bodies of your flies any way that you want. Usually, a gradual taper is desired. With typically sized flies, this is done by simply applying the material a tiny bit thicker as you work forward. On large flies, you might apply the dubbing in layers, first wrapping forward, then spinning on more dubbing and working rearward, then spinning on yet more dubbing and working forward again.

Note: It's advisable to treat the wing-case strip with an adhesive ahead of time. Any flexible cement or glue will do, such as Pliobond, Dave's Flexament, or AquaFlex. You can coat the strips individually or simply coat the entire feather and, after it's dry, separate it into strips with a needle or scissors tip. In either case, be attentive to proportions. The wing-case strip should be slightly wider than the widest part of the thorax. Have a piece of waxed paper at hand on which to lay the feather during drying. Allow for thoroughly drying before using the strips.

Tying Steps

1. Tie on near the front and wrap to the bend. Then tie in the tail with a few pinch wraps, followed by several reinforcing wraps.
2. If you intend to rib the fly, tie in the tinsel now, adjacent to the tail butt.
3. Wrap the wire per instructions for the Woolly Bugger (see page 243), leaving some space in back and in front. Use the tying thread to create little "ramps" front and rear, in order to compensate for the diameter of the wire. Coat with a clear adhesive of some sort.
4. Now for the dubbing. Position the thread a few turns ahead of the tail butt, and expose a few inches of it. Hold the bobbin in your left hand and apply tension to the thread.
5. Remember the dubbing notes. Tease out a very small puff of the dubbing material, and spin it onto the thread with your right thumb and forefinger. It's okay to spin in either direction, but don't roll the material, because the reverse motion will loosen what was spun on. I emphasize: Tease out the dubbing in tiny wisps, lay it on parallel to the thread, insofar as that's possible, and build up the dubbing a little at a time. This enables effective thread contact and a smooth application.
6. Apply enough material to cover up to the middle of the thorax. Refer to the step 5 photo for proportions.
7. Transfer the bobbin to your tying hand and wrap to the rear, the idea being that the "worm" of material will begin to deploy around the hook precisely at the base of the tail. Then wrap progressively forward. The material will tend to loosen as you wrap, so re-spin it as required during the process.

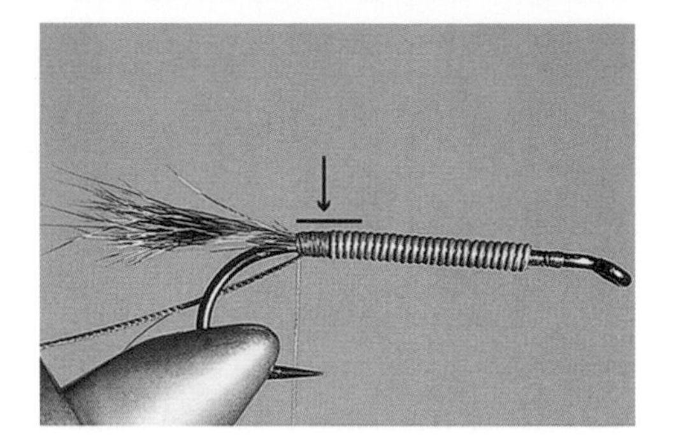

Tail, tinsel, and wire in place (steps 1–3).

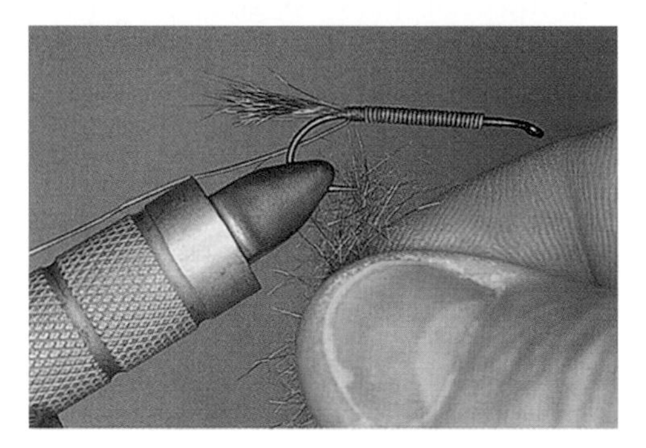

Beginning to apply the dubbing (steps 4–5).

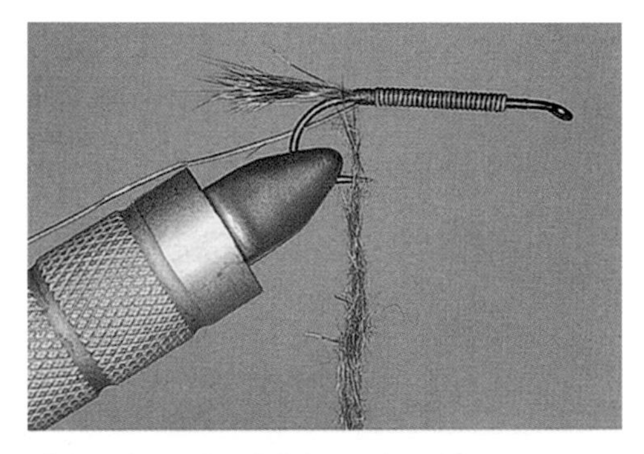

This is how the dubbing should appear on the thread (step 5).

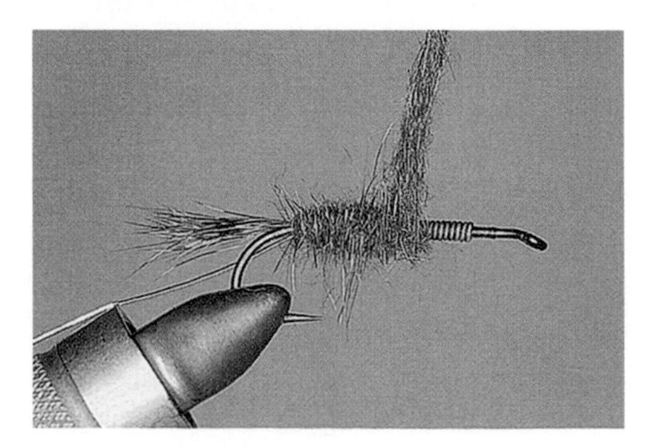

Wrapping the dubbing (step 7).

Tying Steps

8. Ideally, you'll have run out of dubbing when you reach the midpoint of the thorax, which is about 20 percent of the shank length to the rear of the eye. Now wrap the thread a few turns back over the dubbed material. The reason for doing this is to create bulk over which to tie on the wing-case strip. Keep in mind that the thorax is the widest part of a nymph, both natural and artificial. Your thread should now be positioned about 35 percent of the shank length to the rear of the eye.

Body completed. Note thread position (step 8).

9. If you're doing ribbing, wrap it now, keeping the turns evenly spaced and not too close together. Tie off in the area where you wrapped back over the dubbing. Trim off the tag.

Ribbing in place (step 9).

10. As I previously mentioned, the wing-case strip should be slightly wider than the widest part of the dubbed thorax. Because it will be folded forward over the thorax subsequently, it is tied in by the tip or fine end, good-side down, and hanging off to the rear. "Good side" refers to the darker or exterior side of the feather. Center the strip accurately and sneak the thread over, so that it doesn't pleat or fold. Bind it in place securely, and trim off the excess.

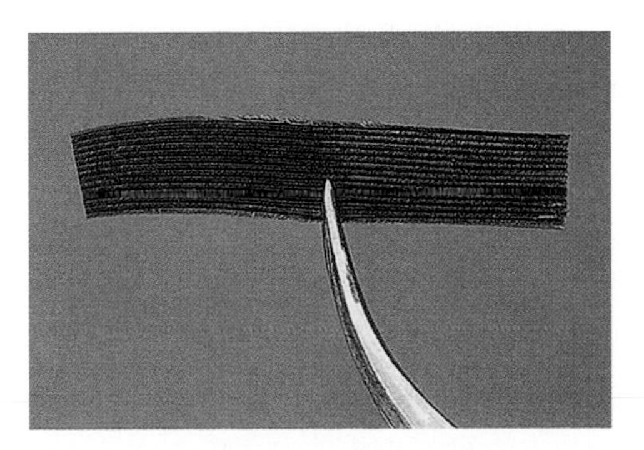

The wing-case strip tied in place (step 10).

A wing-case strip (step 10).

Tying Steps

The thorax dubbed on (step 11).

Folding the wing case into place (step 12).

11. Dub the thorax, using the techniques just described. Don't crowd the eye.
12. Bring the wing-case strip forward over the dubbed thorax and tie it in place. Keep it centered, and don't allow the thread action to cause it to fold back over itself. After securing it, trim off the excess, wrap a neat head, and make the whip-finish.
13. With a needle, carefully pick out a little of the dubbing at the front of the thorax to simulate the legs of the insect. Then apply your lacquer to the head.

The completed fly (step 13).

NOTES ON SPINNING-LOOP DUBBING

As I've mentioned, some dubbings are more difficult to work with, especially on larger flies, such as the Casual Dress pattern listed at the end of the chapter. That's where the spinning-loop dubbing method comes in handy. Here's how it goes:

1. Expose from the bobbin a little more than twice the length of thread you would normally use for the single-thread dubbing process.
2. Spin on the dubbing. You may wish to make the worm a little thicker, because the loop will pack the material tighter when it is twisted.
3. With your hackle pliers, seize the thread just below where the dubbing material ends. Hold the pliers in your left hand and keep tension on the thread.
4. Take the bobbin in your right hand and pass the thread over the hook at the point where it was hanging when you applied the dubbing. Wrap the thread forward to where the body will end.
5. Spin the hackle pliers, tightly twisting the dubbing within the loop.
6. Using the plies as a handle, wrap the dubbing around the hook, thus forming the fly body. Re-spin as necessary.

NYMPH ENHANCEMENT

Enhancements of nymphs of this type include the use of soft, attractively marked feathers for tails and legs. Hungarian partridge and speckled hen are two very popular types. Simply tie on a small bunch of barbs for the tail, and another for the legs. The appearance of the legs can be improved by deploying the barbs to the sides, as well as on the bottom.

Rather than apply ribbing, tyers sometimes add **flash** to their nymphs by mixing some sort of glittery material with the dubbing. This is easy to do with the detergent-and-water method described earlier (see page 262). There are plenty of high-brilliance materials that accommodate this, Lite Brite being one of them. Usually, it's necessary to chop up this material with strong scissors before doing the mixing.

My own little contribution to the embellishment of nymphs is the use of the **bead thorax.** We looked at beads in chapter 25, remember? To substitute a bead for a dubbed or fur thorax, proceed as follows:

1. Select a bead of the desired color, large enough to make a properly sized thorax on the fly you'll be tying.
2. Slide the bead onto the hook, inserting the point into the smaller hole, as described at the end of the soft-hackle chapter (see page 258), and move it to the front.
3. Tie the fly in the normal manner, but don't dub in the thorax area, and avoid excessive thread buildup. Omit the wire underbody.
4. After tying in the wing-case material, tie off, and slide the bead back over the thread wraps.
5. Tie back on in front of the bead. If you wish, and if there's enough space, add legs. Then fold the wing case forward over the bead, tie it down, and finish off the fly.

One note: When you're making bead-thorax nymphs, things work better if the wing-case material isn't too bulky. Thin Skin is a good choice. I've included in the group photo a nymph that incorporates the embellishments of a bead thorax and Hungarian partridge legs.

Some Nymph Patterns

Note: The hooks and thread colors for these flies vary with the designs. Please refer to the hook chart in chapter 22 (page 240) for specifics.

1. ***Pheasant Tail/Bead Thorax***

HOOK:	As specified in the tying lesson.
THREAD:	Brown.
THORAX:	Copper bead.
TAIL & BODY:	Cock ring-necked pheasant tail fibers.
RIBBING:	(optional) Very fine copper wire, reverse-wrapped.
WING CASE:	Bugskin, Thin Skin, or section of goose feather treated with adhesive.
HACKLE:	Hungarian partridge, speckled hen, or cock ring-necked pheasant tail fibers.

2. ***Amber Flashback Nymph***

HOOK:	As specified in the tying lesson.
THREAD:	Tan, brown, or rust.
TAIL:	Brown mallard flank feather fibers or Hungarian partridge, tied fairly long.
RIBBING:	Brown Uni-Stretch, or thin floss twisted fine, or thick thread.
UNDERBODY:	(optional) Fine lead wire or substitute.
BODY/ THORAX:	Amber dubbing, either natural or synthetic.
WING CASE:	Wide Mylar flat tinsel, either gold or silver.
HACKLE:	Brown mallard flank feather fibers or Hungarian partridge.

3. ***Zug Bug***

HOOK:	1XL or 2XL.
THREAD:	Black.
TAIL:	Three peacock sword fronds.
UNDERBODY:	(optional) Fine lead wire or substitute.
RIBBING:	Oval silver tinsel.
BODY:	Peacock herl.
LEGS:	Brown hackle fibers.
WING CASE:	Barred mallard flank feather, trimmed to shape and tied on at the head.

(*Continued on page 270*)

An armada of nymphs. Top left: Zug Bug. Top right: Amber Flashback. Center: Casual Dress. Lower left: Black Montana. Lower right: Pheasant Tail/Bead Thorax.

Some Nymph Patterns (*continued*)

4. ***Casual Dress***

HOOK:	3XL or 4XL.
THREAD:	Black.
TAIL:	A small bunch of fur from the back of a muskrat, with the guard hairs left in.
UNDERBODY:	Lead wire or substitute.
BODY:	Dubbing from the back of a muskrat, with the guard hairs left in.
COLLAR:	A bunch of fur from the back of a muskrat, with the guard hairs left in.
HEAD:	Black ostrich herl or dubbing.

5. ***Black Montana***

HOOK:	3XL or 4XL.
THREAD:	Black.
TAIL:	Black hackle.
BODY:	Black chenille.
HACKLE:	Soft black feather, wrapped over the thorax material.
THORAX:	Orange or yellow chenille.
WING CASE:	Black chenille, three strands.

27 The Winged Wet Fly

Having begun my fly fishing on the fabled rivers of New York's Catskills, I was introduced early on to the winged wet fly. My first two fly-caught trout came to either a Leadwing Coachman or a Hare's Ear, I can't remember which. Such dressings were part of the Catskill tradition in those days, and we never questioned their effectiveness. If we weren't catching fish—well, it was our own ineptitude, or else they just weren't biting.

Or perhaps we were using the wrong pattern. Attempting to cover all bases, we often fished a three-fly cast: a tippet fly and two "droppers," as they were called. Typically, I'd tie on a Leadwing Coachman as my end fly, and a Hare's Ear and either a Dark or a Light Cahill as my dropper flies. If the fish showed a preference for any one of them, I'd cut off the others and fish three of the hot pattern!

Now that you've learned how to tie the peacock and the dubbed bodies, the next step is to learn the wet-fly wing, which is also called the **down wing.** The one we'll tie here is made out of the same sort of wing quill we used for the nymphal wing casing, but it is tied in a different manner, and there's no impregnation. Other types of down wings are made of bunches of flank fibers from birds such as the wood duck, mallard, and teal, and of small bundles of fur and hair.

In the last chapter, I mentioned that one factor in the demise of the winged wet fly was the relative difficulty of tying the wings. Don't be frightened: The key word is *relative.* These wings aren't all that tough to tie, given a little orientation and instruction, and I think you'll be very pleased with the results.

First, the orientation. Selecting a feather that's suited to the task is paramount. The flight quills from the wings of Canada geese and larger ducks are what we generally use. Those from smaller ducks are fine for winging smaller flies. The ones that form the leading edge are called **primaries** and have some useful material on them. The feathers a little farther back are called **secondaries** and are usually the best. After that come the **tertials,** which may have some decent winging material but are usually relegated to nymph wing-casing work.

Prime winging feathers have only moderate curvature and are large enough that the strips we cut out and use for the wings are long enough to be manageable and to allow us to work outside of the coarse portion near the butt end. If you inspect a typical flight quill, you'll see a sort of line that runs parallel to the quill. The material to the quill side of that line is pretty rough stuff. It's fine for holding on to during tying, but otherwise not at all tyer friendly. This is why we operate on the portion to the outside.

It is necessary to have two opposing feathers, meaning a right and a left. The closer they are in size, shape, and texture, the easier your task will be.

The most common wing mistakes that beginners make include:

1. Using strips that are too wide and, less frequently, ones that are too narrow.
2. Poor selection of feathers.
3. Failure to lay down a proper thread base before tying on the wings.
4. Crowding the front of the body.
5. Poor technique with the pinch wrap.
6. Failure to mount the winging strips in proper position.
7. Tying on the strips upside down.
8. Upsetting the finished wings while trimming the butts.

That's quite a list, but don't let it unnerve you. All of these problems are easily solvable; I'll go into all that in detail as we tie the fly. As to selection of feathers, I've already touched on that.

One other item that I'll address here is the matter of what *right-side up* means, with reference to the winging strips. Picture the feather standing up in front of you, with the butt end of the quill on the table. A strip cut with the feather in this position is considered right-side up. This is sometimes referred to as **pointed-end up.**

Sometimes, looking at finished flies can be deceptive, especially in the case of featherwinged salmon flies. This is because the tyer has manipulated the winging strips in such a manner that it appears as though they were tied on with the bottom, or curvy, edges upward. Actually, what happened was that the tyer "humped" the strips, thus altering their configuration. You'll see how this is done in the tying sequence.

Okay, why pointed-end up? The reason is that if the strips are tied on upside down, the pressure of the thread has a tendency to work against the texture of the strips, causing the fibers to separate. You may not encounter this while tying the fly, but you may well see it evidenced after a few casts. So while there are a few exceptions, we generally tie on our winging strips pointed-end up.

Since both the Leadwing Coachman and the Hare's Ear take the same wings, we could do either or both, based on what we've already covered. I've chosen to show you the Leadwing here. In either case, it's important that the wings not be interfered with by the front of the body. This implies not ending the body too far forward or making it too bulky. It also means laying down an adequate thread base.

In addition to the lesson in wings, which is the main thrust of this chapter, we'll examine the simple beard hackle commonly found on this type of fly. Let me discuss this briefly. Remember the discourse on folding a feather late in the soft-hackle chapter (see page 258), and my statement that this was an important technique that would be used in many fly-tying operations? This is one of them. This is good practice for working on dry-fly tails in forthcoming exercises.

The procedure starts out the same way as was described. Stroke the barbs on a feather to 90 degrees from the quill. Now either cut or pull them off in a bunch, being careful to keep the tips even. A note here: Some feathers are symmetrical—the length of the barbs is the same on both sides of the quill—whereas some are not. With symmetrical feathers, you can gather barbs from both sides of the quill at once by stroking them all together as you would when folding a feather. However, if the barb lengths differ, use only one side at a time; otherwise, the tips won't come out even.

There's also a little tag of gold tinsel, but that's pretty much a no-brainer. I should tell you that there are variations of this pattern, as there are of so many. This is one of several that were popular in the Catskills when I was getting started.

Leadwing Coachman Dressing

HOOK:	Typical wet fly, standard or 1XL shank length, typically sizes 10 to 14.
THREAD:	Black 6/0 or 8/0.
TAG:	Narrow flat gold tinsel.
BODY:	Peacock herl.
HACKLE:	Soft dark brown barbs, tied as a beard.
WINGS:	Gray goose or duck, as described.

Tying Steps

1. Tie on near the front and wrap to the bend. Then tie in a piece of narrow flat tinsel with the gold side against the hook shank. Why? Because this material has a tendency to flip over with the first wrap, and we want the gold side to face outward! Trim off the excess.

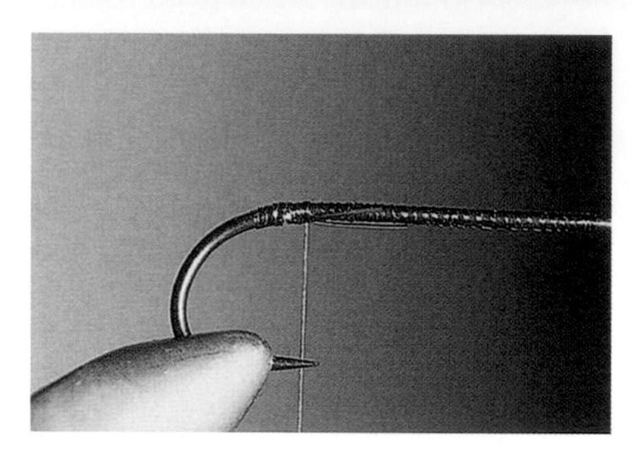

The tinsel tag tied in place (steps 1–2).

2. Make a small tag, using just a few turns, working just a bit down around the bend and back. Secure and trim the tinsel.

3. Either tie in a 5- or 6-inch (125 to 150 mm) piece of thread, or make a loop of that length and cut off one side of it, whichever is easier for you. This, of course, is the reinforcing thread for the peacock. Why didn't we simply leave the excess thread hanging as we did before? Because it gets in the way when the tinsel tag is being tied!

Peacock body completed, beard hackle being measured (steps 3–5).

4. Construct a peacock herl body, following the instructions in the soft-hackle exercise (see page 255). Don't crowd the front; refer to the photo for proportions.

5. Per instructions in the discourse on folding a feather and gathering barbs, procure the hackle material (see page 258). Gather and either cut or pull off a small bunch, being careful to keep the tips even.

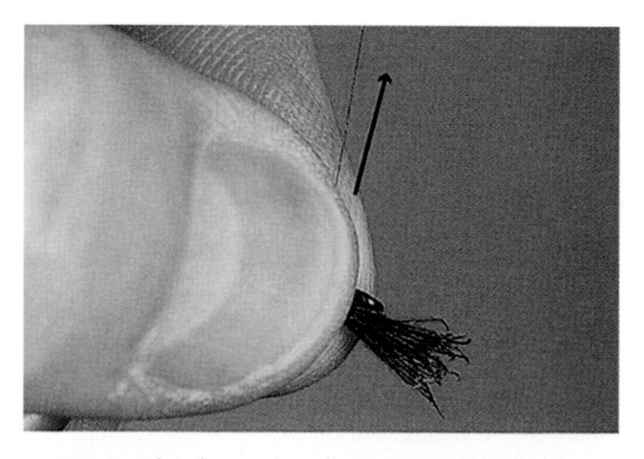

Tying in the beard with an upside-down pinch (step 6).

6. Hold the bunch beneath the hook—at the throat, so to speak. Tie it in with a few upside-down pinch wraps, secure with several more tight wraps, and carefully trim off the excess.

7. Working very carefully and neatly, wrap a thread base on which to mount the wings, as shown. End up with the thread a bit ahead of the front of the body, but not abutting it.

Tying Steps

Beard in place, thread base wrapped in preparation for the wing (step 7).

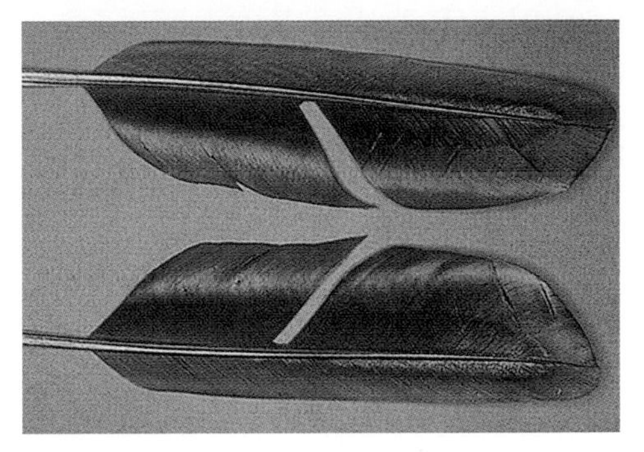

Two opposing goose flight feathers from which a set of winging strips have been removed (step 8).

8. Cut a section from each of the two flight feathers—the left and the right. The closer to identical, the better. As to width: I'm working on a size 10 hook, and the strips are about 3⁄16 to 7⁄32 inch (6 to 7 mm) wide.

9. Match the sections with the concave sides facing inward, so that the respective curvatures cancel each other out, and the wing strips are straight and flat. They need to be perfectly aligned.

10. Hold the wing set with your right thumb and forefinger and place it atop the hook. The wings should extend rearward until the tips touch, or barely break, an imaginary line that runs straight upward from the rear extremity of the bend of the hook.

11. With your left thumb and forefinger, hump the wing set slightly by stroking the tips downward. This establishes the desired shape and counteracts the effect the thread will have during tie-on.

12. Transfer the wing set to your left hand. Place the feathers precisely atop the hook and reestablish the length. Make sure they are perfectly centered and aligned with the hook shank.

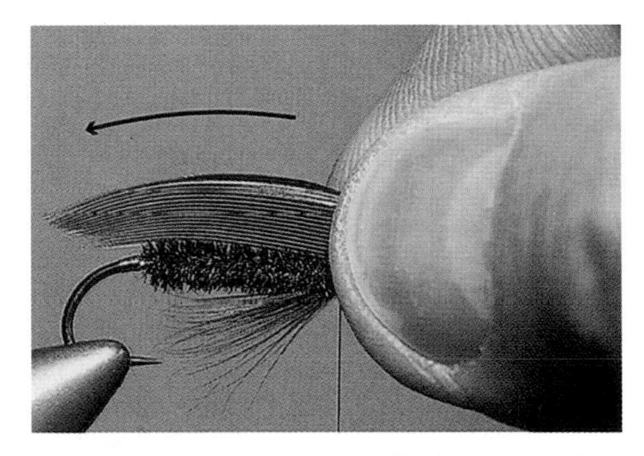

Winging strips in position for being tied on (steps 9–11).

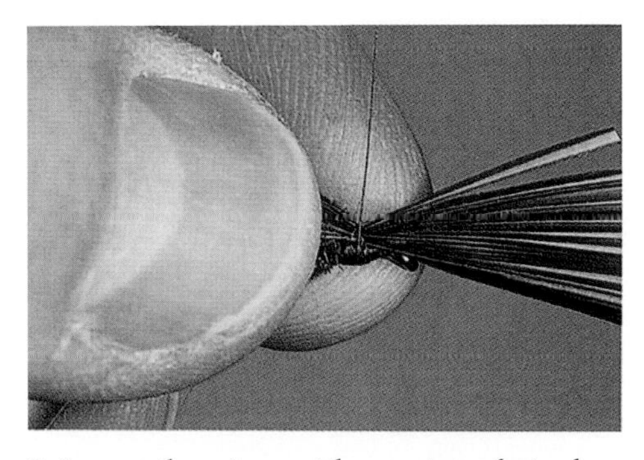

Tying on the wings with a series of pinch wraps (steps 12–15).

Tying Steps

13. Sneak the thread up between your fingers, then over the wing set, and between your fingers again on the far side of the hook. Execute your class-A pinch wrap, crushing the wing set down onto the thread base. Repeat this several times. Do not allow the torque action of the thread to move the wings off center. Keep pressure against the far side of the hook with your left index finger, in order to prevent the wings from slipping downward.

    Note: Some people find it helpful, with the first pinch wrap, to come under the hook and sneak the thread up under the fingers a second time, then tighten by pulling upward. If you have trouble, you might give this technique a try.

14. Inspect what you've done. If the wings are not positioned as desired, back off the thread wraps and do the process over again. If they are correctly positioned, seize them with your left hand again, hold them steady, and secure them with several firm wraps of thread. Keep in mind that there is still thread torque happening, which can alter the position of the wings. Don't let this take place.

15. Inspect the wings again, and adjust, if necessary. Remember: Until you have trimmed them off, the wing butts can be used as handles for making subtle adjustments.

16. With the tips of your sharpest scissors, cut off the wing butts flush with the thread wraps. Hold the wings firmly in place while cutting, because the shearing action of the scissors can also work to upset the wing position. Use several chops, instead of trying to cut everything at once, which would exacerbate shearing action.

17. While still holding the wings, cover the trimmed butts with a few more wraps. Then do the whip-finish, and sit back and admire the beautiful fly you've just created.

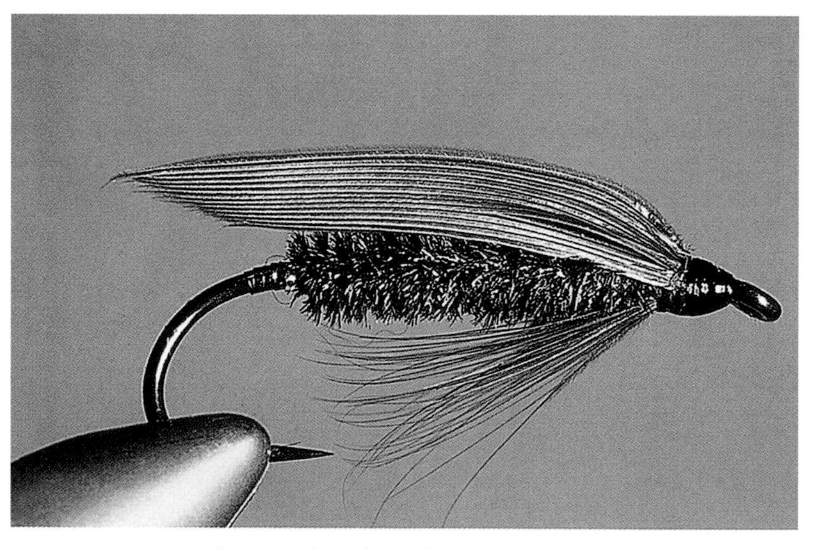

The completed Leadwing Coachman (steps 16–17).

There are literally hundreds of wet-fly patterns out there, using all sorts of materials for wings, bodies, hackle, highlights, and so forth. As mentioned, one of the all-time greats is the Hare's Ear. My favorite version of it uses either Hungarian partridge or speckled hen barbs for the tail and hackle, these being very similar materials. The gold rib is optional. I've included the dressing in the group that follows.

Some Wet-Fly Patterns

Note: The hooks for these patterns are the same as for the tying lesson. Please refer to the hook chart in chapter 22 for specifics (page 240).

1. *Dark Cahill*

TAIL:	Medium brown barbs.
BODY:	Gray dubbing.
HACKLE:	Soft brown, beard-style.
WINGS:	Barred wood duck flank or dyed imitation.

2. *Light Cahill*

TAIL:	Cream barbs.
BODY:	Cream dubbing or yarn.
HACKLE:	Soft cream, beard-style.
WINGS:	Barred wood duck flank or dyed imitation.

3. *Black Gnat*

TAIL:	(optional) Black barbs.
BODY:	Black chenille, yarn, or dubbing.
HACKLE:	Soft black, beard-style.
WINGS:	Dark goose wing quill sections.

4. *Brown Turkey*

TAIL:	None.
HACKLE:	Brown rooster, wrapped palmer-style over the body from the bend to the throat.
BODY:	Brown floss, yarn, Uni-Stretch, or the like.
WINGS:	Mottled brown turkey sections.

5. *Hare's Ear*

THREAD:	Preferably brown 6/0 or 8/0, but black is allowable.
TAIL:	A small bunch of either Hungarian partridge or speckled hen barbs.
RIBBING:	(optional) Fine oval gold tinsel.
BODY:	Hare's Ear dubbing.
HACKLE:	Hungarian partridge or speckled hen barbs, beard-style.
WINGS:	Sections from opposing gray goose or duck wing quills. The gold rib is optional.

A covey of wet flies. Top left: Dark Cahill. Top right: Brown Turkey. Center: Light Cahill. Lower left: Hare's Ear. Lower right: Black Gnat.

28 The Hair-Winged Streamer

Perhaps the most underused type of fly in all of fly fishing is the streamer. It is intended to imitate, or at least to suggest, some sort of baitfish. The two general categories are the **imitator** and the **attractor,** or suggestive type. That's for the convenience of us humans. Fish are not admirers of the fly tyer's craft. To them, there's no such thing as an "attractor." They think it's real food, or they would never try to eat it.

Streamers are also divided into other subgroups that are defined by the primary material used for the main part of the silhouette. This is called the **wing,** which of course is a complete misnomer, because baitfish don't have wings. Since the component goes on in the same position as would a wet-fly wing, however, we call it by that name. In actuality, it's the upper part of the body of the baitfish, if indeed it's anything identifiable at all.

The most common of these subgroups are the **hairwings** and the **featherwings.** The latter includes streamers with marabou wings. The former includes a large number of patterns that are tied with all sorts of hair. Some of them are called bucktails, because the original dressings used deer tail hair, which is still probably the most commonly used material in streamer tying.

If you're anything like me, you'll enjoy streamer tying, because to a large degree it releases you from the disciplines of imitative tying. Much of the time, you'll be working on large hooks with pretty materials that are easy and fun to use. I also hope that you'll give them a fair workout on the water. My basic method of fishing a streamer is to keep it moving and swimming in a lifelike manner, but with little pauses, so that the predator fish gets the idea that this morsel is easily catchable. I think you'll find the results truly exciting.

The first fly I ever tied was a bucktail called the Mickey Finn. It's still a popular and effective fly today, and no one is exactly sure why, because it certainly bears no resemblance to any natural baitfish a trout might encounter. Apparently the answer lies in the visibility of the fly, which uses the two colors that are best seen underwater, plus some silver flash.

Today, various hairs other than bucktail have become popular. Recently, I've begun to see goat hair of several types arriving from Scandinavia, along with arctic fox, both body and tail hair. These are very nice materials to work with and have justifiably gained favor. Certain sheep also produce hair that is suitable for streamer work. Calf tail is sometimes used, but I don't favor it for this particular design of streamer, because even the straightest calf tail is rather crinkly, which makes it hard to obtain the well-defined layers and slender silhouette that I strive for.

More important than the actual variety of animal from which the hair comes is its texture. For smaller streamers—"trout sized," as they are often called—you'll want finely textured hair from a smaller bucktail. (Incidentally, while I'm not going to try to change the terminology that's developed over the past century, it would be more appropriate to refer to this material as deer tail, since we have no way of knowing whether it came from the male or female of the species.)

While bucktail is often used in its natural coloration, the stuff we are using here is, quite obviously, dyed. Today's suppliers have, for the most part, learned how to dye such materials very well indeed, which wasn't always the case when I first tied the Mickey. Look for bright, uniform coloration when selecting tails. If you find that the dye readily comes off on your fingers while tying, you might point this out to your dealer.

I depart from the original dressing in one respect: I use embossed tinsel instead of flat ribbed with oval. This is flat tinsel with little indentations patterned into it, which are quite suggestive of the scales of a small fish. I feel that the embossed tinsel yields a more attractive effect and is far more durable than the relatively delicate oval. However, if you want to be faithful to the traditional dressing, that's fine with me, in which case I suggest that you use a fairly substantial oval tinsel for the ribbing.

All flat tinsels, including the embossed type, are usually applied in two layers, meaning that they are tied in near the front and wrapped to the rear and back, so as to hide any little spaces between wraps. That's what we'll do here. However, if at some point in the future you want to use a single layer of embossed tinsel for this type of body, and have acquired sufficient skill to cover the hook efficiently and smoothly, that's fine. You'll need to overlap the edges very slightly. This is helpful on small streamers, where you're trying to avoid too much bulk. Several widths of embossed tinsel are available. Except for very small streamers, I prefer wide tinsel, as it goes on more smoothly and with fewer turns.

Today, softer alloys are being used in the manufacture of embossed tinsels, the Uni Products version being a prime example. This material is much less lethal and is easier to work with than the old metallic stuff. Still, you must be careful not to run the thread along the edge of embossed tinsel, because it has sawlike properties.

I want to mention one more difference between the original flat-and-oval configuration and the embossed version. When you're using the former, I advocate finishing the body well short of the eye of the hook and tying off the oval ribbing underneath the shank. This avoids interference with the wing. With the embossed type, I find it helpful to work forward with a couple of turns of tinsel ahead of the tie-in point and then to apply a smooth thread base and set the wings at this spot. In this manner, I avoid the wing hairs' being cocked upward by the front of the body. It's desirable that the wing lie flat along the top of the hook.

I have one particular technique that might be considered a departure from traditional wisdom. When possible, I like to wrap flat and embossed tinsels over a bare hook. This allows the material to slide into place in perfectly adjacent turns. The fact that the wraps, if properly done, abut each other prevents them from slipping around during fishing. However, many streamers have tails, butts, or something else that must be tied in at the rear, which disallows wrapping the body material over the bare hook shank. This brings certain thread- and materials-management disciplines into play. I'll explain further after we tie the Mickey.

A word about hooks for streamers. Usually, a long-shanked model is called for. This allows you to closely emulate the shape of a small fish. It also enables the positioning of the "wing" material in such a manner that it won't tangle around the hook shank so readily during casting. If the wings are tied too long, this tangling can be a problem, especially when soft materials such as marabou are used.

Several manufacturers offer streamer hooks with what is called a **looped eye.** In this design, the wire that forms the eye is brought back down the shank a little way, rather than stubbed off at the closure of the eye. Two things are thus accomplished: The potential for a rough edge at the eye is eliminated, and a double-wire base is established. This can be very helpful in mounting wing materials on streamers, both hair and feather.

There are a couple of downsides. First, the return wire, as it is called, must be well tapered and must lie adjacent to the main shank; otherwise, there's a bump that's difficult to work around during tying. The other factor is that properly made looped-eye hooks can be a bit pricey. Personally, I feel the advantages offset the negatives, and I tend to favor looped-eye hooks for streamer work.

While on the subject of hook eyes, let me briefly address the matter of design, meaning turned down, turned up, or straight. I prefer either a turned-down or straight eye, as I feel that a turned-up eye may cause the streamer to plane like a water ski in the current. Still, I would counsel you to avoid hooks with eyes that are too sharply turned down. About 30 degrees is a good turn-down angle. This allows you to use whatever knot you want for attaching the fly to the leader: either the **turle knot** (see page 36), which is formed around the neck of the fly behind the eye, or the **improved clinch knot,** which sets ahead of the eye. Hooks with a radical turn-down angle may cause the fly to behave erratically in the water.

With that, let's tie a Mickey Finn, adhering to the original design and proportions, with the exception of the aforementioned embossed tinsel.

Mickey Finn Dressing

HOOK:	A longer-shanked (4XL to 7XL) model, as shown; typically sizes 4 to 12.
THREAD:	Black 6/0 or 8/0.
BODY:	Silver embossed tinsel.
WING:	Yellow and red hair (bucktail or similar), configured according to the instructions.

Tying Steps

1. Be sure your vise is properly adjusted for the size—meaning the wire diameter—of your hook. Long-shanked hooks have a tendency to work loose in the jaws of the vise, due to their inherent increased leverage.

2. Tie on near the eye and wrap neatly rearward a little way. Refer to the photo for dimensions.

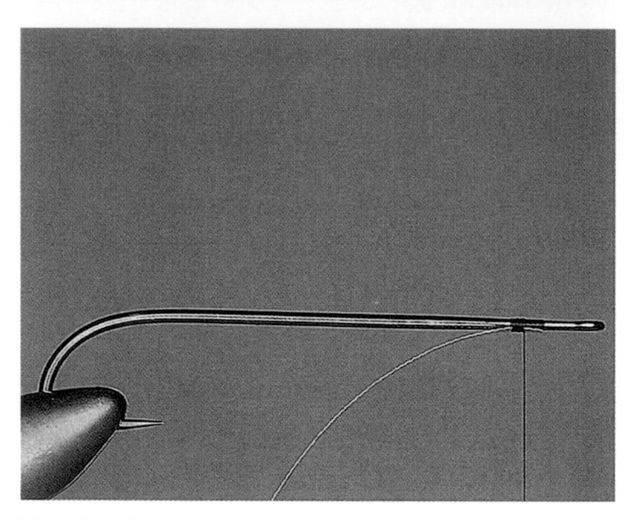

Tinsel tied in (steps 1–3).

3. Cut off a piece of tinsel of sufficient length to allow you to wrap two layers and still have enough left at the end for easy handling. In the case of a size 6, 6XL hook, this would be about 6 or 7 inches (150 to 175 mm). Tie it in lengthwise with the shank beneath the hook, and wrap neatly forward, using one layer of thread, avoiding the buildup of bulk. Trim off the tag end of the tinsel and bind it down. The thread should now be positioned as shown in the photo.

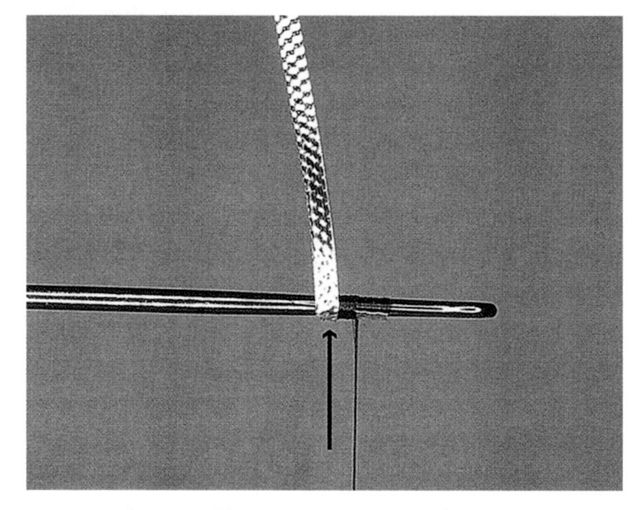

Starting the tinsel by crimping it into this position (step 4).

4. Start the tinsel by folding it over itself. This forms a little "pleat," which you can flatten and smooth out with your fingernail or with flat-jawed pliers or tweezers, if necessary. This brings the tinsel into wrapping position.

5. Wrap rearward, using the following technique: Overlap the wraps very slightly, then with the next turn let the previous wrap slip down off the edge into an adjacent position. You'll hear and feel a little click as this happens. This produces smooth, uniform turns.

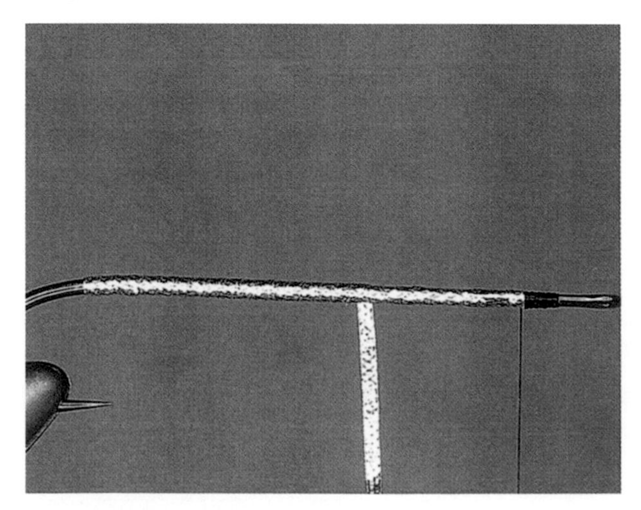

Wrapping the tinsel (steps 5–6).

6. When you reach the bend of the hook, start working forward over the first layer. Use the same overwrap-and-slip-off technique.

7. When you reach the tie-in point, wrap past it two or three turns. This is a single

Tying Steps

layer, so be attentive to making the wraps abut, with no space between.

8. Tie off the tinsel against the bottom of the hook. This is the most dangerous time with regard to cutting the thread, so be careful to work against the flat of the tinsel, and don't let the thread scrape along the edge.

9. Trim off the excess tinsel, then lay down a smooth thread base, using two or three layers of thread, working up to the hook eye, then back over the single layers of tinsel a little. The idea is to establish a perfectly flat base on which to tie the hair.

10. Prepare the first layer of hair as follows: Cut off a small bunch of the yellow hair (check the photos for proportions), and prune out any and all the underfur and short hairs. You can do this with your fingers by holding the hair bunch by its tip end and stroking toward its butt end. A fine-toothed comb makes this even easier. Also, prune out any aberrant hairs that are too long, twisty, or curly. However, don't use a stacker to neaten up the tips, because this produces a whisk-broom effect and results in a chopped-off image that doesn't suggest the streamlined silhouette of a small fish.

11. Establish the length of the hair by setting it atop the hook and observing how far the tips extend beyond the rear of the bend. I suggest that this dimension be about one-third of the shank length, and definitely no more than one-half. Then transfer the bunch to your left hand.

12. You now have a choice: You can tie the bunch onto the hook as is and trim the butts later, or you can pretrim to length now. I prefer the latter method, but if you opt for it, care must be taken. Make sure

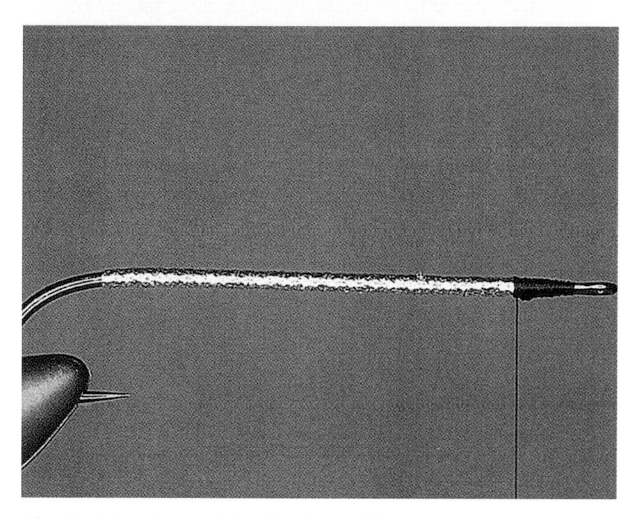

The finished tinsel body, thread base wrapped preparatory to winging (steps 7–9).

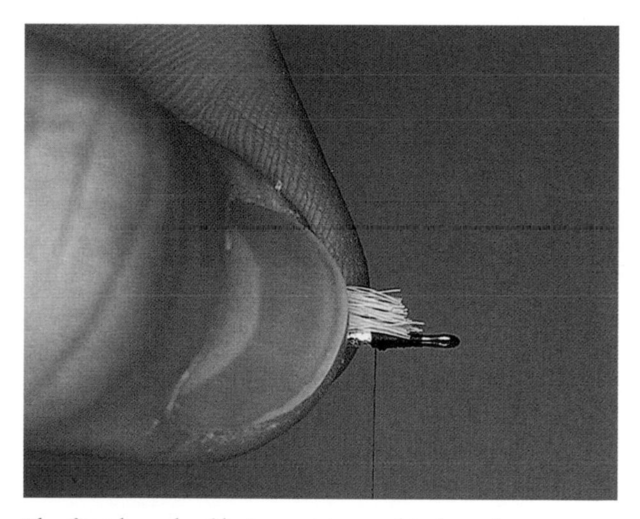

The first bunch of hair, pretrimmed to length (steps 10–12).

Tying Steps

you've established the proper length. When trimming the butts, slope-cut them slightly, but not too much, or you won't have enough material on top to enable a secure tie-down.

13. With the hair bunch sitting flat on top of the thread base and perfectly aligned with the hook shank, tie it on by sneaking a couple of soft wraps over the bunch, followed by a series of very firm ones. Make sure all the hair stays on top of the hook.

14. Establish another thread base as you did the first one, meanwhile binding down the butt end of the first hair bunch.

15. Cut off a small bunch of the red hair equal in thickness to the yellow, and manicure it as instructed in step 10. Then repeat the tie-in process, pretrimming or not as you choose. Be sure to mount the hair on the thread base, and don't let it mix with the first bunch; a red stripe is what you want. You'll need to ramp back and forth a little near the eye, in order to shape the front end properly and to avoid having too severe a slope. In the process, establish yet another thread base.

16. Cut off a second bunch of yellow hair somewhat thicker than the first. The traditional dressing specifies that it should be equal to the first two bunches combined, but that gets pretty tough to manage, so you'll need to use some discretion here. If the first two layers appear to be on the thick side, be a little conservative with the top layer, or you'll have a battle on your hands. It takes a little practice to learn how to properly proportion streamer materials. The initial tendency is to make the bunches too thick.

The first layer of hair in place, new thread base established (steps 13–14).

The red layer of hair in place, new thread base established (step 15).

Tying Steps

17. Tie on the top bunch, again working on the thread base but not wrapping rearward too far to cause the hairs to mix instead of layer.

18. Neaten, smooth out, and shape the head with discrete thread wraps, whip-finish, and apply at least two coats of head lacquer. Instructions for adding eyes follow. If you decide to do this, you may wish to build up the head a bit before tying off, depending on the size of the head at the end of your tying process.

The completed Mickey Finn (steps 16–18).

ADDING EYES

Adding eyes to streamers of this type has always been popular and, with the recent advent of several new types of materials, has become even more so. The traditional method is to paint on the eyes, and that works just fine, though it's somewhat time consuming. You must work on a smooth base—specifically, the aforementioned head lacquer, completely dried. You'll need two colors of lacquer, yellow and black, and two cylindrical applicators, one considerably smaller in diameter than the other. These could be round toothpicks or matchsticks cut to size. However, the rear ends of small drill bits work better than anything I've yet found. Here's the process:

1. Work on the edge of a table, or some similar place; the head of your fly must hang off an edge.
2. Shake the yellow lacquer well. With the larger of the applicators, dip into the lacquer, collecting a globule.
3. Carefully apply the globule to the head of the fly. If you have just the right amount of lacquer, the globule will spread out into a perfect circle without the applicator quite touching the head itself.
4. With the head of the fly extending off the edge of the working surface, complete the other side of the head, creating a mirror image. Set the fly aside and allow the lacquer to dry completely.
5. Shake the black lacquer well. Then, using the smaller applicator, repeat the dotting process, centering a black pupil in the yellow. Allow for thorough drying, then cover with a protective coat of clear lacquer.

A word about the relative proportions of the two applicators. The one you use for the black lacquer needs to be about half the size of the one used for the pupil. In other words, if a ⅛-inch drill bit is the right size for the yellow, use a 1⁄16-inch bit for the black.

Fairly recently, stick-on eyes became available, these being a spin-off from the lure-making industry. There are several types, some made of Mylar, others of a different synthetic. They come in many sizes and colors and are very easy to use. They won't stick to the head of a fly simply by virtue of the adhesive on their backsides, so an effective protective coating is a necessity. This could be clear epoxy or some other tough adhesive that goes on fairly thick. More about this in a bit.

A consideration. If you've been working with waxed thread, you may find that stick-on eyes don't adhere to the head of the fly very well. All that needs to happen is that they stay in place until you apply the protective coating. That probably won't be a problem, but if it becomes one, simply apply one coat of clear lacquer as a base, and let it dry before sticking the eyes on.

Here's the procedure for affixing the stick-on eyes:

1. Have the fly mounted in the vise. With tweezers, peel off an eye from the sheet on which they come, and press it onto the fly head. Do the same on the far side.
2. If you're going to use epoxy, mix it well, per the instructions on the package. Using a toothpick, lay a generous blob of adhe-

WATER-BASED LACQUERS

Recently, a group of new water-based head lacquers appeared on the scene. It offers several colors and also two types of clear: a hard finish and a flexible finish. I was pleasantly surprised to find that the flexible stuff works quite well for coating fly heads as just described. It certainly doesn't have the strength and impregnability of epoxy, but I deem it adequate for the task, and it's a most convenient and quick substitute. One coat will do; two is even better. Again, you'll have to watch out for adhesion to waxed thread—which, incidentally, is also true with epoxy. A coat of well-thinned clear head lacquer solves this problem.

sive on the top of the head. Help it flow evenly over both sides, covering the eyes and the head entirely.

3. For a few moments, you'll have to keep an eye on things and clean off any excess adhesive that collects below the head with your toothpick. Then allow the adhesive to dry completely.

A few notes on epoxy. Make sure you get the clear stuff. I recommend against using two-part rod finishes, because they are too runny. Either the regular or the five-minute type is okay, though the latter doesn't allow much working time. For efficiency's sake, get a group of flies ready to go before mixing the epoxy, and do them all at once. You'll need something to secure them on, as only one can go into your vise. Typically, I do six at a time, because this is about as many as I can keep an eye on at once.

If you can tie the Mickey Finn, you can also tie quite a number of pretty and effective hair-winged streamers. One of the most enduring and popular is the Black-Nosed Dace. This pattern was originated before World War II by Art Flick, a legendary angler and author from New York's Catskills. It falls into the imitator group—it's designed to suggest the baitfish of the same name. However, the fact that this minnow is not found in many watersheds outside the Northeast and Midwest does not seem to alter its effectiveness. A friend of mine who guides on the Bighorn in Montana reports that it's a great fly there, despite the fact that there's probably no natural BNDs within a thousand miles.

I mention this because before leaving the subject of streamers, I want to elaborate on what I stated earlier about wrapping tinsel and certain other body materials over bare steel. The Black-Nosed Dace dressing calls for a tag made of red yarn. This precludes wrapping over bare hook; however, it presents an excellent opportunity to use the technique you learned earlier for adding a tag to the Woolly Worm. It is most helpful in streamer tying, and wet flies and salmon flies as well, and can be employed anytime you encounter a pattern that has a tag or tail of a material long enough and of the right texture to allow you to tie it in near the front and bind it down to the rear. To review:

A Black-Nosed Dace with painted eyes.

1. Tie on as you would for the Mickey.
2. Cut off a piece of red yarn sufficiently longer than the hook shank so that you can grip it from the rear. Tie it in atop the hook about 20 to 25 percent to the rear of the eye, and trim off the tag end.
3. While holding it tightly from the rear, bind it neatly to the hook shank, working all the way to the bend. Then wrap neatly forward, cover the tag at the tie-in spot, and complete the fly. At some point, cut the tag to length. It should be just a short little stump.

Black-Nosed Dace Dressing

HOOK, THREAD, & BODY:	As for the Mickey Finn.
TAG:	As just described.
WING:	Hair in three layers. From the bottom up: white, then black to form a narrow stripe, then brown approximately equal to the white and black combined.

The universe of streamer flies is a very large and diverse one. Broadly defined, it includes the Atlantic salmon flies, certain steelhead flies, and many of our saltwater patterns, the tying techniques and materials of all being at least generally similar. For the versatile angler, this is a very important school of fly tying, and one I hope you'll find interesting and enjoyable.

Some Streamer Patterns

Note: All of these flies are tied on streamer hooks of various lengths. They may all be tied with black thread, with the exception of the Edson Tigers, which call for yellow thread.

1. ***Warden's Worry***

TAIL:	Two opposing sections of red-dyed goose, tied like a wet-fly wing.
RIBBING:	Flat gold tinsel.
BODY:	Fuzzy orangy yellow yarn or dubbing.
THROAT HACKLE:	Yellow barbs.
WING:	Natural tan or light brown bucktail.

2. ***Marabou Black Ghost***

TAIL:	A bunch of yellow hackle fibers.
RIBBING:	Flat silver tinsel.
BODY:	Black floss or stretch nylon.
THROAT HACKLE:	Yellow hackle barbs.
WING:	White marabou.
CHEEKS:	(optional) Jungle cock or substitute.

3. ***Llama***

TAIL:	Hen grizzly hackle barbs.
RIBBING:	Oval gold tinsel.
BODY:	Red floss or stretch nylon.
WING:	A bunch of woodchuck body hair, with the guard hairs left in.
HACKLE:	Soft grizzly tied as a collar.

4. ***Edson Tiger, Light***

THREAD:	Yellow.
TAIL:	The tip of a barred black-and-white wood duck feather.
BODY:	Peacock herl.
WING:	Yellow bucktail or similar hair.
WING TOPPING:	A short section of red goose or duck.
CHEEKS:	Jungle cock or substitute, tied short.

5. ***Edson Tiger, Dark***

THREAD:	Yellow.
TAIL:	Two yellow hackle tips, tied short.
BODY:	Yellow chenille.
THROAT:	Two red hackle tips or a small red beard hackle.
WING:	A bunch of hair from the brown portion of a yellow-dyed bucktail.
CHEEKS:	Jungle cock or substitute, tied short.

A school of streamers. From the top: Light Edson Tiger, Warden's Worry, Marabou Black Ghost, Llama, Dark Edson Tiger.

29 Introducing the Dry Fly

Dry-fly fishing is easily the most popular form of the sport, while not necessarily the most effective at all times. Fortunately, it's sufficiently productive that those who embrace the puritan ethic are not victims of asceticism, per se. And I do not use the term *ethic* in the moral sense. Despite what a certain faction within the fly-fishing fraternity might think, choice of angling method has absolutely nothing to do with either ethics or morality.

The truth is that dry-fly fishing is just sheer joy. I do a lot of subsurface fishing with all sorts of creations, but if I had my druthers, I'd be fishing dry all the time. The fact that I don't is an expression of my Dutch-German practicality.

The most common design of dry fly—what many refer to as the classic, or Catskill, school—consists of four basic components: wings, tail, body, and hackle. This is where we encounter hackle in its purest and most hallowed form: the stiff, glossy fibers that imbue our beloved dry flies with form and function. In the broadest definition, however, any fly that is fished on or in the surface can be considered a dry fly. Some of these do not, and are not intended to, imitate a winged form in either the subadult (dun) or adult (imago) stage. Rather, they are intended to suggest an insect struggling to reach that stage, and perhaps doing so unsuccessfully. Thus we have the floating emerger and stillborn dun schools. And we have imitators of terrestrial insects as well.

As I related in the streamer chapter, we have that very fuzzy dichotomy between so-called imitators and attractors. Actually, with the exception of virtual laboratory models tied as objects of art, the dry flies we fish with don't look a whole lot like the real bugs. However, the visual distortions caused by water and the manner in which light interacts with it, and the effect of the movement of currents, compensate in a very real sense for the dissimilarities. These factors also discipline fly design and the selection and use of materials. It's not so much what the fly looks like in the vise; it's how it performs on the water.

Without going into excruciating detail, let's examine the nature of **dry-fly hackle** and its quality points. From a functional standpoint, particularly with regard to the classic design, the job of the hackle is to support and float the fly on the surface of the water. It also lends coloration, shape, size, an impressionistic image, and the general illusion of a natural insect.

Here are the main attributes to look for in dry-fly hackle feathers:

1. A fine, flexible quill.
2. Stiff, strong barbs, relatively web-free.
3. High barb count—that is, a dense deployment of barbs on the quill.
4. Long "sweet spots," meaning quality throughout a large portion of the feather.
5. Consistency of barb length, which is what determines size.
6. Beautiful coloration, or sheen.

These attributes will become more meaningful as you develop your tying skills. I might comment further on the matter of **web,** because it has long been a major factor in hackle quality. This is the soft portion of a feather near the quill. In top-quality feathers, it may not be present at all, or at least not in the portion that constitutes prime hackle. If present in quantity, it's quite visible; you can see the web line running lengthwise along the quill. If there's a significant amount of it, that's bad, and you should avoid using such feathers for dry-fly work. A little web is tolerable.

There are some other considerations that pertain as much or more to making prudent purchases as to actual hackle quality or characteristics. An excellent case in point is the Hoffman line of saddle hackle, produced by Whiting Farms of Delta, Colorado. The grading system—#1, #2, #3, and so forth—is based almost entirely on the number of feathers on a pelt and their length. Feather quality, as defined above, is virtually the same throughout the three grades. So it comes down to how many flies can be tied from that pelt.

Having mentioned saddles, I should quickly sidetrack to describe **necks,** or **capes** (these two terms may be used interchangeably). Necks, which have long been the standard source of dry-fly hackle, are just what they sound like: the necks of roosters. They have been developed to a very high level of quality over the past several decades by such growers as Henry Hoffman, Ted Hebert, and Dr. Tom Whiting, who now raises both the Hoffman and Hebert strains. Necks are characterized by having a large range of hackle sizes. A top-grade cape might yield feathers for as many as eight or nine sizes of fly, from large size 10s to tiny size 24s and 26s. Material for tails may also be found on the larger feathers around the edges.

With cape feathers, we look for a long **sweet spot,** which is that portion of the feather that yields prime hackle. It is defined as follows:

1. Uniformity of barb length.
2. Relative absence of web at the center.
3. Narrow, flexible quill.

When you're tying with neck hackles, you must strip off everything that isn't part of the sweet spot; otherwise, you're simply crowding the hook with poorer-quality hackle and thicker quill, and there will be no space left for the prime stuff. Many tyers, beginners in particular, have a tendency to try to use as much of the feather as possible; it's a projection of the "I-paid-for-it-and-by-golly-I'm-going-to-use-it" mind-set. Please don't do this to yourself. Be assiduous in your assessment of each and every cape feather, and strip down to the sweet spot without compromise. Usually, this means discarding half or more of the feather. That's not a bad thing; it's to your great advantage to do so.

Saddles come from that part of the chicken where you would mount the saddle in order to ride the animal, if such were possible. Years ago, saddle feathers were seldom suitable for dry-fly work. With the careful and informed development of genetic hackle in recent years, however, saddles have caught up to, and in several respects passed, cape hackle. The feathers are long; in prime saddles, very long, sometimes exceeding a foot (30 cm) in length. On top-grade saddles, almost the entire length of the feather is of dry-fly quality, and most of the feathers on the pelt are of such quality. In other words, almost the whole feather is one huge sweet spot. The very best feathers are found along the sides of the saddle patch. There are usually some softer ones in the center, which make very good Woolly Bugger hackle.

Quality saddle feathers rate very high with respect to the points mentioned earlier. They usually have thin quills, and an extremely high barb count, which translates to more hackle per wrap. This enables you to get several or more flies out of one feather. In fact, I've gotten as many as a dozen in sizes 14 and 16 from a single feather. This is what justifies the price of such pelts.

Another great advantage of such long feathers is the ease with which they are handled. Usually, you don't need to resort to the use of hackle pliers until the feather is virtually used up, and you're down to the tip. It is also possible to wrap two feathers at the same time, thus obtaining a mix, such as that called for in the Adams and many other patterns. The fineness of the quills facilitates this.

At this point you might be wondering: Why use necks at all? There are several reasons. First, saddles have a very limited range of sizes—three at the most. They don't tie down to the very small sizes that, as you'll find out eventually, can be of great importance to the fly fisher. They do not yield tailing material, nor do they yield tippets for the wings that many patterns require. So both capes and saddles have their place in your war chest.

Another difference between necks and saddles is that with necks, unless you're tying smaller flies, you'll usually need to use two feathers. With very high-quality cape hackles, you might be able to obtain sufficient hackle with one feather for a size 14, but usually you have to get down to a 16 or 18 before this is true. With top-grade saddle feathers, one feather will usually do the trick, the reasons being (1) the extraordinarily high barb count, (2) the strength of the barbs, and (3) the ultra-fine quill, which enables tighter packing.

Before we move on to our first dry-fly pattern, a few closing thoughts on hackle selection. In addition to applying the aforementioned criteria when evaluating a cape or saddle, look for aberrations. This is of particular importance when choosing saddles. Sometimes you'll encounter a saddle that has shorter barbs on one side of the quills than the other. If this difference is modest, it's not a big problem. However, if the disparity is significant, and a lot of the feathers display it, don't buy the saddle.

Also, you should be aware that the occasional long saddle feather will change sizes in the middle. In rare cases, I've encountered three different sizes on one feather! If the quality is good in other respects, go ahead and use the saddle; just keep an eye on how the size runs. If it suddenly changes to larger or smaller than you want, switch to another feather, laying the initial one aside for later use on a different-sized fly.

One more aberration to watch out for in saddles is what I call **cupping.** This refers to feathers that manifest an inward curvature of the barbs. A little of this is tolerable, but not much. Stay away from saddles that have more than a slight amount of cupping.

I'd like to begin the dry-fly section of the book with a style of dry fly that represents the ultimate in simplicity: the Bivisible. It has only two components, both of which are hackle feathers wrapped around a fine-wire hook. The second, or frontal, hackle is always white, which gives the fly its "bivisibility." The other, or main, hackle can be any color you desire.

A word about sizing hackle. The size of fly for which a particular feather is proper is determined by the length of the barbs *in the wrapped position.* Thus, when gauging the size of a feather, you must flex it into a simulation of that wrapped position, so that the barbs protrude and you can see how long they are. This can be a bit deceptive, especially with saddles, where the barbs in repose tend to lie at a severe angle. A hackle gauge is most helpful for beginners.

On a conventional fly, using a standard hook, the rule of thumb is that the hackle should be 1½ times the gap of the hook. We'll deal with this in subsequent exercises. In the case of the Bivisible, the fly works better with shorter hackle—approximately equal to the gap, or slightly longer. These flies are designed for use in faster, more diffused currents and balance better when they ride lower on the water.

As I mentioned, this fly is composed entirely of hackle. The style used here is known for some obscure reason as **palmered hackle,** which means that it is wrapped over the length of the hook shank, rather than concentrated fore and aft of the wings, like conventional hackle. As you might suppose, saddle feathers are ideal for this sort of work. They have adequate length and all of the other requisite attributes. We're talking about the main hackle here; the few turns of white at the front can be done with either cape or saddle hackle and can be a bit longer than the main hackle, if you wish. As stated, the main hackle can be whatever color you want. Here, we'll use brown.

Brown Bivisible Dressing

HOOK:	Fine-wire dry fly, standard shank length, typically sizes 10 to 16.
THREAD:	Fine black or brown, 6/0 or 8/0.
MAIN HACKLE:	Brown, preferably a saddle feather.
FRONT HACKLE:	White, either saddle or cape.

Tying Steps

1. Select a brown hackle and prepare it by stripping off any soft material at the butt end that doesn't have dry-fly characteristics. In other words, strip back to the sweet spot. Leave about ¼ inch (6 mm) of quill for tying in.
2. Tie on a little way to the rear of the eye and wrap neatly and smoothly to the rear. The smoother the thread base, the better the hackle will deploy.
3. Tie in the feather with the front, or more colorful, side of the feather facing you; this will result in the colorful side being in front during wrapping, which is very important. Leave a tiny bit of bare quill exposed. This permits the feather to rotate to a position perpendicular to the hook shank, which ensures that no barbs will deploy prematurely and end up slanted rearward at an angle. We want all barbs to protrude at virtually a right angle to the shank.
4. Wrap the thread forward, binding down the quill butt in the process. Be very neat, and cut off any excess quill well short of the eye area. Stop about 25 percent of the shank length before the eye.
5. With a nice, long saddle hackle, you're better off not using hackle pliers; they would only get in the way. Pick up the feather and start wrapping forward, with each turn adjacent to the preceding one. Be sure the colorful side of the feather is in front; otherwise, the barbs will start to lean forward after a few turns. Maintain moderate tension, well short of the breaking point of the quill.
6. When you reach the spot where the thread hangs in wait, hold the feather under tension with your right hand. Pick up the bobbin with your left hand, and ex-

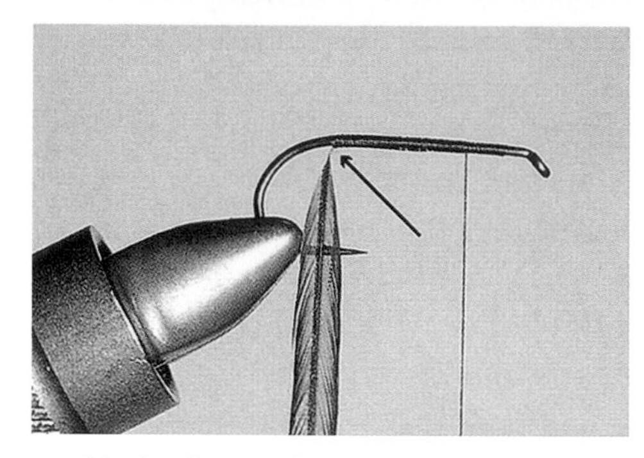

Hackle feather tied in. Note tiny bit of quill exposed (steps 1–4).

The hackle feather being wrapped. Note that the pretty side is in front (step 5).

Tying off the hackle. Note that the thread intercepts the quill (step 6).

Tying Steps

ecute several lift-over moves, thus binding the quill to the hook. Then switch the bobbin to your right hand and take several more firm wraps. When you are sure the feather is secure, trim off the excess, and lay it aside for future use. Then take a few wraps over the spot where you trimmed, smoothing it out.

7. Prepare a white feather as you did the brown, and tie it in such that the first turn will be contiguous to the last of the brown. Advance the thread forward, but don't crowd the eye.
8. Take a few turns of white, then tie that feather off, as you did the brown.
9. After trimming and securing, make a whip-finish.

The white feather for the front hackle tied in (step 7).

The completed fly (steps 8–9).

HACKLE COLORS

As I mentioned, there are as many Bivisibles as there are hackle colors; more, in fact, because you can mix two colors to form the main hackle. Grizzly works great, as do dark dun and a brown and grizzly mix. Pale colors, such as cream, tend to neutralize the effect of the white front hackle, because there is little contrast.

The major hackle colors are:

Brown Just as it sounds. It can range from a light brown, also called dark ginger, to a rich, chocolate brown, also called Coachman brown.

Ginger A lighter brown, or tan.

Cream As it sounds. It can range from pale to very rich and golden, which is also called straw cream.

Dun This color is somewhat controversial. The Brits have their own definition. Here in America, *dun* is synonymous with *gray.* There are many shades, ranging from very light, which is known as pale watery dun, to almost black, which is known as dark dun. There's slate, which is a rich, dark gray, and medium dun, which is lighter than slate but darker than pale watery. There are also complex duns of many shades that show rust and golden tints. They can be gorgeous.

Black As it sounds.

Grizzly Barred gray or black and white. Also known as barred rock.

Cree Barred with multiple colors. Very rare.

Furnace Brown with a black center stripe. Somewhat rare.

Badger White or cream with a black center stripe. Somewhat scarce in paler shades.

There's a lingering controversy over dyed versus natural colors. It has some historical basis in fact, because until fairly recently, the dye jobs done on hackles were pretty poor, not only from the standpoint of the colors themselves, but also because of what the process did to the feathers.

This is no longer the case. The dye jobs we get today from the top suppliers are excellent, and the colors may, in some respects, be better than the naturals. The only possible exception is with dun: The dyed grays, while very pretty, tend to be flat, whereas the naturals often have highlights and overtones. I find these attractive, but I can't tell you how the fish feel about them. In summary—I wouldn't, and in fact don't, hesitate to use dyed hackles.

Some Bivisible Patterns

Note: These patterns all use the same hook called for in the tying lesson. Please refer to the hook chart in chapter 22 for specifics (page 240).

1. ***Black***
   Black hackle tied palmer-style, fronted by white.
2. ***Grizzly***
   Grizzly hackle tied palmer-style, fronted by white.
3. ***Cree or Barred Ginger***
   Cree or barred ginger hackle tied palmer-style, fronted by white.
4. ***Brown/Grizzly* (*Adams mix*)**
   Mixed brown and grizzly hackle tied palmer-style, fronted by white.
5. ***Grizzly/Peacock Palmer***
   A peacock herl body, over which grizzly hackle is tied palmer-style, fronted by white.

Common hackle colors. Top row, left to right: Coachman brown, fiery brown, light brown or dark ginger, ginger, barred ginger, cream. Bottom row, left to right: grizzly or barred rock, badger, furnace, medium gray dun, pale watery dun, cree.

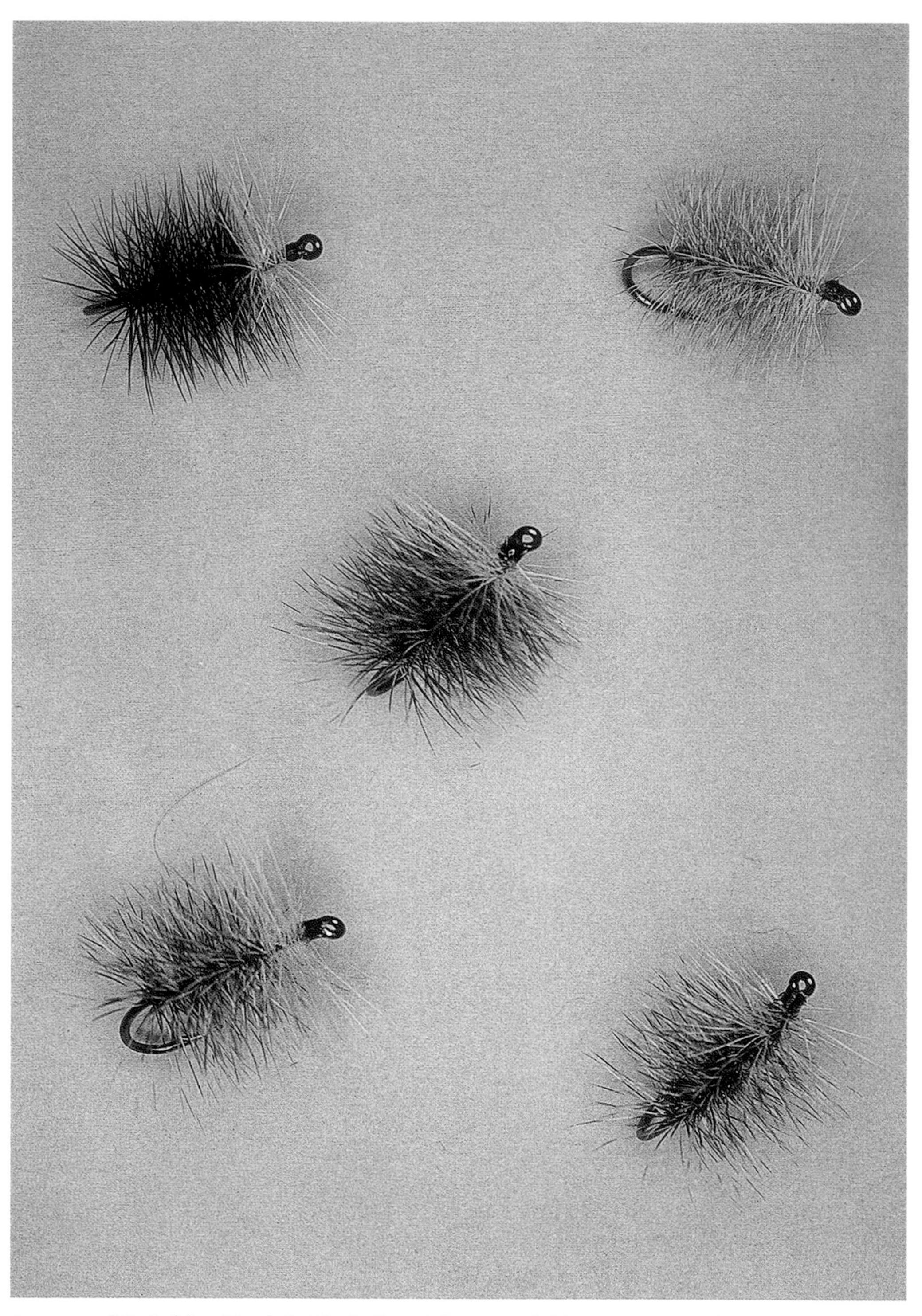

A swarm of Bivisibles. Top left: Black. Top right: Barred Ginger. Center: Adams Mix. Lower left: Grizzly. Lower right: Grizzly/Peacock Palmer.

30 The Hair-Winged Caddis

Continuing to build on the lessons of the Bivisible exercise, let's tie a fly of a design that will enable you to imitate a very important order of insects: the caddisflies. Entomologists tell us that there are a couple of thousand different caddis in North America, quite a number of which are of importance to the fly fisher. They vary widely in size, color, and behavior.

Many anglers believe that caddis have become more important than mayflies in certain watersheds. This may well be true, because they seem to withstand environmental changes better than the ephemeral mayflies, which must undergo a final metamorphosis into the delicate imago stage before becoming fertile and, thus, capable of reproduction.

A few words about fishing the adult caddis. You'll often see caddisflies popping off the water and fish rising like crazy all around. You are sure that you have a good imitation of the insect, yet you can't seem to entice a single trout. The reason is that certain caddis rise very quickly through the water and take wing directly, sort of like a rocket fired by a submarine. What you see is the rise of fish nabbing the escaping pupae just under the surface. Often, they aren't quick enough, and a caddis can be seen flying virtually out of the riseform.

A technique that's worked quite well for me under such circumstances is this: Instead of casting above these riseforms in the conventional manner, I smack my fly right into the riseform as quickly as possible. If there's a hungry and frustrated trout lying there, it will often react immediately, thinking it's getting a second chance at the bug that eluded him a moment earlier. Try this—I think you'll be rewarded. And it's easier than learning how to imitate and present the emerging pupa, which is your other alternative.

The fly we are about to tie is a variation of a great western pattern known as the Troth Caddis. Al Troth immigrated from his native Pennsylvania to the Beaverhead Valley in Montana, in order to pursue the fly-fishing lifestyle. He's now a legend in those parts. The simple but deadly pattern he created to dupe the cautious and selective brown trout of the Beaverhead has become a universal pattern, and we all owe Al a debt of thanks for it.

As I understand it, Al's original dressing didn't have hackle. It relied on elk hair to give it both form and flotation. One of the popular dressings that evolved from this is the simple palmered Hair-Winged Caddis, which has only three components: body, wing, and hackle. This will serve as an introduction to winging the dry fly, which is the part that seems to give the beginner the most trouble.

You probably know already that the caddisfly, when in repose, carries its wings tented over its body in mothlike fashion. This is known in fly-tying parlance as the **down-wing** dry-fly style. It is easier to emulate than the wings of mayflies, which are carried in several positions, depending on whether the fly is in the subadult or adult form. We'll explore that in subsequent chapters.

> If you're at all interested in scientific terminology, the four major orders of aquatic insects the angler has to deal with are identified by the Latin word for "wings," which is *ptera*. Caddisflies are of the order Trichoptera, which means "tented wings." Mayflies are of the order Ephemeroptera, which means, in general terms, "ephemeral, delicate, or temporal wings." Stoneflies are of the order Plecoptera, which means "plaited wings." The other major aquatic order is Diptera, which is the largest and includes such beloved insects as the mosquito and the blackfly. *Diptera* means "two-winged."

There are several types of materials you might use for the body. Here, I want to introduce you to a material of fairly recent vintage known as **stretch nylon.** Its most common application is as a substitute for the traditional material called floss (see page 258). Like floss, stretch nylon comes in stranded form, but it possesses some different attributes. It's a tough, durable material that resists fraying during handling and holds its color well when wet. It's a good floater, and thus suitable for dry-fly work. It can be used for almost any size of fly, simply by wrapping layers or using multiple strands. It comes in a wide array of attractive colors. Also, it can, in certain applications, be mounted in a bobbin and used as both thread and body material at once.

Another material you'll meet for the first time here is deer body hair. This is a broad subject, because there are so many varieties of the stuff and a number of ways to use it. Additionally, hair from other animals—elk, caribou, antelope, reindeer—can be substituted for deer hair to obtain certain results. If you get into spun-and-clipped hair tying, which is required for such patterns as the Muddler Minnow, the Irresistible, and hair bass bugs, you'll be exposed to all sorts of hairs.

Depending on the species of animal, and the part of its body from whence the hair is taken, deer hair can range from soft and pulpy to hard and bristly. The soft stuff is what is used for spinning. It flares under thread pressure and can then be trimmed to shape. Very hard hair is used for streamer wings, such as those of the Mickey Finn. It comes from the tail of the deer. Between these two extremes, we have hair that is more manageable, is fairly fine of texture, flares enough to form nice-looking wings, and has good floating properties. That's what this dressing requires.

Natural caddisflies come in many colors. Various shades of green and olive are quite ubiquitous, so we'll use green stretch nylon here. For the hackle, which is wrapped palmer-style, I favor grizzly, as I believe the barred hackle looks more alive on the water and is suggestive of movement. Caddisflies are nothing if not peripatetic. These short-legged insects ride low on the water, so the hackle is undersized, like that of the Bivisible.

Palmered Hair-Winged Caddis Dressing

HOOK:	Standard fine-wire dry fly.
THREAD:	6/0 or 8/0, preferably of a fairly light neutral shade, such as tan.
HACKLE:	Grizzly, preferably high-grade saddle.
BODY:	Stretch nylon, green.
WING:	Medium-textured deer body hair, natural color.

Tying Steps

1. Size and prepare a hackle per the instructions for the Bivisible (see page 294).
2. Tie on about one-third of the shank length rearward of the eye, wrap to the bend, and tie in the hackle, as you did on the Bivisible. Remember to leave the tiniest bit of bare quill exposed.
3. Wrap neatly to the tie-in point, meanwhile trimming off and binding down the quill butt.
4. Tie in a piece of the stretch nylon about 5 inches (125 mm) in length, and trim off the excess. An easy way to control such soft, floppy material when tying it in is to stretch it between the fingers of your two hands, then press it against the backside of the hook while passing the thread over it. This works for yarn, tinsel, or whatever.
5. Wrap the material back to the bend of the hook and forward, forming a double layer. If you wish, you may take one turn of the body material behind the tie-in point of the feather. This helps position the feather for wrapping.
6. Tie off and trim the stretch nylon. Note that these operations take place well to the rear of the hook eye.

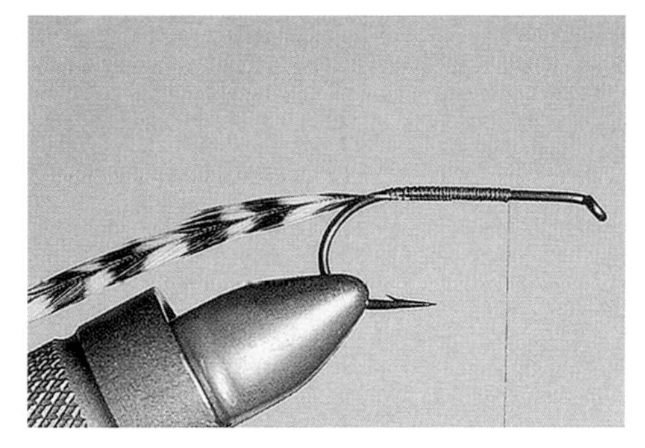

Hackle tied in. Note thread position (steps 1–3).

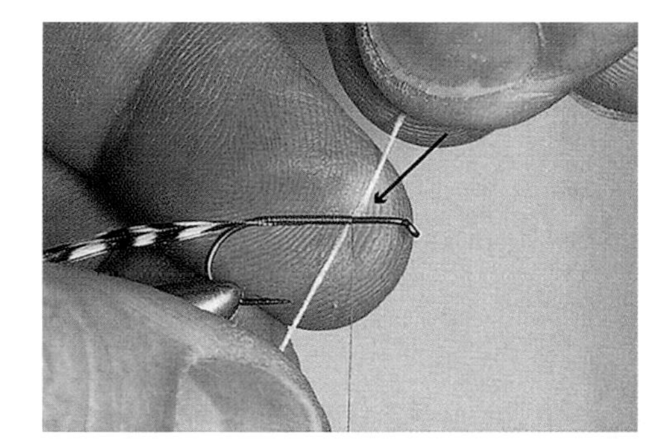

An easy method for tying in materials that have no "backbone" (step 4).

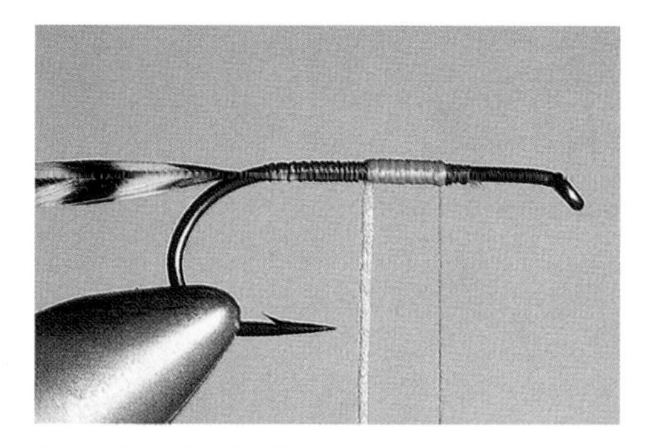

Wrapping the body (steps 5–6).

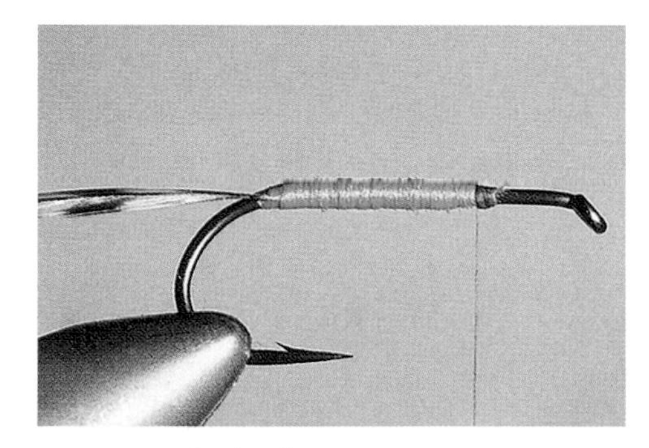

Wrapping the body (steps 5–6).

Tying Steps

7. Palmer-wrap the hackle in spirals over the body, allowing the green to show through between turns. When you reach the front of the body, secure the feather with a few thread wraps, but don't cut anything off; you'll need it to complete the fly.

   Note: If you don't happen to own any long saddle feathers, and are using shorter cape hackles for this fly, you may have to tie off the first feather, make the wing, then tie in a second feather for the front hackle.

The body hackle wrapped and secured in place for subsequent use (step 7).

8. With the remaining feather hanging out of the way, run the thread back and forth to the eye two or three times, thus laying down a base for the wing.
9. Cut off a small bunch of hair, and clean out all underfur and shorties. As I mentioned in the streamer chapter (see page 279), a fine-toothed comb helps.
10. Even up the tips of the hairs. A stacker is useful here, but if you don't have one, simply remove aberrant hairs with your fingers.

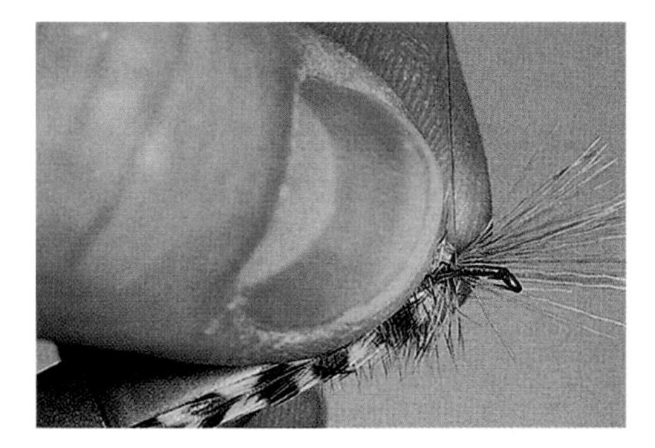

Tying the wing in place (steps 8–13).

11. Now you have an option. If you wish, you can cut a channel lengthwise out of the hackle on top of the hook. It would look like a wedge of pie from the front. This isn't mandatory, however—you can mount the wing successfully without doing it.
12. Hold the winging bunch in your left hand and establish the length. It should extend to, or just beyond, an imaginary line tangent to the rear of the bend of the hook.
13. Set the wing in place and tie it on adjacent to the front of the body. The recommended method for doing this is to take several soft, or gathering, wraps, then gradually add tighter wraps. This helps keep the hair from flaring all over the place and interfering with what you're doing.

Wing butts trimmed, thread base wrapped to accommodate the front hackle (step 14).

Tying Steps

14. When you feel that the wing is secured, trim off the butts, while holding the wing with your left hand, to prevent inadvertent movement. Then, as neatly as possible, bind down the butts, ending up with the thread just rearward of the eye in tie-off position.
15. Pick up the feather and wrap a front hackle. Here, the wraps should be well packed, or adjacent to one another. Tie off and secure the feather, and make a whip-finish.

The finished Caddis (step 15).

A little trick: If you have a second bobbin, you can mount the stretch nylon in it and use it for both thread and body material. After tying in the hackle and completing the body, tie off the stretch nylon, substitute the regular tying thread, and proceed with the rest of the fly.

Using these techniques, you can create a host of down-wing flies of whatever sizes and colors you wish. One of my favorites for western waters is the Dark Olive Sedge, the dressing for which follows.

Some Down-Wing Dry-Fly Patterns

1. ***Black (Chimarra) Caddis***

HOOK:	Standard dry fly; please refer to the hook chart in chapter 22 for specifics (page 240).
THREAD:	Black.
HACKLE:	Black or darkly barred grizzly, tied palmer-style over the body, then conventional-style ahead of the wing.
BODY:	Black floss, stretch nylon, or fine dubbing.
WING:	Black deer hair.

2. ***Dark Olive Sedge***

HOOK:	Standard dry fly.
THREAD:	Brown or dark olive, 8/0.
HACKLE:	Slate gray saddle, tied palmer-style over the body, then conventional-style ahead of the wing.
BODY:	Dark olive floss, stretch nylon, or fine dubbing; on very small sizes, just the thread.
WING:	Slate-dyed hair.

3. ***Royal Trude***

HOOK:	Long dry fly (2XL), typically sizes 8 to 14.
TAIL:	A small bunch of golden pheasant cape tippet fibers.
BODY:	Two short sections of peacock herl with a red floss or equivalent belly band in between (like the Royal Wulff; see chapter 32).
WING:	A small bunch of white calf tail, tied down-wing-style.
HACKLE:	Brown, tied in front of the wing.

4. ***Lime Trude***

HOOK:	Long dry fly (2XL), typically sizes 8 to 14.
TAIL:	A small bunch of golden pheasant cape tippet fibers.
BODY:	Lime-colored dubbing.
WING:	A small bunch of white calf tail, tied down-wing-style.
HACKLE:	Mixed brown and grizzly, similar to the Adams in the following chapter, but tied in front of the wing.

5. ***Stimulator***

HOOK:	Long (2XL, 3X, or 4X) dry fly.
THREAD:	Tan or similar.
TAIL:	A short bunch of deer body hair, stacked.
HACKLE:	High-quality grizzly saddle feather, tied palmer-style over the body and thorax, with the turns closer together ahead of the wing.
BODY:	Yellow stretch nylon or fine yarn.
WING:	A longer bunch of deer body hair, stacked.
THORAX:	Orange dubbing.

A select group of down-wing flies. Top left: Dark Olive Sedge. Top right: Lime Trude. Center: Stimulator. Lower left: Royal Trude. Lower right: Black (Chimarra) Caddis.

31 A Classic Dry Fly—The Adams

When asked that age-old angling question, "If you had to fish dry with only one pattern, what would it be?" I'm willing to bet that most experienced fly fishers would answer, "The Adams, of course!" For while this fly may not look exactly like any one insect, it is very suggestive of insect life in general and has an alluring "bugginess" about it that trout have had trouble resisting for well over half a century.

The Adams is credited to one Len Halliday, a well-known northern Michigan tyer of the earlier part of the 1900s. The original dressing was somewhat different from the one most people tie today. The wings were tied **spent,** meaning that they were set at a flat attitude and lay dead-man's-float on the water; there was also a little yellow ball of dubbing at the rear that represented an egg sac. If I'm correctly informed, the fly was tied without a tail—which figures, because it was supposed to look like an egg-laying caddis, and caddisflies are tail-less.

As the fly went through immigration to other parts of the country, especially the Catskills, it was altered to suit the fishing conditions and conventions of each region. The version that seems to have gained favor as the standard is British/Catskill in all respects. It has the four main components—wings, tail, body, and hackle—and the proportions are what we know as **standard,** or traditional.

Even the most standardized patterns of dry fly take various forms: thicker or thinner bodies, longer or shorter wings and tails, more or less hackle, and so forth. Here, we'll tie the textbook style, and you can take it from there to suit your local fishing conditions and preferences.

This fly represents a major step forward in your development as a fly tyer. You'll learn the upright tippet feather wing, the standard dry-fly tail, the dubbed dry-fly body, and the two-feather hackle. This opens up major areas of dry-fly tying, because these components, and the techniques for constructing them, are the very essence of the art.

An observation. In most of the previous tying lessons, you've seen how the execution of procedures early on in the tying of a fly affects subsequent ones. Efficient fly tying is a progressive process of integration. In a sense, it's like shooting pool: What you do now sets up what you do next. This becomes more critical as you move into the delicate and discrete disciplines of dry-fly tying. Being neat and precise when tying on the wings and tail sets up making a neat, well-proportioned body and properly formed hackle. In fact, you'll soon find out that neatness *does* count, big time. It's easier to tie flies with care and precision than quickly and sloppily. Why rush? This isn't a race.

Adams Dressing

HOOK:	Standard fine-wire dry fly, typically sizes 10 to 18.
THREAD:	Black 6/0 or 8/0.
WINGS:	Grizzly (barred rock) tippets; soft rooster or hen.
TAIL:	Long, stiff hackle barbs; brown or grizzly, or a mix of the two.
BODY:	Gray dubbing, finely packed.
HACKLE:	Brown and grizzly mixed.

A few preparatory notes before we start with the tying. Len Halliday and the tyers of that era used grizzly rooster tippets, meaning small hackle feathers, for the wings. Considering the quality and characteristics of the rooster hackle back then, this was appropriate. With today's materials, many tyers—myself included—favor hen grizzly, which produces a better-looking wing and is very economical.

Initially, I was taught to strip off all materials that weren't to be part of the actual wings. Later, I found that simply folding back the excess stuff nearest the butts worked better, because it provides something to hold on to and helps keep the quills from rotating and skewing the wings. Another plus is that if you miscalculate and make the wings too short, you can easily back off and repeat the folding-back process, whereas once you've stripped off material, it's history. If you prefer to try stripping the quills bare, go ahead, but I think you'll find my method preferable.

The dubbing can be either natural or synthetic, so long as it is very smooth and fine in texture. Personally, I find the new synthetics hard to beat. A brown and grizzly mix is my preference for the tail, but I don't believe the fly suffers a great deal if only one or the other is used, so don't worry about this too much.

As to proportions, the rule of thumb is that the hackle should be 1½ times the gap of the hook in length and should be distributed fairly equally fore and aft of the wings. The wings should be about the length of the hook shank and should be seated about 25 percent of the shank length rearward of the eye. The tails are also approximately the length of the shank, but they can be very slightly longer, if this is required to achieve proper balance. The idea is that the fly should rest on the tips of the tail and hackle, with the hook barely clearing a flat surface.

It is quite important that the tails be spread a little. This not only improves balance, but aids flotation as well. Tails that are tied as a tight clump tend to behave as a wick and draw up water. Tails that are spread or fanned out a bit emulate a snowshoe on the surface of the water, distributing weight over area. You'll see how this is done in the tying sequence.

Tying Steps

1. Tie on near the eye and wrap a neat thread base on which to mount the wings, using perhaps three layers of thread. End up with the thread hanging about 25 percent of the shank length to the rear of the eye.

2. Select two matching tippets (small hackle feathers) from a grizzly neck, and prepare them as previously described, either folding back (my recommendation) or stripping off all of the fluff and lower barbs that won't be part of the wings. Keep in mind that the wing length is equivalent to the hook shank, meaning from the eye to where the bend begins.

3. Hold the wings with the thumb and forefinger of your left hand with the convex sides against each other, so that they flare apart. Get the tips absolutely even, so that the wings will come out equal in length.

4. Set the wings in position atop the hook at the thread position. Hold them in such a manner as to expose the quills at the point where the thread will intersect them. Keep them centered. Tie them in place with several pinch wraps, followed by several securing wraps.

5. When the wings are almost, but not quite, locked in, gently stroke them upright. This helps set the wings in perfect position and alignment, because it corrects for any slipping or rolling that went on during the tying-in process.

6. Gently crimp the wings into an upright attitude, then lock them in that position with a few thread wraps tight to the front of the quills.

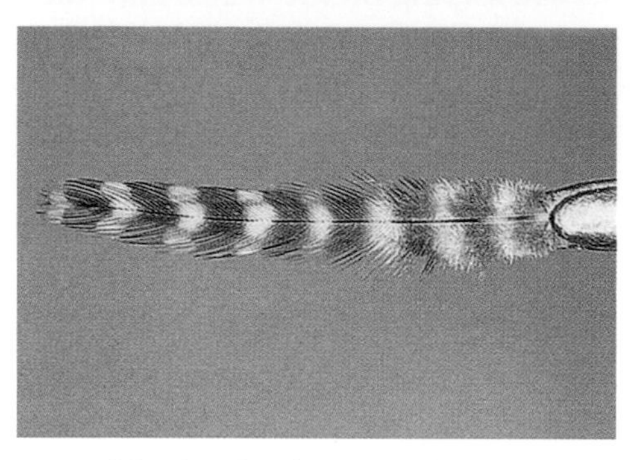

Typical feather for this type of wing (step 2).

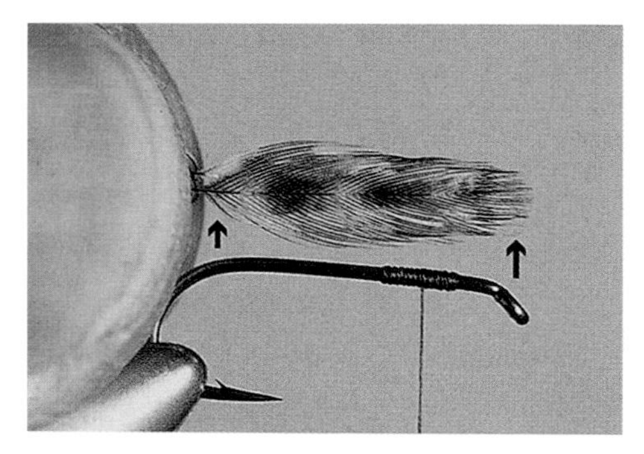

The winging feathers are measured with the hook shank. Note how the barbs are held back to expose the quill precisely at the tie-in point (steps 2–3).

The wings tied on (step 4).

Tying Steps

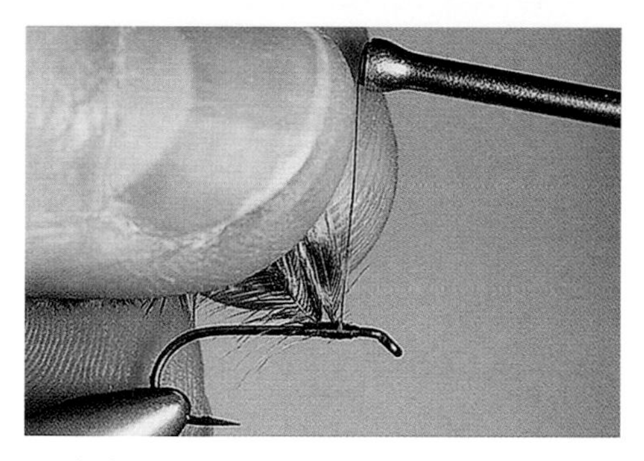

Lock the wings into an upright position and, after trimming the butts, wrap to the bend (steps 5–7).

Lock the wings into an upright position and, after trimming the butts, wrap to the bend (steps 5–7).

7. Slope-cut the butts and excess material, then neatly bind it down as you wrap to the rear. This forms a smooth, nicely tapered underlayer and establishes the shape of the finished body.

8. Just at the bend, make a tiny bump with the thread—two or three turns only. This will help spread the tail fibers.

9. For the tail, select a large hackle feather with long, stiff barbs. Complete the barb-gathering procedure per earlier instructions—stroking the barbs to perpendicular, then cutting off or pulling off a bunch. Remember: If the barbs are of equal length on both sides of the quill, you can fold the feather and take from both sides at once. Otherwise, use one side at a time. The tail should be sufficient to support the fly on the water, but not so heavy as to be unsightly. Check the photos for proportions.

10. While keeping the tips as evenly aligned as possible, set the tailing bunch in position, meanwhile gauging the length, as specified.

A large feather from the edge of a cape, with good tailing barbs (step 9).

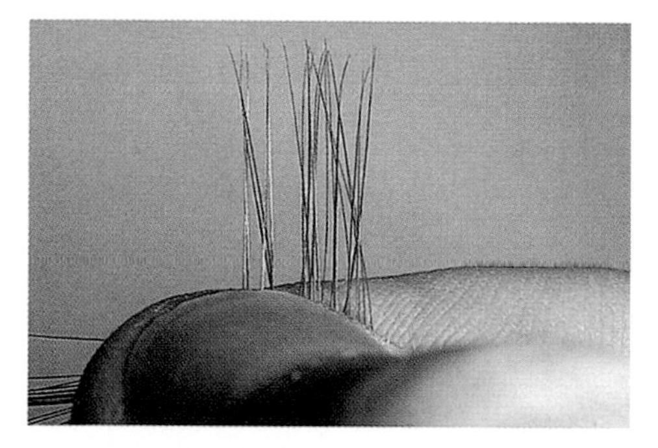

How to gather barbs neatly for a dry-fly tail (step 9).

Tying Steps

11. Tie on the tailing bunch with either a couple of pinch wraps or a couple of soft wraps, followed by securing wraps. In the process, jam them against the little thread bump, so that they spread a bit.

12. Trim the tail butts in such a manner that they integrate smoothly with the wing butts, then wrap neatly forward to just short of the wings and back to the rear. Try to avoid building up any unnecessary bulk immediately behind the wings, because this interferes with the hackling process.

13. Dubbing the typical dry-fly body is a study in minimalism. Tease out the dubbing and spin it on gradually in very tiny amounts. Try to lay the fibers parallel to the thread. If possible, build in a slight taper. As to proportions, if you are working, for example, on a size 12 hook, 1¼ to 1½ inches (32 to 38 mm) of dubbing is about right. It's important to end the body short of the wings, so that you won't be winding hackle over dubbing.

14. Wrap the dubbing. The first turn hides the little thread bumps that spread the tails.

15. Prepare two hackles—a brown and a grizzly—per previous instructions. When selecting them, make sure that both are the right size. Either cape or saddle feathers will work fine. In either case, don't cheat. Strip off any material that's not prime.

16. Lay the two feathers together spoon-style, with the brown one in front. Tie them in by the quill butts just behind the wing, underneath the hook, pretty-sides forward, with a tiny bit of quill exposed.

17. Lock in the quills with neat, tight thread wraps, coming forward under the wings. Trim off the quills neatly short of the eye, and neaten up as necessary with some discrete thread wraps. The thread should

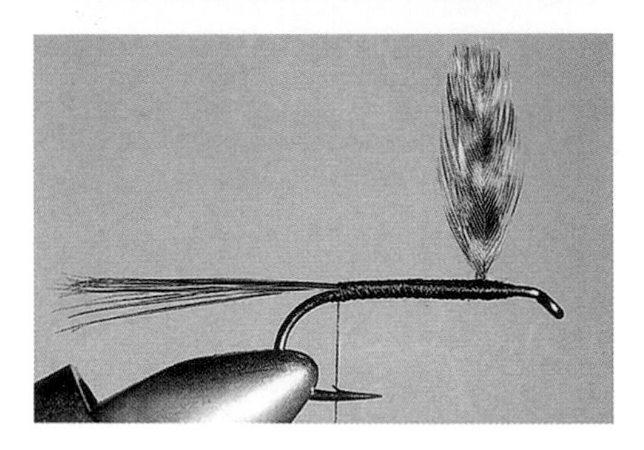

Tail tied on, butts neatly buried, thread in position to receive dubbing (steps 10–12).

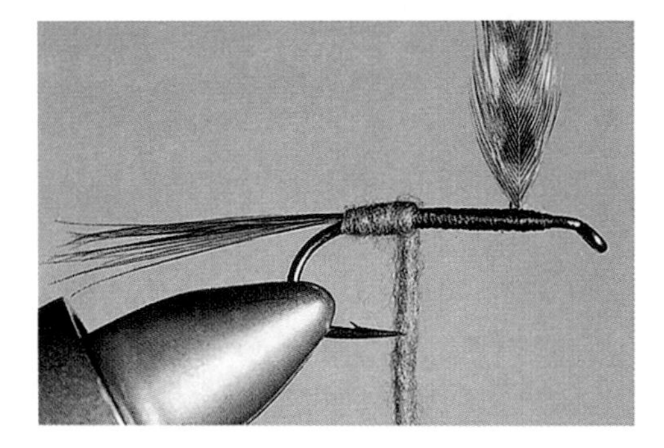

Dubbing the dry-fly body (steps 13–14).

Dubbing the dry-fly body (steps 13–14).

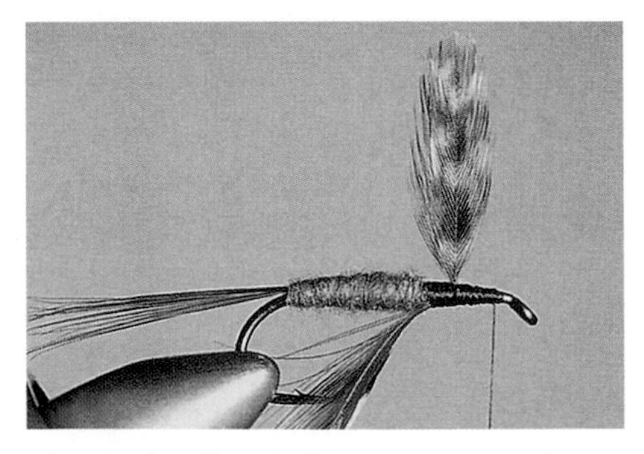

The two hackles tied in. Again, note that a bit of quill is exposed (steps 15–17).

end up positioned so as to allow for tying off each hackle individually and making a whip finish without crowding the eye.

18. If you're using saddle feathers and they're long enough, you won't need hackle pliers, as you will with the short cape feathers. In either case, start with the feather nearest the front—which should be the brown—and wind forward, each turn abutting the one before. Don't worry about leaving tiny crevices for the next hackle to fit into; the quills will seat themselves.

Wrapping the first hackle up to, but not crowding, the rear of the wings (step 18).

19. Depending on just how everything came out, you'll get two or three turns behind the wings. Don't force an extra turn; this would cock the wings forward. Cross over beneath the wings and take the next wrap tight to the front of the wings, which helps support them in an upright position.

Complete wrapping the first hackle in front of the wings, tie it off, and trim neatly before proceeding with the second hackle (steps 19–20).

20. Take another two or three turns forward—whatever there's room for without crowding—then tie off and trim the feather, as you've been doing.

21. Pick up the second feather and repeat the process. It should integrate neatly with the first one. If you notice any twisting, matting, or whatever, back off and rewrap.

22. Finish wrapping the second hackle, trim, whip-finish, and admire.

Wrapping the second hackle completes the fly (steps 21–22).

You've now learned two of the most important types of dry-fly wings. Many patterns call for tippet wings similar to those for the Adams, but using feathers of different colors and markings. There are two things to be avoided: using feathers with too heavy a quill and making the wings too wide. Both will produce skewed wings with too much air resistance. They are guaranteed to turn your leader into a Slinky.

One last note on the Adams tail. As I stated earlier, the dressing accepted as standard today specifies a mix of grizzly and brown for the tail. If you decide you want to tie it this way, here's my easy method for handling and mixing the two colors:

1. Procure a bunch of either color sufficient for half the amount needed for the tail and tie it in place with only two turns of thread.

2. Procure a similar bunch of the other color, take it in your left hand, and hold it just above the first bunch. Match up the tips, so that all barbs are equal in length.

3. While holding both bunches, back off the two thread wraps used to tie in the first bunch. Roll the barbs around between your fingers a bit, mixing them. Then tie them both on together.

Some Classic Dry-Fly Patterns

Note: These patterns all use the same standard dry-fly hook called for in the tying lesson. Please refer to the hook chart in chapter 22 for specifics (page 240).

1. *Hendrickson*

THREAD: Tan or brown.
WINGS: Barred wood duck flank feather, tied as for the hair wing on the Royal Wulff; see chapter 32.
TAIL: Medium gray hackles, stiff.
BODY: Dubbing: pale tan, reddish tan, pinkish lavender, depending on region (varies considerably).
HACKLE: Medium gray.

2. *Quill Gordon*

THREAD: Tan, gray, or olive.
WINGS: Barred wood duck flank feather, tied as for the hair wing on the Royal Wulff; see chapter 32.
TAIL: Medium gray hackles, stiff.
BODY: Light/dark segmented stripped quill from the eye portion of a peacock tail feather.
HACKLE: Medium gray.

3. *Blue-Winged Olive*

THREAD: Olive or brown.
WINGS: Gray hen cape hackles, small, tied as was done in the tying lesson.
TAIL: Medium gray hackles, stiff.
BODY: Fine, soft olive dubbing.
HACKLE: Medium gray.

4. *Gray Fox*

THREAD: Tan, gray, or pale yellow.
WINGS: Barred teal or mallard flank feather, tied as for the hair wing on the Royal Wulff; see chapter 32.
TAIL: Mixed straw cream and grizzly hackles, stiff.
BODY: Cream dubbing.
HACKLE: Mixed straw cream and grizzly.

5. *Pale Morning Dun*

THREAD: Pale olive or tan.
WINGS: Pale gray hen cape hackles, small, tied as was done in the tying lesson.
TAIL: Pale watery gray hackles, stiff.
BODY: Fine, soft pale yellowish olive dubbing.
HACKLE: Pale watery gray.

A flight of make-believe mayflies. Top left: Quill Gordon. Top right: Gray Fox. Center: Buff Hendrickson. Lower left: Blue-Winged Olive. Lower right: Pale Morning Dun.

32 The Royal Wulff— An American Monarch

I'd be willing to bet that almost all of the fly fishers who answered the question posed at the beginning of the previous chapter with a pattern other than the Adams would opt for the Royal Wulff. There are few flies indeed that have accounted for as many fish and as much excitement as this improbable creation. Its original name was the Hair-Winged Royal Coachman, or just the Hair-Wing Royal. Lee Wulff began tying and fishing his novel flies in 1931, but he didn't name them after himself. Allegedly, Dan Bailey did that.

I became pretty good friends with Lee in his later years, but I never pumped him for information about the hairwings. He did say that the two original dressings that he developed were the White Wulff and the Gray Wulff, as they eventually became known. The great success of these new flies motivated other tyers to dream up Wulffs of their own, and also to fit existing patterns with Wulff-style wings, which is how the Royal came into being. I would guess that there are two dozen Wulffs at this writing, and maybe that's a conservative estimate.

These flies are very American. They were designed for the brawling freestone rivers of the mountainous Northeast and would seldom have produced on the placid chalkstreams of England and Normandy. I say that, and yet every now and then some crazy fish takes exception. My late and much-lamented friend Matt Vinciguerra took his wife Judy (née Darbee) to Silver Creek in Idaho, where the fish can calibrate a leader with the best of them. Judy tied on a huge White Wulff and proceeded to nail a rainbow that weighed as much as any two of the properly behaved trout Matty duped with his 22s and 7X. Her father would have been proud of her.

The only tricky aspect of Wulff tying is doing the wings, but once learned, this becomes pretty easy. As a bonus, the two combined techniques—the X-wrap and figure-8—are the same as for the popular wood duck flank wing that so many terrific patterns use. This opens up a vast array of tying possibilities.

A number of hairs can be used for Wulff wings. Size has quite a lot to do with the choice. Smaller hook sizes, quite logically, require fine hair. Lee's favorite was calf tail, but surprisingly, he also used bucktail. At first glance, bucktail doesn't look like it would work, and some of it won't, at least not very well. For winging, fine-textured hair from small bucktails works best. It yields silhouette without unmanageable bulk, and has enough flexibility to be conformed into wings without an all-out wrestling match. Using a stacker is the key.

Getting back to calf tail: Selection is all-important. Length is not the primary issue; you can leave the really long-haired tail for the salmon flies and streamers. What is important is texture and relative straightness—relative, because no calf tail is really straight. As to texture, some tails are much wirier than others, and while they may be usable on larger hook sizes, they are not pleasant to work with.

I should mention that calf body hair can be a great Wulff wing material. It's much straighter and a little softer than the tail hair, and a lot more manageable. The only drawback is that it tends to be on the short side. If you can find some that runs about an inch (25 mm), buy it and treasure it.

Lee used to tease me about the style of my Wulff wings; he said I made them too neat. We who write about fly tying and have to look at macro photographs of our creations do have a penchant for cosmetics. Lee liked rough-looking flies, and who would argue the point with him? Not me, for sure, but I still prefer to make them at least somewhat tidy. With calf tail, even the neatest wings are plenty bushy.

Lee and I never did discuss tails. I noticed that he used calf tail for this component also, and, judging from the number of fish he caught, it obviously worked, so we'll use it here. Still, I prefer a straighter hair, such as bucktail, moose body, or woodchuck tail. I like to stack these hair bunches, because I feel that the neater the tips, the better the balance. On smaller hook sizes, I prefer feather barbs. I should also mention that I don't worry about the color of the tail very much.

In consideration of the types of currents in which I fish Wulffs, I use somewhat more hackle than with my more delicate and insect-specific dry flies. Either cape or saddle feathers will work, but in my opinion this is where the high-quality saddles really stand out. The barb strength and count, along with the very narrow quills, have revolutionized the way we tie Wulff-style hackles. It is perfectly feasible to dress a medium to large Wulff with a single feather of this type, because the hackle will pack densely. All that's required is that you leave enough space to the rear of and in front of the wings. You can also use two feathers, as you did in the Adams exercise. It's often possible to wrap them both at the same time, but that doesn't always work, and it's not a procedure I would recommend for beginning tyers. If you do want to give it a try, don't use hackle pliers. The feathers have to slip around a little between your fingers, in order to compensate for small but significant differences in circumference. It's like the differential on a car, which enables turning corners.

Before we begin, I want to identify three sources of trouble having to do with the wings; these three are responsible for more heartburn than everything else combined. The first, and worst, is trying to use too much material. The second—and it's related to the first—is not manicuring the winging bunch properly and thoroughly. You must get rid of all the junk and short stuff in the bunch and work with only those hairs that will contribute to the formation of the wings. The third is sizing the wings properly. Please adhere closely to the length-of-shank prescription. Hair wings are heavier than other types, and too long a wing will cause your fly to tip over on its side when it's floating down the stream.

One more comment on that first no-no. If you use too much hair for the wings, it follows that your wing butts will be thicker than need be. This gets you into trouble with the hackle, because besides creating bulk, the wing butts create a nonlinearity. There is no such material ahead of the wings, which means that the hackle has two unequal diameters around which to travel. If it's minimal, you can live with this disparity, but if it's significant, the hackle length will be uneven front and back.

I've mentioned several times how useful a little fine-toothed comb can be, and there is no task in which it is more helpful than in manicuring winging hair. It can be used to clean out the trashy stuff and to unlock the kinky hairs, so that they can be evened up in a stacker. In fact, the first thing I do when I buy a new calf tail is to thoroughly comb it. You'll be amazed at the difference this makes.

Royal Wulff Dressing

HOOK:	Standard dry fly, typically sizes 8 to 16.
THREAD:	Black 6/0 or 8/0.
WINGS:	White calf tail or substitute, as described.
TAIL:	Same as the wings.
BODY:	Two short sections of peacock herl with a red floss or equivalent belly band in between.
HACKLE:	Brown, preferably of rich, fairly dark coloration.

Yes, I believe in stacking Wulff wings. The primary reason—and this is much more important than many tyers realize—is that by evening up the tips, you know exactly how much hair you have. Otherwise, there's liable to be a lot of short stuff hiding within the bunch that will contribute nothing to the wing silhouette, but will create unwanted bulk at the worst possible place, and will cause major tying difficulties.

Despite what's been written elsewhere, calf tail *will* stack—but you'll need a fine-toothed comb and a wide-tubed stacker. Remember: You can stack small bunches with a big stacker, but you can't work on big bunches with a small one. This is true in spades with calf tail, because of its kinky texture, which causes the hairs to billow out and bind inside the tube. Also, you'll need to "unlock" the hairs that are bound together by the natural twists in the material. This is done by combing toward the tip ends a few times.

Okay, you don't yet have a stacker. Be sure to clean out the bunch thoroughly; as I've stated, combing is most helpful. Then even up the tip ends as best you can with your fingers, discarding any wild, unruly hairs. You'll be preparing the tailing bunch in exactly the same manner.

Tying Steps

1. Tie on just rearward of the eye and create a thread base on which to mount the wings, as you did with the Adams, ending up with the thread about 25 percent to the rear of the eye.

2. With the foregoing comments clearly in mind, cut off a small bunch of the hair and go through the various steps to prepare it. Clean out the junk, comb out the tips, and either stack them or even them up manually.

3. Hold the winging bunch in your left hand, tips forward, and gauge length. Then tie it in place on the thread base, using either a series of pinch wraps or a couple of soft gathering wraps, followed by some securing wraps.

4. Before locking the bunch down completely, gently stroke the hairs into an upright position a few times. This ensures that all of the hairs are squarely on top of the hook and compensates for any effect that torquing action of the thread may have had.

5. Take a few more firm wraps, then cut off the butts on a long slope.

6. When you're sure the hair is locked down and won't slip under pressure, crimp it into standing position with your thumb, thus building in some "memory."

7. While holding the hair upright with your left hand, build a dam of thread against the front. Use only enough thread to position the wing directly upright, and not one wrap more. As you're building this dam, run the thread toward the eye and back now and then, smoothing things out so that you don't create a bump that will interfere with wrapping hackle later on.

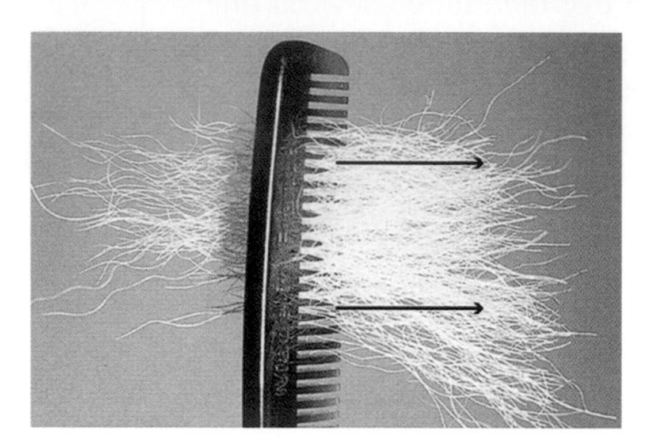

It is very important to clean all extraneous material from the winging bunch. A fine-toothed comb is a great help (step 1).

It is also very important to even up the tips of the hair bunch. This is how it is done in a hair stacker (step 2).

The winging bunch tied in and locked into an upright position (steps 3–7).

Tying Steps

8. Now divide the hair into two equal bunches, using a dubbing needle or toothpick. Then take hold of the two bunches with your thumbs and forefingers and spread them, so that they assume a winglike attitude.

9. Now for the first of the two thread operations that form the wings. I call this one the **X-wrap.** Start with the thread just ahead of the wings. Pass it between the wings to the far side of the hook, behind the far wing. Then pass it underneath the hook, come up behind the near wing, and pass it through between the wings again, ending up on the far side of the hook, ahead of the wings. One X-wrap is usually sufficient, but if you need to add another, that's fine.

10. Now for the second thread operation, the **figure-8.** Begin as though you were doing an X-wrap, working the thread between the wings to the far side of the hook, behind the far wing. When the thread is slightly below the plane of the hook shank, take hold of the far wing with your left thumb and forefinger, and, while holding the wing under tension, pass the thread 360 degrees *around the base of the wing*—that is, the hair itself. Bring it back between the wings, then down behind the near wing on the near side of the hook, maintaining thread tension at all times. Don't let go of the far wing until you've completed this maneuver and the bobbin is hanging straight down.

11. Now take hold of the near wing and pass the thread *around the base of it*, maintaining thread tension throughout. The thread ends up behind the far wing on the far side of the hook.

12. Repeat the figure-8 at least once, and a third time if it's necessary to form the wings as desired—which is straight up and separated at an angle of between 35 and 45 degrees.

Top view of the X-wrap, which divides the wings (step 9).

Top views of the figure-8 wraps that shape and position the wings (steps 10–12).

Top views of the figure-8 wraps that shape and position the wings (steps 10–12).

Tying Steps

13. Wrap neatly to the bend, covering the wing butts that you slope-cut earlier.
14. Cut a small bunch of hair for the tail and prepare it as you would a winging bunch. Gauge the length: It should be equal to or slightly longer than the hook shank.
15. Tie the tail hair precisely on top of the hook, as you would a winging bunch. After securing it, trim the butts in such a manner that they dovetail with the wing butts. Cover them with thread, wrapping almost to the wings and back to the bend. This results in a smooth, even underbody.
16. Tie in a bunch of four or five peacock fronds by the tips, as you did in the soft-hackle in chapter 25 (see page 256). In the process of securing them, form a thread loop about as long as the fronds themselves. Wrap to the rear, locking in the loop, so that it doesn't matter which end you use. Then cut off one side of the loop and trim the thread to the length of the peacock. Be sure that both the peacock and the thread are co-located at the bend of the hook and that there is no space between the two; otherwise, the thread will come across the peacock and may cut it. If you find it easier to simply tie in another piece of thread instead of doing the loop process, you may do so.
17. Pick up the tag end of thread and start twisting it together with the peacock fronds, in effect forming a virtual chenille. Don't take too many twists at first, because the thread might sever the herl.
18. Wrap the twisted herl and thread around the hook, forming a small ball of herl. Remember: If you run into difficulty with twisting, you can resort to the electronics clip, or regular hackle pliers. Then bind the herl/thread to the hook, creating

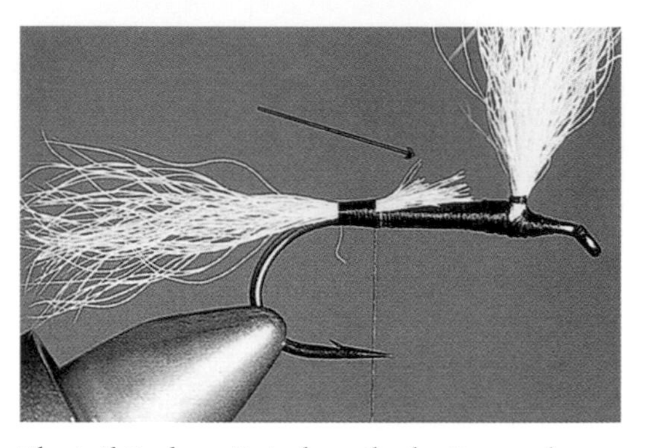

The tail tied on. Note how the butts are slope-cut so that they dovetail with those of the wings and form a smooth base when bound down (steps 14–15).

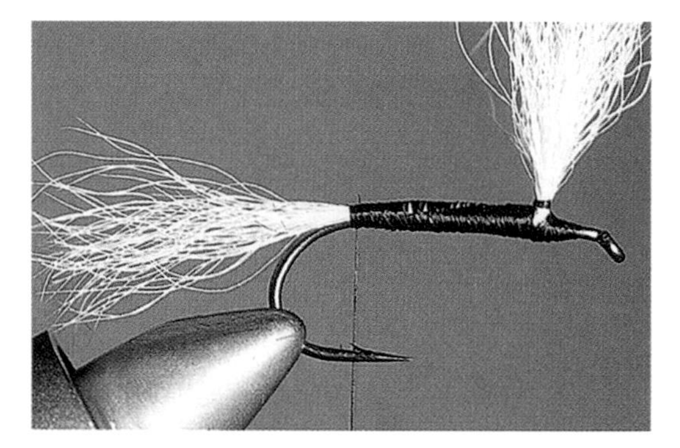

The tail tied on. Note how the butts are slope-cut so that they dovetail with those of the wings, and form a smooth base when bound down (steps 14–15).

The first bump of peacock herl wrapped in place, and the thread positioned for the next operation (steps 16–18).

Tying Steps

space for the center portion of the body. The herl is left hanging to the front; it will be used to form the third segment of the body.

19. At the front end of the little thread base you just created, tie in a short piece of red floss or, preferably, stretch nylon. Wrap a little "belly band," working to the rear and forward. Secure it and trim off the excess.

20. Work the thread forward a bit; then pick up the herl/thread, retwist, and make another little ball. Be sure to stay well behind the wings. Then tie off and trim the peacock.

21. As I stated previously, you can use one or two feathers for the hackle. In the case of cape hackles, you'll surely need two. One high-quality saddle feather may yield enough hackle, given its high barb count and narrow quill, but don't hesitate to use two, if necessary.

22. Prepare the hackle feather or feathers per instructions in the three chapters preceding. When selecting them, make sure they are the right size, about 1½ times the gap.

23. I recommend doing the feather tie-in a bit differently with Wulffs than with, for example, the Adams. Tie it (or them) in by the quill butt(s) ahead of, rather than behind, the wing; on top of, rather than beneath, the hook. This allows you to use the quill butt(s) to compensate for and balance out the wing butts. Remember: Pretty-side(s) forward, and leave enough quill exposed so that after you wrap rearward to position the feathers, there will be a tiny bit of quill showing.

The belly band and second peacock bump completed. Note the space behind the wing and the neat thread base (steps 19–20).

The hackle tied in, as described (steps 21–24).

Tying Steps

24. Hold the feather(s) under moderate tension with your left hand. Then lock in the quill(s) with neat, tight thread wraps, working rearward. When you reach the wings, move the feather(s) downward and bind them to the near side of the hook, wrapping back to the front of the body. Then wrap forward again and trim short of the eye. Neaten up and even up as necessary with some discrete thread wraps. The idea is to create as even and flat a base as possible.

25. Wrap the feather(s) per previous instructions, and finish off the fly in the usual manner.

The finished Royal Wulff (step 25).

The alternative method for tying in hackle feathers may seem tricky to the beginner, so if you want to revert to the methodology used for the Adams, that's okay. I would recommend that once you become more adept at hackling dry flies, you learn the Wulff method, because it will improve your final product.

Not all hair-winged flies are part of the Wulff pack. However, the winging techniques you've learned here will enable you to tie a wide variety of patterns. Hair-winged dry flies are wonderful in the proper environment. They work great in faster water, and sometimes even in slower currents. They can be used as strike indicators by suspending a nymph or something else below the main fly on a dropper. Once in a while, you might hook two fish at once, one on the dropper and one on the hairwing. That's always quite a thrill.

Some Wulff Patterns

Note: These patterns all use the same standard dry-fly hook called for in the tying lesson. Please refer to the hook chart in chapter 22 for specifics (page 240).

1. ***Grizzly Wulff***

WINGS:	Brown hair: calf tail, or other.
TAIL:	Same as wings.
BODY:	Yellow floss, yarn, or dubbing.
HACKLE:	Brown and grizzly mixed.

2. ***White Wulff***

WINGS:	White hair: calf tail, or other.
TAIL:	Same as wings.
BODY:	Cream dubbing.
HACKLE:	Light badger hackle (cream with dark center).

3. ***Gray Wulff***

WINGS:	Brown hair: calf tail, or other.
TAIL:	Same as wings.
BODY:	Gray muskrat fur or similar dubbing.
HACKLE:	Slate gray.

4. ***Black Wulff***

WINGS:	Dark blackish brown hair: moose body or woodchuck tail.
TAIL:	Same as wings.
BODY:	Pink floss.
HACKLE:	Dark furnace (brown with black center) or dark brown.

5. ***Ausable Wulff***

THREAD:	Hot orange.
WINGS:	White hair: calf tail, or other.
TAIL:	Woodchuck tail or brown bucktail.
BODY:	Rusty orange dubbing or originally dyed Australian possum.
HACKLE:	Brown and grizzly mixed.

While there are a lot of new and innovative materials and methods in the world of fly tying today, I believe you'll find that what we've covered in this book has equipped you with the skills to handle most fly-tying situations and has established a base for progression into more advanced and sophisticated techniques. Best wishes for tying success and enjoyment.

A Wulff pack. Top left: Gray Wulff. Top right: Grizzly Wulff. Center: White Wulff. Lower left: Ausable Wulff. Lower right: Black Wulff.

Appendix: Publications and Organizations for Fly Fishers

BOOKS ON FLY TYING

Most Important

Fly Tying Made Clear and Simple by Skip Morris

Flies (new edition) by J. Edson Leonard

Fly Tying Materials by Eric Leiser

Universal Fly Tying Guide by Dick Stewart (excellent for beginners)

Excellent

American Nymph Fly Tying Manual by Randall Kaufmann

Art of Tying the Dry Fly by Skip Morris (excellent for beginners)

Bass Flies by Dick Stewart

Designing Trout Flies by Gary Borger

The Fly Tyer's Almanac by Robert Boyle and Dave Whitlock

Popular Fly Patterns by Terry Hellekson

Salt Water Flies by Kenneth Bay

Tying the Swisher and Richards Flies by Doug Swisher and Carl Richards

Tying Bass and Panfish Flies by Skip Morris

Good

Atlantic Salmon Flies and Fishing by Joseph D. Bates Jr.

Bug Making by C. Boyd Pfeiffer

The Complete Book of Fly Tying by Eric Leiser

Dick Surette's Fly Index by Dick Surette

Dyeing and Bleaching Natural Fly-Tying Materials by A. K. Best

Flies for Alaska by Anthony Route

Salmon Flies by Poul Jorgensen

Streamers and Bucktails by Joseph D. Bates Jr.

Tying and Fishing Terrestrials by Gerald Almy

Western Trout Fly Tying Manual by Jack Dennis

BOOKS ON FLY FISHING

Most Important

Dave Whitlock's Guide to Aquatic Trout Foods by Dave Whitlock

Fishing the Flats by Mark Sosin and Lefty Kreh

Fly Fishing in Salt Water by Lefty Kreh

L.L. Bean Fly-Fishing for Bass Handbook by Dave Whitlock

Masters on the Dry Fly, edited by J. Migel

Masters on the Nymph, edited by J. Migel and Leonard Wright

Selective Trout by Doug Swisher and Carl Richards

Steelhead Fly Fishing by Trey Combs

Excellent

Bonefishing with a Fly by Randall Kaufmann

The Caddis and the Angler by Larry Solomon and Eric Leiser

Caddisflies by Gary LaFontaine

The Essence of Flycasting by Mel Kreiger

Fishing the Dry Fly as a Living Insect by Leonard Wright

Fly Casting with Lefty Kreh by Lefty Kreh

Fly Fishing for Trout by Dick Talleur

Fly Fishing for Trout—Imitating and Fishing Natural Fish Foods by Dave Whitlock

Fly Fishing Strategy by Doug Swisher and Carl Richards

Naturals by Gary Borger

Presentations by Gary Borger

Strategies for Stillwater by Dave Hughes

Through the Fish's Eye by Mark Sosin and John Clark

FLY-FISHING PERIODICALS

These magazines have up-to-date features and advertisements to keep you abreast of all you need to know about fly fishing today.

The Flyfisher, P.O. Box 1595, Bozeman, MT 59771

The official magazine of the Federation of Fly Fishers (FFF), published quarterly. FFF membership includes a subscription to the magazine.

Flyfishing, P.O. Box 02112, Portland, OR 97202

Features fly fishing and fly tying.

Fly Fisherman, Box 8200, Harrisburg, PA 17105

Features articles on fly fishing and fly tying throughout the world.

Fly Rod and Reel, P.O. Box 370, Camden, ME 04843

Interesting fly-fishing articles.

The Roundtable, United Fly Tyers, Inc., P.O. Box 732, Boston, MA 02102

Membership in United Fly Tyers, a nonprofit international organization, includes subscription. Articles on fly tying with how-to instruction.

Salmon Trout Steelheader, P.O. Box 02112, Portland, OR 97202

Often describes how to tie the best western patterns.

Scientific Angler's Handbooks, Scientific Anglers, P.O. Box 2001, Midland, MI 48640

Annual handbooks on general fly fishing, bass fly fishing, panfish fly fishing, and saltwater fly fishing.

Trout, 1500 Wilson Boulevard, Arlington, VA 22209

The official magazine of Trout Unlimited (TU), published quarterly. TU membership includes a subscription.

American Angler, P.O. Box 4100, Bennington, VT 05201-4100

Fly Fishing and Fly Tying, Game and Fish Publications, 8 The Square, Aberfetdy, Perthshire, PH 15 2DD

Fly Fishing in Salt Water, 2001 Western Avenue, Suite 210, Seattle, WA 98121

Fly Tackle Dealer, Roxmont, Route 1, Rockport, ME 04856

Infisherman, Infisherman Inc., 2 In-Fisherman Drive, Brainerd, MN 56401-0999

The Nature Conservancy, 1815 North Lynn Street, Arlington, VA 22209

Saltwater Fly Fishing, P.O. Box 4100, Bennington, VT 05201-4100

Wild Steelhead and Salmon, 2315 210th Street, SE, Bothell, WA 98021-4206

MAJOR FLY-FISHING ORGANIZATIONS

Federation of Fly Fishers, P.O. Box 1595, Bozeman, MT 59771

The federation has hundreds of clubs nationally and many internationally, conducting all types of fly-fishing, fly-tying, and conservation activities. With membership you receive an excellent news bulletin and *The Flyfisher* magazine.

Trout Unlimited, P.O. Box 1944, Washington, DC 20013

Trout Unlimited has chapters throughout the United States and Canada. It emphasizes trout and salmon fishing and conservation activities. Local chapters are active in fly-fishing and fly-tying seminars. With membership you receive a news bulletin and *Trout* magazine.

United Fly Tyers, Inc., P.O. Box 723, Boston, MA 02102

Active in all types of fly-tying and fly-fishing promotion and instruction. Has excellent magazine, *The Roundtable*, on fly tying.

Saltwater Fly Rodders Of America, P.O. Box 304, Cape May Court House, NJ 08120

Active in all types of saltwater fly fishing and fly tying. Also has magazine with membership.

The Nature Conservancy, 1815 North Lynn Street, Arlington, VA 22209

Most fly fishers discover that tying your own flies is easily as much fun and rewarding as fly fishing . . . I consider it to be the other half of fly fishing!

FLY-FISHING AND FLY-TYING VIDEOTAPES

Videotapes are excellent for home educational viewing and practicing.

The Essence of Flycasting by Mel Krieger. An excellent tape on learning Mel's fly-casting methods.

The Skills of Fly Fishing by Gary Borger. Good introduction and teaching tape on fly fishing.

Anatomy of a Trout Stream by Rick Hafele. Excellent tape for learning about trout, how and where they live and feed.

Dave Whitlock's Fly Fishing for Bass. Excellent and exciting tape on how to fly fish for bass.

Strategies for Selective Trout by Doug Swisher. An excellent tape on how to read water and fish for trout more successfully.

Fly Fishing for Steelhead by Lani Waller. Good tape for the beginner steelhead fly fisher.

L.L. Bean Introduction to Fly Fishing with Dave Whitlock. An excellent companion tape to this handbook for beginners.

Bass Pro—Tying Bass Flies with Dave Whitlock. Dave ties his four favorite bass flies, the Most Whit Hair Bug, Frog Diver, Shad, and Harejig.

Fly Tying Basics with Jack Dennis. A good tape with which to learn to tie flies.

Glossary

Abdomen—The main part of the body of an insect.

Action—A word that expresses the flexibility and power of a fly rod.

AFTMA—American Fishing Tackle Manufacturers Association. American fishing-tackle manufacturers organized to maintain standards of fishing tackle, public information, product quality, marketing, and conservation of the resource.

Arbor—The spindle of a fly-reel spool that the backing line is attached to and wound on.

Aquatic insects—Those insects that live some part of their normal life cycle beneath the water.

Attractor (color)—Unnaturally bright color in a fly pattern.

Backing (braided)—A line most commonly composed of several filaments of either nylon or Dacron braided into a single component. Used to extend fly line's length.

Bank—The higher and steeper sides above a lake or stream, usually created by water cutting or eroding the shoreline.

Bar—A mounded structure in streams and some lakes caused by accumulation of rock, sand, sediment, and dead vegetation, usually protruding out of the water or very near the surface.

Barb (hook)—The raised cut section of a hook immediately behind the point. It is designed to prevent the hook from coming out of the fish's mouth.

Barb—The raised-cut section of a hook immediately behind the point.

Barbless hook—A fly hook without a barb.

Barbs (feather)—The tines of a feather that constitute hackle.

Bass—A general descriptive term for a group of larger freshwater sunfish, particularly largemouth bass, smallmouth bass, and Kentucky or spotted bass.

Bass bug—A floating or diving bass fly that is tied out of deer hair.

Beaching—A method of landing a fish by coaxing or forcing it to swim or drift itself aground in the shallow water of a lake or stream shoreline.

Beard—A small bunch of hackle fibers tied under the hook shank just in back of the head of the fly. Commonly employed on nymphs, wets, and salmon flies.

Beaver pond—A small lake, usually less than 2 acres, that has been formed by the damming of a small brook or stream by beavers.

Belly—The larger midsection of a fly line. Also may refer to the curve of a fly-line midsection when wind or current pushes it into a C shape.

Bite—A term often used by fly fishers to describe the strike of a fish. *Bite* also may refer to the distance from the hook point and the extent of the bend.

Bite tippet—A short tippet of heavy monofilament or wire that prevents a sharp-toothed fish from biting the fly off the leader. Also called a *shock tippet.*

Blue dun—One of several commonly used colors in hackling, especially on dry flies. A shade of gray, possibly tinted with ginger.

Body—The main portion of a fly, tied on the hook shank from the tail forward.

Brackish water—Water that has less salt content than true ocean salt water. Occurs most commonly where freshwater streams meet or mix with saltwater bays and estuaries.

Braided loop—A loop connector that slides over either end of the fly line and is fixed there with glue or a heat-shrink sleeve. Used for loop-to-loop connections of the leader or shooting line to the fly line.

Breakoff—The accidental or purposeful breaking of the leader tippet from a hooked fish, freeing it.

Bucktail—A deer tail; also, a streamer fly tied with the hair of a deer tail.

Bug—Usually refers to a floating bass fly that might imitate various large insects, frogs, mice, and so on.

Butt cap—The end of a fly-rod handle used for resting and protecting the fly rod and fly reel when stored upright. At times it is rested against the fly fisher's stomach when fighting a large fish.

Canal—A man-made, water-filled ditch used to join lakes or swamps to rivers, or to straighten and quicken the flow of a stream's runoff.

Cast—The act of delivering the fly to the fishing area with fly rod, line, and leader. *Cast* is also used as a descriptive term by English fly fishers to denote the fly leader.

Catch and release—An expression for catching fish, with immediate release alive and unharmed.

Catch-and-release net—A shallow, soft, fine-mesh, knotless dip net that enhances the ability to capture, unhook, and release a fish without harming it.

Channel—The main depression caused by flowing water (current).

Char—A group of popular freshwater fish that includes brook trout, lake trout, arctic char, and Dolly Varden.

Cheek—A feather tied just behind the head of a fly.

Chenille—A popular fly-tying material consisting of fine fibers of rayon, wool, nylon, and so on that are found together in a uniform cord with two or more twisted threads. Especially popular on underwater flies such as the Woolly Worm.

Chum line—A series of fish food pieces put into the water to attract and congregate hungry fish in a specific area near the angler.

Class tippet—A tippet that is accurately calibrated in pound test for world-record fly-fishing catches.

Clippers—A small tool used to cut and trim the fly line, leader, or tippet material.

Coaster—A local term, especially along the northeastern Atlantic coast, for a brown or brook trout that goes into brackish or salt water for a period of its life and then returns to freshwater streams to spawn.

Cold-water fish—Fish that thrive best in water temperatures ranging from 40 to 60 degrees F. For example: trout, char, grayling, and salmon.

Collar—Wet-fly hackle wrapped 360 degrees around the front of a fly.

Cool-water fish—Fish that thrive best in water temperatures ranging from 50 to 75 degrees F. For example: smallmouth bass, shad, walleye, northern pike, whitefish, striped bass.

Corkers—Rubber sandals with sharp, hard-metal cleats in their soles that are worn over waders, boots, or shoes to increase grip or traction on very slippery rock stream bottoms.

Cork rings—Rings of cork that are glued together and shaped to form the fly-rod handle.

Cove—A small water indentation in the shoreline of a lake or ocean.

Crayfish—A freshwater, lobsterlike, small crustacean very popular as fish food.

Cree—A multicolored chicken feather, having markings of brown, gray, white, and possibly black.

Creel—A container cooled by water evaporation, used to keep and carry dead fish.

Crossbar (fly reel)—A part of a fly-reel frame that is chiefly for structural support between the two sides. Sometimes referred to as a *post.*

Cruising (fish)—An expression describing a fish that is moving about in a lake or stream in order to find food.

Crustaceans—An important group of fresh- and saltwater aquatic invertebrates that are fed upon by many fish. Shrimp, scud, sow bugs, crabs, and crayfish are examples.

Current—The flowing or gravitational pull of water in rivers, streams, lakes, and oceans.

Dead drift—The drift of a fly downstream without action other than what is given it by the natural current flow. It means no drag.

Deer hair—Body hair from a deer. It's known for its superior floating characteristics and commonly used for making fly bodies, and sometimes wings. Elk, caribou, and antelope hair are similar.

Density—Refers to the weight of fly line, leader, or fly compared to the weight of the water. *High density* means much heavier than water and fast sinking. *Low density* means slow sinking or even floating.

Dip net—The device used to scoop up and hold a hooked fish. Also called a *landing net.*

Double hook—A fly-hook design that has two points, barbs, and bends, and one common shank. Most commonly used for making Atlantic salmon flies.

Drag (guides)—The rod's guides and fly line create points of friction that are often referred to as *drag.*

Drag (line)—An expressive term used to describe a current or wind pull on the fly line that results in pulling the fly unnaturally over or through the water.

Drag (reel)—A part of the fly reel that adjusts the spool's tension when line is pulled off the reel by the fly fisher or a fish.

Dress—The application of waterproofing or flotant material to the fly line, leader, or fly.

Drift—Describes the path a fly travels while it is fished down the stream's current.

Dry fly—A basic fly design that floats on the water's surface. It is usually made of low-density, water-resistant materials to hold it in the water's surface film.

Dry-fly paste—A paste compound used to waterproof materials to hold them in the water's surface film.

Dry-fly spray—Aerosol spray compound used to waterproof the water-absorbent materials of a dry fly.

Dubbing—A fly-tying material consisting of natural hairs and/or synthetic fibers blended into a loose felt and used to form the body of many floating and sinking flies; also, the procedure by which fur or materials of similar consistency are spun onto a thread to form a fly body.

Dun—The term used to identify the first adult stage (subimago) of mayfly aquatic insects. Also a descriptive term generally referring to a gray or dull color common on mayfly duns.

Eddy—A calm, slowly swirling (upstream) water flow in a stream behind an obstruction such as a boulder, log, bar, or moss bed.

Emerger—A term to identify the stage of a natural or a fly imitation of an aquatic insect as it swims to the surface to hatch or transform from nymph or pupa to adult.

Eye—Used to simulate the eye of a small fish on a streamer fly.

Feather—The epidermal outgrowth covering the wings and body of birds. Feathers commonly used in fly tying include: breast, flank, neck hackle, saddle hackle, herl, crest, pointers or primaries, secondaries, flight, and tippets.

Feeding—A fish's eating or striking period.

Fibers—Small filaments that make up a feather. The term also refers to other fine components, such as hair.

Fighting—The act of tiring a hooked fish in preparation for landing it.

Fingerling—A general term used to describe various fish species (trout, bass, catfish, and so on) when they are about finger length in size.

Fishery—A body of water that sustains a healthy fish population and has potential for fly-fishing success.

Fish for fun—Catching and immediately releasing fish alive and unharmed. Usually it is illegal to keep or kill fish caught in these designated areas.

Fish locator—A common name for various electronic sonars that are used to locate fish, the structures wherein they live, their depth in the water, and the depth of the water itself. Also called a *fish finder*.

Fishing vest—A vest with assorted pockets for carrying the various flies, reels, and accessories used while walking, wading, or fly fishing.

Flat—A wide shallow-water section of a lake, stream, or ocean. Flats usually have a relatively uniform smooth surface.

Floss—A stranded material commonly used in making fly bodies.

Flotant—Material used to waterproof fly lines, leaders, and flies.

Fly—The artificial lure used in fly fishing.

Fly design—Describes type of fly or purpose of fly.

Fly pattern—The color and material makeup of a particular fly design.

Fly tyer—A person who makes or "ties" flies for fly fishing.

Foam line—An accumulation of air bubbles on the water's surface caused by water turbulence, winds, tides, or currents. Fish often concentrate and feed under foam lines.

Freestone stream—A stream that has a relatively high bottom gradient and so is swift flowing made up mostly of coarse gravel or rubble and whose source of water is mainly runoff rain and melting snow.

Fresh water—Water with little or no salt content. It also refers to fish species that are adapted only to freshwater environs.

Fry—The first stage of development of a fish after hatching from the egg or live birth. Usually from ½ to 2 inches in length.

Gaff—A hook-and-handle tool used to hook and capture larger fish. Also refers to the act of hooking and capturing a fish once it has been tired with rod and reel.

Gamefish—A general term used to denote those species of fish that will readily strike or attack an artificial lure or fly. Also deals with the ability and willingness of the fish to fight very hard after it is hooked.

Gap, Gape—The space between point and shank of the hook.

Gill—The respiratory organ of a water-breathing fish, located just behind the head.

Giving tip—Holding the rod tip forward and high to provide maximum shock absorption to prevent the leader's tippet from breaking and the fly from being pulled out of the fish's mouth.

Grab—A term often used to describe a brief period fish go through when they are willing to strike a fly.

Grain—The unit of measurement used for calibrating fly-line weights.

Grease—The application of paste or fly dressing to line to enhance flotation.

Grizzly—Feather from a Plymouth rock or barred rock chicken; gray, white, and black markings.

Hackle—Usually neck and back feathers of a chicken; however, it can also be from other chickenlike birds such as grouse or partridge. Also, the part of a fly that is composed of the above.

Half-hitch—A basic knot used in fly fishing and fly tying.

Handle (reel)—A crank on a fly-reel spool used for reeling the fly line onto the fly reel.

Handle (rod)—The grip used for holding the fly rod while casting, fishing, and fighting a fish.

Hauling—A method of increasing fly-line speed during pickup, backward, or forward casting. It is accomplished by the hand pulling on the fly line between the rod's stripper guide and the fly reel.

Herl—The fuzzy material found on certain feathers, such as peacock tail.

Hold—A place where a fish, such as a salmon, trout, or bass, rests or remains stationary for a period of time.

Holding fish—Describes a fish that remains in a particular spot in a lake or stream.

Hook barb—The raised metal slice off the hook point and bend. The barb helps prevent the hook from backing out of the fish's mouth tissue.

Hook bend—The curved or bent section just behind the hook shank.

Hook eye—The closed loop part of a fly hook to which the leader or tippet is attached.

Hook (fly)—The device used to hold a fish that strikes or attempts to eat the fly.

Hook shank—The length of hook exclusive of its eye and bend. Generally it's the section to which fly-tying materials are tied.

Hooking fish—Setting the hook in a fish's mouth tissue after the fish has struck.

Hookkeeper—The small clip or eyelet at the front of the fly-rod handle used to store the fly when not in use.

Hook point—The needlelike point on the end of the hook bend. It enhances faster penetration into the fish's mouth tissue.

Hook size—The distance or amount of gap on a fly hook or fly. Also refers to the overall length and size of wire the hook is made from. Generally hook sizes range from the largest, 5/0, to the smallest, 36.

Immature insect—Refers to insects that have not reached sexual maturity or full growth.

Inlet—The area of a lake, pond, or ocean where a stream flows in.

Jack—A common term usually referring to one- or two-year-old sexually mature male salmon or trout that join older fish in their spawning run.

Jump—When a hooked fish comes up out of the water in an attempt to shake the hook or break the leader.

Kick boat—A small, one-person fishing craft that is propelled by the angler's legs and swimfins. Some kick boats have oars as a second method of propulsion.

Knotless—A leader that has no knots tied in it to join different-sized sections or tippets.

Landing—Capturing a hooked fish after it has become tired.

Larva—A term denoting the worm or grub-like stage between the egg and pupa of the caddis and midge aquatic insects. Also the common descriptive term of the artificial-fly imitation of the larva.

Leader—The transparent part of the fly-fishing line between the fly line and fly. It may include the tippet section.

Leader straightener—A rubber or leather pad used to heat and straighten the coils from a leader.

Leader wallet—A convenient pocketed container for storage of extra leaders to be carried while fly fishing.

Leech—A bloodsucking, wormlike aquatic invertebrate or a fly imitating it.

Levels—The amount of water or depth of a stream or lake.

Line—Short expression for a *fly line*. When the fly line scares a fish it is commonly referred to as *lining* it.

Line guard—The part of a fly reel that the fly line passes through or over as it is wound on or off the reel spool. It acts as a guide and reduces wear from line friction.

Loop—The general term describing the U shape of the fly line as it unrolls forward or backward during the casting cycle.

Loop to loop—An expression used to describe the joining of the fly line to the leader or leader to tippet, where a closed loop in each is joined to make the other connection.

Lure—An imitation fish food with one or more hooks on it. As a verb it refers to attracting a fish to strike a fly.

Manipulate—Generally refers to a more intricate fly presentation and actions accomplished with fly rods of 9 feet or longer.

Marabou—Soft, flowing feathers, usually from a turkey body, commonly used in tying streamers.

Mature insect—Insects that have reached sexual maturity or full growth.

Matuka—Generally refers to a special fly design in which feathers are uniquely wrapped to the length of a hook shank and/or body of a fly so that they appear as part of the body. The word *Matuka* originated from a bird, the matukar, whose feathers were popularly used for this type of fly.

Meadow stream—A low-gradient stream that flows in a meandering course mainly through meadows or valleys.

Mending—The act of lifting or rolling the fly line with the rod to reposition it in order to avoid fly drag due to current speeds or wind.

Mesh—The net bag or seine of a dip net or landing net.

Minnow—A general term used for many species of smaller fishes (1 to 6 inches long), as well as the same sizes of immature larger fish.

Monofilament—A single filament or strand of nylon used for fishing line, leader, or tippet material.

Moss bed—A large underwater growth of aquatic plants.

Mudding—The term used to describe a fish stirring up a visible cloud of mud or silt as it feeds and swims on the bottom.

Muddler—A very popular and effective type of artificial fly that has a large, clipped deer hair head and usually incorporates hair and feathers for its body parts.

Neck (fly tying)—Usually refers to the pelt taken from that part of a chicken; neck feathers are used in fly tying.

Neck (geography)—A long, narrow body of water usually found at a stream's inlet to a lake.

Net—Refers to the act of landing a fish with a dip net or landing net.

Neutral color—Color and pattern of a fly or natural food that does not contrast with its surroundings.

No-kill—A fishery policy of catching and releasing unharmed live fish.

Nongamefish—A general term used to describe those species of fish that never or seldom strike or attack artificial lures or flies.

Nymph—Refers to the water-breathing or immature stage of aquatic insects. Also, a fly that imitates these insects.

Nymphing—Fly fishing with aquatic nymph imitations. Also used to describe a fish that is foraging for aquatic nymphs.

Outlet—That part of a lake where water flows out.

Palmering—A method of applying hackle over the length of the hook shank or body of a fly.

Palming the reel—The application of a palm against the fly reel's outer spool flange to add extra drag pressure on a fish pulling line off the fly reel.

Panfish—A large group of abundant freshwater gamefish species, generally under 2 pounds in weight. Included are sunfish, bluegill, yellow perch, white bass, crappie, to name a few.

Parr—The second stage of development of salmonoids, usually termed fingerlings. The term comes from large dark bands of oval marks on their sides.

Perch—A group of fish including the yellow perch, white perch, darter, and walleye pike.

Pickup—The lifting of a fly line, leader, and fly off the water as the backcast is begun.

Pike—A group of cold and cool freshwater gamefish including northern pike, pickerel, and muskie. Sometimes the walleye pike (which is not a true pike but a perch) is included.

Pocket—A depression in the bottom of a stream located in the riffle or run of a stream.

Pocket water—A series of bottom depressions or pockets in stream riffle or run section.

Point—Refers to the narrow, pointed section of land that juts out into a lake or stream.

Polaroids—A popular term for sunglasses that polarize or filter out certain angles of light rays. They reduce reflective sunlight off water so fish beneath are more easily seen.

Pond—Usually refers to a small lake less than 5 acres in surface area—except in Maine, where the term is often used interchangeably with *lake*.

Popper—A type of surface fly, commonly used for bass and warm-water or saltwater fish. The body is usually made of cork, balsa wood, hair, or a buoyant plastic material.

Pound test—Refers to the strength of a fishing line, leader, or tippet. Sometimes called *breaking strength* or *test*.

Power (rod)—The degree of efficiency a rod has in casting, hooking, and landing a fish.

Predator fish—A fish that eats live fish, insects, and other animals.

Presentation—The placement of the fly on or below the water. Also describes the fly's path and action on the water.

Pressure (rod)—How hard a fly fisher pulls, restricts, or fights a hooked fish with the fly rod, reel, and leader determines the amount of pressure being used.

Pumping a fish—Pulling a large fish by using a pumping or rod-butt-lifting action as the fish sounds or pulls away. As the rod is quickly lowered after the pump-up, the reel takes up the line gained on the fish.

Pupa—Generally refers to the stage between larva and adult of the caddis and midge aquatic insects. Also common descriptive term used for the artificial fly imitation of the same insects.

Putting down—Fish that have been scared by the fly fisher and stop feeding have been *put down*.

Put and take—A fisheries management policy that involves artificial stocking of catchable fish and encouragement of killing and removing these fish when caught.

Quill—The "spine" of a feather; the stem.

Rapids—A section of a stream that has a high gradient and fast, rough-surfaced flowing water.

Reading water—Visually examining the surface of the water to evaluate fishing potential, depth, and fish location.

Reel—To wind in or retrieve the fly line, leader, backing, and so on. Also a short expression for *fly reel*.

Reel hand—The hand and arm used to hold or reel in the fly line. Same as *line hand*.

Reel saddle—The part of a reel that provides means for attaching the reel to the rod seat and/or handle.

Reel seat—The part of a fly rod, just behind the rod handle, where the fly reel is fastened.

Reel spool—The part of a fly reel where the line is wound and stored.

Rib, or Ribbing—Spiral-wrapped material over the body of a fly.

Riffle—The section of a stream where the water flows shallowly and rapidly over an irregular bottom so that the surface riffles. Also refers to a water surface slightly disturbed by the wind.

Rising fish—A fish that is visibly feeding just below or at the water's surface.

Rod blank—A fly rod before it is fitted with guides and handle or other finished fly-rod accessories.

Rod guides—Also *fly-rod guides*, the closed loop structures fastened to the fly-rod shaft that hold the fly line on the rod's length.

Roll—The movement of a fish when it arches up and down from the surface as it feeds.

Run—The fleeing swim of a fish that has been hooked and frightened. Also describes a stretch of stream just below a riffle and above a pool.

Salmon fly—An artificial fly used most commonly for Atlantic salmon. Also refers to a common name given to several larger species of stonefly aquatic insects.

Salt water—A general term used to describe the fish or fishing in salty oceans, seas, and other similar saltwater areas.

Saltwater fly—An artificial fly that is made principally to be fished in salt water. Its hook must resist salt corrosion.

Selective—Refers to the feeding habits of fish preferring special flies or special presentation of flies.

School—A group of the same species of fish swimming together.

Scud—A small shrimplike crustacean or a fly imitating it.

Shoal—A shallow-bottomed area in a lake, stream, or estuary.

Shock tippet—see *Bite tippet*.

Shocking the tip—This happens when the forward-and-down fly-casting stroke is begun too quickly and with too much acceleration, causing the fly-rod tip to dip back and down sharply, creating a tailing-loop cast.

Shooting—A term referring to the fly line or shooting line that is pulled out from the force or momentum of the casting power and extended fly-line weight.

Shoreline—The area immediately adjacent to the water's edge, along lakes and streams.

Shoulder—Any feather tied to the front of a fly just behind the head, in order to obtain a particular effect.

Shrimp—A widely distributed, important crustacean; also, its fly imitation.

Sidefinder—A special electronic sonar fish locator that detects fish on a horizontal plane (to the side) of a boat or float tube that it is mounted on.

Skater—A design of floating fly that has a very long hackle or hair around the hook to enable it to sit high or skate across the water's surface.

Slack line—When the fly line has little or no tension on it between the fly reel, the rod, and the fly.

Slough—A sluggish or nonflowing narrow, dead-ended body of water usually created by a stream changing to a new path or channel. The old channel becomes a slough if water still connects it to the stream.

Smolt—The third stage of development of sea-run salmonids (trout, salmon, char), usually in lengths of 4 to 10 inches.

Snag guard—A device on a fly that prevents the fly hook from snagging or hanging on various obstacles (rocks, logs, moss, and so on) near or in the fishing water.

Snake guide—A simple two-footed, open, wire-loop fly-rod guide, designed principally to reduce friction and overall weight, and to hold the fly line close to the fly-rod shaft. It slightly resembles a semicoiled snake in shape.

Snelled fly—An artificial fly with a short permanent section of gut or monofilament attached to it. On the opposite end is a fixed closed loop to attach the snell to the leader.

Spawn—The act of fish reproduction. Also refers to a mass of fish eggs.

Spawning runs—The movement of a fish or a number of fish from their resident water to a more suitable area to mate and to lay their eggs.

Spillway—The outlet section of a lake where the water flows over a particular section of the dam.

Spinner—The term used to identify the second adult stage (imago) of mayfly aquatic insects. The wings are generally transparent or translucent and often lie flat, or spent, when the insect is expiring on the water. Also, a small shiny metal blade that revolves on a metal wire shaft when pulled through the water to attract a fish to the fly.

Spinning—A method of lure casting that utilizes a fixed-spool reel in which the line spins off as the weighted lure pulls it out.

Splice—The joining of two fly-line sections together.

Spook—Scaring a fish so much that it stops feeding and/or swims away and hides.

Spring creek—A stream in which the water originates from the flow of subsurface springwater.

Spun deer hair—Hair applied in such a manner that it flares and spins around the shank of the hook and is then trimmed to a specific shape.

Steelhead—A migrating rainbow trout that lives part of its life in freshwater streams and other parts in saltwater oceans or large freshwater lakes.

Steelhead fly—An artificial sinking fly designed specifically for catching steelhead.

Stillborn—A term that describes an insect, or its imitation, that is having difficulty emerging in the normal manner.

Straightening (fly line or leader)—The removal of coils or twists in the fly line or leader caused by their storage on the fly reel.

Streamer—A subsurface fly that imitates small fish or similarly shaped natural creatures a fish might strike or eat.

Strike—A fish hitting or biting the natural food or artificial fly. Also the action a fly fisher takes with fly rod and line to set the hook in a fish's mouth.

Stringer—A length of cord, rope, or chain for retaining, keeping alive, and carrying caught fish.

Stripper guide—The first large guide on the butt section of a fly rod above the rod handle. It is designed to reduce friction and enhance casting and retrieving.

Stripping—The act of rapidly retrieving a fly and fly line that involves making a series of fast pulls on the fly line with the line hand.

Structure—Describes objects in the water that fish would live near. Used more in lake fishing than in stream fishing.

Studs—Metal protrusions on the soles of wading shoes or boots for improving footing on very slick wet rocks, ice, or the like.

Swim—The way a sinking fly moves through the water as it is being fished. It may move like a minnow or a nymph, for example, or simply swim as an attractor.

Synthetic tying materials—Fly-tying materials that are man-made; for example, Orlon, Mylar, and FisHair.

Tackle—A general term covering all equipment used in fly fishing.

Tag—A component on certain types of flies, located at the rear. Also may refer to the excess, or tag end, of a fly-tying material.

Tag end—The forward end of a leader or tippet.

Tail—The caudal fin of a fish. Also refers to capturing and/or landing a hooked fish by grasping it just in front of its tail. Also, the lower or end (downstream) portion of a stream pool.

Tailer—A tool for tailing (landing) fish. It has a locking loop on the handle that locks around the fish's tail.

Tailing—A term often used to describe a fish feeding in a position along the bottom in shallow water so that its tail sometimes sticks above the surface of the water.

Tailwater—A stream coming from a large man-made dam.

Tailwater trout—Trout that live in the cold-water streams below man-made dams.

Take—The fish's action in catching food or a fly.

Taper—The shape of a fly line or leader. May also be used in describing fly-rod shape.

Terrestrial—Insects that are land-born air breathers. Included are grasshoppers, crickets, ants, beetles, and the like. Also, a fly that imitates such an insect.

Thorax—The "chest" area of an insect's body.

Tide—The periodic rising and lowering of water levels in streams, lakes, and oceans due to gravitational forces or releases of impounded waters.

Tie—Describes the making of artificial flies. Also, a term used to describe forming various line, leader, and fly knots.

Tinsel—Metallic body materials used for the ribbing or bodies of flies.

Tippet (fly tackle)—The small end of a leader or additional section of nylon monofilament tied to the end of the leader.

Tippet (fly tying)—Commonly refers to small feathers from various birds used in fly tying.

Tip-top—The fly-rod line guide that is fitted over the rod's tip end.

Topping—Refers to that component of certain feathers—generally peacock swords or golden pheasant crest feathers—that lies above the wing. Most common on Atlantic salmon flies.

Treble hook—A fish hook with three bends, barbs, and points joined on a common shank.

Trolling—Fishing a fly or lure by pulling it behind a boat. Less commonly, fishing by wading or walking with the fly dragging in the water behind.

Trout—A group of very popular freshwater gamefish that live in cold, pure water. Includes rainbow trout, golden trout, brown trout, cutthroat trout, brook trout, to name a few.

Twitch—A small movement given to the fly by using the rod tip or a short fly-line strip.

Underbody—The "foundation" of a fly body. Commonly wire for weighting.

Vest (Fishing vest)—A vestlike garment containing a number of various-sized pockets used to carry flies and other fishing accessory items while fly fishing.

Wading—Walking on the bottom of a stream, lake, or ocean in water no deeper than your chest.

Waders—Waterproof combination of shoes and pants used for wading.

Wading shoes—Shoes used over stocking-foot waders for wading.

Wading staff—A walking cane used to assist in wading, particularly on slick, irregular bottoms and in swift water.

Warm-water fish—Fish that thrive best in water temperatures ranging from 65 to 85 degrees F.

Water clarity—The degree of transparency water has; how far below the surface you can see an object.

Water color—Refers to a water's color tint. It is affected by suspended particles and the bottom color reflection.

Water condition—A general expression fly fishers use to describe the combination of level, temperature, and clarity.

Web—The softer, triangular-shaped, shadowy area in the center of a hackle feather.

Weed guard—A simple wire or nylon device on a fly that prevents it from hooking vegetation in the fishing area.

Whip-finish—A special-purpose knot used for securing the tying thread at the completion of a fly.

Wiggle nymph—A two-section, hinge-bodied, artificial nymph fly.

Wind knot—A simple but troublesome overhand knot that is accidentally tied on the fly line or leader while casting.

Wing case—That part of an immature aquatic insect (nymph) that houses and protects what will later become the wings. Located on the top of the thorax.

Wings—The term used both in fly tying and in describing natural insects in reference to that component.

Woolly Worm—A design of sinking fly that has a fuzzy or woolly body, and hackle spiraled around and over the body's length. Also the larvae of terrestrial moths or butterflies.

Index

G

H

I

J

K

L